Radicalism and the Origins of
the Vietnamese Revolution

RADICALISM and the ORIGINS of the VIETNAMESE REVOLUTION

Hue-Tam Ho Tai

Harvard University Press
Cambridge, Massachusetts
London, England

Copyright © 1992 by the President and Fellows of Harvard College
All rights reserved
Printed in the United States of America
Second printing, 1996

First Harvard University Press paperback edition, 1996

Library of Congress Cataloging-in-Publication Data

Tai, Hue-Tam Ho, 1948–
    Radicalism and the origins of the Vietnamese revolution / Hue-Tam Ho Tai.
      p.   cm.
    Includes index.
    ISBN 0-674-74612-0 (cloth)
    ISBN 0-674-74613-9 (pbk.)
      1. Vietnam—Politics and government—1858–1945. 2. Radicalism—Vietnam—History. I. Title.
DS556.8.T34   1992   91-16930
959.7'03—dc20   CIP

To Andrew and Matthew

Contents

Acknowledgments	ix
Introduction	1
1 Our Fathers' House	10
2 Different Roads to Freedom	57
3 Daughters of Annam	88
4 Scandal Sheets	114
5 Prodigal Children	146
6 Organizing Revolution	171
7 Freedom and Discipline	196
8 Communists, Trotskyists, and Progressives	224
Conclusion	258
Notes	267
Index	311

Acknowledgments

This work was originally conceived as a companion to my first book, in which I analyzed the role of millenarian sectarianism among peasants of southern Vietnam in the nineteenth and twentieth centuries. My idea was to study the career of Nguyen An Ninh, the urban radical who was as much at home in Paris salons as in peasant huts. But I soon realized that, in order to make sense of his life, I had to follow the itinerary of his contemporaries. Thus, instead of a biography of a single individual, I have tried to write the collective story of a whole generation.

It gives me great pleasure to acknowledge the many debts I have incurred while writing this book. I will be forever grateful to my parents, the late Ho Huu Tuong and Nguyen Hue Minh, whose involvement in anticolonial politics dated from the 1920s. This book was begun after their death; but while I was growing up, they provided me with a wealth of information about events with which they were intimately connected, and in so doing, inspired in me an abiding love of history. Thanks are due to Walter Slote and Mrs. I. Milton Sacks for giving me a copy of the written transcripts of a set of interviews which Walter Slote conducted with my father in 1966.

The late Huynh Kim Khanh, whose untimely death is greatly mourned, generously provided me with a copy of the memoirs of Nguyen An Ninh's widow. My analysis of the events of the 1920s and 1930s has also been influenced by his excellent study of Vietnamese Communism during this period. Other Vietnam scholars from whose advice and support I have benefited include Georges Boudarel, Pierre Brocheux, William Duiker, Daniel Hémery, David Marr, Nguyen The Anh, Samuel Popkin, and Alexander Woodside.

As always, the Fairbank Center for East Asian Research continues to provide a supportive and intellectually rewarding environment in which to do research and writing. Among my colleagues at the Center, I would like particularly to thank Philip Kuhn, Joshua Fogel, and

Benjamin Schwartz for helpful comments on various stages of the manuscript. My thanks also go to Albert Craig for his careful reading of an earlier version.

I have been fortunate in my dealings with the staff of various libraries, in particular, the Widener and Harvard-Yenching libraries at Harvard University and the Dépôt d'Archives d'Outre-Mer of the French Ministry of Colonies in Aix-en-Provence.

All scholars of Vietnam are indebted to Huynh Sanh Thong for his magnificent translations of Vietnamese poetry. I have reprinted in the Introduction two lines of verse by Nguyen Du from *The Tale of Kieu: A Bilingual Edition,* edited and translated by Huynh Sanh Thong, copyright 1983 by Yale University Press. Also quoted in the Introduction and in the epigraphs is poetry by Tran Te Xuong, Nguyen Dinh Chieu, and Nguyen Cong Tru, from *The Heritage of Vietnamese Poetry,* edited and translated by Huynh Sanh Thong, copyrighted 1979 by Yale University Press. Grateful acknowledgment is made to Yale University Press for permission to quote from these sources. The epigraph from *A Call to Youth* is included in Thai Bach, *Thi van quoc cam thoi thuoc Phap* (Saigon: nha Khai Tri, 1960). The translation is my own, as are all translations from the French or Vietnamese not otherwise noted.

I would like to thank Aida Donald and Elizabeth Suttell of Harvard University Press, who patiently shepherded the manuscript through the various stages of the publication process, and Elizabeth Gretz, whose careful editing greatly improved it.

As always, my husband, Patrick, has been unfailingly supportive. His knowledge of computers has been invaluable, and his willingness to do more than his share of household work when I needed to write made it possible for me to finish the book. Although my two sons, Andrew and Matthew, helped delay its completion, their beloved presence also gives me an added reason for wishing to preserve the past for the sake of future generations.

Introduction

THIS BOOK is about the role of radicalism in the early phase of the Vietnamese Revolution and its eventual displacement by Marxism-Leninism as the dominant force in reshaping anticolonial politics and as the source of language for discussing cultural, social, and political issues.

The phenomenon I am labeling radicalism came to the forefront of Vietnamese politics in the mid-1920s, when young, mostly urban, Vietnamese left home by the hundreds, like so many prodigal children, to seek knowledge and freedom in exile.[1] I propose to examine the intellectual and social forces that spurred Vietnamese young people on their odyssey and turned them from rebels into revolutionaries. So much attention has focused on the rise of communism that the role of radicalism in the anticolonial movement has been overlooked. Although Marxism-Leninism eventually won over large numbers of Vietnamese revolutionaries, many of them were introduced to anticolonial politics through radicalism. By radicalism, I mean an essentially nonideological current of reaction, both to colonial rule and to native accommodation to that rule, whose chief characteristics were iconoclasm and the marriage of the personal and the political. In this sense, radicalism is not a true "ism" as conventionally understood, but more of a political mood.

At the origin of the youthful exodus was a series of student strikes. Intertwined in the strikes, and in their causes and their aftermath, are two themes: the yearning of a newly urbanized and Westernized youth for freedom, at both the personal and the collective level, and their quest for a glimpse into the future. But although Vietnamese radicalism was presented as a break with the past, its themes were not new. They can be summed up in the traditional literary trope which pits talent *(tai)* against destiny *(mang)*. Every Vietnamese is familiar with the lines from the nineteenth-century classic, the *Tale of Kieu:*

> One hundred years; in this life span on earth
> Destiny and talent are apt to feud.[2]

The history of Vietnamese radicalism is the story of a generation's search for the proper role of human will *(tai)* and history *(mang)* in revolution.

The root causes of radicalism are easy to identify: it was a delayed reaction to colonial conquest. The first stage of French conquest was completed in the 1860s, with the creation of the colony of French Cochinchina in the South. A second campaign ended in 1884 with the establishment of the protectorate of Tonkin in the North and the protectorate of Annam in central Vietnam. By the 1920s, therefore, Vietnam had been under French rule for at least forty years, and southern Vietnam for sixty. The experience of conquest was by no means novel. Vietnam as a people, a nation, and a culture had been forged over two millennia of resistance against Chinese domination. To survive, the Vietnamese had borrowed freely from Chinese social, political, and cultural institutions and values. But the new enemy from the West posed a different challenge. Confucian literati, who constituted Vietnam's ruling elite, sought at first to preserve the social and moral order they had inherited. Eventually, they were forced to acknowledge the futility of trying to restore national sovereignty by force of arms and appeals to Confucian principles.

The impetus for change came with the discovery of Social Darwinism, via the writings of reform-minded Chinese literati such as Liang Ch'i-ch'ao and K'ang Yu-wei. To an elite more at ease promoting the ideals of equilibrium and harmony, its emphasis on struggle and competition was not easy to accept. But Vietnam's loss of independence enhanced the suasive power of Social Darwinism and also gave it a peculiarly poignant slant. Its Western proponents might see in Social Darwinism an essentially optimistic worldview, in which those endowed with the proper spirit of competition and the will to strive were rewarded with success. But Vietnamese and Chinese saw mostly its bleak corollary. Equating independence with survival, patriotic literati believed that they were engaged in a desperate race against annihilation as a people and a culture. Their country appeared to them to be a "weak and small" *(nhuoc tieu)* nation in the process of being swallowed up by a stronger and fitter France. Language reinforced this cannibalistic vision of colonialism as a "people-eating system" *(che do thuc dan)*, an even more evocative description than the usual "dog-eat-dog" metaphors of Social Darwinism. Accustomed as they were to employing cultural yardsticks to measure national health, these literati opted to follow the path already taken by their Chinese counterparts in attempting to strengthen their country by reforming its culture. But the zeal of the Vietnamese literati in embracing what they called "New Learning" from the West compounded the profound changes which colonialism had brought to the political, economic, and social landscape of Vietnam. It also undermined the power of Confucian orthodoxy and the moral authority of tradition.

The spiritual crisis which resulted from this assault on traditional sources of social cohesion provided the impetus for lively debates among members of the elite. These often amounted to little more than monologues, however, for by the 1920s the elite had become fragmented according to educational and social backgrounds, interests, and values. The very language in which the debates were conducted was not uniform. In the South, French was used even by those who sought to overthrow French rule. In other regions, older anticolonial activists stuck to Chinese. Increasingly, however, the Vietnamese vernacular, in its romanized writing system once despised as a tool of the invaders, was employed by enemies and upholders of the colonial order alike. But whether written in Vietnamese, Chinese, or French, many of the words were unfamiliar; others were old terms which had been given new meanings and a different resonance. They became weapons in a struggle for control over ruling metaphors and symbols. Friends and foes of change alike used the rhetoric of the family, the metaphor of adolescence and immaturity, and above all, the emblematic figure of Vietnamese womanhood to illustrate their particular vision of both present and future.

The focus of many of these debates was the generation of young Vietnamese born after the colonial regime had become entrenched. Educated in French schools very different from the academies of old, they no longer possessed a sense of rootedness and had fallen prey to a deep spiritual malaise. To understand the forces that produced this anomie, it is important to trace the students' educational experience, the ambiguous lessons of the past, the weight of conflicting values and expectations under which they labored, the political and cultural choices open to them, and the models they could emulate. Among these models were restorationist patriots as well as patriotic reformers; southern Constitutionalists as well as northern neo-traditionalists; staunch cultural conservatives as well as critics of "ossified

Confucianism" *(hu nho);* defenders of the French colonial enterprise as well as anticolonial activists of various ideological persuasions operating inside and outside Vietnam.

To many of these young Vietnamese, revolution came to seem the only possible solution to an existential predicament that bound their personal concerns to those of the nation in a tight and seemingly natural unity. They saw a symmetry between the national struggle for independence from colonial rule and their own efforts to emancipate themselves from the oppressiveness of native social institutions and the deadweight of tradition. It was this perceived symmetry which gave rise to radicalism.

Radicalism was strongly influenced by anarchism in both its collective and its libertarian strains. Though anarchism was introduced into Vietnamese anticolonial politics in the 1900s, its influence was greatest during the 1920s. Unlike Social Darwinism, anarchism was preoccupied not with survival and competition but with freedom and the relationship between the individual and society. Anarchism inspired many acts of violence, but it was also responsible for the humanist tone of the revolutionary discourse of the 1920s.

This discourse was fundamentally changed by the introduction of Marxism-Leninism. Whereas radicals conceived of independence as arising organically from their struggle toward self-emancipation, Marxists established a new symmetry between national liberation and the pursuit of social justice along class lines. The emergence of communism in Vietnam is well documented, but the process through which Marxism-Leninism triumphed over radicalism, after it had brought so many young Vietnamese into the revolutionary cause, remains obscure. In brief, this triumph can be attributed to a peculiar conjunction of international trends and domestic problems. Although a few exiles, most notably Nguyen Ai Quoc (better known as Ho Chi Minh), became converted to Marxism-Leninism in the early 1920s, most Vietnamese revolutionaries were not introduced to it until the close of the decade. By then, revolutionary organizations were in disarray. The introduction of Marxism-Leninism also coincided with a critical juncture in the history of world communism. In the wake of the failure of the United Front in China, the Comintern adopted a revolutionary strategy more suited to the needs of movements of decolonization in predominantly agrarian countries such as Vietnam.

To study the history of Vietnamese radicalism is to be made aware of its proponents' abiding concerns: freedom, security, the needs of the individual, and the interests of the community. Both supporters and foes of the colonial status quo defined their political choices in terms of the issues of freedom and security. To some, security was more important than freedom, predictability more desirable than perfection. This meant accepting inherited institutions, no matter how oppressive, and the colonial system, no matter how unjust. Others, however, were drawn to freedom in its multiple meanings: liberation of the nation from colonial rule and emancipation of the individual from the patriarchal family system, outdated moral values, and authoritarian social institutions. But the corollary of freedom was uncertainty, and even those committed to the revolutionary enterprise needed reassurance. Ready as they were to sacrifice the present to the future, they too, sought certainty, albeit of another kind: not the belief that tomorrow would be like today, and therefore endurable, but the sure knowledge that it would be utterly different, and therefore better. Only then would their sacrifices and their transgressions against conventional morality not be in vain. Amid the vagaries of revolutionary life, the Marxist promise of certain victory must have seemed irresistible. In the meantime, the Leninist party balanced iron discipline with comradely warmth, and acted as substitute for the despised patriarchal family.

The person most closely associated with the events of 1926–1927 is Nguyen An Ninh, a non-Marxist who did not live to witness the triumph of revolution. By making him the central figure of this study, I am challenging an assumption prevalent in earlier works on the Vietnamese Revolution that its history can be compressed into the history of communism. Eschewing teleology, I have tried to present intellectual and political options as they appeared from the vantage point of the 1920s, when the revolutionary process began, rather than of August 1945, when independence became a reality.

IN MARSHALING my data and constructing my narrative, I have taken heed of Tocqueville's formula: "to interweave the thread of ideas with the thread of facts; say enough of the latter to make the former intelligible and make the reader understand the importance of these ideas yet not write a history [of events] as such."[3] In this spirit, I have tried to place the origins of the Vietnamese Revolution in the framework of the interplay between cultural discourse and political action. Thus, although this is primarily a study of the young Vietnamese who made the transition from student rebels to revolutionaries, it is also about their elders: those who continued to resist the invaders when all hope was lost as well as those who surrendered without a fight; those who plotted the overthrow of the French as well as those who preached accommodation to the colonial state; those who advocated total assimilation as well as those who called for a blend of Western ideas and Eastern values. This work is also about the rhetoric of *mission civilisatrice* and the realities of colonial life: in the yawning gap between the two lay the breeding ground of radicalism and revolution.

My concern is to analyze the relationship between political culture and cultural politics, and between rhetoric and action in the 1920s. To do so, I have made use of different types of sources. For what was said, the obvious sources are journals, newspapers, and contemporary fiction both in French and in Vietnamese. For reasons discussed in Chapter 4, the most significant publications in northern Vietnam (Tonkin) and central Vietnam (Annam) were in Vietnamese, whereas in southern Vietnam (Cochinchina), most of the debates were conducted in French. Fiction, in the form of short stories, plays, and novels, began to take on importance after World War I.[4] For what was done, the single best source of information is without doubt the French colonial archives. These include not only official records of all kinds but also rich data on the activities of Vietnamese expatriates in France and translations of Vietnamese journals and newspapers of the 1920s and 1930s.

In addition to these sources and to the secondary materials in French, Vietnamese, and English available for this period, I have made use of another kind of record which, for lack of a better description, I call personal sources. I was raised among survivors of the generation of 1926: my parents, their parents, other relatives, friends, and sometimes foes. One man, who liked to recite French Renaissance poetry by the hour, had organized the funeral of Phan Chu Trinh. Another had been selected by Nguyen Ai Quoc to succeed him as the head of a Vietnamese expatriate association; in the 1960s, he was living on memories, sharing them with his friends' children in exchange for an occasional bottle of French cologne. A neighbor had once masterminded the sending of Vietnamese students to the Workers' University of the East in Moscow from the headquarters of the Anti-Imperialist League in Berlin. Other people, long dead, were like friendly ghosts, spoken of so frequently and so casually that they seemed as vivid as if they had just left the room. A few others, though their number is fast dwindling, today occupy the highest positions in the country's leadership. In their youth, many of these people had pooled together their meager resources in crowded students' digs and sometimes had shared even more crowded prison cells. For this study of what is, after all, the generation of my parents, their friends as well as their adversaries, I have drawn on my father's unpublished memoirs, on his published works, and on a set of interviews conducted with him in 1966, and also on the reminiscences of many others who form an indelible part of my memory of growing up in decidedly postrevolutionary South Vietnam.

For the sake of Vietnamese readers and Vietnam specialists, I have included as much information as possible, at the risk of drowning a more general audience in details. Conversely, for the benefit of a more general audience, I have supplied information which Vietnam specialists may find somewhat elementary.

Readers are often frustrated by the similarity of Vietnamese names. It is an understandable frustration; half the population shares the same surname, Nguyen, and there are only eleven other common surnames. Common usage dictates that a person be referred to by his or her personal name, ordinarily the last element. Exception is made when a person—usually a man—has attained such stature that the only way to indicate respect is to refer to him by his family name. This usage has nothing to do with power or social position, but with something more intangible, such as moral authority and, above all, historical importance. Hence, Ho for Ho Chi Minh, but Diem for Ngo Dinh Diem. In calling some by their given names and others by their surnames, I do not wish necessarily to indicate approval or disapproval, but merely to follow established usage.

Colonial conquest deprived the Vietnamese of the right to call their country by its proper name and think of themselves as Vietnamese; instead they had to use the names of Tonkin, Annam, and Cochinchina. Despite memories of national unity conjured up by the name of Vietnam, the division of the country under colonial rule was a real and painful one. Loss of linguistic autonomy was so internalized that even revolutionaries referred to themselves by the name given them by their French masters—Annamites—a label that resonated with echoes of an earlier period of colonial rule under the T'ang dynasty.

It goes against the grain to use terms laden with pejorative connotations and imposed on the Vietnamese by others, but because one of my aims is to explore the ideas of contemporary Vietnamese, I have decided to adopt the terminology they used.

This concern to write from the perspective of contemporary Vietnamese also informs my interpretation of a whole range of terms which formed part of the public discourse. There was nothing subtle about the political and cultural discourse of the 1920s. The rhetorical needs of the moment yielded an extraordinary number of emphatic pronouncements on Vietnamese culture, society, history, and "tradition" quite at variance with observable or recorded facts. Confucianism came in for a great deal of distortion, both by those who sought to preserve its supposed legacy and by those who sought to undo its perceived damage. Interestingly, both its supporters and detractors held, quite sincerely, to a rather narrow and impoverished definition of Confucianism. But, ultimately, what is important is not how historically accurate a particular statement was, or whether certain teachings correctly distilled the essence of Confucian values, but that they formed part of a cultural discourse which shaped political choices as much as it was shaped by them.

In the early decades of the century, the Vietnamese were exposed to a large number of neologisms, many of them originally coined by the Japanese and introduced into the Chinese discourse by Liang Ch'i-ch'ao and other Chinese reformers. In adding these neologisms to their language, the Vietnamese often departed from the words' meanings or gave them a peculiar twist. Though I have tried here and there to draw attention to the way in which local usage differed from the original meaning, by and large, I have presented these terms as they were understood by contemporary Vietnamese, for, ultimately, it was local interpretation rather than original meaning which guided their actions.

Anticolonial struggles the world over share a number of similarities. It is therefore tempting for the historian to try to draw comparisons among the historical experiences of different peoples, especially if they are considered part of the same world. No doubt some readers will wish at different points that I had drawn parallels with other countries of Southeast Asia that were undergoing decolonization at the same time as Vietnam. Contemporary Vietnamese, however, knew little of what went on in Southeast Asia. As the poet Tran Te Xuong (1870–1907) wrote:

> *Kung-hsi! Merci!* I know all foreign tongues.
> If not to China, I'll run off to France!⁵

It makes sense, therefore, to content ourselves with following the prodigal children of Vietnam on their travels to China and France in search of the knowledge that would set them free and restore their hope in the future.

1 Our Fathers' House

> An old family, in the old abode of its fathers, still covered with traditional respect and surrounded by memories dear to it and to the surrounding population, these are the debris of a society that is falling to dust and which soon will leave no traces. Happy are those who can tie together in their thoughts the past, the present, and the future.
>
> Alexis de Tocqueville, letter to his wife, 4 May 1858

LUNAR New Year 1920, in a Cochinchinese village. Bedecked in his mandarin's finery, a magistrate lay sprawled on the floor of his old teacher's front room, being caned like a naughty schoolboy.[1] The day had begun conventionally enough for the hapless magistrate. After offering New Year's wishes to his father, he had walked over to the house of his former teacher to repeat the performance. But his greetings were no sooner over than his teacher scolded him: "Peasants from your prefecture who were passing through here recently complained of maladministration. The duty of every mandarin is to care for the welfare of the people. What have you to say for yourself?" Before he could defend himself, the magistrate was ordered to lie down to receive his punishment.

Even in the precolonial era, which such a scene evokes, it was probably rare for a grown man to be so chastised. It must have been even rarer in Cochinchina, whose newly settled population, concerned with wresting a living from the land, showed only lukewarm enthusiasm for classical learning and Confucian values. But foreign conquest had generated a powerful nativism which led southerners to glorify a past made all the more luminous by the moral quicksands of colonial life.[2]

Dao Duy Chung, the teacher in this story, was emblematic of this patriotic nativism. He was an immigrant, like many southerners, having come from central Vietnam in the 1880s with the intention of mobilizing local peasants against the French. He soon found his cause hopeless, the French having become well entrenched after nearly twenty years of colonial rule. He stayed on, nevertheless, married into a local family, and opened an academy. That southerners were no longer allowed to sit for the civil service examinations was apparently no obstacle to its success; Dao Duy Chung continued to groom students in the traditional curriculum and prepare them for the duties of public office. A carefully protected enclave of classical studies and old-fashioned principles, his academy helped maintain the illusion that the past was still alive.[3] The same nativistic impulse kept the magistrate from pointing out that his was a purely honorific title; he preferred instead to accept his teacher's chastisement as a way of reaffirming his commitment to the values of earlier days, when mandarins had truly held sway over the lives of common people.

But younger Vietnamese, whose entire life had been spent under colonial rule, could not hide from present unpleasantness by retreating into the past. By the 1920s, colonialism had wrought massive changes in Vietnamese politics, society, and culture, eroding both the cohesiveness of the elite and its faith in the ideology that had sustained it over the centuries. The formerly uniform system of education was replaced between 1917 and 1919 by a hodgepodge of French schools, Franco-Annamite schools, and, in Tonkin and Annam, reformed "traditional" academies, each with its own curriculum and constituency. The first intimation of trouble among the new generation of students came soon afterward. Two hundred students went on strike at the Collège Chasseloup-Laubat in December 1920; unrest broke out a few days later at the Collège de My Tho.[4] The press paid little attention to these brief and unconnected shows of discontent. But the demonstrations that erupted in 1926 were more sustained and spread rapidly through the elite schools of the country. The students' unruliness came as a shock to their elders. It seemed all the more incomprehensible because educational opportunities were limited and those who could attend school were universally considered highly fortunate.

As the magistrate could attest, old-style instruction had formerly been accompanied by the liberal application of the cane; in the 1920s corporal punishment had not disappeared from colonial schools, but it was no longer deemed a natural aid to the acquisition of knowledge. Yet, although poor conditions or harsh discipline triggered some instances of rebellion, they were not the fundamental cause of student unrest. The cause was a profound crisis of authority, in which teachers were the first, but by no means the only, targets. Unable to restore discipline in the classroom, teachers turned for help to their charges' parents. In the imperial capital of Hue, court mandarins were even brought in to preach obedience to their sons and daughters. But this only crystallized youthful suspicions that parents, teachers, and officials worked in collusion to repress students' generous instincts and idealistic aspirations. Why and how did young Vietnamese become alienated from both old values and new teachings and rise up to defy a once hallowed triad of authority figures?

The Scholar's World

Dao Duy Chung's success in operating an academy long after civil service examinations were abolished in the South is testimony to the selective nature of nativism. When Vietnamese waxed nostalgic, it was seldom about the examination system, even though it was the culmination of classical education and the entry into the world of officialdom.

Students generally progressed from village or subprefectural schools to academies such as the one Dao Duy Chung ran. A typical school was usually no more than the teacher's private home and could accommodate only a half-dozen students.[5] Academies, which prepared students for the grueling triennial regional examinations, were just as modest in size. The examinations themselves usually attracted several thousand candidates.[6] Those who won a coveted *cu nhon* (Ch. *chu jen*) degree in the regional contests could go on to the imperial capital to be examined for the *tien si* (Ch. *chin shih*) degree, with hopes of a brilliant career in the mandarinate. Those who failed, or obtained only the lower degree of *tu tai* (Ch. *hsiu tsai*), returned home to become village teachers; the more talented and respected opened subprefectural schools or academies.

The most eloquent memorial to the vanished world of the scholar came from the pen of Ngo Tat To, a northern scholar who had failed the regional examinations of 1915, the last to be held in Tonkin. In 1941, Ngo Tat To published a novel entitled *Tents and Bamboo Beds (Leu chong)*, in which he described the harrowing ordeal of being a degree candidate. The novel's hero was a brilliant young scholar who, in the later stages of the examinations, fell afoul of a taboo prohibiting the use of imperial names and was nearly executed for lèse-majesté. Providing a counterpoint was his less original classmate, who won the prestigious degree and then was appointed to a post for which his book learning had ill prepared him. When he proved unable to quell a local uprising, the court punished him by sending him to an even more conflict-ridden district in the highlands. This allowed the novel's hero to reflect on the pleasures of pure scholarship as contrasted to the dangers of political office.

Ngo Tat To did not despise politics, but only bureaucratic careerism. He was also ambivalent about the intellectual legacy of Confucianism. Not long before he began work on his novel, To declared: "It is Confucianism which in the past elevated Vietnam to the rank of civilized nations. It is also Confucianism which has brought Vietnam to the brink of perdition."[7] Yet he went on to make important contributions to classical scholarship, his ire being reserved for the brand of Confucianism which the Nguyen emperors had been promoting since the nineteenth century.

The Nguyen dynasty had come to power in 1802 after decades of civil war and nearly two centuries of national division. To bring back stability to the nepotism-ridden political system they had inherited, the dynasty's emperors made the Confucian civil service examinations the sole avenue to official appointment. Reacting also to the populist cultural policies of their Tay Son predecessors, they banned the demotic script used to transcribe the Vietnamese vernacular. The demotic script was looked upon by rulers and officials as a tool used by the devious to undermine Confucian orthodoxy, and with it, their legitimacy.[8] Instead of the Vietnamese vernacular, scholars considered Chinese characters to be their own language. Students were taught to read and write Chinese; they learned the Confucian classics, T'ang-style poetry, and Ch'ing-style eight-legged essays. Their ideal was to approximate as closely as possible the learning and the life of their Chinese counterparts. But because of the vagaries of cultural exchanges and their own emphasis on examination-centered learning, Vietnamese literati had only a limited exposure to the range of ideas circulating in China. Furthermore, the generally small size of the academies did not allow for the lively scholarly exchanges that went on in Chinese institutions. What Vietnamese students absorbed, therefore, was often a formalistic kind of knowledge *(van hoc tu chuong)* that sacrificed originality to the goal of passing exams. Required to concentrate on Sung neo-Confucianism, they overlooked the contributions of philosophers whose ideas did not form part of the Nguyen examination curriculum.[9]

His distaste for the examination system did not prevent Ngo Tat To from entertaining a deep nostalgia for the world of the Confucian scholar away from the hurly-burly of mandarin politics. Both his father and grandfather, failed degree candidates like himself, had eked out a living as village teachers. Making a virtue of their necessity, Ngo Tat To paid homage to the relationship that had once existed between his rural scholar forebears and their charges. In that idealized world, teachers and students were bound by a tie as strong and enduring as the tie that bound fathers and sons. As the saying went, teachers ranked second only to fathers.[10] This idea was vividly illustrated on New Year's Day when students, after extending greetings to their fathers, immediately went to their teachers' home to do likewise before paying their respects to their mothers. In Tonkin, where the Confucian ethos was far stronger than in Cochinchina, the same word *thay* applied to both father and teacher, emphasizing their overlapping duties in promoting the material and moral welfare of the young men in their care. Just as fathers performed tutorial duties, so did teachers act as surrogate fathers. They cooperated together in transmitting the accumulated wisdom and values of past generations. In return, they expected lifelong respect and obedience.[11]

The avowed goal of traditional education was to turn a scholar into a "superior man" (*quan tu;* Ch. *chun tzu*) through self-cultivation. But self-perfection was only a first step toward political office. The motto of the superior man was: "Cultivate thyself, set thy house in order, govern thy country, pacify All-Under-Heaven."[12] Underlying this motto was the assumption that individual self-cultivation led naturally to family management and thence to political rule. An official was regarded as the "father and mother of the people" *(dan chi phu mau)*. It was his responsibility to look after their welfare and, like any father, he expected to be obeyed and respected by them. Teachers, therefore, were supposed to prepare their students not only for the examinations but also for their future role as "fathers and mothers of the people." Vietnamese officials clung to this self-image long after French administrators, having usurped the mandarins' power, assumed the rhetorical role of fathers of the immature and wayward Vietnamese population.

Familial relationships did not remain immune from such rhetorical shifts or from the effects of change in politics and education. Few parents, however, realized how deep was their children's frustration over being given an inferior education that led to menial positions in the colonial administration. Their titles conveyed a glamour at odds with the workaday reality of their jobs. Thus were interpreters and clerks allowed to sit at the highest table at village feasts, side by side with traditional degree-holders.[13] Paradoxically, it was the more prestigious schools that turned out the most alienated students, for the presence of French administrative and teaching staff usually led to tense race relations.[14] But unhappy experiences in school and blighted career prospects do not explain the emergence of radical politics, or the rebellion by young Vietnamese against parents, teachers, and mandarins. The seeds of crisis lay in Confucian social theory itself, in the tension between piety and patriotism. This tension was largely unacknowledged in normal times; the experience of foreign conquest, and more directly, the educational reforms of 1917–1919 brought it to the fore, albeit with a long delay.

Piety and Patriotism

Because Confucian social theory conceived of the country as a family writ large, filial piety and family harmony were the twin bases of social and political stability. The various relationships that existed within the family and society were articulated by the Three Bonds: loyalty (*trung;* Ch. *chung*), which a subject owed to his ruler; piety (*hieu;* Ch. *hsiao*), which governed the behavior of a son toward his father; and fidelity (*nghia;* Ch. *i*), which bound husband and wife together. Ideally, each of the Bonds reinforced the other two. The relationship between ruler and ruled was patterned after the unequal but reciprocal relationship between father and son; the rapport between the emperor and his officials was likened to conjugal fidelity. A husband might repudiate his wife if she proved unsatisfactory (there were seven legitimate grounds for such a move), but a wife owed her husband total fidelity, even after his death. Similarly, the emperor could dismiss his mandarins, though not entirely without cause; but, just as "a chaste woman may not serve two husbands, a loyal official may not serve two rulers."[15] Piety was the bedrock upon which the lives of ordinary peasants were built, loyalty the cornerstone of a mandarin's career.

In normal times, public service and family interest neatly dovetailed: a mandarin could at the same time show loyalty to the reigning monarch and promote his family's fortunes, while acting as the father and mother of the common people in his jurisdiction. History, however, often tested the relative strength of the Three Bonds and forced men to choose between them. Plenty of mandarins chose to collaborate with the French and were predictably likened to unchaste women by their detractors.[16] French conquest, however, highlighted the conflict that could erupt between the demands of dynastic loyalty and filial piety.

Each principle was eloquently defended by two men who came from the same village of Dong Thai in Ha Tinh province (Annam) and were even distantly related through marriage: Phan Dinh Phung and Hoang Cao Khai.[17] Both had risen to high positions and enjoyed the respect of their fellow officials. Hoang Cao Khai won a *cu nhon* degree at an early age, then proceeded to gamble away most of his patrimony.[18] Phan Dinh Phung, less brilliant, did not obtain his degree until he was thirty-nine (he became a *tien si* the following year). But he was less erratic than Hoang Cao Khai and was admired for his rigorous, even rigid, adherence to Confucian principles.

This principled inflexibility led to Phan's ouster from the Regency Council in 1883, when he refused to go along with his fellow regents and depose Emperor Tu Duc's chosen heir in favor of another. Phan was too widely admired for the other regents to have him executed, so he was merely confined to his native village. Two years later, the crisis of succession was temporarily over, the regents having installed the twelve-year-old Ham Nghi on the throne and wielding power in his name. By then, the whole of the country had passed into French hands; protectorates had been created in Annam and Tonkin. Belatedly, the regents whisked the young emperor away from the capital and issued a decree ordering a general uprising in his name. In the hills of his native Ha Tinh, Phan Dinh Phung responded by launching the Aid the King Movement (Can Vuong). This was essentially a movement led by scholars and officials like himself and directed at other literati (the French called it the Scholars' Revolt). Hoping to put an end to the Aid the King Movement, the French tried to win Phan Dinh Phung over to their side by playing on his family feelings. They captured his brother and used him as a bait to draw Phan into submission. If Phan agreed to collaborate, he would be rewarded with a high office; if he did not, death awaited his brother and his many relatives in Dong Thai village. This was the message which an old friend, who had surrendered to the French, relayed to Phan in 1886: "I have to tell you that I passed through Dong Thai recently and saw your ancestral temple and your ancestral tombs all in ruin through neglect; I was so overwhelmed that I cried. Brother Phan, the safety of your relations and your neighbors depends entirely upon you; whether your brother lives or dies also depends entirely upon you."[19]

In reply, Phan is said to have explained to his comrades-in-arms that he considered the whole nation his family: "From the time I joined with you in the Aid the King movement, I determined to forget questions of family and village. Now I have but one tomb, a very large one, that must be defended: the land of Vietnam. I have only one brother, very important, who is in danger: more than twenty million countrymen. If I worried about my own tombs, who would worry about defending the tombs of the rest of the country? If I saved my own brother, who would save all the other brothers of our country? There is only one way for me to die now."[20]

Phan may have been unwilling to put piety before loyalty, but not everyone agreed with his interpretation of the primary duty of a Confucian official. Phan was rare, if not unique, among his contemporaries in speaking of his compatriots as his brothers, and in suggesting that love of country (*ai quoc;* Ch. *ai kuo*) rather than dynastic loyalty (*trung;* Ch. *chung*) was the wellspring of his struggle. There had always been officials who knew how to bow with the prevailing wind in order to protect their families, their tombs, their villages and who believed that Confucian ideology sanctified their priorities. Many were those who looked upon colonial conquest as merely another case of dynastic struggle which could be used to win merit for themselves (*cong;* Ch. *kung*) and safety for their kin by serving the new ruling house. They had an articulate spokesman in Phan's fellow villager, Hoang Cao Khai. In 1894, Khai, who was by then viceroy of Tonkin, wrote to Phan:

> When the capital fell and the emperor had to flee, you rose up in his support. In the context of that time, you did what was right, no one gainsays you. But the situation has changed now; can things go on as before? Even unintelligent and uneducated people have concluded that they cannot. With your superior understanding, is it possible that you do not realize this? I think I perceive your train of thought. You are determined to do whatever you deem right, to devote to it all your efforts and talents. It lies within man's power to do what must be done, though whether it succeeds or not depends on Heaven; one can only give of oneself to one's country, unto death. Therefore, it is up to you to persist in your endeavor, and no one may deter you from your goal.

And yet, when I see the misery our country is plunged in, I am filled with sorrow ... I have always been taught that mandarins should consider the care of the people as fundamental; there has never been anyone who did not love the people and yet was considered loyal to the emperor ... What you have done so far is truly loyal, but what sin have the common people committed that they should be caught in such suffering? It is fine to say that since you are working for the benefit of all, you no longer care for your own family; but how can you also abandon the hundreds of families of your region? I am not concerned only with the green grass of our village of Dong Thai: I am afraid that if you fight on, the whole region around Lam River and Mount Hong will turn into a lake.[21]

Phan Dinh Phung died of hunger and dysentery in the hills one year after that exchange. When a collaborating mandarin discovered where his body was buried, he had it exhumed and burned. Phan's ashes were then shot into the river out of the mouth of a cannon, as was done to the ashes of common criminals.[22] His name and his deeds were proscribed. Hoang Cao Khai, in contrast, died covered with riches and honors, held up by the colonial authorities as an example of true patriotism. Two of his sons became provincial governors; one of them married a royal princess and was a prominent figure in political and cultural circles in the 1920s. Who would not recoil at the cost to himself and his kin that Phan Dinh Phung paid for his interpretation of duty, or be tempted to emulate Hoang Cao Khai's brilliant career? Realizing that Phan was impervious to appeals to his family feelings, Hoang Cao Khai tried in vain to play on his regionalist sympathies. Other literati did not even bother to think in regional terms. Buttressed by unimpeachable Confucian logic, they found it more convenient and profitable to choose family piety over dynastic loyalty.

The exchange between Hoang Cao Khai and Phan Dinh Phung also illustrates competing interpretations of the causes of national defeat. Their differences, anchored in the same basic vision of human life, were a harbinger of future disagreements over the role of personal heroism and historical forces in revolution. According to popular wisdom, a person's life was determined by the interplay of two forces: talent (*tai;* Ch. *tsai*) and destiny (*mang;* Ch. *ming*). Women were popularly considered to be entirely at the mercy of fate, their happiness dependent on the men in their life. Men, however, had the power to exert control over their destiny by making use of whatever talents they possessed and were therefore not supposed to "fold their arms and accept defeat" *(khoanh tay danh chiu thua)*. Instead, they were expected to emulate King Hsia Yu, the mythical flood-tamer, or Yu Kung, who had moved mountains.

This belief in free will coexisted with the fatalistic orientation of much of Vietnamese culture, as evidenced in the poetry of even the most activist of Vietnamese statesmen. Fatalism informed the response of Emperor Tu Duc to French conquest. Having committed fratricide in his fight for the throne, he tended to interpret the loss of national independence as his personal punishment. For his part, Hoang Cao Khai claimed that in surrendering to the French he was bowing to the Will of Heaven, which had ordained the country's fall to alien rule. Others, however, believed that the history of the country did not condone defeatism. They saw resistance, rather than acceptance, as Vietnam's recurring theme. It was in the crucible of unceasing struggle against loss of national independence (*vong quoc;* Ch. *wang kuo*) that the meaning of Vietnam as a nation, a people, and a culture had been forged. Phan Dinh Phung refused to blame Heaven for the country's woes and hinted broadly that colonial conquest had been facilitated by the collective failure of the ruling elite to uphold traditional principles: "Over the millennia, our country has only used its civilization to survive from generation to generation. It does not have a large territory, its army is not powerful, it does not possess great wealth; the only thing it has to support it is the bond between ruler and subject, the bond between father and son, and the five cardinal virtues ... This is why, though China is our neighbor and is vastly more powerful than our country, yet, in the end, it has never been able to swallow it up."[23]

Phan Dinh Phung seemed to suggest that, if only the correct principles were upheld, then virtue would prevail, and the enemy would be driven out. Hoang Cao Khai conceded that belief in a preordained fate did not relieve men of the duty to uphold righteousness. But he was right in pointing out that Phan was more concerned with acting morally than with pursuing success.

As time went on, success indeed became increasingly elusive. Phan Dinh Phung's dogged resistance in the face of almost certain defeat was of a piece with his earlier refusal to follow the lead of his fellow regents: it was imbued by a very traditional concept of duty. Inspirational as they would be to future generations, his feats of heroism were performed in the service of a purely restorationist cause. Phan and other participants in the Aid the King Movement did not contemplate the reform of Vietnamese society or of its ruling ideology; they sought only to restore the old order by clinging to traditional values. The death of Phan Dinh Phung in 1895 signaled not only the end of his movement but also the beginning of a reappraisal of these values.

The Social Darwinian Critique of Culture

In the bitter aftermath of failure, patriotic literati had to come to terms with the fact that nostalgia for a lost independence was no longer sufficient to sustain the spirit of resistance. They must be willing to learn from a new enemy, just as they had once learned from the Middle Kingdom. Out of this painful process of cultural reorientation was born the Reform Movement. Like Phan's guerrilla war, it was led by scholars and aimed mainly at other scholars.

This reorientation came about largely as a result of the Social Darwinian critique of Vietnamese culture. Once this critique was internalized, it was never stated as explicitly as in early reformist writings. From the beginning, Social Darwinism was used to discuss inequality between nations; only later was it applied to individuals as well. But survival of the nation remained the underlying theme of political discourse.

To the Vietnamese, Social Darwinism was a revelation. It provided an explanation of their country's downfall which was both familiar and startlingly new: Vietnam had indeed fallen prey to a mightier country, but its conqueror's might lay in its cultural superiority. Accustomed to using cultural criteria to gauge a country's health, Vietnamese literati easily accepted the thrust of this argument. At the same time, much of the suasive power of Social Darwinism lay in its unfamiliar worldview which, instead of celebrating equilibrium and harmony, exalted the notion of unceasing competition for supremacy and survival among actors endowed with unequal gifts and resources.

Vietnamese reformers were first exposed to the ideas of Herbert Spencer, the father of Social Darwinism, by K'ang Yu-wei and his disciple Liang Ch'i-ch'ao. But it was K'ang's contemporary, the scholar and translator Yen Fu, who introduced Herbert Spencer to the Chinese reading public. In Vietnam, the first mention of Herbert Spencer came in an anonymous pamphlet written in 1904 to launch the Reform Movement, *The Civilization of New Learning (Van minh tan hoc sach)*.[24] Its preamble could have been written by Yen Fu himself, so closely did it follow his logic. It argued that ideas alone were insufficient for the maintenance of civilization; competition, too, was required. In fact, the more ideas, the more competition; and the more competition, the more ideas were generated. Vietnam, however, had a passive rather than a dynamic civilization, which venerated the old and native and despised the new and foreign, thus inhibiting the generation of new ideas. It undervalued the importance of self-strengthening. The West exalted the people; the Vietnamese revered the ruler and paid no attention to rural conditions. All this, argued the anonymous author, should be changed.

Whereas for its Western and Chinese advocates, Social Darwinism seemed an essentially optimistic vision, to the Vietnamese it offered a bleaker scenario for the future.[25] If only the fittest prevailed, would the country, whose weak state had already led to foreign conquest, be able to survive? Was the annihilation of the Vietnamese nation, people, and culture already determined or would human effort succeed in reversing course? Yen Fu had tempered the determinism inherent in Social Darwinism with a voluntarist dimension; so did the Vietnamese literati who embraced it. The proposals contained in *The Civilization of New Learning* were close kin to Chinese self-strengthening programs. But Vietnamese reformers dared not hope, as their Chinese counterparts did, that the reforms they advocated would enable their country to compete with the West on more equal terms and emerge victorious. All they dared hope for was survival. Their pleas thus had a more urgent and desperate ring than the pronouncements of the Chinese writers who inspired them.

The difference in outlook between Chinese and Vietnamese reformers is illustrated in an exchange that took place in Tokyo between the Vietnamese scholar Phan Boi Chau and the Chinese scholar-statesman Liang Ch'i-ch'ao in 1905. Liang, reports Phan, had been moved to tears by his description of Vietnam's loss of independence and urged him to publicize it.[26] Vietnam's loss of independence could serve as a warning to Chinese people of the danger they themselves were facing. He advised Phan to produce "a serious literary presentation to the world of the plight of Vietnam in the face of France's policy of extermination." Such a work would also encourage "Vietnamese youth to study overseas as a start to awakening popular consciousness and improving the general level of education." Heeding this advice, Phan wrote his *History of the Loss of Vietnam (Viet Nam vong quoc su)*. Liang provided a preface and arranged to have the book published in his journal *Renovation of the People (Hsin-min ts'ung-pao)* in 1905.[27]

What for Liang Ch'i-ch'ao was a cautionary tale was for Phan a national tragedy. "For a human being, the greatest suffering comes from losing his country." Thus began the *History of the Loss of Vietnam*. It was this sense of loss that spurred Phan and others to reform.

Reform and Its Advocates

Phan Boi Chau's advocacy of foreign learning formed part of a larger program of self-strengthening measures. Its centerpiece was a call to jettison Chinese characters, upon which the whole edifice of classical learning reposed, in favor of the romanized script. First developed by traders and missionaries in the seventeenth century, the romanized script faithfully reproduced the sound and syntax of spoken Vietnamese; it thus had the potential for bridging the gap between elite and popular cultures, an objective whose importance to the anticolonial struggle was gaining recognition. But it was also associated with foreign rule. The colonial authorities promoted its use because it was easier to master than Chinese characters; furthermore, they hoped that abandoning Chinese characters would lead to the decline of classical learning and with it the legitimacy of the scholarly elite and the values that had nurtured resistance to French rule. It was therefore not without a great deal of agonized soul-searching that scholars in Tonkin and Annam allowed themselves to be persuaded of the need to learn the romanized script and new ways of looking at the world. In 1907 a group of scholars, inspired by Fukuzawa Yukichi's Keio University, opened the Tonkin Free School (Dong Kinh Nghia Thuc). There they taught the rudiments of the new script, expounded the ideas of Chinese reformist scholars, and introduced names associated with the Enlightenment or with European nationalism into the political discourse.

The men who participated in the Reform Movement were a mixed group. Some wanted cultural change for its own sake, others because they saw it as a prerequisite for the success of anticolonial action. Phan Boi Chau was the foremost representative of the instrumentalist perspective on linguistic and educational reforms. Born in Nghe An in 1867, Phan was already eighteen when Annam fell to the French. After he became involved in the Aid the King Movement, he soon found out that his lack of a degree was a handicap among status-conscious literati. After his father became ill, he temporarily forsook political engagement for family affairs, all the while trying to succeed in the examination system. Finally, in 1900, Phan passed the regional exams with highest honors.[28] Around that time, calls for cultural reform, which had fallen on stony ground in the 1860s, began circulating again among Vietnamese literati in the wake of the Chinese Reform Movement of 1898. Phan Boi Chau was introduced to the ideas of Rousseau and Montesquieu and to the names of nineteenth-century nationalists such as Mazzini and Cavour through the writings of Liang Ch'i-ch'ao, K'ang Yu-wei, and other Chinese reformers.

Despite his own inability to master it, as well as lingering misgivings, Phan became an enthusiastic advocate of using the romanized script as the vehicle for the new Western-inspired learning which he deemed necessary for a modern nation. For him, as for Yen Fu, the recovery of independence rather than the preservation of culture was paramount, for without the nation, how could the people and culture survive? The transformation of culture was thus less a matter of intrinsic value than of strategic necessity. But Yen Fu had been a true scholar, whereas Phan was more action oriented. Knowledge, for him, was not so much the key to self-discovery as part of a panoply of anticolonial devices. When Phan launched the Eastern Travel Movement in 1905, it was to enable students to go to China and Japan to accumulate the knowledge necessary to eventually overthrow foreign rule. His first commitment remained to political struggle, including armed struggle.[29] In his *History of the Loss of Vietnam*, he interspersed veiled incitements to armed struggle with calls to study abroad. His basic lack of interest in cultural issues for their own sake resulted, however, in a lack of ideological sophistication, which was to vitiate his tireless efforts to create viable anticolonial movements.

A more truly culturalist approach was advocated by Phan Chu Trinh. Phan Chu Trinh, who also hailed from central Vietnam, received a degree in the metropolitan examinations of 1900, the year that Phan Boi Chau passed the regional exams. Unlike Phan Boi Chau, he had been too young to take part in the Aid the King Movement. His father, who had been involved, was assassinated during its dying days for reasons that remain obscure. Although his father died at the hands of fellow insurgents, Phan Chu Trinh blamed the monarchy for his death. Perhaps because of this event, which occurred when he was entering his teens, Phan Chu Trinh remained a lifelong foe of violence. Believing that a gradualist path was the way to avoid bloodshed, he was willing to defer independence until such time as the Vietnamese had undergone a thorough cultural and social transformation. While critical of colonial rule, he reserved his undiluted hatred for the Vietnamese imperial court, which he held responsible for the sorry state of the nation. He spent fourteen years in exile in France and, although he never learned French, he found much in French culture and political institutions worth adopting. Phan Chu Trinh was at heart a true reformer; Phan Boi Chau, the pioneer of the Revolution.[30]

Though the Reform Movement was dominated by classically trained scholars such as Phan Chu Trinh and Phan Boi Chau, it also attracted a considerable number of graduates of the School of Interpreters. The School had opened in Hanoi in 1886 to train staff for the lower ranks of the colonial administration in Tonkin. In embracing Western learning and becoming part of the apparatus of foreign domination, graduates of the School, who were known as scholars of New Learning to distinguish them from Confucian literati, laid themselves open to suspicions of disloyalty. But many of them sincerely believed that they were working for the betterment of their country. They took part in the Reform Movement out of conviction that Vietnamese culture and society had reached a dead end.[31] Their enthusiasm for linguistic and educational reform also derived in no small measure from the fact that, at one stroke, it vindicated their own training and careers and transformed them from cultural brokers of uncertain social standing and suspect loyalties into members of the intellectual and patriotic avant-garde.

The most prominent of these scholars of New Learning within the Reform Movement was Nguyen van Vinh. A 1898 graduate of the School of Interpreters, he had worked for several years as a secretary to the Résident of Lao Kay. After attending the Marseilles Colonial Exhibition in 1906, he resigned his job to go into journalism. The next year, together with Pham Duy Ton, another graduate of the School of Interpreters, Vinh drafted an application to the Résident Supérieur on behalf of fellow reformers for permission to open the Tonkin Free School and acted as its official sponsor.[32]

In Cochinchina, the Reform Movement took on distinctive characteristics.[33] After four decades of colonial rule, most educated southerners were already conversant with the romanized script. There was thus no need to fight a battle that had already been won. Southern patriots even succeeded in using Vietnamese-language newspapers such as *Agrarian Tribune (Nong Co Min Dam)* and *News from the Six Provinces (Luc Tinh Tan Van)* to spread reformist propaganda discreetly. Instead of emphasizing the need for new ideas and a new educational system, southern reformers concentrated on launching business ventures in competition with Chinese traders (and less overtly, with French settlers). They opened rice mills, fish sauce plants, hotels, restaurants, servicing shops, grocery stores. Revenues from such ventures went into supporting various anticolonial activities, in particular the sending of students to Japan and China.

Similar attempts to overcome elitist disdain for trade and business met with indifferent results in Annam and Tonkin, where the mandarin mentality was more entrenched. Literati were willing enough to swallow their prejudices, but they had no experience in heading businesses or managing stores, a task that was usually left to women. They also lacked the common touch. Potential shoppers were intimidated when, expecting to see a woman behind the counter, they saw instead a man dressed in the flowing robes of a scholar, with a servant standing by to fan him and serve him tea. Some literati could not bring themselves to demand that their female customers settle their accounts promptly, and ran up huge debts instead of making money for the cause.[34] The Tonkin Free School stayed afloat only because the wife of its principal sold a store she owned in Hanoi to provide the necessary funds: "My hand shook as I held the sales contract. From childhood, I had never dreamed of selling off a piece of my patrimony. The school was closed down a month after I sold that store; if it had not, I don't know where money would have been found to sustain it."[35]

Getting scholars involved in the grubby world of commercial endeavor was only one component in a wide-ranging attempt to update Confucian values. Trade was made palatable by being presented as a patriotic endeavor. But it was filial piety, the bedrock of Vietnamese society, which attracted the most discussion. The redefinition of filial piety was occasioned by the recognition that the rift between filiality and loyalty must be healed so that piety could serve the cause of patriotism. The first efforts were quite modest. In the past, it had been argued that it was unfilial to cut one's hair or nails: like the rest of the body, they were gifts from one's parents. Now, reformers claimed it was more hygienic, and thus a higher form of piety, to keep them trimmed and clean. The demands of family duty remained unquestioned; what had changed was their concrete expression. In retrospect, therefore, the redefinition of filial piety was much less revolutionary than it appeared at the time, despite the anguish and controversy it provoked.

These attempts to reconcile piety and loyalty occurred as the institution of the monarchy was becoming increasingly hollow. Ever since Ham Nghi had fled the capital in 1885, the French had controlled the imperial succession. In 1907 they deposed Thanh Thai, whom they had installed on the throne two decades earlier, and replaced him with his son, the child emperor Duy Tan. In the absence of a strong imperial presence, an imperceptible shift from dynastic loyalty to a less narrow patriotism was taking place. This shift had already begun during the Aid the King Movement. Despite Hoang Cao Khai's aspersions, Phan Dinh Phung had been motivated not by blind loyalty to the emperor but by love of country. Patriotic literati could draw strength from his example, but they could not agree on the concrete meaning of patriotism, and hence on the ultimate goal of cultural innovation. This lack of consensus ultimately unraveled the fragile unity of the Reform Movement.

The End of the Reform Movement

The introduction in 1908 of a new and unpopular iron currency triggered a wave of antitax protests in Annam, where the Reform Movement had been particularly active. Reformist scholars produced inflammatory poems and songs, which the authorities held responsible for the peasant riots that took place in Quang Nam. The demonstrators were swiftly crushed. The Tonkin Free School and other makeshift schools patterned after it were closed down.[36] The University of Hanoi, which had been opened in 1902 in response to Vietnamese demands for better education, was also a casualty of the backlash. Scores of literati were jailed. The colonial authorities arrested the father of Duong Ba Trac, a minor figure in the Reform Movement, to lure Trac into surrendering. At first, Trac defiantly tried to live up to the new notion of filiality and patriotism and wrote to his own son: "If the nation has no father, that is not important; but what it must not lack is sons."[37] But, as the authorities expected, he was too filial to leave his father to their tender mercies and soon surrendered. Phan Chu Trinh was sent to the penal island of Con Son. Phan Boi Chau, who was in Japan with a party of students, escaped arrest. But in

1909, the French Sûreté was able to infiltrate the network of his southern supporters and halt the movement of students to Japan and China. That same year, at the request of the French authorities, Phan was ordered out of Japan.[38] The Reform Movement was over as a political force, but the cultural reorientation it had launched continued.

French settlers, who regarded concessions to the natives as signs of failure of colonial will, fully supported the repression; but in Paris, the unrest reinforced the government's conviction that sweeping changes were needed in Indochina. Such changes, moreover, though ultimately aimed at curbing Vietnamese unrest, would also greatly curtail the power of the settlers. The man chosen for the task was Albert Sarraut, a popular Deputy with a liberal reputation. He arrived in Indochina in 1911, armed with a mandate for wide-ranging reforms.[39] In particular, he was to streamline the relationship between the Government-General of Indochina and its five constituent states as a precondition for giving more autonomy to Indochina in its dealings with the French metropolitan government. The target of this effort was the powerful Cochinchinese Colonial Council, whose stranglehold over the Indochinese budget undermined attempts to achieve fiscal stability. Sarraut was also to enlarge native representation in various legislative and advisory bodies, revise procedures for naturalization, and introduce educational reforms. But by the time ill-health forced him to return home two years later, Sarraut could point to very few accomplishments. He had created new advisory bodies in Tonkin and Cochinchina on which Vietnamese were allowed to sit, he had bullied the imperial cabinet into accepting the creation of provincial assemblies, he had reduced somewhat the numerical difference between French and Vietnamese members of the Cochinchinese Colonial Council, he had revised rules for naturalization, and he had set in motion the abolition of the Confucian examinations.[40] More fundamental problems, however, had been left untackled.

Sarraut's term had not been without incident, duly seized upon by those who opposed reforms. In 1911, the Manchu dynasty had been overthrown in China and a Republican government installed in power. Inspired by the success of the 1911 Revolution, Phan Boi Chau created the League for the Restoration of Vietnam (Viet Nam Quang Phuc Hoi) in 1912 among Vietnamese expatriates in southern China. Phan had originally wanted to lead a movement dedicated to the overthrow of French rule and the creation of a Vietnamese republic. But he had to yield to the preference of his southern supporters (who provided most of his funds) for a monarchical government. The League was therefore headed by a descendant of the Nguyen dynastic founder, Prince Cuong De; Phan himself assumed the role of Prime Minister of its provisional revolutionary government-in-exile.[41]

To give visibility to his newly formed League, Phan Boi Chau masterminded a series of terrorist incidents and distributed funds to his adherents to purchase bombs for use inside Vietnam.[42] Two French army officers were killed in Hanoi in early 1913; another victim was the Vietnamese governor of Thai Binh province.[43] Meanwhile, acting under the influence of Phan's emissaries, members of secret societies and religious sects in Cochinchina staged attacks on the French police headquarters in Saigon.[44]

The violent activities of the Restoration League provoked a split among veterans of the Reform Movement, dividing those who espoused cultural reform as a weapon against foreign domination and the scholars of New Learning who had made their peace with colonialism. The latter had already been rudely awakened from their rosy images of themselves as fearless cultural warriors when the colonial authorities cracked down on the Reform Movement in 1908. Nguyen van Vinh and Pham Duy Ton, the two official sponsors of the Tonkin Free School, were brought back to Ha Dong to face its governor, Hoang Trong Phu. Phu, a son of Hoang Cao Khai, was well aware of their disinclination toward political activism and ordered them released after a brief detention.[45] Indeed, the experience had been enough to chasten them.

Nguyen van Vinh subsequently made clear his distaste for political violence when he became editor-in-chief of a new weekly, *Indochina Review (Dong Duong Tap Chi)*. The *Indochina Review* was hastily launched on 15 May 1913, soon after the bombing incidents. In a prefatory note, Vinh explained that, although preparations for the first issue had not been finalized, it had been decided to bring forward the date of its publication in order "to use literature and art, to use the cultural benefits of France to shut out seditious noises, so that the explosions caused by the rebels will not drown out the drums of civilization."[46] Phan Boi Chau, Vinh thundered, was a "mean and foolish man who has fled abroad and incites others to violence so as to sow disorder and bring trouble to the people."

Having thus paid his political dues, Nguyen van Vinh was free to concentrate on the cultural pursuits which had originally led him into the Reform Movement. His journal was a landmark in the history of Vietnamese-language publishing.[47] A prolific translator of French literature ranging from La Fontaine's Fables to Hugo's *Les Misérables*, Vinh was an early champion of the vernacular script. He advocated education in Vietnamese and was the first to think of using the national classic *Tale of Kieu* as a basic text in Franco-Annamite schools. He was thus no assimilationist. But he had internalized the Social Darwinian (and hence Western-derived) critique of Vietnamese culture and used *Indochina Review* to launch a sustained assault against it. For twenty-three issues the journal ran a series of articles entitled "Examining Our Defects," in which Vinh attacked nearly everything Vietnamese.[48] This included the bankruptcy of village institutions in the hands of corrupt notables (no. 10); the tendency of the Vietnamese toward indiscriminate superstition, which undermined sincere faith so that no spiritual strength was left to undertake great enterprises (no. 13); the shallow and wrong-headed kind of learning which created intellectuals "who know only two or three characters but sit from morn till night shaking their thighs, well fed, warmly clothed . . . , despising all those who toil, mud up to their knees, hands covered in dirt," and dismissing them as so many "uncouth and brutish peasants" (no. 11). There were many other faults to criticize: the Vietnamese lust for gaming, gossip, cynicism, and so forth (no. 12). In another column entitled "Women's Words," which he wrote under the feminine pen name of Dao thi Loan, Vinh gave full vent to his mysogyny. He decried what he considered the silly habits of Vietnamese women, from their child-bearing and child-rearing customs to the way they treated their husbands and their friends, the funny way they liked to lie down in their kitchens (no. 9); their obsession with mediums, which he interpreted as disguised female libidinousness (no. 20); their fondness for betel-chewing, which some thought the height of elegance, but was "still a rather barbaric custom" (no. 49);[49] and "their liking for dirty talk, for which, surely, they must be unsurpassed" (no. 50).[50] Few areas of Vietnamese learning and few customs or social institutions escaped his barbs.

Like other cultural progressives of the post-Reform decade, Nguyen van Vinh had been won over by Sarraut's justification for continued colonial rule and his scheme for preparing the Vietnamese for eventual independence. Sarraut readily conceded that French dominion over the Vietnamese had been established against their will, and through much violence. But that was past history. What was now at issue was whether the Vietnamese were ready for self-rule; and his answer was a categorical no. Their customs, their institutions, their level of education, their mentality put them in the category of backward people who would profit from the firm guidance of a Western nation. Sarraut stressed that he condemned a "colonial pact" in which the natives were considered as something less than human, or were kept in a state of perpetual childhood. He took pride, instead, in advocating a period of tutelage. During such a period, political concessions would be gradually granted as natives proved themselves capable of profiting by them and of using their newly acquired rights wisely. Only when they had finally reached cultural and political maturity would this tutelage no longer be justified.[51] Its civilizing mission accomplished, France would then graciously bestow independence. If Sarraut's argument was carried to its logical conclusion, the Vietnamese would not be fully mature until they had become exactly like the French in their thinking, their customs, their institutions. In other words, they would deserve independence from French rule only when they no longer desired to be Vietnamese, but Frenchmen in yellow skin.

Nguyen van Vinh, however, never confronted the logic of Sarraut's reasoning. The French colonial presence continued to work changes in Vietnamese culture; other Vietnamese reformers emerged, who had been totally, instead of partially, educated in French. As they did, Nguyen van Vinh turned effortlessly from innovator to preservationist. His retreat from innovation began just before Sarraut launched his far-reaching educational reforms.[52] It is unclear whether his backtracking was motivated by political considerations, as was later the case for his close associate, Pham Quynh. The best explanation perhaps is that Nguyen van Vinh was essentially a transitional figure who, after two decades of introducing Western learning to the Vietnamese public, was ready to return to his cultural roots just as a new generation of students with a more thorough understanding of French culture was coming of age.

By and large, graduates of the School of Interpreters in Tonkin and of the Franco-Annamite establishments in Cochinchina were still not sufficiently numerous and had not yet risen high enough in colonial society to counter their lack of traditional scholarly credentials. But events that occurred during and immediately after World War I wrought a real transformation of Vietnam's political elite and educational system, which in turn brought into the open further schisms in the Reform Movement. Advocates of violent opposition to French rule were temporarily marginalized by either imprisonment or exile. In the North, scholars of New Learning who had once championed cultural innovation became advocates of the cultural and political status quo; in the South, interest in business and trade, already apparent during the Reform Movement, became even more noticeable with the emergence of the bourgeoisie.

Wartime Unrest

When Indochina was put on a war footing in 1915, local authorities began drafting "volunteers" for the European front. The forcible recruitment of thousands of peasants and workers provoked riots throughout Cochinchina, led by members of religious sects and secret societies. Three months later, a plot against the French garrison in Annam was discovered. Implicated in the plot, the sixteen-year-old emperor Duy Tan was dethroned and replaced by the more amenable Khai Dinh.[53] It was claimed that the mastermind of both sets of events was Phan Boi Chau, then operating out of South China and Siam. French public opinion became hysterical. The settlers, invoking the state of war, clamored for blood. Military tribunals were convened to dispense summary justice to the rioters in Cochinchina. Thirty-eight men were publicly executed, over a thousand more were detained; the southern countryside was turned upside down in search of adherents of sects and secret societies.[54]

Worse soon followed. The French Résident of Thai Nguyen province in central Tonkin, Darles, was an unsavory character whose sadism provoked a rebellion which united the prisoners and the colonial troops located in the garrison under his command. In the first eight months of 1917, 670 prisoners held at the Thai Nguyen garrison had died, some because of unsanitary conditions, others killed by Darles himself or by their own hand.[55] Luong Ngoc Quyen, the leader of the uprising, had been part of the Reform Movement since its inception and had been one of the first recruits into the Eastern Travel Movement.[56] Since going to Japan in 1905, he had remained in exile, mostly in South China. Captured there in 1915, he spent two years in a tiny and dank prison cell whose size did not allow him to stand or to lie down. By the time of the uprising, he had lost the use of his legs.

The uprising began in August 1917 and was not quelled until December, at a cost of five hundred lives.[57] Although a military commission of investigation put the blame squarely on Darles for provoking the uprising and the subsequent carnage, he escaped with no more than a fine of one hundred piasters—enough to buy a couple of coffins—and was dismissed from office only after he was photographed torturing a Vietnamese.[58]

French settlers, however, were not interested in the commission's findings. What little tolerance for reform they had previously harbored had vanished. Sarraut, who had arrived back in January 1917 for a second term as Governor-General, thus suffered a decisive setback in his ability to carry out the rest of his program. Already unpopular among the settlers, he had little choice but to set aside his planned overhaul of the governmental structure of Indochina: in their current mood, the settlers were likely to provoke administrative paralysis in order to thwart him.

Sarraut tackled instead the less explosive question of educational reform. He attempted to introduce uniform standards throughout the country in order to address two problems. First was the growing clamor for more educational opportunities, which came not only from anticolonial reformers but also from those segments of the population most supportive of his policies, the emerging urban and landowning middle class. Second was the need to recruit more natives into the colonial civil service. Until 1914, French-educated Vietnamese had been given only clerical assignments. But by 1917, it was clear to Sarraut that, once the war was over, there would be a severe shortage of personnel in France. The colonies would therefore have to rely on locals to fill administrative slots.[59] This meant that natives would have to be given greater responsibilities. But first, they must receive a proper education. Educational reform, long a rallying cry of the Vietnamese elite, became an initiative of the colonial regime.

Educational Turmoil

Western learning had been introduced to the three regions of Vietnam in the haphazard fashion that characterized the whole colonial enterprise.

Traditional schools and academies had largely disappeared from Cochinchina by the 1890s. But for a long time, there was only one French *lycée,* Chasseloup-Laubat, which was located in Saigon. Modeled after metropolitan schools, it was designed primarily for the sons of European residents but also admitted a few Vietnamese, sons of large landowners or members of the colonial service. Under Vietnamese pressure, the colonial authorities established a Franco-indigenous system where both French and the romanized script were taught. Whereas traditional schools and academies had been spread throughout the countryside, the new Franco-indigenous schools were concentrated largely in urban centers, out of the range of rural children. At first, the new schools were intended to offer instruction only in the first three grades; subsequent decrees later added another three years of schooling.[60] After 1910, secondary education began to be provided at a few select institutions such as the Collège Chasseloup-Laubat (which occupied the same premises as the *lycée*) and the Collège de My Tho.[61]

The situation was even bleaker in the two protectorates. Owing to imperial inertia, the traditional examination system was maintained in Tonkin until 1915 and in Annam until 1918. In Tonkin, the Collège du Protectorat, a Franco-indigenous school similar to those of Cochinchina, had been established prior to 1918 as a result of pressure from Vietnamese who wanted a nontraditional education but whose entry into the local *lycée* (renamed Lycée Albert Sarraut after 1919) was barred by local settlers. But in Annam, imperial mandarins, clinging to the tattered remnants of their authority, refused to allow the creation of either French *lycées* or Franco-Annamite schools. The imperial court argued that the curriculum of such schools ran against the spirit of the treaties signed between the two countries, for it demanded that students pledge loyalty to France.[62] Until 1919, the only institution where Franco-Annamite education was allowed was the Imperial College, which had been created in 1896 to fill the personnel needs of the colonial regime. Education in French was slowly introduced between 1914 and 1917, but it began only in the third year of schooling.[63]

After Confucian examinations were abolished, Sarraut tried to bring coherence into the educational system, using the Franco-Annamite schools of Cochinchina as a model. At every educational level, the curriculum was to be adapted to local circumstances; this meant in practice that Indochinese education was far inferior to that dispensed in French schools. Only with the decree of 12 October 1930 did the *baccalauréat indochinois* become valid for entry into French universities.[64] To cap the new system, the University of Hanoi was reopened in 1917. When it was founded in 1902, it had consisted only of a medical school designed to train natives to become paramedics rather than qualified medical doctors. The reopened University added a School of Law to train native civil servants and a Normal School to turn out staff for the Franco-Annamite schools.

The new educational policies were not universally welcomed and implemented. The mandarins of Annam continued to resist the introduction of Franco-Annamite education. They preferred to overhaul the traditional curriculum to provide for the teaching of the romanized script alongside Chinese characters. All academies and schools established earlier to prepare students for the Confucian exams were ordered closed down by imperial decree on 14 July 1919.[65] This made it possible for the court to bring traditional education under greater control and to eradicate a source of continued hostility toward "all innovation of Western origin."[66] The reformed indigenous schools became the sole avenue for recruitment into the mandarinate after 1919. At the apex of this system were two institutions, the Imperial College for boys and Dong Khanh School for girls, which opened in 1919. Both were located in Hue and were reserved primarily for the sons and daughters of the imperial clan and of high mandarins; other students were admitted in limited numbers and under more stringent entry requirements. In Tonkin, the number of Franco-Annamite schools increased after 1919, mainly in urban centers, and especially in the two French concessions of Hanoi and Haiphong. By and large, however, reformed traditional schools were more numerous, for the local elite continued to be attracted to careers as mandarins.

Another feature of Sarraut's educational reforms was numerical expansion. Each village was to build a new school at its own expense. Villagers proceeded to build schools only to close them down almost immediately, lacking funds for maintenance, supplies, equipment, or staff salaries.[67] The expansion of Franco-Annamite schools did little to fulfill the educational needs of the population. Official figures put at 144,300 the total number of students who were enrolled in primary schools in 1921.[68] A negligible number received post-primary education. Things improved only marginally over the next ten years. In 1924–1925, 187,000 children attended school, of which only 17,000 were in secondary schools.[69] Statistics produced for the Colonial Exhibition of 1930 showed that, out of a total population of slightly over seventeen million, 323,759 children of all ages were attending public school.[70] Another 60,000 were enrolled in private establishments founded with Sarraut's blessing, and which, like the public schools, were concentrated in urban centers.[71] Finally, there were also about 3,000 Vietnamese enrolled in French *lycées* (Albert Sarraut in Hanoi, Chasseloup-Laubat in Saigon, and the Dalat *lycée* for residents of Annam). Assuming the school-age population to be one-fourth of the total population, the totals suggest that only 10 percent of school-age children actually went to school. Most villages continued to lack schools, or were able to offer education only in the first grade. Rural children who wanted to continue beyond the first grade had to go to township schools, many miles away from home.[72] Despite these problems, owing to popular respect for knowledge, literacy was somewhat higher than the levels of school attendance would suggest.[73]

Many of the reforms launched by Sarraut were nullified by Governor-General Martial Merlin, who arrived in Vietnam in July 1923. Under the guise of maintaining standards, Merlin severely reduced the level of secondary and post-secondary education. On 14 May 1924, he issued stringent regulations for the opening of new secondary schools, declaring that the secondary school sector was "overdeveloped."[74] He also closed the School of Law, which, with an enrollment of six hundred students, was the largest of the schools of the University of Hanoi. When Vietnamese protested, he retorted that, whereas they were interested only in vertical education for the few, he was interested in horizontal education for the many.[75] In actuality, Merlin's move was largely aimed at rooting out teachers in both traditional and independent Franco-Annamite schools whose loyalty to the colonial state was suspect, a problem that was more acute at the secondary and college levels than at the primary level. Besides issuing restrictive standards for private Franco-Annamite schools, he also cracked down on traditional schools which had failed to close in 1919. In 1924, 1,800 traditional schools were forcibly shut down in Annam and Tonkin.[76] Despite Merlin's strictures about the overdevelopment of secondary education, only a few secondary Franco-Annamite schools actually provided instruction at all levels.[77]

Though he continued to be accused of pursuing a policy of obscurantism, Merlin won praise in some quarters for his efforts to expand primary education in Vietnamese.[78] These efforts were designed to cope with the acute scarcity of French-speaking teaching personnel in the two protectorates, particularly in Annam. In 1924, Merlin allowed three-year schools, with teaching in Vietnamese, to be established. Teachers in these schools were required to have only five years of schooling themselves. To save money, only a handful were put on the regular government payroll; others were hired as auxiliaries by villages, which could only afford to pay them by the day. Only nine teachers were on the regular payroll in Annam; there, the rate for village auxiliaries in 1931 ranged from twelve to twenty-eight piasters per month.[79] Educational cleavages between rural and urban areas that resulted from the uneven distribution of schools were deepened by these curricular differences. In villages, students were taught in their own language by poorly trained, poorly paid teachers; in the cities, students learned from better qualified and better remunerated teachers, but in an alien language.

The elite that emerged from the conflation of scholars of Old and New Learning, graduates of reformed traditional academies, and French and Franco-Annamite schools was inevitably fragmented. It was divided by differences not only in what had been learned but also in how it had been learned. In precolonial times, students had spent endless hours learning by rote long passages in what was, after all, a foreign language, and had been beaten for every peccadillo and failure of memory. But they and their teachers had been united by a shared ethos and a common purpose. In the French and Franco-Annamite schools, no longer was a single mentor responsible for the intellectual and moral growth of a group of disciples bound to him for life by ties of quasi-kinship; instead, students were taught by a variety of instructors, none of whom was responsible for the welfare or behavior of his students outside school. Teachers, and in particular French teachers, were no mere transmitters of a new kind of learning: they represented the colonial state, just as once Confucian teachers had been a link to the world of officialdom. But though the colonial administration inspired fear, its moral authority was low. And low as well, by this time, was the moral authority of the monarchy and of the traditional mandarinate.

Crises of Authority

Constant French meddling in the imperial succession and in the day-to-day running of the imperial cabinet had fatally undermined the prestige of the monarchy. When Emperor Khai Dinh went to France in 1922 to visit the Marseilles Colonial Exhibition, the exiled Phan Chu Trinh issued a savage Seven Point Indictment (That Dieu Thu) against him, holding him, in traditional fashion, personally accountable for the sorry state of his subjects.[80] Nguyen Ai Quoc (alias Ho Chi Minh) ridiculed Khai Dinh in his one-act play, *The Bamboo Dragon,* whose message was that the Dragon of Annam had no more substance than a piece of twisted bamboo.[81] When Khai Dinh died in November 1925, he left as his heir the twelve-year-old Bao Dai, whom he had taken to France in 1922 to be raised in a manner befitting the future ruler of a colonized country. Bao Dai was whisked back to France immediately after the funeral, leaving the throne empty for the next seven years and the French Résident Supérieur in total command.

The monarchical state was moribund, but the traditional equation of nation with family proved useful to the shrewd Sarraut, who appropriated it to propound his vision of colonial Vietnam as one big family ruled by a firm but benevolent paterfamilias promoting the welfare of his children. Eager to be perceived as a bringer of enlightenment, he stressed the uplifting dimension of France's *mission civilisatrice.* It was not easy to sustain this vision in the face of settler callousness. In 1914 Sarraut had felt it necessary to remind Indochina's highest officials that "the natives are human beings just like us, and should be treated like human beings." [82] But he managed to convince an impressive number of Vietnamese of the sincerity of his sentiments. Before leaving for France in the spring of 1919, Sarraut made one last rousing speech. Standing on the steps of the Temple of Confucius, he told his delighted supporters that he would go on fighting for their interests in his new position in the "mother country" (he was Minister of Colonies between 1920 and 1924). He intoned: "A father does not abandon his children." [83]

The choice of venue was full of ironies. Sarraut, who had dismantled the traditional system of education, was using as his platform the place where the names of generations of laureates of the civil service examinations were engraved; the foremost representative of foreign domination stood in front of the most sacred shrine of Confucianism, addressing the fathers and mothers of the people as if they were mere children. Despite this jumble of contradictory symbols and meanings, Sarraut's grand gesture worked. His language appealed to tradition-minded scholars willing to make peace with the French for the sake of preserving a semblance of order. As for the more Westernized advocates of Franco-Annamite collaboration, they saw nothing objectionable in being considered as immature children in need of paternal guidance. It was, after all, the premise upon which the policy of collaboration was based. Both groups remained dazzled by the unfulfilled promises of Sarraut's rhetoric for the next decade and beyond. But under the weight of so many discordant claims and interpretations, the symbols of family and country became debased.

The legitimacy of the mandarinate eroded even more quickly than the moral authority of teachers. Although it was preserved in Annam, Tonkin, and even in Cochinchina in an atavistic form, the mandarinate had little real power. The standard of living of the mandarins was inferior to that of even the lowliest French colonial employees, increasing the mandarins' appetite for corruption. Popular hostility toward officials was nothing new, but in the changed circumstances, it took on added substance. It had been no part of Sarraut's program to destroy the Vietnamese elite, though this was an unintended effect. The public buildings of Indochina might display the slogans of the French Revolution: Liberty, Equality, Fraternity. But for Sarraut, "The existence of an elite is the absolute prerequisite for normal life in any country . . . Therefore, in firmly supporting a policy of ever closer collaboration with native elements duly qualified through their knowledge, their past, their services, their social situation, the 'French Protector' remains faithful to itself."[84]

But who among the Vietnamese could lay claim to being the elite? The Vietnamese intelligentsia represented an infinitesimal proportion of the population, and by 1920, the different educational trajectories available to it had left it deeply divided in its outlook. On the surface, the elite of Annam was least affected by cultural shock, since French education and ideas made fewer inroads there. Even so, Annam's intelligentsia was divided between those who sought success in traditional fashion through a career in the mandarinate and those who, following in the footsteps of Phan Dinh Phung and Phan Boi Chau, eschewed officialdom in favor of anticolonial engagement. The elite was also seriously handicapped in its ability to participate in the intellectual life of the country, for, backed to the hilt by the French Résidents Supérieurs, the imperial court and its mandarins were able to stifle most discourse through censorship and accusations of lèse-majesté. Natives of Annam had to move to Hanoi or Saigon in order to become involved in journalism, the preferred vehicle for discussing cultural or political matters. Only in 1927 did Annam gain a newspaper in the Vietnamese language. In Cochinchina, the prestige of the French *lycées,* higher than that of the Franco-Annamite schools, contributed to the rise of a strongly assimilationist party which, though numerically small, largely preempted the debate on cultural renewal. Southerners tended not to discuss the content of education, except to claim that it was inferior to that available in France; mostly, they demanded more of it. Southern debates were largely political, focusing on issues such as electoral reform and native participation in decision-making bodies. But Tonkin, Vietnam's traditional center of intellectual life, where illicit traditional schools, court-sanctioned "reformed" indigenous schools, and Franco-Annamite schools now coexisted uneasily, became a cultural battleground.

Judging by the rules for naturalization passed in 1915, there is no doubt that Sarraut's ideal elite was a thoroughly Westernized one. Among the information required of applicants was whether they ate bread or rice, sat on chairs, slept on mattresses, and so forth.[85] Such an elite did exist in Cochinchina. But Sarraut was realistic enough to recognize the need to win over the Confucian literati of Tonkin and Annam, whose prestige and influence had not yet been irreversibly undermined by graduates of Franco-Annamite schools. When he returned to Vietnam in 1917, Sarraut immediately cast about for suitable men to publish newspapers that would serve as his unofficial platform. The newspapers would help counter the relentless hostility of the settlers by winning the Vietnamese elite, old and new, over to his program of reforms. With the help of Louis Marty, an erudite scholar fluent in both Chinese and Vietnamese whom he named Director of the Indochinese Sûreté, Sarraut identified two men to run two papers, one in Hanoi and one in Saigon. Both papers were launched with funds provided by Sarraut's office and began publication almost simultaneously in July and August 1917, but they were aimed at very different audiences. The journal that appeared in Hanoi was called *Southern Wind (Nam Phong)* and was designed to win over northern neo-traditionalists; the newspaper published in Saigon was called *Tribune Indigène* and was meant to mobilize the opinion of southern, French-educated assimilationists.

Tame Heretics: The Southern Bourgeoisie

Tribune Indigène was aimed at both the French-educated Vietnamese elite and the French settlers of Cochinchina. Because its publisher and its editor-in-chief both enjoyed French citizenship, it was permitted to discuss politics (a rubric very broadly interpreted by the authorities to mean anything that might arouse the slightest controversy). The publisher of *Tribune Indigène,* Nguyen Phu Khai, was a wealthy landowner who had once been a protégé of the writer Pierre Loti and had studied in France.[86] But the real soul of *Tribune Indigène* was its editor-in-chief, Bui Quang Chieu. Only five years separated Bui Quang Chieu from Phan Boi Chau; like Phan, Chieu was born in a scholarly family, possibly of higher status.[87] But a gulf of experience lay between them, for, by 1872, the year of Chieu's birth, all of the South had passed under French rule. Chieu was given a thoroughly French education. He went to France in 1893 to attend the Ecole Coloniale and later to Algeria for further studies. Upon his return in 1897, he entered the colonial bureaucracy as an agronomic engineer. He acquired French citizenship and became involved in cultural endeavors, contributing to the expansion of the Société d'Enseignement Mutuel (Hoi Tri Tri), of which he eventually became president. His efforts to rise above the herd paid off in 1917 when Sarraut, casting for Vietnamese allies, selected him to be the editor of *Tribune Indigène.*

Bui Quang Chieu believed himself to be working for the good of his country in advancing the interests of members of his own class: the French-educated businessmen, landowners, and civil servants who formed the emerging Cochinchinese bourgeoisie. The composition of the bourgeoisie was fairly diverse in terms of social origins, wealth, and occupation. A small number enjoyed French citizenship. Some, though not all, owed their wealth to collaboration with the French during the early phase of conquest; they or their parents had been rewarded with high positions and the opportunity to acquire land cheaply. Others had been quick to make the most of new economic opportunities. Still others were civil servants of far more modest means. They were, however, united in their pride in their Western education and contemptuous of old-style village officials and mandarins. When France, having accomplished its *mission civilisatrice,* granted independence to the Vietnamese, the bourgeoisie would be the class best suited to become the new ruling elite. In the meantime, it was happy to shelter in the protective shade of the French mother country. With its newly acquired wealth and Western education, the bourgeoisie considered itself the enlightened class par excellence as well as the motive force of progress. Its members wanted political power and social recognition with all the fervor of most *nouveaux riches* and were obsessed with the goal of replacing the mandarinate as the native elite. They shared Sarraut's conviction that the elite, by which they meant those empowered to vote and sit on legislative bodies, should be made up of people who, like themselves, possessed a solid French education, were devoted to French ideals and culture, and had achieved wealth and social position.

The emergence of the Cochinchinese bourgeoisie since the turn of the century had already become discernible in the mercantile orientation of the southern Reform Movement, although it had been overshadowed by the Movement's political agenda. The repression which was visited upon opponents of colonial rule from north to south in 1917 allowed the bourgeoisie to become more visible. It also became more vocal in its demands. In April 1919, just as Sarraut was preparing to leave for France, *Tribune Indigène* began printing on its masthead the announcement that it was the "Organ of the Indochinese Constitutionalist Party," thus serving notice that while Sarraut would carry on the fight for an Indochinese Constitution in France, the paper would do likewise in Vietnam. The combative tone was not simply a journalistic flourish. The bourgeoisie believed itself to be an embattled minority surrounded by enemies intent on undermining its economic and political interests: French settlers who tried to prevent the Vietnamese bourgeoisie from gaining more economic power and political rights as French citizens, Chinese businessmen who exercised disproportionate control over the economy, mandarins who refused to yield to the bourgeoisie their position of preeminence, and finally, the masses of workers and peasants who were showing signs of increasing restlessness.

Francophile by both education and self-interest, members of the bourgeoisie were ideal advocates of the kind of reforms Sarraut envisaged. But, though their interests and those of Albert Sarraut converged on many points, they were not always identical. Sarraut's aim in bolstering native elites was merely to provide the social stability needed for economic prosperity. As Minister of Colonies, Sarraut, who had not been able to balance the Indochinese budget, became concerned with making the colonies profitable. In 1921 he launched a program of colonial development which inaugurated a period of unbridled economic exploitation in Vietnam, fueled by the inflation that had set in as a result of heavy financial contributions to the war effort. Reflecting on his program ten years later, Sarraut justified it on the ground that "the time of 'hermit nations' has passed. No country has the right to exist in hostile isolation, leaving in incompetent hands the empty ownership of unutilized riches."[88] Although members of the Vietnamese bourgeoisie agreed on the need to develop the riches of Vietnam (and Laos), they much preferred that the task be left to them rather than to the get-rich-quick entrepreneurs who were attracted to Indochina by Sarraut's economic policies.

The basic ideas underlying the political program of the Constitutionalists were set forth in a speech given by Diep van Cuong on 21 September 1917.[89] Cuong, who sat on the Cochinchinese Colonial Council, proposed that local government be restructured along French lines, so that the Westernized elite could play a bigger role in running the country. His reformist zeal was directed against the policy of selecting Vietnamese representatives to the legislative and advisory bodies of Cochinchina from among members of what he called the *ancien régime,* products of the traditional educational system. A few weeks later, he called for suffrage for men who held a business license, for property owners, and for (French) educated elements.[90]

The new assertiveness of the bourgeoisie evidenced in these proposals rested on a sense of accomplishment and self-righteousness engendered by its successful wartime fund-raising campaign and its awareness of having shown due devotion to France in its hour of need. After Indochina formally became involved in the war effort in 1915, approximately six hundred million francs were raised in outright donations, treasury bonds, and loans. In addition to aiding the French war effort, the campaign highlighted the financial clout of native landowners and businessmen.[91]

But there were also the ninety-four thousand natives of Indochina who had been sent to serve as "volunteers" in Europe, ostensibly as a token of their gratitude for the benefits showered on them by the colonial regime.[92] Although a small minority of better-educated men went to Europe as interpreters, most of the so-called volunteers were poor peasants and workers.[93] The draftees were expected to return home by 1919, raising the problem of how to reward them for their war service. The possibility of granting them the time-honored reward of full French citizenship, which included suffrage, was raised,[94] a thought that brought to the fore all the more elitist traits of the bourgeois politicians. Bui Quang Chieu was a strong advocate of easing rules of accession to the rights of French citizenship for members of the bourgeoisie (natives of Cochinchina already being French subjects).[95] At the time, enfranchised Vietnamese numbered about one thousand.[96] If granted full citizenship, returned veterans would have swamped the few members of the Vietnamese bourgeoisie who so prized their own right to vote. This caused Chieu to "shudder at the thought of admitting undesirables into the great French family: people without means of livelihood or without culture." [97] Chieu was vociferous in his opposition to an enlargement of the electorate which would have altered the balance of power not only between the races—something he desired—but more important, between the classes, which he considered catastrophic. "Mass Naturalization? Never," ran the editorial of *Tribune Indigène* on 31 January 1918: "I cannot help being seriously disturbed when I think that if, by some extraordinary measures, mass naturalization was decreed in Cochinchina, the result of a legislative election could depend on the vote of our rickshaw boys and our cooks." Inequality was a fact of life. It was the ordering principle among individuals as it was among nations and races. To the vast mass of peasants and workers Chieu conceded only "the right to exist": "How can there be equality in life? Let me give an example: thanks to his efforts to educate himself, thanks to chance and circumstances, thanks to his wealth and achievements, a man rises into the elite or the bourgeoisie; naturally he has the right to enjoy more privileges than a street sweeper. The latter is ignorant, he cannot do anything else. All he has a right to is to exist, that is as it should be." [98]

Chieu's invincible elitism, personal vanity, and horror of disorder were so many weapons in the hands of the authorities, severely limiting his effectiveness as a reformer, even on behalf of his own class. One way for the colonial authorities and the settlers to check Chieu's ambitions was to charge him with sympathy for Phan Boi Chau, who was accused of inspiring all the violent attempts to overthrow colonial rule that had occurred over the last fifteen years. Unfailingly, Chieu hastened to refute such accusations. In an unmistakable, if oblique, swipe at Phan Boi Chau, Chieu declared in 1923: "Some people advocate obtaining independence through the gun, I advocate obtaining it through culture." [99]

Bui Quang Chieu's personal experience had turned him into an ardent assimilationist who lost few opportunities to proclaim his loyalty to France. In his view, the French had the right to rule over the Vietnamese by virtue of their white skin and their inherent moral superiority. Even when faced with blatant miscarriages of justice caused by the settlers' insistence on preserving French prestige, Bui Quang Chieu could only reiterate his love of order and his faith in the rule of law. To the end, Chieu could not sympathize with efforts to make the romanized script the official written language of Vietnam. He saw it as an unnecessary delay on the road to complete fluency in French, the language of the ruling class and therefore the only one worth knowing. He even admitted that he very seldom read the Vietnamese-language press.[100] His detractors claimed that he seldom spoke his native tongue, either. Having opted for total assimilation, Chieu was utterly uninterested in cultural matters. For all his pride in his education, he was not an intellectual and cared little about what children were learning, as long as they attended school. He was an ardent supporter of educational expansion: "Schools, more schools, always more schools!" was the motto of the Constitutionalists.[101] In the wake of Sarraut's educational reforms, Chieu had opened a private Franco-Annamite school of his own. However, for him, the goal of education was not political empowerment for the masses, but the ascendancy of the Western-educated bourgeoisie over the remnants of the Confucian elite. Others, like Pham Quynh in Tonkin, might wish for a more "judicious blending of East and West." Such questions do not seem to have bothered Chieu; on that issue, his perceived adversaries were the settlers. He had enough trouble already fending off their warnings that mass education would merely teach the natives to rebel against their masters. On the contrary, he argued, spreading French ideas among the Vietnamese could only bind the latter closer to France. Recognizing the "moral superiority of the French," Chieu editorialized:

> By inculcating French ideas in the minds of the Indochinese peoples, there need be no fear that we will see a reawakening of Annamite nationalism, for it can be satisfied with the present regime which suits our collective aspirations much better than the *ancien régime* could have . . . Now that we have shown France our deep attachment to her, now that we have brought her irrefutable proofs of our loyalism, we come to respectfully but firmly ask of the protector nation: "Educate us, as you educate your own children . . . Tell us what we must pay so that the Annamites do not remain the least educated people in East Asia despite French protection. Our rice fields are rich, our plains are fertile; we want to have schools that are worthy of you and of us. Then our happiness will be complete."[102]

Though Bui Quang Chieu's detractors dismissed him as nothing more than a French puppet, he was above all an articulate advocate of the interests of his class. As the mouthpiece for this assimilationist, but also increasingly assertive, bourgeoisie, *Tribune Indigène* was perceived as such a thorn in the side of the colonial regime that in 1919, acting Governor-General Georges Maspéro, a less liberal administrator than Sarraut, decided to fund another newspaper with the hope that its publisher would prove less cantankerous.[103] The man chosen for the job was Nguyen Phan Long, a self-taught employee of the Customs service, who was an occasional contributor to *Tribune Indigène*. Despite its beginning, Long's journal, *Echo Annamite*, quickly became more critical than *Tribune Indigène* had ever been, for it reflected more closely the concerns and experiences of Long's fellow civil servants. Though resentful of their subordinate status and often demeaning jobs, these colonial clerks were nonetheless afraid of losing what status and jobs they had. Their ambivalence was fully reflected in Long's personality. Although less elitist than Bui Quang Chieu, he was only mildly effective as a reformist editor. He had the pompous manner of the autodidact, yet at the same time lacked Chieu's abundant self-assurance.

Thus neither Bui Quang Chieu nor Nguyen Phan Long was an assertive presence. Caught between the intransigence of the settlers, the pressure of the colonial administration, and their own dislike for "mob rule and anarchy," which made them unwilling to mobilize popular opinion in support of even the most modest demands for reforms, both men were forced to walk a political tightrope. As far as the authorities were concerned, they were meant to perform a necessary function as counterweights against the sometimes unbearable pressure exerted by the settlers. The head of the Cochinchinese Sûreté observed to the incoming Governor in 1921: "In a certain sense, an opposition is a desirable thing. It is good for a democratic government to face an opposition in order to balance it, stimulate it, and control it. The Apostle has already uttered these profound words: 'there is a need for heretics.' The evil does not lie in the existence of an opposition; it lies in the absence of a counterweight to this opposition so that it is allowed to become strong enough to impede, paralyze or distort the actions of the government. We need heretics, but not too many." [104]

Tame heretics: this was the role allotted Bui Quang Chieu, Nguyen Phan Long, and the bourgeois politicians who rallied around them under the banner of Constitutionalism. Bui Quang Chieu regularly sought reassurances from the Cochinchinese Sûreté that his criticisms did not trespass the bounds of gubernatorial tolerance and invariably toned down his editorials when he was told they did.[105] For all of his much-prized French citizenship, Bui Quang Chieu's position was thus as precarious as that of any other Vietnamese, all the more so since he was still employed in the Indochinese bureaucracy as an agronomist. In January 1925, he was transferred against his will to Phnom Penh in retaliation for having headed a successful campaign to defeat a scheme by Maurice Cognacq, the Governor of Cochinchina, to grant monopoly rights to a French consortium to develop new facilities in the port of Saigon. Chieu agonized for a whole month, for he had just invested a considerable fortune so that *Tribune Indigène* could appear five days a week instead of three; but, in the end, loath to be dismissed from office so close to the date of his retirement, he meekly went to Phnom Penh.[106] The newly expanded *Tribune Indigène* folded almost immediately.

Tradition and Innovation: The Northern Literati

For Sarraut, French settlers posed fewer problems in the North than in the South. They were less numerous in the North, and could be fended off with the intricacies of the protectorate system. Nor, in 1917, were there yet enough graduates of Franco-Annamite schools to sustain a French-language publication similar to *Tribune Indigène* or *Echo Annamite*. At any rate, the Vietnamese whose opinion Sarraut and Marty sought to court were not the few who were already won over to the cause of French rule, but the far more influential classical scholars whose hopes of appointment to the imperial mandarinate had disappeared along with the examination system, and whose erudition was becoming obsolete. There was a risk that, out of a sense of intellectual disaffection and blighted career prospects, formerly quiescent scholars would unite with their anticolonial, antimonarchical brethren to spearhead a backlash against the reforms instituted by Sarraut. *Southern Wind* was meant to serve as a haven for these disoriented scholars, as well as a means of rallying local public opinion behind the idea of Franco-Annamite collaboration.

Pham Quynh, who was selected as publisher of *Southern Wind*, had first caught the eye of Louis Marty when he was writing for Nguyen van Vinh's *Indochina Review*. Pham Quynh, who was born in Tonkin in 1892, came from a prestigious lineage that went back to the thirteenth century.[107] His great-grandfather, an educational officer during the reign of Emperor Minh Mang (1820–1840), was included in the "Twenty-Four Exemplars of Filial Piety" *(Nhi thap tu hieu)* by Hoang Thai Xuyen.[108] Pham Quynh might have followed in his ancestors' footsteps and become a mandarin had he not lost both his parents before he was ten. Instead of providing him with a classical education, his paternal grandmother enrolled him at the age of twelve in the School of Interpreters. Four years later, he had acquired a good command of French and of the romanized script, and a basic knowledge of Chinese. A Certificate of Primary Education in hand, he went to work at the Ecole Française d'Extrême-Orient. In 1913, while still working at the Ecole Française, he joined the editorial staff of *Indochina Review*.

In 1915, Pham Quynh and Nguyen Ba Trac, another contributor to *Indochina Review*, were selected by Marty to publish a Chinese-language "History of the War in Europe." It was designed to counter German influence in China, where France had a number of concessions, and among the Chinese-reading public of Tonkin. When Sarraut decided to look for means of both sustaining Indochinese support for the war and publicizing his program of reforms, Pham Quynh was chosen, at Marty's suggestion, to receive funds. He proceeded to launch *Southern Wind*. The first issue of the journal, which appeared monthly, bore the phrase "The Annamite Dragon spits out silver to overthrow the German bandits," which had been adopted as the slogan of the fund-raising campaign for the war.[109] In the second issue, Duong Ba Trac, one of the journal's early contributors, piously wrote: "Pray that God protect our adoptive mother so that she may destroy all the demons and restore our nation."[110] Only nine years earlier, the same Duong Ba Trac had declared that it did not matter if the country had no father.

Unlike *Tribune Indigène*, which was written entirely in French, *Southern Wind* came in three parts: one French, one Vietnamese, and one Chinese. The first, always the shortest, was the least interesting; often, it merely reiterated what was contained in the Vietnamese section. At the beginning, the Chinese section featured important scholarship, but once *Southern Wind* had fulfilled its mission of wooing the Confucian literati, it became what Pham Quynh had always wanted it to be: a journal written primarily in the Vietnamese vernacular of which he was an ardent champion. Since it was essentially a Vietnamese-language paper, it was subject to prior censorship and was theoretically not allowed to discuss political matters. In fact,

Southern Wind was meant to represent official French views on matters of domestic and international politics.[111] Within the limited compass in which Pham Quynh operated, *Southern Wind* seems to have changed direction with each successive Governor-General. One critic charged in 1930: "Following only the wind causes the ship to change ideology as often as people change shirts."[112] Yet, if Pham Quynh was effective in carrying out a program mapped out by the colonial authorities, it was because his political shifts were fairly trivial, and because he sincerely believed in the cultural line he propounded.

Unlike *Tribune Indigène,* which sought to engage the authorities and the French settlers in dialogue, *Southern Wind* was directed exclusively at the Vietnamese themselves. Pham Quynh was not concerned with political representation, which was unavailable to natives of the protectorates, but with finding solutions to the acute cultural malaise from which, everyone now realized, the nation suffered. He wrote, "the nation is like a ship in the middle of a wide river; it has long ago left one shore, but it is still far from the other."[113] It was Pham Quynh's self-imposed duty to guide it through the perilous journey from the shore of tradition to the shore of modernity. Pham Quynh shared with Nguyen van Vinh and Bui Quang Chieu the belief that Vietnamese society was backward, and that many of its customs and mores bordered on the barbaric. Before they could be considered mature enough for self-rule, the Vietnamese would have to undergo a thoroughgoing cultural transformation. Indeed, he argued that without that transformation, it would be useless for the Vietnamese to win political concessions from the French, for these would not take hold.[114] But he did not believe that assimilation was the solution to Vietnam's cultural backwardness.

What Pham Quynh wanted was to strike a proper balance between native tradition and Western modernity, for those were the terms in which he conceived Vietnam's cultural dilemma. Like so many others, he had been influenced by Social Darwinism. Phan Boi Chau had opted to work for the survival of the Vietnamese nation. Pham Quynh worried over the survival of Vietnamese culture and the preservation of what he considered to be its national essence *(quoc tuy)*.

Pham Quynh had been deeply affected by Tagore's call for a new culture based on a synthesis of what was best in East and West. A disseminator of Western learning of fairly catholic tastes (because he accepted the inherent superiority of all things Western), he was particularly concerned with isolating what was best in Eastern culture.

In this he followed the traditional (and elitist) habit of thinking in East Asian rather than purely Vietnamese terms. From his copious delving into contemporary Chinese writings, but without acknowledging his intellectual debts, Pham Quynh had absorbed the idea of preserving the national essence.

But it was national essence with a major difference. The Vietnamese national essence movement was, like much of 1920s politics, a purely elite phenomenon. Its interpretation of tradition was more narrow than in China. Leaders of the Chinese National Essence Movement such as Liang Shu-ming were receptive to Western intellectual influences, but they were also classically trained scholars, for whom Confucian learning was still a living and diverse tradition. Furthermore, their interpretation of national essence was not limited to Confucianism, but was broad and inclusive. It contained a strong agrarian and democratic component which manifested itself variously in the campaign for the vernacular and in other efforts to bridge the gap between elite and popular cultures, between intellectuals and peasants.[115] The 1904 manifesto of the Reform Movement, *The Civilization of New Learning,* had criticized the Vietnamese for neglecting rural conditions; since then, the countryside had become a target for reform but was not viewed as a source of knowledge. Had Vietnamese neo-traditionalists valued rural mores and institutions more, they might have come up with a different understanding of national essence. But Pham Quynh and other neo-traditionalists had no interest in returning to Vietnam's agrarian roots. They shared their contemporaries' almost unanimous conviction that the village was the repository of antiquated and downright harmful customs and usages. Though Pham Quynh did not advocate turning the village into an approximation of a French municipality as did Bui Quang Chieu and his southern supporters, his journal published numerous proposals for reforming village institutions, and these invariably began with a catalogue of the evils of rural life.

For Vietnamese neo-traditionalists, the national essence of their country was synonymous with Confucianism. But even in the etiolated Vietnamese context, it was a pale echo of the more muscular Confucianism that had flourished in the nineteenth century. With the end of the civil service examinations, interest in classical scholarship was being kept alive by a dwindling band of Confucian literati. Waning interest in the study of the Chinese language and difficulties in obtaining Chinese-language materials caused by an overzealous censorship bureau cut off Vietnamese scholars from much of their literary and philosophical heritage and from ongoing Chinese cultural debates. As a result, the meaning of Confucianism became so impoverished that what came to be understood by that term was a certain type of morality which emphasized decorum, orderliness, family relationships, and reciprocity, and could be encapsulated in a few mottos: the Three Bonds, the Five Cardinal Precepts, the Three Submissions, the Four Virtues. It had become a set of behavioral principles and had lost its potency as a personal philosophy or method of government. Its detractors called it "ossified Confucianism" *(hu nho)*. Yet, whether they defended tradition or attacked it, commentators from all sides believed that tradition began and ended with this particular brand of Confucianism.

Pham Quynh scorned the idea that the sum total of human knowledge could be found in the Four Classics and strove to define a new culture for a modernizing Vietnam. He interpreted national essence as a vaguely defined blend of Vietnamese literature, Confucian morality, family institutions, and modestly progressive education in the Vietnamese vernacular rather than in Chinese or French. His motto was: "As long as our language endures, our country will endure." His ardent advocacy of the romanized script as the language of choice in the school curriculum led him to seek to enrich the Vietnamese vernacular with neologisms borrowed from China (and ultimately Japan). He enthusiastically welcomed Merlin's establishment of Vietnamese-language education at the elementary level. When he became Imperial Minister of Education in 1932, he argued strenuously against the extension of French-language education to Annam. Pham Quynh liked to think of himself as a cultural innovator, but his obsession with protecting what he imagined to be the national essence and his advocacy of old-fashioned morality made him Vietnam's foremost neo-traditionalist. Although lacking classical credentials, he was closer in spirit to the conservatives he was supposed to woo than to the progressives among whom he imagined himself to be. At heart he belonged to the transitional generation of scholars of New Learning like Nguyen van Vinh, who, having once pioneered Western education, now saw salvation in the reaffirmation of traditional values.

Southern Wind was neatly complemented by the Hanoi-based Association for the Intellectual and Moral Formation of the Annamites (Hoi Khai Tri Tien Duc), also known by its French acronym, AFIMA. The creation of AFIMA in 1919 was the work of a group of high-ranking mandarins, including Hoang Trong Phu and Than Trong Hue, an uncle of Emperor Khai Dinh. In 1922, Hoang Trong Phu served as its president, but the real decision-makers within the Association were its vice-president, Nguyen van Vinh, and its secretary-general, Pham Quynh, who represented AFIMA at the Marseilles Colonial Exhibition that year. Because culture was a form of politics in colonial Vietnam, it is no surprise that the guiding hand behind AFIMA belonged to the ubiquitous Marty, who had put the idea of creating AFIMA in the minds of its founders in the first place.[116] Nguyen van Vinh thus explained AFIMA's mandate:

> We must constantly react against the demoralization that could result from too rapid Westernization, which would destroy the framework of our national past without substituting a new discipline for the old one. We are abruptly introducing a sense of responsibility and a critical spirit among individuals who belong to a collectivity which, for centuries, practiced blind self-effacement before family, clan, village, ruler. We must not lose our balance when the notion of individual rights penetrates a world where everything was sacrificed to duties toward the collective, cleverly hierarchical, structures which formed the Annamite social edifice.[117]

Considering himself no less a patriot than Phan Boi Chau, Pham Quynh shared the southern collaborationists' abhorrence of violence and disorder. He was not opposed to change on principle. He understood that a certain amount of disarray was unavoidable, but if change was introduced gradually, disorder and anomie could be averted. In 1930, he explained his motto as follows: "We must ensure that in the process of constant progress, society remains stable and peaceful."[118] His interpretation of order was anchored in traditional thinking: a state of equilibrium, of harmony, and above all an absence of disorder *(loan)*. *Disorder* in the Vietnamese language is a term that is almost protean in its range of meanings. It can mean simple untidiness; mental or emotional confusion; immorality, or amorality; disorderliness; lawlessness; political unrest and rebellion; cosmic disorder. In its most profound and broadest sense, it means total chaos, anarchy and anomie encompassing the individual, society, the world, the cosmos.

Despite the difference in their preferred language of expression, Pham Quynh and Bui Quang Chieu shared a static notion of order which boiled down to the absence of visible disorder. They did not delve below this surface calm to look for deeper tensions. Notwithstanding their reservations about specific aspects of colonialism, they feared the disruptive effect of too rapid change even more, and thus were drawn to adopting a collaborationist stance. Both were reluctant to rock the colonial boat lest they find themselves engulfed in treacherous waters. They were unwilling to confront the possibility that colonial rule was inimical to true order. Paradoxically, they had married their static notion of order to the dynamism of the Social Darwinian vision of history to produce a rationale for prolonged colonial rule: by reason of their superiority, the French had earned the right to be in Vietnam. Their continued presence was needed to provide stability while the country was in the throes of cultural transformation. Through this theoretical sleight of hand, the collaborationists transformed the predatory conqueror into a nurturing father, setting aside the notion that the struggle for survival is a constant state of war and precarious equilibrium. In the process, order became as morally suspect as the other values and institutions they tried to uphold.

The Making of Prodigal Children

Although they occupied opposite ends of the cultural spectrum, Bui Quang Chieu and Pham Quynh set the burden of colonialism squarely on Vietnamese shoulders. Chieu urged total assimilation; Pham Quynh called for the preservation of tradition even while he blamed the backwardness of Vietnamese society and culture for colonial conquest. It was a burden that, increasingly, young Vietnamese refused to bear.

Concerned as he was with the survival of Vietnamese culture, Pham Quynh wanted to exert an influence over Vietnam's youth. But his chosen persona ill-fitted him to serve as their mentor. He was not much older than they—he was only thirty-one at the time he spoke about the moral malaise of Vietnamese youth, though with nearly a decade of involvement in journalism behind him. Yet he had turned himself into a pundit, honing an editorial style which seldom betrayed traces of youthful excess. Only occasionally, as in his account of his 1922 trip to France, did he become carried away by enthusiasm, leading later observers to marvel that he had ever been young.[119] Usually he spoke in measured accents, as befitted his chosen mission as Vietnam's premier cultural arbiter and teacher, with *Southern Wind* as his pulpit and the whole country as his parish.

Pham Quynh underestimated the extent of Vietnam's cultural crisis. Baffled by the melancholy which seemed to hold Vietnam's youth in its grip, he attributed it to youthful self-centeredness. Such a conclusion left him unable to empathize with those caught in the maelstrom of change. Pham Quynh still thought in terms of obligations embedded in networks of relationships. Why should young people be despondent? He thought there were several possible reasons for their sadness: unfulfilled, unattainable ideals; a dull daily life; and unhealthy bodies which rendered them prone to vicarious sorrowing over fictional tragedies.[120] Were young people depressed because they had failed in their exams? Because they could not find employment? Because their lovers were faithless or their valued friends turned out to be cheats? Or because they had not yet found spouses? If so, Pham Quynh maintained that these were petty and unimportant reasons for apathy and sorrow. "Melancholy is justified when great enterprises that are undertaken remain unfinished. But what has today's youth done to justify its sadness?"[121] Many youths, chafing under parental authority, pressured into suitable but loveless marriages, and pushed into demeaning bureaucratic jobs for the sake of providing for their families, found in their predicament cause enough for despondency. But Pham Quynh, proud of his past and orphaned at a young age, had never experienced the full weight of patriarchal authority and was unable to comprehend the demoralizing effects of familism coupled with colonial rule. Illogically for a man who fashioned his politics after those of whichever Governor-General happened to be in power, he trotted out heroes of Vietnam's tradition of resistance to foreign rule as examples of great men who had earned the right to feel despondent over their unfulfilled ambitions. Happy with his personal circumstances, he refused to see that, by his standards, the only great enterprise whose failure would have justified dejection was the overthrow of colonial rule.

The family had become the last bastion of traditional values and the repository of career ambitions that had remained intact despite the change of regime. The less parents understood what their children were learning at school, the more functionalist a view they took of education. Its content might have become inaccessible, but it still served as a path into the civil service and as a means of advancing the interests of one's family. This purely pragmatic view of education has found echoes in a number of interpretations of the origins of the Vietnamese Revolution. Thus, a strike that took place in 1927 has been described as "a student assertion of elite status . . . Their vision of an elite was not one that bowed and scraped and allowed itself to be bullied. The strike was a clear and simple statement that students wanted to be a real elite, not minor fonctionnaires."[122]

But there is a different interpretation for student unrest. Caught in the cross fire of old expectations and alien ideas, young Vietnamese were becoming aware of the pervasiveness of what the anarchist Kropotkin called "conventional lies." Although fathers no longer shared with teachers common ideas on how to promote the intellectual and moral development of their sons, at the least hint of unruliness, they were called in to bring their offspring into line. Students were appalled to see their fathers, including high-ranking mandarins, abase themselves in front of the school authorities, abusive and unjust though the latter had been. Few had the heart (or nerve) to confront their own fathers, but they had less compunction about lashing out at others'. Nguyen Thuong Huyen, a *cu nhon* degree-holder whose father was a magistrate in Ha Dong, wrote an anonymous letter to the provincial governor to castigate the mandarins of Vinh Yen for kowtowing to visiting French officials, thus forcing all other Vietnamese present to follow suit.[123] Perhaps the students who jeered when mandarins kowtowed in front of their teachers were less unsettled by the prospect of bleak futures devoid of power than by the discrepancy between Confucian ideals and colonial reality, the undisputed power of the paterfamilias at home and the abject servility of the mandarin abroad.

Many were consumed by guilt over their lives of idle privilege and were appalled to discover that their own fathers were oppressive and corrupt. Indeed, the ranks of the Vietnamese Revolution contained an unusual number of sons and daughters of the Confucian elite. Nguyen The Truyen is perhaps the prime example of this group of early participants in the Revolution. Truyen, named delegate for Indochina in the French Communist Party in 1923, was fifteen when his grandfather, the governor of Thai Binh province, was killed in 1913 by adherents of the Restoration League.[124] Truyen could not have failed to know that his grandfather was held in deepest contempt by his peers. As the Sûreté delicately put it, "the governor of Thai Binh was known among the natives for his devotion to the Protectorate and for the sternness with which he had suppressed the activities of instigators of disorder."[125]

In order to account for this preponderance of children of Vietnam's

Confucian elite among the leadership of the Revolution, a number of scholars have eschewed the idea that it had its origins in their frustrated career ambitions, and have discerned instead continuities between Confucianism and communism which eased the transition from the one to the other. Chief among these was the Confucian preoccupation with moral action and collective welfare. This preoccupation, however, could take many guises. Piety and loyalty could lead to collaboration as easily as they did to rebellion. Those who argue for continuity tend to emphasize a linear progression from Phan Dinh Phung, through the Reform Movement, to the Vietnamese Youth League and eventually the Indochinese Communist Party. But Phan Dinh Phung, deeply conservative as a regent, was ahead of his time as an advocate of fatherland over family, an exception rather than the norm among his peers. Depending on circumstances, filial piety could lead to avoidance of political engagement in favor of personal advancement; it could mean following one's father into opposing foreign rule; or it could mean attempting to redeem a father's shameful acquiescence to that rule through rebellion. Indeed, rebellion and conformity coexisted within the same families—sometimes within the same individual. Fathers who deeply disapproved of their offsprings' activities seldom cut off their funds.[126]

But there were also those for whom anticolonialism was a family tradition. They were often the sons and daughters of rural literati rather than of high-ranking mandarins. The prestige of rural scholars may have been reinforced by the disappearance of the examination system. Such scholars were typically described as lower degree-holders or men of high learning and probity who had failed to win a degree, the implication being that they were worthy of greater recognition. Sometimes, their marginal position within the new colonial order was due to their refusal to compromise their principles. Despite the disappearance of their schools and academies, they still managed to spread anticolonial, antimonarchical propaganda. They passed on their political values to their children, but not their cultural vocabulary, which had been publicly appropriated by conservative accommodationists. When it came time for their children to express their patriotic feelings, they did so, like the rest of their peers, in the language of iconoclasm. Nguyen Khac Vien, the Communist son of a Confucian scholar, tried to explain the success of Communist ideology in Vietnam by pointing out the ways in which it resonated with Confucian values; but he also recalled his early distaste for what passed for tradition in the 1920s, a distaste he had shared with others of his generation and which their elders failed to comprehend.[127]

In 1920, when the radicalization of Vietnamese youth was just beginning, an elderly scholar named Nguyen Ba Hoc wrote to *Southern Wind* to warn of the pitfalls of Westernization. Vietnam, declared Hoc, was like a grand old house bequeathed by parents to their children, who had allowed it to become dilapidated. The children had then cast covetous eyes on someone else's beautiful house, and decided to destroy their own and build a new one like it. But they did not know how to go about it, and the new house let in the wind and rain.[128] The real problem, however, was not that the house of Vietnam had become leaky, but that conservative scholars like Nguyen Ba Hoc had accepted the presence of the usurper for the long term. The older generation's obsequious gratitude toward the Mother Country *(Mau Quoc)* of Great France *(Dai Phap)* was the very reason that younger Vietnamese had lost interest in preserving the paternal house. Huynh Kim Khanh continues the metaphor: "Unlike his counterparts elsewhere, [the Vietnamese radical] had no home to return to. His inheritance was a home destroyed and a soil desecrated by bandits. His memory was haunted by the shameful resignation of his elders to colonialism. The Vietnamese radical of the 1920s had to face a task not borne by radicals elsewhere: he had to dislodge the bandits and construct a new home." [129]

Furthermore, if the young were estranged from their roots, it was the result of a culturalist strategy of adaptation to French rule shared by accommodationists and anticolonialists alike. For, despite the upheavals that successive waves of reform had caused in the educational system, one theme remained constant: self-cultivation was the first step toward bringing order to All-Under-Heaven. This strategy of adaptation had created such a burden of conflicting values and expectations that it left the youth of Vietnam disoriented, not knowing what its beliefs ought to be or where its loyalties ought to lie: a youth with a divided self. Whatever qualms their evident crisis of faith might provoke, the students were universally deemed to represent the future of the country. Thus they easily persuaded themselves that their plight was the plight of the nation, that their efforts to emancipate themselves from all forms of authority would advance the cause of national independence, and that a new order would arise from their struggle toward self-realization. Out of this marriage of the personal and the political emerged the urban radicalism of the 1920s.

2 Different Roads to Freedom

> He's standing there alone—a stray, a waif.
> He's waiting—will he meet a friend or guide?
> The streams and hills are empty of all life.
> Some strangers shuffle past, forlorn and wan.
> He's seeking men but only sees blue clouds.
> He'll tarry for the ride till his hair turns gray.
> Who will show him the path through this vast world?
> How long, how long, must he stand there and wait?
> Tran Te Xuong (1870–1907)

ONLY recently has the role of anarchism in the Vietnamese Revolution attracted scholarly analysis, despite anarchism's unmistakable influence on the revolution's early phase.[1] One reason for this neglect is the remarkable diversity of opinions and general orientation among those who fell under its spell, reflecting not only the amorphous character of anarchism but also its dual provenance: China and Japan on the one hand, France on the other. After World War I, many Vietnamese, especially if they were from Annam or Tonkin, still went to China in search of the knowledge denied them at home; but for natives of Cochinchina, France had become the preferred destination. The fractured history of anarchism and of revolution in Vietnam is inextricably linked to the split pattern of Vietnamese emigration in the early decades of the century. Vietnamese exiles started out with rather diverse backgrounds; abroad, they went through very different experiences. To the extent that they were influenced by anarchism, they were also exposed to different aspects of this protean ideology. Those who went to China and Japan were more likely to encounter it in its collectivist orientation as a component of anarcho-socialism; those who were influenced by French anarchism came to know its libertarian and individualist strain, which owed much to the influence of Nietzschean philosophy.

The combination of different experiences of exile and different political and social contexts at home produced multiple revolutionary cultures. In Tonkin and Annam, where political discourse was severely constrained, anticolonial sentiments often found an outlet in activism, sometimes of a violent nature. This emphasis on action rather than discussion, coupled with concern for collective liberation from colonial rule, provided the stimulus for attempts at political organization. In the South, where the press was freer, participation in journalistic debates acted as a sort of safety valve, defusing political tensions. Nguyen An Ninh made use of journalism to exhort his contemporaries to merge their quest for personal emancipation and self-realization with the struggle for national independence, but his emphasis on self-realization made him less interested in the practical problems of anticolonial action. Phan Boi Chau and Nguyen An Ninh thus represent different sides of Vietnamese anarchism, along with its promises and its limitations.

Eastern Travels

Research on Vietnamese anarchism has so far focused on Phan Boi Chau. When he arrived in Japan in January 1905, Phan was already thirty-eight years old and was already fixed in his basic ideas, in particular in his utilitarian orientation. He apparently remained oblivious to what did not seem directly useful to his patriotic purpose.

Remarkably little of the new ideological universe open to Phan in Japan is discernible in his writings. They are singularly unenlightening about the political currents to which he was exposed, even though these ranged from constitutionalism to anarchism and socialism. At the time of his arrival, the Chinese expatriate community in Japan was sharply divided. On one side was the group headed by Liang Ch'i-ch'ao, which advocated a constitutional monarchy for China through its journal *Renovation of the People;* on the other was the staunchly republican group which published the *People's Journal*.[2] Phan managed to retain the good will of both sides, his criterion for choosing foreign associates being their willingness to help the Vietnamese overthrow the French. He became friends with Chang Ping-lin, who was then editor-in-chief of the *People's Journal;* he made the acquaintance of Chang Chi, Hu Han-min, Sun Yat-sen, and of members of the Japanese Socialist Party.[3] He thus had a wide circle of acquaintances, but, uninterested in theoretical subtleties, he remained at the periphery of their debates.

Indicative of his lack of ideological depth is the speed with which

Different Roads to Freedom 59

he adopted and discarded political labels, and his confusion over the political beliefs of some of his closest associates in Japan. In mid-1907, Phan Boi Chau founded the Constitutionalist Association (Cong Hien Hoi) among students who had come to Japan under the aegis of the Eastern Travel Movement he had launched.[4] Phan says nothing about the political program of the Constitutionalist Association, but its very name hints at the influence on Phan of Liang Ch'i-ch'ao's advocacy of a constitutional monarchy. Only one year later, however, the Constitutionalist Association was disbanded after the Japanese authorities, acceding to a French request, ordered its student members to leave.[5] Phan then joined an organization named, he later wrote, the East Asia League (Toa Domeikai). According to him, the East Asia League was created that year with the enthusiastic support of Chang Ping-lin, Chang Chi, and a number of Japanese Socialists.[6] However, research by Shiraishi Masaya suggests that Phan's memory must have been faulty, for by 1908, the individuals he mentions had either left Japan or had been arrested.[7] The organization he joined was not the East Asia League but another one, known variously as the Asian Friendship Association (Ashu Washinkai) or the League of East Asian Lost Countries (Tung-ya Wang-kuo Tung-meng-hui). Although its constitution was written by Chang Pin-lin, the real moving force behind this organization was Liu Shih-pei, the editor of the anarchist journal *Natural Justice (Tien I)*.

Natural Justice was launched by Liu Shih-pei, his wife, Ho Chen, and Chang Chi, an anarchist acquaintance of Phan's, at about the time when Phan himself was establishing his short-lived Constitutionalist Association. Liu Shih-pei, in the words of Arif Dirlik, "was the first Chinese intellectual to see in socialism a means to liberate China from Western oppression"; he wrote articles about colonialism in Asia in *Natural Justice*.[8] Considering his friendship with Chang Pin-lin and Chang Chi and his political affinities, it is unlikely that Phan never met Liu or read his journal. Shiraishi indeed suggests that Phan and Liu moved in the same circles and knew each other quite well.[9] Yet, though Phan makes repeated references to Chang Ping-lin, he never mentions Liu; it must be assumed that Liu as a person or thinker made so little impact on him that Phan forgot him completely. Three months after launching *Natural Justice,* Liu, together with Chang Pin-lin, created the Society for the Study of Socialism. Despite its name, the Society was dedicated to the cause of anarchism. Liu Shih-pei declared: "Our aim is not only to practice socialism but to have anarchism as our goal." [10] In 1911, Sung Chiao-jen reiterated the idea that socialism was only a stage toward true anarchism: "If you advocate true socialism it will not succeed unless you support anarchism and communism; neither social democracy nor state socialism are worthy of respect." [11] However, fine distinctions between these two currents of thought seem to have made no impact on Phan Boi Chau.

After he was ordered out of Japan in 1909, Phan Boi Chau spent several years in the wilderness, shuttling between Siam, Hong Kong, and the Chinese mainland. Things improved after the fall of the Ch'ing in 1911. He received invitations from his old friends Chang Ping-lin and Ch'en Ch'i-mei to come to China and arrived there in January 1912.[12] Phan now counted a number of powerful friends and acquaintances in Republican China. Hu Han-min, whom Phan calls "my friend" in his memoirs, was governor of Kwangtung and shielded Vietnamese expatriates from the long arm of the Sûreté.[13] When he founded the League for the Restoration of Vietnam in 1912, Phan was drawing inspiration from the success of Sun Yat-sen's Revolutionary Alliance in overthrowing the Ch'ing dynasty. The League's name was derived from Chang Ping-lin's own Restoration League, perhaps because it was better known in Southeast Asia than the Revolutionary Alliance, perhaps also because Phan was personally closer to Chang than to Sun Yat-sen. Phan obtained a small sum of money from Ch'en Ch'i-mei, who had become governor of Shanghai. But it was far from enough to finance his activities.[14]

Another of Phan's benefactors in this enterprise was the prominent anarchist Liu Shih-fu. Liu was instrumental in popularizing the ideas of both the Paris and the Tokyo groups of Chinese anarchists and integrating them into contemporary domestic revolutionary politics.[15] Committed to internationalism, Liu cultivated the friendship of Vietnamese exiles in South China. In 1912, he gave two hundred piasters to Phan to launch the Restoration League and proposed a scheme to raise additional funds.[16]

That same year, under the advice of Liu Shih-fu and Teng Ching-ya, Phan created a League for the Prosperity of China and Asia (Hoi Chan Hoa Hung A), which aimed to foster solidarity between China and the colonized countries of Asia, in particular Vietnam, India, Burma, and Korea.[17] Also in 1912, Phan Boi Chau and Nguyen Thuong Hien, the former head of the Tonkin Free School, joined a clandestine anarchist society in Shanghai called the Worldwide League for Humanity (The Gioi Nhan Dao Hoi), which included one

Japanese and fifteen Chinese members. Its extreme-left program caused the newly formed Republican government to withhold recognition, and as a result, the League never really expanded in either membership or activities.[18] In Kwangsi, nearer the Vietnamese border, expatriates were also joining internationalist organizations, in particular one called the League of the Partisans of Universal Brotherhood (Dai Dong Lien Lac Cam Tinh Hoi). This organization enjoyed the open protection of the head of the local police, in whom, according to a French official, a four-year sojourn in France had not induced greater sympathy for French aims in Asia.[19] Phan Boi Chau and other Vietnamese expatriates in Japan and China thus came into contact with a large number of Chinese anarchists and joined a variety of organizations either dedicated to or influenced by anarchism. But whatever intellectual debt Phan owed to Chinese anarchism was built from the advice and experience of others, rather than from a reasoned consideration of the philosophy itself. This has led Shiraishi to conclude that Phan was not influenced by anarchism but that he was instead "a nationalist who accepted a Social Darwinist idea of struggle between the stronger and the weaker nations."[20]

There were, however, certain aspects of anarchism which resonated with Phan's own thinking. Phan had come into contact with what scholars describe as the "Tokyo strand" of Chinese anarchism, to distinguish it from the strand which emerged among Chinese expatriates in Paris. Whereas the latter was focused on the individual, the Tokyo strand focused primarily on society. Chinese anarchists in Japan emphasized the collective plight of the people, and particularly of rural society. Their interest in rural problems made them far more eager than their iconoclastic counterparts in Paris to preserve Chinese tradition; indeed, despite their commitment to anarcho-socialism, some of them turned away from issues of social transformation in post-revolutionary China. Chang Ping-lin believed that once Manchu rule ended and a republican government was installed, the work of the Restoration League, which he had founded in 1903, would be done.[21] Liu Shi-pei, whom Dirlik describes as antimodernist, eventually turned against the Chinese revolution.[22] Both men became associated with Chinese neo-traditionalism. The nativistic orientation Chang and Liu gave to Chinese anarchism must have been attractive to Phan Boi Chau, for it resonated with his own fairly conservative, but at the same time inclusive, ideas on culture. Woodside suggests that, except on the question of women, Phan Boi Chau was more conservative and more elitist than Chang Ping-lin, whose own commitment to anarcho-socialism did not long outlast the 1911 Revolution.[23] Despite his failure to persuade his southern associates to abandon their commitment to monarchist restoration, Phan was an early advocate of republicanism in Vietnam. But, like his good friend Chang Ping-lin, he had no clearly articulated vision of post-independence society, and his concept of revolution remained predominantly political. He viewed reform as a form of self-strengthening in the cause of national independence rather than as a means of ensuring long-lasting social and cultural change.

The one aspect of anarchist thinking which resonated most forcefully with Phan's own was the willingness to use violence in the service of a just cause. Phan was dismayed when Hu Han-min and Ch'en Ch'i-mei failed to provide substantial sums of money and lectured him instead on the need to educate the populace before contemplating the violent overthrow of the French.[24] Phan fully concurred with the anarchist position that violence was justified as a revolutionary tactic to move people's hearts and arouse mass support.[25] Aside from these practical considerations was the traditional appeal of heroic self-sacrifice, of the righteous deed whose moral significance overrode its tactical futility, the grand gesture of the knight-errant redressing political and social wrongs to restore cosmic order. Such a notion found an immediate response among Vietnamese who avidly read the translations of Chinese historical romances that were then flooding the market and whose own national literature abounded with ringing calls to heroism. Phan himself often talked admiringly of various attempts to assassinate the first Chinese emperor, Chin-shih huang-ti.[26] When urged by Ch'en Ch'i-mei to give priority to propaganda and education, he defended his predilection for direct action by citing the example of Mazzini.[27]

The bombing incidents of 1913 in Hanoi were the result of this predilection. They brought publicity to the League, as Phan Boi Chau had intended, but they also brought reprisals against it. At home, seven members of the League were executed (Phan Boi Chau was sentenced to death in absentia); abroad, the French and British authorities cooperated in cracking down on anticolonial activity. The various internationalist organizations in China disintegrated under the pressure. Soon afterward Phan Boi Chau fell prey to a reversal in the Chinese domestic politics in which he was so active a participant. When Yuan Shih-k'ai seized power, he was arrested by Yuan's crony,

Different Roads to Freedom 63

Lung Chi-kuan, at Sarraut's request. Lung, however, did not deport Phan to Indochina as Sarraut had asked.[28] Phan spent three years in a Chinese prison. Then Yuan Shih-k'ai's death once again turned the tide in favor of the Republican government and Phan was released.

After his release in February 1917, Phan retired to Hang-chou, where he continued to turn out polemical writings. But Phan had been overtaken by changes in the political landscape and was betrayed by his own trusting nature. In 1918, he came under the influence of Phan Dinh Phung's son, Phan Ba Ngoc. The younger man had been one of his trusted disciples and associates, but he had become a double agent during Phan Boi Chau's incarceration.[29] Unaware of this change of heart, Phan Boi Chau took Phan Ba Ngoc's advice and produced a tract advocating Franco-Annamite collaboration, for submission to Albert Sarraut as a basis for discussing French colonial policy in Vietnam. Negotiations between Phan Boi Chau and Sarraut never took place, and Phan later disavowed the tract, claiming that he had been misled by Phan Ba Ngoc.[30] But the very fact that he had allowed himself to be persuaded to write it suggests he had run out of ideas on how to revitalize the anticolonial movement and hasten the demise of French rule.

Whether by choice, or more probably because of circumstances, Phan Boi Chau by the early 1920s had become marginalized by the disappearance of his contacts among the Chinese left. Liu Shih-fu had died of tuberculosis in 1915; Ch'en Ch'i-mei was assassinated the following year while Phan was still in jail. Chang Ping-lin, with whom Phan managed to renew contact, had not only abandoned anarcho-socialism but had given up politics altogether in favor of intellectual pursuits.[31] In 1920, Phan was again drawn by his concern for the people's welfare to give renewed consideration to socialism. He translated into Chinese an account of the Soviet Union, originally written by a Japanese syndicalist, with the title, "Inquiry into the True Character of the Soviet Union."[32] He intended to use this translation to introduce himself to the Soviet and Chinese Socialist parties, but nothing came of this effort.

Phan Boi Chau had also become a marginal figure in the Vietnamese émigré community. Two of his followers, Dang Tu Man and Dang Thuc Hua, had tried with only modest success to keep the League for the Restoration of Vietnam alive during the war. In 1919, Dang Thuc Hua abandoned the futile effort and issued a stinging critique of the League. He excoriated it for its elitism, which he saw exemplified by the figurehead role given to Prince Cuong De. In tones reminiscent of the May Fourth Movement which burst out that year, he advocated total immersion in the population: "We must go barefoot into the streets and byways and live the life of the common people."[33] His call remained unanswered, for Vietnamese anticolonialism in the early 1920s remained an elitist affair.[34] Revolutionaries expected to set an example for the common people, not to learn from them. But Hua's analysis of the weaknesses of the Restoration League bore fruit in 1923 with the regrouping of former followers of Phan Boi Chau into a new organization, known as the Society of Like Hearts (Tam Tam Xa), and also as the New Vietnam Youth Corps (Tan Viet Thanh Nien Doan).

According to Phan, who was not involved in it, the Society of Like Hearts was inspired by the One Heart Society (I hsin she) of Liu Shih-fu.[35] It was therefore anarchist in orientation. It had as its motto to "unite all Vietnamese of perception and energy without distinction between parties as long as they are resolved to set aside their prejudices and personal interests and to devote themselves entirely to the accomplishment of all tasks needed to restore the Vietnamese to their dignity as human beings."[36] The Society's Manifesto went on to explain that in the sixty years since the loss of independence, there had been no dearth of patriots calling on the people to rise up against the oppressors, yet the population still suffered under the colonial yoke; this was due to the absence of solid political organization, effective support, and true spirit of self-sacrifice. It deplored the loss of morale among the Vietnamese people at home and the atomized situation of the expatriates. The Society saw the persistence of personal rivalries and lack of collective spirit as the main reason for the failure of earlier anticolonial efforts. It therefore proposed to mobilize popular energies and to act on the basis of collective decisions to restore the human dignity which had been stolen from the Vietnamese people and to work for its happiness. Despite repeated references to the restoration of "human dignity," there was no discussion of how the Society of Like Hearts proposed to restructure society. Indeed the phrase apparently meant little more than the recovery of national independence and the introduction of universal suffrage. The Manifesto declared: "What kind of political system we have after independence is recovered will be up to the whole people to decide by a majority vote so that it conforms with international trends and the situation of our country." In other words, the Society's unitary view of the struggle for independence masked an inability to envisage the social dynamics of post-independence Vietnam.

The Manifesto went on to give the specifics of its proposed organization, criteria for admission, and the punishments that awaited those who did not carry out their assignments to the full or who betrayed the Society. Recruits were to be admitted without discrimination on the basis of party affiliation or gender, as long as two members in good standing vouched for them. Eventually, they would be certified by the Society's Central Committee or Branch Committee. The Society was to be organized into cells and branches and led by a Central Committee, but the precise relationship between each of these levels was left vague, although the Manifesto insisted on the importance of collective decision-making. The tone of the Manifesto and of another document setting forth the circumstances of the Society's founding, both of which were written in Chinese, and the references to a cell-based organization, suggest that the seven founders of the Society of Like Hearts were inspired by the Kuomintang and possibly by the recently formed Chinese Communist Party. Indeed, members of the Society made contact with Soviet advisors at the Whampoa Military Academy, which opened in the spring of 1924, and both the Manifesto and the document relating the founding of the Society ended up in the Comintern Archives.[37]

The Society of Like Hearts turned out to be as elitist as Phan Boi Chau's Restoration League and relied excessively on veterans of the Reform Movement. In the spring of 1923, Le Hong Son, one of the Society's founders, made his way from Canton to Hanoi to meet the former principal of the Tonkin Free School. Over the next several months, he discussed with his contacts in Nam Dinh and in his native province of Nghe An the creation of a network linking patriots from all three regions of the country with émigrés in China. After he reported back to his associates in Canton that winter, the Society decided that another member, Ho Tung Mau, would make a follow-up trip to publicize its existence. This would be done by distributing copies of a letter written by Prince Cuong De calling for a reawakening of scholarly patriotism. A copy of this letter was sent to Emperor Khai Dinh and to his uncle and Minister of Rites, Than Trong Hue. Mau also carried letters from Nguyen Thuong Hien and Phan Boi Chau addressed to various eminent individuals.[38]

Another point of similarity between the Society of Like Hearts and the Restoration League was the use of direct action as a means of destabilizing the colonial regime, gaining publicity, and mobilizing popular opinion. Le Hong Son assassinated Phan Ba Ngoc in 1922, his treachery having finally been exposed.[39] In mid-1924, the Society decided to assassinate Governor-General Merlin, then on an official visit to China. The plan was to attack him while he attended a banquet in the international concession in Canton. The attack would be carried out by Pham Hong Thai, whom Le Hong Son had recently recruited into the Society. According to Phan Boi Chau, Thai procured a bomb from a chemical engineer who taught at Whampoa.[40] Posing as a reporter, Thai hid the bomb inside a camera and threw it at the gubernatorial party as it settled down to dinner at the Victoria Hotel. Three people died, two were grievously wounded, but Merlin escaped unhurt. Thai, with the police at his heels, threw himself in the river and drowned.

Though Pham Hong Thai's bomb did not kill its intended target, it achieved its ultimate objective, proving that political violence had its uses: it reawakened Vietnamese anticolonial sentiment as the assassinations of 1913 had not succeeded in doing. This was partly a matter of timing. Vietnam's newly assertive youth found in the twenty-four-year-old Pham Hong Thai a model to emulate. His elevation to the status of a revolutionary martyr also owed something to the anti-French politics of the Kuomintang, and in particular of Hu Han-min, who was again governor of Kwangtung province. After Pham Hong Thai's death, two prominent members of the Kuomintang, Liao Chung-k'ai and Wang Ching-wei, had his tomb moved to Huang Hua-kuan, across from the monument to the seventy-two martyrs of the Wuchang Uprising.[41] Inscribed on the stele was a text, which officially came from the pen of Hu Han-min, depicting Pham Hong Thai as a scion of Vietnam's Confucian elite. It told how Thai had been angered by the obscurantist educational policies of the French and had therefore quit school to work in a factory, where he had risen to the post of foreman. Thai, the text continued, supported the strategy, pursued by certain Vietnamese patriots, of working to mobilize colonial troops in Tonkin, Annam, and Cochinchina against the French and spreading anticolonial propaganda, but he had come to think also that only violence could strike terror among the enemy and fire the people with revolutionary zeal.[42]

Publicity, however, was no substitute for ideas. Although Pham Hong Thai's tomb became a site of pilgrimage for patriotic exiles, the Society of Like Hearts was floundering, at a loss as to how to follow

Different Roads to Freedom 67

up on his exploit. In the wake of Pham Hong Thai's aborted assassination of Merlin, Phan Boi Chau became eager to open an academy similar to Whampoa to train Vietnamese revolutionaries. He also discussed with Chiang Kai-shek the possibility of turning the Restoration League into a Vietnamese Nationalist Party on the model of the Kuomintang.[43] On Chiang's advice, Phan traveled from Canton to Peking to meet Ts'ai Yuan-p'ei, the president of Peking University. Ts'ai introduced him to two Comintern agents, but no academy materialized from these meetings and Phan retreated to Hang-chou without further pursuing his plans of creating a Vietnamese Nationalist Party. It was at this juncture that Nguyen Ai Quoc, later known as Ho Chi Minh, arrived from Moscow as part of Borodin's entourage.

From Fraternity to Intercolonial Union

Prior to his sojourn in Moscow Nguyen Ai Quoc had spent several years in France, where there lived another group of expatriates. Though many came from the same literati background as the China exiles, the French exiles had moved further away from their intellectual roots. Through his link with the two communities of Vietnamese expatriates in China and France, Nguyen Ai Quoc, who emerged as a severe critic of radicalism, serves as a link between the different strands of anarchism to which they were exposed.

Nguyen Ai Quoc had originally left for France in the summer of 1911. He was then about twenty.[44] Nguyen Tat Thanh, as he was then known, was the son of an old friend of Phan Boi Chau. A graduate of the Imperial College in Hue, Thanh had been briefly involved in teaching the romanized script in a school of the Reform Movement before going to Saigon to find passage for France. He paid his way by working as a cook's assistant on the ship Latouche-Treville. Upon arriving in Marseilles, he requested permission to attend the Ecole Coloniale, but was refused admission.[45] After two years working on ships plying the Atlantic, he settled in London in 1913. From London, he maintained a steady correspondence with Phan Chu Trinh, another of his father's old friends. He also seems to have been in contact with another émigré, Phan van Truong, whom he probably met for the first time when Truong came to London to meet an emissary from Prince Cuong De.[46]

Phan van Truong, who had come from Hanoi to France in 1910, was a qualified lawyer, and enjoyed French citizenship. But he also had two brothers who were deported for life in 1913 for their part in the bombing incidents of that year.[47] As for Phan Chu Trinh, after being sent to the penal island of Con Son in 1909, he had convinced a visiting Governor-General of the fundamentally nonviolent nature of his reformism. In a gesture designed to appease Vietnamese and metropolitan French public opinion, he had been granted clemency and released into the care of a Cochinchinese notable. In a further quirk of French colonial policy, Phan and his teen-age son were then sent to France as members of a group of Indochinese educators. The initial period of stay was six months and could be renewed. Phan and his son were even granted funds to buy a suitable wardrobe and a monthly stipend of one hundred fifty francs each.[48] Phan arrived in France in May 1911, enrolled his son in school, and settled down for the next fourteen years.[49]

Soon after his arrival in France, Phan Chu Trinh teamed up with Phan van Truong to found the first association created among colonial expatriates in France, the Fraternité (Dong Bao Than Ai) group. Behind its fraternal character, the group may have had a vaguely reformist program, although this is difficult to ascertain because Phan van Truong thoroughly obscured its true nature in the account he gave of it in the journal *Cloche Fêlée* in 1925. In 1914, after war broke out in Europe, the Sûreté, which was operating a massive sweep of potentially subversive organizations, discovered the existence of the Fraternité group. Phan Chu Trinh and Phan van Truong were promptly sent to prison. After their release in April 1915, Phan Chu Trinh returned to Paris where, having lost his stipend, he eked out a meager living retouching photographs. But Phan van Truong was sent to the Toulon Arsenal to serve as an interpreter for the colonial troops. The Fraternité group, which had counted only a dozen or so members, had disbanded in their absence. Nguyen Tat Thanh, meanwhile, arrived from London in 1917. He immediately tried to revive Fraternité so that it could serve as a springboard for his own political program.

In the wake of the American entry into World War I, Thanh had become fired with enthusiasm by Woodrow Wilson's call for self-determination for colonial peoples. When the Versailles Conference convened in 1919, he cooperated with Phan van Truong and Phan Chu Trinh to produce a document, "Les Revendications du Peuple Annamite," which was sent to the national delegations taking part in the Versailles Conference as well as to the French President on behalf of a "Group of Annamite Patriots in France." Although no evidence exists concerning the founding of this Group, it would appear that it was the successor to Fraternité. The document that was issued in its name bore the collective signature "Nguyen Ai Quoc," Nguyen the Patriot.[50] Introducing himself under that name, Thanh took copies of the "Revendications" to the offices of all the Paris newspapers. Only *Le Peuple*, which was the organ of the Socialist Party, showed interest in publishing the document. Thanh was warmly welcomed by its editor, Jean Longuet, and by various other Socialist luminaries.[51] Discarding the name Nguyen Tat Thanh, he joined the Socialist Party as Nguyen Ai Quoc.

In 1920, Nguyen Ai Quoc, as he had become, was given a copy of Lenin's "Theses on the National and Colonial Question" by a Socialist acquaintance. He found in the Theses something that had eluded earlier anticolonial activists: the theoretical foundations for combining national and social issues. In December, Nguyen Ai Quoc attended the Tours Congress of the Socialist Party as delegate for Indochina and cast his vote in favor of joining the Third International, thus becoming a founding member of the French Communist Party. In 1921, as a member of the Party's Colonial Studies Commission, he was instrumental in creating the Intercolonial Union, an organization designed to win the support of the natives of French colonies who resided in France. The Intercolonial Union brought out a French-language journal, *Paria*, devoted to colonial and working-class issues. Nguyen Ai Quoc was editor-in-chief of the journal and contributed articles on both themes, though his French often had to be polished by Phan van Truong. In fact, Truong sometimes wrote entire articles that appeared under his colleague's byline, for Nguyen Ai Quoc was overextended.[52] Beside his work in the French Communist Party and the Intercolonial Union and his job as editor-in-chief of *Paria*, he also wrote for a variety of left-wing publications, including *Humanité* and *Cahiers du Communisme*. He also assiduously cultivated links with Vietnamese sailors and other manual workers in France, whom the more patrician Phan Chu Trinh and Phan van Truong ignored. Lastly, he eked out a modest living as a photographer and forger of Chinese antiquities.

Emperor Khai Dinh's visit to the Colonial Exhibition of Marseilles in 1922 sparked a resurgence of activism among anticolonial émigrés. But Phan van Truong did not fully approve of Nguyen Ai Quoc's internationalist and proletarian politics. Truong objected in particular to the fact that Vietnamese independence was not a central focus of the Intercolonial Union, so in 1923 he tried to reorganize the Fraternité group.[53] He may also have been concerned about the possibility of competition from a new organization, the Association Mutuelle des Indochinois en France. The Association, founded in 1920, was headed by Nguyen Phu Khai and Bui Quang Chieu and, like a number of other organizations which sprang up among Vietnamese residents in France at that time, it was covertly subsidized by the Ministry of Colonies so that it could compete for influence with the Group of Annamite Patriots. Indeed, the ostensibly apolitical Association Mutuelle threatened to supplant the Group of Annamite Patriots as the preeminent émigré organization.[54] But after meeting no success in his effort to revive the Fraternité group, Phan van Truong conceded to Nguyen Ai Quoc the leadership of the anticolonialist expatriates.

Nguyen Ai Quoc, for his part, was unhappy with the level of support for anticolonial and proletarian causes in France, and his dissatisfaction extended to the Colonial Studies Commission of the Communist Party. He objected to the elimination of a regular column on colonial affairs from *Humanité*. He complained that "capitalist" papers such as *Oeuvre* had been quicker in reporting a major anticolonial uprising in Dahomey, and that *Humanité* had not given enough prominence to news of a workers' strike in Tunisia and famine in North Africa.[55] He was also dismayed by the apathy of the Vietnamese students in France. He compared them unfavorably with Chinese student-workers, who, he claimed, were gaining valuable training in bridging the gap between intellectuals and workers. He charged that either the Vietnamese students were on government scholarship and thus reluctant to displease the authorities, or they came from rich families and had no interest in upsetting the colonial status quo. All they were interested in was satisfying their idle curiosity and seeking pleasure.[56] Nguyen Ai Quoc left for Moscow in mid-1923 to attend a meeting of the Krestintern (Communist Peasant International). He returned secretly to France shortly afterward, but left again in late October or November by a circuitous route to attend the Fifth Plenum of the Comintern. When he arrived in Moscow in January 1924, Lenin had just died.

Before leaving Paris, Nguyen Ai Quoc had groomed another Vietnamese to take over his duties within the Intercolonial Union and the French Communist Party. His choice fell on Nguyen The Truyen, a chemical engineer married to a Frenchwoman of independent means.

A grandson of the governor of Thai Binh who was assassinated in 1913, Truyen had been sent by his family to France, where, to his father's dismay, he gravitated toward anticolonial émigrés.[57] Truyen, however, lacked the empathy with ordinary Vietnamese which was a hallmark of Nguyen Ai Quoc's politics; in this, however, he was no worse than Phan van Truong, who reportedly offended Vietnamese workers in France with his unflattering remarks about them.[58] More or less ignoring workers, Truyen concentrated on reaching the students arriving from Vietnam, but he does not seem to have been much interested in organizing them. Under his leadership, the Vietnamese anticolonial community resembled more a debating society than a political movement. Expatriates met at one another's lodgings or in cafés for prolonged discussions. This was heady stuff for newcomers who in this fashion received their first exposure to the lively intellectual and political climate of France, but little effort was made to turn them into disciplined adherents of a purposeful organization.

Thus, although the two communities of émigré activists in France and in China shared many similarities, there were also important areas of differences between them. Both groups functioned with greater latitude than was possible within Vietnam, but they were still vulnerable to French repression. In China, the effectiveness of the Sûreté was curbed by the anti-French policies of key Chinese officials; in France, repression was softened by French laws and by the fact that the expatriates had the support of prominent political figures and organizations. In both countries, however, the Sûreté was extraordinarily successful in recruiting informers and *agents provocateurs*. Regionalism played a part in guiding emigration. The China émigrés came mostly from Tonkin and Annam; virtually none came from Cochinchina. The demographic profile of the émigrés in France was almost the reverse. They came mostly from Cochinchina, although natives of Tonkin were also quite numerous; none came from Annam. This pattern reflected the differences in educational experiences of natives of the three regions, in particular the persistence of Chinese studies in Tonkin and Annam. But it was also due to the relative ease of travel to France from either Tonkin or Cochinchina. Natives of Annam had to go to Haiphong or Saigon to find passage to France. It was just as easy for them to make their way clandestinely to China via Tonkin or Siam. Particularistic ties of family, locality, and shared mentors also played an important role in the recruitment of members into the Society of Like Hearts, though this was less a factor among the émigrés in France. Both groups of expatriates shared a lack of political direction. But while the expatriates in China focused largely on action and organization, Vietnamese exposed to the debating-society atmosphere of Paris politics stressed the importance of ideas and oratory, but had poor organizational skills.

Prophet of Disorder

For young Vietnamese growing up in the 1920s, it was Nguyen An Ninh, rather than Nguyen The Truyen or the shadowy Nguyen Ai Quoc, who epitomized the experience of exile in France. Ninh had the advantage over his contemporaries of being attuned to contemporary European thought. On his bookshelves could be found works by Renan, Nietzsche, Flaubert, Kant, Plato, Alain, Rousseau, Tolstoy, and Dostoevsky as well as a photograph of Tagore.[59] Léon Werth, who met him in 1924, described him as "the most European" man he had met in Indochina. He did more than illustrate the breadth of ideas available abroad: he embodied the experience of exile as a quest for self-realization as well as a patriotic endeavor.

Phan Boi Chau and his imitators kept alive the anticolonial tradition of Phan Dinh Phung. To those who preferred to define themselves in reaction to the assimilationists and neo-traditionalists then dominating the political and cultural scene, Nguyen An Ninh symbolized rupture and renewal. He rejected Sarraut's argument that the attainment of national sovereignty must be the end result of a slow and gradual process of political maturation. Ninh agreed with Pham Quynh on the nature of Vietnam's predicament to the point of using the same metaphor. In the 10 December 1923 issue of *Cloche Fêlée* (meaning "cracked bell"), the first issue of the journal Ninh founded in Saigon, he wrote: "Vietnamese youth is caught as if in whirling waters, not knowing where to swim for. Faced with a moral choice, it does not know on which morality to base its actions and its judgments."[60] But whereas Pham Quynh used that metaphor to emphasize the need for continuity, Ninh used it to argue for the quest for a new moral order. Ninh believed that the crisis facing the Vietnamese did not revolve around the choice between Old and New Learning; it was a crisis of moral knowledge. He excoriated those who believed in the cultural and moral superiority of the French and in their right to govern benighted natives: "Only a band of former domestics or messenger boys, raised by the colonial government to the highest ranks . . .

sang the praise of French domination . . . The notion of European prestige is based neither on moral nor on intellectual superiority but on skin color." [61]

Nguyen An Ninh, who spent most of 1920–1923 living in France, had fallen under the spell of French anarchism. It was an anarchism heavily tinged with Nietzschean individualism. In 1902, the German anarchist Max Nettlau had written to Peter Kropotkin to suggest that the idea of freedom be stressed over economic issues, and that anarchists particularly address themselves to the problems of the new generation. This had drawn a stinging reply from Kropotkin, in which he criticized the influence on European youth of Nietzschean ideas, which he regarded as baneful manifestations of bourgeois individualism.

> As for French bourgeois youth, it has always liked bold and striking affirmations, particularly between the ages of nineteen and thirty. The negativism, the "nihilism" of anarchy enticed them. On the other hand, they were impressed by the devotion and the self-sacrificing spirit of the young working class. And finally, a movement similar to the nihilism of Bazarov is flourishing in France, a movement concerned with mores, a *Kulturbewegung* whose object is to reject conventional lies . . . It has happened, with this difference: in Russia the nihilist movement [1859–69] was followed by the populist movement *v narod* ["to the people"], whereas in France nothing like this occurred. This is why the revolutionary movement has not gained anything directly from it . . . Who came forward to work for the revolution? Has this young generation produced a single person who could relieve the old one? Nihil.[62]

"A movement concerned with mores, a *Kulturbewegung* whose object is to reject conventional lies" was precisely what interested Nguyen An Ninh. But he would not have agreed to the charge of nihilism, for he wanted Vietnamese youth to reinvent itself, to create its own destiny; not merely to turn its back on the past but to look forward to the future.

When he returned home in 1923, Ninh had become a twenty-three-year-old firebrand. He thrust himself upon a political stage where the dominant tone was moderation and compromise, and thereby became immensely popular among his peers, who were already chafing under the weight of parental authority and the petty tyranny of their teachers. Much of their discontent was not yet overtly political. It tended to manifest itself in short stories, and later, novels, which took as their themes the oppressiveness of the Confucian extended family toward the young of both sexes, and particularly women. Nguyen An Ninh's critique of the narrow moralism of the neo-traditionalists and of their fallacious notions of order struck a responsive chord among his peers, because it addressed both their personal and their social concerns. By exhorting them to break with the past and free themselves from tyranny of all kinds, Ninh helped his contemporaries become conscious of their shared concerns and their collective power and to think of themselves as a unique, iconoclastic, generation.

Ninh was certainly not the only Vietnamese commentator to inveigh against the burden of tradition, or to view revolution mainly in terms of culture. Phan Chu Trinh and others preceded him. Nor was he the only critic of accommodation; Phan Boi Chau had been fighting the French before Ninh was even born. Years before Ninh made his first public speech, Phan himself had lamented the Vietnamese fondness for bureaucratic appointments and resonant but empty titles.[63] But just as Phan Boi Chau and Phan Chu Trinh had needed traditional credentials in order to persuade their peers to discard traditional education, so did Ninh use his Paris law degree to lend weight to his withering attacks on collaborationist leaders who claimed to represent the aspirations of the "French-influenced Annamite elite." Thus, while the exiles in China represented the unbroken link with scholarly patriotism within the emerging revolutionary culture, Nguyen An Ninh represented its radical, youth-oriented side. And yet his background was not wholly dissimilar from theirs. He belonged to that far from insignificant minority for whom patriotism was a family inheritance.

Ninh was born on 6 September 1900 in a suburb of Saigon.[64] His father, Nguyen An Khuong, was a middling landowner who preferred to think of himself as a country scholar. He was a prolific translator of Chinese historical novels, for which, in the absence of genuine Vietnamese fiction, there was a strong demand in the South. When the Reform Movement was launched, Nguyen An Khuong supported it enthusiastically. He opened a hotel to serve as a meeting place for patriotic conspirators and for students on their way abroad. The Chieu Nam hotel also functioned as a center for collecting funds raised in the provinces on behalf of Phan Boi Chau, and for distributing anticolonial propaganda. Khuong's sister managed it while also overseeing her nephew's education (Nguyen An Ninh's mother is never mentioned, raising the possibility that she died in childbirth).⁶⁵ This arrangement freed Nguyen An Khuong to act as business manager for *News from the Six Provinces,* a Vietnamese-language paper which managed to disseminate anticolonial propaganda until the Sûreté managed to infiltrate the Eastern Travel Movement and uncovered its southern infrastructure. Another aunt was also active in anticolonial politics. The widow of a French freemason, she escorted Prince Cuong De on his trip through the South in 1913, bringing along her half-French son to underscore her French connections and avoid awkward questions from the police during the trip.⁶⁶ Ninh's paternal uncle, Nguyen An Cu, a much-traveled practitioner of traditional medicine, also had wide connections in the anticolonial underground. Nguyen An Ninh was thus raised in an intensely patriotic atmosphere.

His father's anticolonial sentiments and classical erudition did not prevent him from having Ninh educated entirely in French schools. Ninh first attended the Institution Taberd run by Jesuit missionaries in Saigon, then the Franco-Annamite Collège de My Tho (which included only the first grades of the secondary level of education), and finally, the most prestigious of all colonial schools, the Lycée Chasseloup-Laubat. He graduated with a *brevet d'études supérieures* in 1917, together with sixteen other classmates.⁶⁷ Ninh was already considered an eccentric: brilliant, image-conscious, ready to do or say outrageous things in order to receive the adulation of his peers which he was said to crave.⁶⁸ For a few months after leaving school, Ninh worked for the newspaper *Courier Saigonnais*. He then went to Hanoi on a scholarship and enrolled first in the School of Medicine, then switched to the School of Law.⁶⁹

During his two unhappy years at the University of Hanoi, Ninh entered into an acrimonious relationship with the man who was to be Governor of Cochinchina between 1921 and 1926. Maurice Cognacq, a native of the French colonial island of Réunion and a medical doctor specializing in tropical medicine, had been chosen by Sarraut in 1917 to head the newly reopened School of Medicine. In 1920, he was named Director of Public Instruction and put in charge of the expanded secondary education sector. That year, dissatisfied with the low standards prevailing at the University, Ninh asked for permission to go to France. Cognacq tried to dissuade him from going, but Ninh persisted.⁷⁰ After he obtained the reluctant permission of the authorities to go, his father sold a piece of land to pay for his voyage. He then took Ninh to the temple of Marshal Le van Duyet, the viceroy of the South in the early nineteenth century. The temple, which was located not far from their home in Gia Dinh, was popularly used as a place to pledge solemn oaths. According to widely circulated stories, Nguyen An Khuong asked his son never to forget his duty to his country, nor to fall victim to bureaucratic ambitions.

Upon arriving in France, Ninh first attended the *lycée* of Bordeaux in order to obtain the French *baccalauréat* (the Indochinese *baccalauréat* not being valid in France at that time), then went to Paris, where he enrolled in the Sorbonne to study law. He was immediately drawn into expatriate politics and probably joined the Group of Annamite Patriots in France. In 1920, he wrote to the Minister of Colonies to complain that he was being harassed by the Sûreté.[71] He also wrote a few articles for *La Tribune Annamite*, edited by E. Babut, which was loosely connected to the *Tribune Indigène* of Bui Quang Chieu but was generally to its left.[72] After obtaining his *license en droit*, he traveled to Belgium, Austria, Germany, and Italy before heading home for a few months in October 1922 to marry the daughter of a rich landowner. After his wedding, he returned to France to try for a doctorate. But his funds were insufficient to support his studies, so he took on a variety of odd jobs, such as working as a proofreader and editor for *Paria*. He is also said to have written articles for *Le Libertaire*, which was the organ of the anarchist movement in France and which welcomed contributions on colonial questions.[73] True to his reputation as an eccentric, he also set himself up as a fortune-teller. But in September 1923, penury, combined with his wife's request for a divorce, forced him to return home.[74]

In January 1923, just before going back to France, he had given a public lecture at the Société d'Enseignement Mutuel on the need for a new Vietnamese culture. According to Ninh himself, the lecture absolutely baffled his audience.[75] There is no extant text of this first talk, but from a later lecture of 15 October 1923, it appears that Ninh discussed the need for a genuinely new culture responding fully to Vietnamese needs, one that was neither unthinkingly assimilationist nor unthinkingly neo-traditionalist. The audience was far more responsive to his attacks against "bureaucratism." Bui Quang Chieu had already deplored the mandarin mentality of his compatriots which caused them to seek careers almost exclusively in the colonial bureaucracy instead of exploring new avenues to success in business.[76] But for Ninh, the major defect of "bureaucratism" was not a matter of career choices. Civil servants, he said in his October 1923 speech, were "slaves in gowns of brocade and embroidered shoes."[77] Thus he seems to have only partially incorporated the anarchist critique of the state into his own thinking. Proudhon had warned of the totalitarian potential of bureaucracy: "Bureaucratism leads to state communism, to the absorption of all local and individual life into the administrative machinery, to the destruction of free thought." But the colonial context obscured this fundamental problem; colonialism appeared to the Vietnamese as such a monolith that it deprived them of the ability to disaggregate its components and effects. They were used to equating colonial rule with state power, and tended to believe that if colonialism disappeared, so would most of their country's problems. Ninh ignored the issue of state power and concentrated entirely on exposing the lack of freedom of supposedly powerful individuals. Young Vietnamese being groomed for jobs in the colonial administration responded enthusiastically to Ninh's critique of bureaucratism.

After his return to Saigon in September 1923, Ninh made known his collaboration on *Paria*. Notwithstanding this, he was invited to speak again at the Société d'Enseignement Mutuel, now under the presidency of Nguyen Phan Long. The speech he delivered on 15 October 1923 was entitled "The Aspirations of Annamite Youth." This second public appearance created a sensation and turned the twenty-three-year-old Ninh into the idol of his generation. Ninh again took up the theme of culture. Referring to the anomie in which his country was mired, he attributed its cause to cultural clash: "After fifty years of French influence, Vietnamese youth today is still very far from France; the conflict of two civilizations which heretofore have ignored each other is intense . . . The resolution of this conflict is surely painful for weak souls. Many small happinesses which old society granted them have been destroyed." In this diagnosis of the Vietnamese crisis of consciousness, Ninh was in agreement with Nguyen van Vinh, Pham Quynh, and the neo-traditionalists; but in many ways, his speech can be viewed as a denunciation of the cures they proposed.

Ninh launched a frontal attack on contemporary Vietnamese culture, taking a swipe at the native bourgeoisie for its imperfect understanding of French culture and its false knowledge aimed only at securing jobs. But his prime target was neo-traditionalism which, in his opinion, was based on erroneous conceptions of Chinese culture in general, and of Confucianism in particular. He began by going over some of the points he had made in his previous talk, attacking Confucianism and its stranglehold on Vietnam's intellectual elite. He acknowledged that "Confucian ideas, when well understood, raise men to a large and generous conception of life. The key to the Confucian doctrine lies in the individual himself, in his self-perfection." He paid lip service to the contribution of Confucianism to the promotion of social order, but spent most of his time lambasting, by invoking Chuang-tzu, "the narrow morality, the stifling ideas of Confucius." The biggest problem, in his opinion, was that Vietnamese Confucianism was "an article of exportation" and therefore not genuine; it had caused havoc among the elite and contributed to the low intellectual level of the country. Now, in the clash of cultures brought about by colonial conquest, "the so-called elite trained in the Chinese classics has been forced to cling to Confucian ideas like shipwrecked people to a raft." If Nguyen An Ninh, son of a classical scholar, so comprehensively attacked Confucian teachings, it was because they had been misappropriated by collaborationists.

Having presented his critique of both neo-traditionalist and assimilationist justifications for Franco-Annamite collaboration, Ninh went on to denounce the very idea upon which the policy was founded: the idea of France's *mission civilisatrice*. Referring to a recently published work, *Le Miracle français en Asie,* he demanded: "What is this miracle? It is a miracle indeed to be able in a short time to plunge a people with an already low intellectual level into thick ignorance; it is a miracle indeed to be able, in such a short time, to plunge a people with democratic ideas into complete servitude."[78] The idea of French tutelage was a dangerous delusion: "I advance this to show to the youth of today that, in everything, it can only rely on itself to rise to the level where man, conscious of his own strength, begins to become conscious of his own dignity."

In January, Pham Quynh had castigated Vietnam's youth for its mood of despondency and its lack of ideals. It was this very issue that Ninh decided to address, calling on his contemporaries to leave their elders behind, set themselves free of the deadweight of the past, and embark on a great voyage of discovery whose very peril would be liberating:

> The greatest idealists have always advised those who wanted to become their disciples to "flee from their fathers' house." We, too, must leave our families, escape from our society, leave our country.

> We need a life of struggle to awaken the little vigor we have left, we need a society which will reveal to us our true worth. We need a milieu which will raise our intelligence and our soul, we need a peak where we can feel all our strength and possess our soul, and in a glance full of life and of love, embrace the whole world and comprehend our harmony with it. And then, we will leave this peak which we have reached and which for a time has been like a land of exile, to return to society where we will then be able to utilize to the full our creative forces.

The overblown language carried echoes of Nietszche, Bergson, and Gide; Social Darwinian images resonated with traditional organicist metaphors. While collaborationists staked their political fortunes on the avoidance of political instability at all cost, opponents of colonial rule believed that the Vietnamese body politic was diseased at the core and that only desperate remedies would work. The antithesis of disorder and anomie in Vietnamese is a term normally employed in the active voice, as a transitive verb. Like *loan, tri* encompasses a variety of meanings; it can mean curing a disease, punishing an unruly child (or a rebellious vassal), or governing the country. It is less a state of mind or affairs than an activity designed to repair wrongs and set the cosmos straight. Phan Boi Chau suggested, in his *History of Pham Hong Thai*, that sometimes only poison can effectively fight poison.[79] Ninh contended that only strong medicine and an infusion of new blood could cleanse Vietnamese society of its ills. The cure would undoubtedly be painful, but there was no other way to restore the country to health. "What we need is curiosity under all its forms, a curiosity that is the last hope and last sign of life, that is capable of every audacity in order to quench its thirst, a curiosity that burrows, seeks, searches, and dissects everything that is life in others so as to find the remedy which will give new vigor to a weakened blood." This rather vampiric imagery betrays the influence of Bergson's concept of *élan vital*, which offered the possibility of countering the prospect of racial and cultural extinction. Although the Vietnamese were indeed a tired people whose blood was running thin, they could reverse this state of affairs by striving to become stronger. Allying Bergson's biological metaphor with Nietzsche's advocacy of the cult of the Superman, Ninh tried to persuade his contemporaries that their personal fate and the fate of their nation were one. The new blood that was needed was new ideas and new values, fully realized and internalized.[80]

The idea that young men must seek their destinies in the great world outside the home was a familiar theme; but that they should reject the values of their fathers was little short of revolutionary. When Ninh exhorted his contemporaries to leave home, there is no question that he had in mind a comfortable if somewhat stifling house, not the dilapidated building to which Nguyen Ba Hoc likened the country. Ninh, who greatly admired André Gide, may have taken his inspiration from Gide's novella, *L'Enfant prodigue,* which was originally published in 1899. In the novella, Gide had reworked the Biblical parable as a series of tableaux in which the Prodigal Son confronts various members of his family. But whereas Gide had used the metaphor of the paternal house to refer to the church, Ninh used it to discuss colonial Vietnam. The elder brother, resentful at the lavish welcome given to the wayward child, can easily stand for advocates of Franco-Annamite collaboration; these elder statesmen, who prided themselves for their loyalty to France ("our adoptive mother," to use the slogan printed in *Southern Wind*) and their love of stability, did sometimes express resentment over the fact that the noisy demands of the young attracted more attention than their own politely worded requests. The last vignette involves an exchange between the Prodigal Son and his younger brother, who, scorning warnings about the dangers that lie ahead, prepares to leave the family home, vowing not to let life defeat him or to return.

Neither the Bible nor Gide made clear what had caused the Prodigal Son to exile himself from the house of his father, nor his younger brother to burn to emulate him. But Ninh, who called imperial mandarins slaves in brocade gowns and embroidered shoes, was wary of the temptations of comfort. There was an element of wanderlust in his personality. He suffered from physical claustrophobia, but he was also afraid of ideological walls. The younger brother stood for all those in whom the hopes of the country rested, the new generation he was trying to reach. Ninh was not persuaded that this generation was particularly eager to leave the comfortable abode of its fathers. He therefore assumed the burden of both exhorting it to leave home and warning it of the difficulties ahead. He agreed up to a point with Pham Quynh on the meanness and poverty of the ambitions of Vietnam's youth. On 24 December, he addressed his readers: "The future we desire today will not come to us in a dream; it is not enough to inscribe in gilt letters on the front of a few public buildings the words 'Liberty, Equality, Fraternity' for liberty, equality and fraternity to reign among us. Fellow countrymen, . . . you demand of others things that they cannot give you, things that it would be dangerous to give to you at the first time of asking, things that you must obtain yourselves, conquer yourselves, to prove that you are mature enough to enjoy what you desire."[81]

It is less easy to find an exact equivalent in Vietnamese society for the father. In Gide's story, he is an aging figure who has relinquished most of his power to his elder son. Possibly this points to the colonial regime, whose false benevolence Nguyen An Ninh repudiated; or perhaps to old reformist scholars like his father, whose day was already gone. The analysis of the family contained in a long article, "Order and Anarchy," which appeared in *Cloche Fêlée* on 31 December 1923, is singularly free of animosity toward that institution, which so many of his peers were beginning to find suffocating. A much-loved only son, Ninh described the traditional family as "a veritable republic where affection and kinship maintain harmony and peace."[82] The initial issue of *Cloche Fêlée* contained an oblique but touching tribute to the generation of scholar-patriots to which his father belonged. In "The First Sound of the Bell," Ninh, using the pen name of Nguyen Tinh (Nguyen the Awakened), conjured up a night scene in which a young man sat at the feet of an old man dressed in the flowing robes of a Confucian scholar. The scholar recalled for his visitor the glory of days gone by in a country that was still independent. As dawn broke over this scene, the young man's imagination soared and was filled with a beautiful dream of the future.[83]

The Sûreté was not unaware of the influence of anarchism on Ninh's ideas. An agent opined that, in choosing for his journal the title *Cloche Fêlée,* Ninh had taken inspiration from the Russian nihilist newspaper *Kolokol.*[84] In his speech of 15 October 1923, Ninh had not elaborated on his observation that Confucianism prized order above liberty, but he was obsessed with the relationship between these two values. Advocates of accommodation liked to raise the specter of chaos and justified continued French rule on the ground that it was necessary to maintain social order. But Ninh forced his audience to distinguish between true and apparent order. He repeatedly asked: "What is order? What is anarchy?" Perhaps the best indication of anarchist influence on Ninh's thought is contained in his 31 December article entitled "Order and Anarchy." Again using the pen name of Nguyen Tinh, and now adopting the perspective of an enlightened Frenchman, he wrote:

He has tried to spread ideas that would force men to impose upon themselves a line of behavior, rules, laws, and discipline in order to realize the greatest creative force allowed man. You will say that, if he seeks order, then the present state of affairs is one of disorder; that, before accusing him, one must find how much truth there is in his ideas. We say to you: he would like the Annamites to become more thoughtful, more disciplined, stronger, and hence, more difficult to govern. The day his ideas bear fruit, Annam will certainly have become a second France, but that day will mark the end of our reign.

Ninh did not extol individual freedom at the expense of the people. But when he spoke of emancipating the Vietnamese masses from exploitation, he talked of spiritual misery as much as material poverty: "Confronted with material misery that is so great, it is not difficult to guess at the spiritual misery of the race . . . The country is still very far from the day when a little well-being will help men escape from ignorance and moral misery, from the terrible darkness that weighs upon them so that they can become conscious of their right to live and of their dignity." [85]

Ninh's advocacy of anarchist ideas took the form of quotes from an astonishing array of sources: from Tagore to Tolstoy, from Claudel to Bertrand Russell. On 17 December 1923, *Cloche Fêlée* ran an excerpt from the German industrialist Walter Rathenau: "He who wants to rule above slaves is himself an escaped slave; the only man who is free is the one who is willingly followed by free men and willingly serves free men." This idea was amplified in the 7 January issue with a quote from Rabindranath Tagore, whom Ninh admired as much as did Pham Quynh, but for rather different reasons: "Those who take pleasure in dominating foreign races abdicate little by little their own liberty and their own humanity in favor of the mechanisms that are necessary to keep other peoples in servitude. Yet, the degradation which we inflict on others through pride or through personal interest degrades our own humanity, and this result is the most terrible of penalties, for we become aware of it only when it is too late."

Nguyen An Ninh was thus concerned with the moral damage which colonial dominion inflicted on both colonizers and colonized. He echoed traditional notions of patriotism and heroic self-sacrifice, and of elitist moral righteousness. But he was also possessed of a strong philosophical streak. During a trip through Cochinchina in the spring of 1924, Werth and Ninh came upon a boy whose face had just been bloodied by a French soldier for peddling copies of *Cloche Fêlée*. They confronted the soldier, whom they found drunkenly leaving a restaurant. As the soldier, taken aback by Werth's presence, lost himself in bluster, Ninh shrugged: "I think we are revenged. He has lied enough this evening." [86]

Ninh's was a profoundly idealistic opposition to authoritarianism, in which national independence was only a logical extension of individual freedom. He was a nationalist who also believed in "the community of aristocrats of the higher spirit." [87] He approvingly quoted Jean Jaurès on the relationship between true nationalism and internationalism: "Far from creating divisions, suspicion, and hatred among nations, nationalism which extends into internationalism contributes to human harmony and beauty." [88] He believed in the possibility of solidarity and fraternity transcending barriers of caste and class. Misplaced nationalism could be inimical to true liberty and justice. In a cinema, a soldier who sat directly behind him suddenly rocked his chair and yelled: "Move, you're blocking my view." Ninh upbraided him for his uncouth manners; the man gripped Ninh by his necktie. Soon the audience was divided into two camps, the French ready to pounce on Ninh and the Vietnamese quaking with fear. Ninh observed to Werth that, throughout the affair, the captain who had sat next to the soldier had remained resolutely silent: deeply disapproving of his subordinate's bullying, but unwilling to take the side of a native against a fellow Frenchman. [89]

Ninh was still something of an adolescent in search of a philosophy of life, too drunk with words and ideas for systematic thinking. He was convinced that action was the path to self-knowledge and self-realization, but could not settle on a particular course. "Dream, dream," Ninh declared, "but act also. To live is to act." He viewed action primarily as an act of personal authentication, as a means of providing youth with an escape from its moral predicament. Ninh argued that it was possible for youth to lift itself out of the moral quagmire into which the national crisis of consciousness had plunged it and to invent its own destiny. But individual liberation and self-realization could only be achieved through selfless dedication to society. As he wrote on 24 December 1923: "Do you know that we are a sacrificed generation, and that we must think only of our task and not of our personal happiness?"

Nguyen An Ninh's conviction that the body politic and cultural was diseased and that its well-being necessitated painful remedies brought him close to the northern opponents of French rule, and made of him a somewhat reluctant convert to revolutionary violence. Truong thi Sau, whom he began courting in 1924, remembers his descriptions of the Soviet Union as a workers' paradise, where everyone had work to do, women were liberated, and all children had access to a good education. He showed her his picture of Lenin, whom he venerated just as Vietnamese students venerated him.[90] But Ninh still recoiled at the human cost of a Bolshevik-style revolution. In his fear of excessive bloodshed, he rejected the violence that was a hallmark of Vietnamese emigré politics in China: "Is revolution possible? I have myself answered in the negative; the reason for my answer is that there does not exist an Annamite elite capable of preparing and leading a revolution and especially of profiting from it so as to achieve its goal with the least possible waste."[91] For the moment, it was sufficient for young Vietnamese to "undermine social inequalities, erode the stupid pride of the insolent few through legal means." He proposed the formation of a league devoted to redressing social wrongs: "To fight against rudeness and violence which are anchored in colonial mores and contribute in no small part to making the atmosphere unbearable."[92]

But Ninh's repudiation of revolutionary violence was far from categorical. Like most anarchists, he was willing to excuse it as the ineluctable consequence of state violence. Increasingly, though he still saw no way of preventing bloody excesses, he began to accept that violent revolution was inevitable. When he again visited France in late 1924, he became convinced of the need for organized, purposeful action, action that was focused not on individual self-authentication but on the achievement of social justice. In a major pamphlet which he finished writing in February 1925, he proclaimed: "Against a modern organization of oppression we must oppose a modern organization of resistance."[93]

Just about this time, anticolonialism was on the rise in Tonkin and Annam. In January 1925, Ton Quang Phiet, a student at the Normal School in Hanoi, published an article in *Southern Wind* commenting on the theme of moral malaise which Pham Quynh had broached two years earlier. He averred that the real problem of youth was not its sadness but its hedonism, which stemmed from an utter lack of ideals.[94] This seemingly unoriginal article was in fact less a commentary on the moral deficiencies of youth than a call to political engagement which had to be couched in the oblique language of cultural discourse because of the strict censorship prevailing in Tonkin. Ton Quang Phiet was involved in a clandestine party called Phuc Viet (Vietnamese Restoration), whose name harked back to Phan Boi Chau's now defunct League for the Restoration of Vietnam.

The Phuc Viet party was originally created by veterans of the Reform Movement who were incarcerated together on the penal island of Con Son.[95] Cut off from communications with the outside, they had drawn up a program of action consisting only of forging an alliance with Phan Boi Chau in South China, studying the causes of previous failures, and spreading anticolonial propaganda within the country. Unaware of the moribund state of the League for the Restoration of Vietnam, two members of Phuc Viet who had made their escape from jail headed for Canton in 1917 with the hope of linking up with Phan Boi Chau. There they were met by Phan Ba Ngoc, who, they hoped, would put them in contact with Phan Boi Chau. Instead, Ngoc led them straight into the hands of the French Sûreté in Shanghai. But while the two men were sent back to prison, other members of Phuc Viet were being released. Once back on the mainland, however, they found that they were totally out of step with the new accommodationist elite that had gained prominence over the last decade. For a time, therefore, Phuc Viet languished in a state of half-life. Meanwhile, young Vietnamese educated in French or Franco-Annamite schools were beginning to graduate and move into low-level jobs in the colonial bureaucracy. The myriad irritations they experienced in these positions fed their hostility toward colonial rule. With the infusion of new blood from these young civil servants, the Phuc Viet party was reorganized in 1924. As before, most of its members were drawn from Annam. While renewed efforts were made to contact the exiles in China, Ton Quang Phiet, one of the new recruits and a student at the University of Hanoi, was given the task of mobilizing opinion in Tonkin.[96] The article he wrote for *Southern Wind* was one of his earliest efforts to fulfill this mission.

It is interesting to contrast Ninh's speeches and writings with Ton Quang Phiet's article. Both men tried to shame their peers into action. But for all his calls to unity, discipline, and action, Ninh was primarily a thinker, albeit not a particularly rigorous one. He was too patriotic to preach assimilation as did Bui Quang Chieu, yet he was also too hostile toward what now passed for Confucianism to call for the preservation of tradition as did Pham Quynh. His consciousness of his and his peers' alienation caused him to cast the task ahead as an intensely personal odyssey, and to think of national liberation in terms of the reinvention of the individual. Ninh's concept of the individual was primarily as an autonomous moral being rather than as a political actor enmeshed in webs of social relationships and responsibilities. Liberty, for him, was more than a political status: it was a spiritual condition. It was not difficult for him to equate political action with moral action and to believe that the pursuit of personal freedom would lead to the liberation of the nation as a whole. In this he owed more to Confucian ideas of self-perfection than he thought. Attracted to the anarchist critique of society and to its libertarian strain which was hostile to all forms of authority, Ninh resisted giving thought to the requirements of effective political organization. As a result, he was unable to unite the many admirers who were attracted by his cultural iconoclasm into the "modern organization of resistance" that he knew to be necessary for the success of revolution. Ton Quang Phiet, less conscious of rupture with the past, was not interested in challenging convention or in creating a new sense of self. Like Phan Boi Chau, he cared more about group rights than individual liberty and thought of liberation as a predominantly political process. Less concerned with the question of authority than Ninh was, he did not shy away from issues of organization. Other northern activists also favored a generalized concern for the welfare and happiness of the people which found its immediate expression in the struggle to recover national independence; in the still nebulous vision of a post-independence society, the state, as representative of the people, was implicitly accorded a crucial role in ensuring equality and justice for all. The need for organization, both to fight for independence and to protect the welfare of the people, was taken for granted. But, like the Society of Like Hearts and the League for the Restoration of Vietnam, the Phuc Viet lacked a clear vision of the future because it had not developed a conceptual framework to analyze society. Without solid ideological foundation, it was capable of wavering between terrorism and Franco-Annamite collaboration in the name of patriotism.

Ultimately, the emergence of anarchism in both its collective and its libertarian strains stemmed from different interpretations of the duties of the elite. Traditionally, these duties were summed up in the Confucian principle linking the individual to the polity through the ethos of self-cultivation and public service. As Nguyen An Ninh himself acknowledged, Confucianism was based on the individual and self-cultivation. His contribution was to redefine the meaning of self-

Different Roads to Freedom

cultivation and give it an iconoclastic ring. Ton Quang Phiet and other epigones of Phan Boi Chau concentrated on the other components of the same principle, and tried to figure out how to rule the country and bring order to All-Under-Heaven. The next few years would test whether it was possible to combine self-cultivation and collective political action in a single ideology of Revolution.

3 Daughters of Annam

> When war strikes close to the home, even women must fight.
> Vietnamese popular saying

IN 1925, my grandfather had a photograph taken of his two eldest daughters, my aunt and my mother. Looking awkward in their flowing gowns and elaborate hairdos, the two girls, then aged seventeen and twelve, seemed demure and untouched by life. There exists another picture of Nguyen Trung Nguyet, the eldest, taken only four years later. In it, she no longer wears the colorful tunic of a scholar's daughter, but the short jacket of a peasant woman. She stares at the camera with defiant eyes: it is a police mug-shot. I found it in the archives of the French Sûreté.

At the time of her arrest, Nguyet was responsible for recruiting women into the Vietnamese Youth League, an anticolonial organization which Nguyen Ai Quoc had founded among Vietnamese exiles in China in 1925. She spent the next eight years of her life in prison after going through a sensational trial, during which her reputation was torn to shreds and she was branded a dangerous revolutionary. The story of Nguyet's brief and tragic involvement in revolutionary politics is of interest not because of its lurid aspects, but because she was so much a product of her times. But, whereas most of her contemporaries in the Vietnamese Revolution generally graduated from personal rebellion to political engagement, Nguyet herself made a different journey. It was filial piety that led her to patriotism and to feminism.

Like Nguyen An Ninh, Nguyen Trung Nguyet came from a close-knit family with scholarly leanings and anticolonial sympathies. And like him, she became, under the influence of patriotic relatives, a dutiful rebel, a pious iconoclast. Nguyen An Ninh appealed to a seemingly gender-neutral but actually masculine youth to combine its quest for personal freedom with national independence. Nguyen Trung Nguyet represents the marriage of feminism and anticolonialism within the Vietnamese Revolution. Until she left home in the wake of the students' strikes of 1926, Nguyet had not shown signs of wanting to take up the cause of women's emancipation. But while she was growing up, the role of women in Vietnam had become a major point of confrontation between cultural progressives and conservatives. Moreover, since disputes on culture and morality usually had a political subtext, the question of women operated as a discourse on freedom, in which differences between personal and national concerns blurred and merged together.

A Family Affair

The connection between feminism and revolution is not unique to the Vietnamese context. Indeed, it can be found in so many other revolutionary settings as to appear organic. Is the link between feminism and communism coincidental or is it made inevitable by some inherent revolutionary logic? The tensions and contradictions between communism and feminism in the Soviet Union and in China have been the subject of a substantial body of scholarship.[1] In each case, early commitment to the emancipation of individual women through the reshaping of familial relationships yielded to a more economistic, class-based, vision of society that relegated gender to a minor role. Some scholars of the Vietnamese Revolution have suggested a natural alliance between national liberation and women's emancipation.[2] But as Alexander B. Woodside has observed, the marriage between feminism and revolution was "far from a foregone conclusion."[3] So how did this marriage come about? And how harmonious was it? Answers to the second question will be proposed in subsequent chapters. To the first, it can be replied that in their different ways, in the early stages of the Revolution, the struggle to liberate women and the struggle to liberate the nation were family affairs.

As the arena where the individual became part of society and the polity, the family was subject to the conflicts that inevitably arose when consensus over the meaning of these concepts broke down. The paternalistic rhetoric of the colonial state reflected traditional Vietnamese views of the family and of the polity. Yet, though the authority structure of the family might be patriarchal, its anchor was definitely feminine. The continuity of the lineage depended on male offspring, but the task of ensuring cultural and social continuity fell to their mothers. Men were traditionally expected to "roam the lakes and mountains" *(ho thi tang bong)*; women represented the welcoming stability of home and hearth where the weary adventurer or responsibility-laden official could return to find solace.

Gender acted as a coded language for debating a whole range of issues without overstepping the limits imposed on public discourse by colonial censorship. The French rhetoric of empire which presented France as the mother country, the Governor-General as a father figure, and the colonial people as children at various stages of immaturity met its match in the Vietnamese literary practice of commenting on the human condition through the device of female characters. The Vietnamese woman stood like an emblematic figure against the canvas of tangled meanings and crumbling institutions that colonial society had become and made personal and concrete abstract issues of morality, social structure, independence, collaboration, empowerment, liberty, and equality.

Disdaining traditional literary representations of feminine self-abnegation beloved of neo-traditionalists, young Vietnamese chose a character out of French Romantic fiction to incarnate both their plight and their aspirations: Camille. To them, Camille represented the struggle of youth against age, class-transcending passion against worldly hypocrisy: the quest for freedom made feminine. Debates on women thus represented a body of reflection on their condition and a commentary on a whole range of cultural, social, and political questions. Woman was youth; woman was also the only possible symbol of a colonized nation. Not the buoyant, self-confident personification of European imperialism, such as Marianne, Germania, or Britannia, nor one modeled after the tragic heroines of Vietnamese history, such as the Trung sisters or any female warrior, ruler, or poet who came after them, but woman-as-quintessential-victim. In her plight was her strength, for it undermined the legitimacy of both the Vietnamese paterfamilias at home and the French "father" of the colonial people abroad. Later on, woman would assume yet another symbolic role in public discourse as the representative of the disenfranchised masses. This multiplicity of functions ensured that the question of women would continue to be hotly debated over the years, but there also existed the danger that the condition of women as women would be lost from view in the welter of symbolism.

In Cochinchina, where rules governing political speech were more relaxed than in Annam and Tonkin, the Constitutionalists, who dominated the native press, were too obsessed with expanding their own electoral representation and furthering their economic interests to pay attention to women. Even in France, after all, women did not yet enjoy the right to vote. Equally important was the fact that education and Confucian morality, the two issues around which early debates on women were constructed, aroused little controversy in Cochinchina, which was less bound by tradition than Tonkin or Annam. Nary a protest was uttered when the Constitutionalists proposed equal education for men and women in 1919. Nguyen Phan Long tried to contribute to the debate by writing a highly mannered novel about a modern young woman, which was serialized in *Tribune Indigène* under the title *Le Roman de Mlle Lys* in 1919. In 1924, Nguyen An Ninh ran a series of articles on Indian women by Ananda Cooramaswamy in his own journal, *Cloche Fêlée*. That was more or less the extent to which the question of women was debated in the South in the early years.

But in northern Vietnam, where political discourse was so circumscribed by censorship as to be rendered meaningless, debates on women became primary vehicles for arguing about topics that could not be addressed forthrightly, in particular the meaning of freedom and the best way of achieving it. The strain of individualism which asserted itself in these debates was different from the one represented by Nguyen An Ninh. His notion of freedom was the realization of the highest potential of the individual as an autonomous moral and social being. The debates on women focused on a more practical and structural approach to freedom: emancipation first from ignorance, and later from the webs of familial relationships and social responsibilities in which young people of both sexes found themselves enmeshed.

The question of women, first debated exclusively among male writers, eventually attracted contributions from women, some timid, others full of barely controlled rage. To describe as feminism the many solutions offered is to obscure the range of opinion on the matter. Just as the proper role of women was perceived differently in different quarters, so was the meaning of emancipation: from whom, from what, how, and to what purpose? Should women receive formal education? What kind of education and how much of it? What for? Were women, by virtue of their domesticity, really untouched by political currents, or were they doubly enslaved by male domination at home and colonial rule abroad? Should women leave their quiet corner by the family hearth and plunge into public life? Should they leave politics, including the making of revolution, to the men? Should they merely aspire to be ornaments to their husbands' salons? These questions and many more were earnestly examined alongside equally earnest debates about new culture, new morality, new bases of social organization, and new politics. At bottom, the question was: "What kind of society do we want?"

The link between women's emancipation and radicalism was initially (and unwittingly) forged by conservative opinion-makers who had abdicated to the French the responsibility of ruling the country but worried that traditional values were being eroded and that Vietnamese society was drifting, anchorless, on the sea of change. It was in articles dealing with women's education and family morality that their calls for preserving the national essence rang loudest, for they clung to the illusion that the traditional family could provide a haven of stability in a swiftly changing society. Since national essence was supposedly synonymous with Confucianism, the debates on women thus helped shape perceptions of Confucianism among a generation of students emerging from Franco-Annamite schools without exposure to classical studies. Ironically, the self-professed champions of a synthesis between Western learning and national essence turned out to be their own worst enemies. By choosing to defend neo-traditionalist values in the context of a debate almost entirely concerned with domestic morality, they emptied Confucianism of intellectual substance as well as of its larger social and political relevance. It was reduced to a code of personal behavior which was perceived as narrow, hidebound, elitist, moralistic, and even anti-intellectual. Thus, having set the terms of the debates, conservative moralists soon lost control of them: instead of steering Vietnamese youth in the direction of slow, steady, incremental change, these debates uncovered a generational divide that made paternal authority a focus of the radical critique of society.

The Education of Women

Until the twentieth century, women had not had the right to formal education. Prohibited from taking the civil service examinations, women had been taught, if they were taught at all, at home. This consisted of instructing them in household skills and morality, the latter being summed up by the Three Submissions and the Four Virtues *(tam tong tu duc)*. Women were supposed to be perpetual minors. When young, they were under the authority of their fathers;

when married, they came under the authority of their husbands; when widowed, they were required to acquiesce in the decisions of their sons.⁴ Their everyday behavior was guided by the Four Virtues: housewifery, appearance, speech, and conduct *(cong, dung ngon, hanh)*. They were expected to be skilled and diligent in the various chores needed to run their household smoothly; additionally, they must be good managers of the family finances, thrifty in their expenditures, and good at earning money at their market stalls or shop counters. They must maintain a neat appearance and modest expression at all times; their speech must be mild and conciliatory.⁵ Under the Nguyen legal code, a wife's loose mouth or sharp tongue was considered cause enough for repudiation. Above all, women must be chaste.

Women's lives were circumscribed by injunctions and taboos which filled manual upon manual of "family education in verse" *(gia huan ca)*. They constituted a flourishing literary subgenre which went as far back as the fifteenth century, the oldest example being attributed to the scholar and statesman Nguyen Trai (1380–1442). Other famous scholars through the ages had also tried to lay down the law to women. Written in verse for easy memorizing, these manuals combined in haphazard fashion instruction in household management and morality. As Pham Quynh acknowledged, they were long on prohibitions and made for depressing reading. In one, he counted one hundred "don'ts."

> Do not talk to a man who is not a relative;
> Do not say hello to him, so as not arouse suspicion.
> Do not frequent women who are not virtuous;
> Do not alter your clothing without reason;
> When sewing do not let your needle be idle;
> When alone, do not sing or declaim poetry;
> Do not look out the window with a pensive air.
> ... Do not shrug, do not sigh;
> Do not laugh before you have even said a word;
> When laughing, do not show all your teeth;
> Do not gossip, or talk crudely ...

As Pham Quynh noted, these injunctions and restraints were as "inconsistent as children's stories, tedious, trivial and petty."⁶

Not all women could live up to the ideals of domestic femininity these rules were meant to enforce. When debates on women first began in the pages of *Southern Wind,* Than Trong Hue, the Imperial Minister of Rites, pointed out that women had not always been kept within the home, but had traditionally worked in the fields alongside their husbands, or had been market stall-holders, and producers of handicraft.[7] Few traditional moralists, however, could be found to praise the free and easy demeanor of peasant women. Although the rules contained in family education manuals truly applied only to the wives and daughters of the elite, they represented the dominant ethos, values to which women of all classes were expected to aspire even if they could not apply them in their daily conduct. Women who did absorb the teachings of the family education manuals and fulfilled the criteria of the Three Submissions and the Four Virtues were praised as "wholesome daughters, gentle wives, and caring mothers."[8] There was no positive way of describing an independent woman of the elite. The best-known and most admired woman of the early 1920s, the Widow Nguyet Anh, wore her widowhood like a cloak. Daughter of Nguyen Dinh Chieu, the most famous scholar and poet the South had produced, she could boast a considerable erudition and no small talent at poetry. Nor was she a fragile hothouse plant who could not bear being taken outdoors. Having lost her husband early, she supported herself and her children through a variety of businesses. In 1919, she launched the first women's magazine, *Women's Bell (Nu Gioi Chung),* in Saigon. Yet she preferred to be remembered as the chaste relic of her husband rather than as a woman of talent and achievements. The title "widow" which she affixed to her name became an integral part of her identity. Her insistence on being a living monument to Confucian values, her scrupulous avoidance of political discussion (forbidden in the Vietnamese language press in any case) in order to dispense sage and entirely conventional advice to female readers, made this grandmotherly figure seem not so much a feminist pioneer as the representative of traditional womanhood at its best. In fact, the creation of *Women's Bell* resulted from Pham Quynh's efforts to coopt, on behalf of the French colonial authorities, the descendants of Nguyen Dinh Chieu. In addition to his fame as a poet, Nguyen Dinh Chieu was the symbol of southern patriotism.[9]

At the time the Widow Nguyet Anh began publishing *Women's Bell* in Saigon, women in Annam and Tonkin had just won the right to formal education. The drive to grant them that right had been slow in gathering force. The Reformers wanted to build a more egalitarian society, and when they opened their classrooms in 1907, they decided that perhaps girls and married women could also be taught how to use the romanized script. In fact, women, not having undergone a rigorous classical education, were more receptive to New Learning than many a scholar. Finding that his daughter was already familiar with the new script, Luong van Can put her in charge of the women's section at the Tonkin Free School. At least two poems were produced for use in her class. One, entitled "A Mother Draws Glory from Her Children," exhorted young people not to forsake their duty to their country in the pursuit of riches and position. The other, entitled "Advice of a Wife to Her Husband," exuded patriotic fervor. The anonymous author invited her husband to strive to become a Bismarck or a Gladstone, while she would try to emulate Joan of Arc or Mme. Roland.[10] The reference to these two French heroines was not uncommon either in Vietnam or in China, from which the Reform Movement drew its inspiration. More important, both poems conceived of women as wives and mothers, as nurturing figures whose essential function was to provide assistance, succor, and backstage advice to the male actors on the public stage. Their identity was defined in relation to others. In this, the Reformers followed the spirit of the contemporary Chinese women's press.[11]

Phan Boi Chau, who was perhaps the first Vietnamese to discuss the role of women in Vietnamese society, viewed women primarily as effective anticolonial warriors whose services it would be foolish to sacrifice to traditional notions of feminine decorum. Phan knew the value of women in the anticolonial movement. Women (even those belonging to the elite) ran small businesses which could be used as fronts for anticolonial activities. They could travel without exciting undue suspicion, and they were less likely than men to be detained and searched by the police. Phan, who subsumed everything to the cause of independence, was not open to arguments such as those advanced by Ho Chen in *Natural Justice* when he was still in Japan. Ho Chen argued against conceiving of sexual equality purely as a means of strengthening the nation and presented it as a natural right and a class issue.[12] In his drama on the Trung queens, written in 1911, Phan made it clear that feminism must serve the cause of the nation.[13] The Trung sisters, who had led a rebellion which briefly overthrew Chinese rule in A.D. 39, had long symbolized Vietnamese patriotism. Phan depicted them as women whose love of country had led them to rise above ordinary feminine weaknesses. Turning these two icons of Vietnamese patriotism into paragons of Confucian femininity, he made them ask themselves how to reconcile the resoluteness and strength necessary to wage war with the docility and meekness traditionally expected of women.

Since self-strengthening was the primary objective of the Reform Movement, the education of women was decidedly secondary to the need to rethink the education of (male) literati. Nor was it the exclusive concern of the Reformers. In 1907, classes were organized within the Imperial Citadel in Hue to provide formal education for the daughters of the imperial family and court mandarins. There were forty-seven pupils who learned French, arithmetic, and sewing under the supervision of the French director of the school; a Vietnamese auxiliary taught the romanized script, the French alphabet, and Chinese characters. The school was moved outside the Imperial Citadel the following year. Finally, in 1919 the foundations of the Dong Khanh College for girls were laid down in Hue amid much fanfare.[14] That year marked a turning point in women's education. Until then, only a handful of girls had attended school, usually only in the first three grades. In the South, where innovations were introduced first, it had become possible in 1910 for girls to attend secondary school in Saigon, whereas previously, only elementary education had been available to a tiny, privileged minority.[15] However, with the end of the Confucian examinations and the expansion of secondary education, older girls began to receive formal schooling.

Articles on women began appearing in the northern press soon after the promulgation of Sarraut's educational reforms. Pham Quynh himself launched the first salvo in his article "The Education of Women and Girls," in one of the first issues of his journal.[16] The prospect that young women would emerge from behind the "high walls and closed gates" *(tuong cao cong kin)* of home to attend school, and that, away from parental supervision, they would absorb new ideas and come into contact with people of different backgrounds was highly disturbing to conservative moralists. Nguyen Ba Hoc lamented that good women were traditionally not supposed to exchange even names with strange men, let alone engage in conversation with them; but now women felt free to speak out on topics normally reserved for men and, worse, did so publicly.[17] At any rate, he argued, there was no point in educating women when even educated men could not find jobs.

Pham Quynh, younger and less hidebound in his notions, conceded: "Until now, the world has been the exclusive property of men.

Now, it belongs also to women."[18] But what kind of women? Though in general Pham Quynh supported the idea of granting formal education to women, he too had grave qualms. Like Nguyen Ba Hoc, he feared that education might lead women to moral turpitude. He had met the "New Woman" and did not like her. In a talk given in May 1924, he offered a savage portrayal of this dreaded breed in his account of two young women traveling on a train. They were coiffed in the latest style, rouged and lipsticked, and wore objectionable clothes. One had propped her feet on the seat across from her and was languidly smoking a cigarette. The other affected a pair of sunglasses even though the train compartment was darkened. Supremely oblivious to the silent disapproval of their fellow passengers, they talked in carrying, self-assured voices about card parties, French food, and other frivolous pleasures in which they had recently indulged.

For all his endorsement of women's education, Pham Quynh was an old-guard moralist at heart, as were other advocates of national essence. In his eyes, the "New Women" were little better than brazen hussies: idle, self-centered, and pleasure-seeking, loud and free in their manners to a point bordering on immorality. They were a sad contrast to "Traditional Ladies," who behaved as "true daughters of Confucius."[19] The prejudices of these moralists were revealed in their choice of adjectives: "New Woman" *(thi tan)* and "Traditional Lady" *(cuu nuong)*. The latter was a paragon of feminine decorum, shunning public display, mindful of the welfare of her family, and always putting duty before pleasure. Becomingly modest and obedient, she always deferred to her father or husband in every way. The New Woman was bold and brash; she wore make-up and revealing clothes, and was acid-tongued. She was not truly worthy of being the daughter of mandarins.

If neo-traditionalist opinions on the issues of women's education and morality seem unreal, even for the 1920s, it is because they concerned only a tiny minority of women. Than Trong Hue had already pointed out the important economic role of peasant women. In the cities, too, young women who were good at making money *(dam dang)* were deemed highly marriageable. A small number of unmarried women chose to live on their own, supporting themselves by working as seamstresses or shopkeepers. The debates, however, were not about these ordinary women, but about the development of a new Western-educated elite and the role of women in that elite. The talk in which Pham Quynh had presented his picture of the New Woman was given under the auspices of AFIMA. Gracing the proceedings with her presence was Princess Thieu Bao, the wife of AFIMA's president, Hoang Trong Phu. The rest of the audience was made up of the very type of Western-educated, upper- and middle-class women he was caricaturing in his speech. Pham Quynh was not concerned about the damage formal education might do to women of the lower classes: in all probability, they would continue to have no access to it. He was concerned only with the small number of women whose families could afford to keep them cloistered behind high walls and closed gates, as in the past, or to send them to school, as was now being proposed.

Underlying Pham Quynh's gradualist philosophy was the belief that the world was composed of those who ruled and those who were ruled. Individuals should receive the training and education most appropriate to their nature, their station in life, and their future calling. Since it was the duty of the rulers to provide leadership and the duty of those whom they ruled merely to follow their lead, Pham Quynh concerned himself only with the cultivation and development of the elite. He acknowledged that the great majority of Vietnamese (he put it at 75 percent but it was closer to 90 percent) would never receive any schooling beyond the third grade. As secretary-general of AFIMA, he worked hard to remedy the situation, spearheading the opening of nursery schools in villages and towns and the general expansion of schooling for boys.[20] He was of the view that the education of boys was aimed at cultivating talent for the country; because talent knew no social barriers, it followed that all boys should have the chance to attend school.[21] Women, however, were made of different stuff. Pham Quynh had begun by welcoming the idea of sexual equality. But in the next breath, he argued that men and women had different natures:

> Men are like clouds in autumn
> Women are like smoke in the hearth.
> Though they reach different heights
> They are both capable of soaring.[22]

These images so delighted him that he used them on several other occasions.

As for clouds, the natural domain of the male resided well above the mundane concerns of home; but women, like smoke, would always be linked to the hearth. Clouds and smoke could both soar, but they would always reach different heights. To prevent smoke from soaring at all would be to deny its very nature, but how high it reached depended on the hearth it came from. A woman's place was still in the home, even though Pham Quynh claimed that the world outside also belonged to her. But why consider her contribution to society negligible because her domain was domestic? Indeed, in oriental civilizations the family was considered the very basis of society, and therefore the woman's role must be appreciated more fully. As Nguyen Don Phuc, a frequent contributor to the debates on women, noted, "The virtue of the Oriental woman is not in quelling revolt in the East or bringing order to the North [*danh Dong dep Bac*]; it does not reside in competing with men for sexual equality, nor in studying the stars, or algebra. Even if they are educated, they should learn only the Four Virtues [*tu duc*]."[23] He further argued that women were entirely responsible for the education of their children, since men, busy with work outside the home, had no time left for the task. This was how he explained the meaning of the popular saying, "If a child turns out badly, that is his mother's fault."[24]

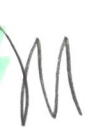

Pham Quynh's family history, replete with women who devoted themselves to the welfare of their menfolk, reinforced his belief in their nurturing vocation.[25] Pham Quynh did not propose to take elite women out of their domestic sphere and into public life, but to equip them with the new skills their changing duties demanded. Until now, the women's sphere had been the kitchen, where they cooked, worked, and ate, in strict segregation from their men. According to Pham Quynh, women should now prepare to emerge from their kitchen hearths to grace the salons of their husbands. And for that, they needed to learn a whole new set of skills. In days past, it had not been unusual for daughters of scholarly households to acquire a smattering of book-learning while their brothers prepared for the Confucian exams. In families of more modest means and aspirations, a girl probably would not be taught how to read and write; all her education would be concentrated on the acquisition of domestic skills that would make her a desirable match. For centuries, women had dominated trade, though mostly at a petty level. The poorer sold fruits and vegetables or handicrafts at market stalls. The more prosperous owned shops. But these activities were considered part of family management; they were not supposed to lead women into the public arena of cultural or political debate. As conceived by Pham Quynh, the education of middle-class girls, who would have to perform their own household chores, should emphasize practical skills. They must learn sewing, weaving, embroidery, arithmetic, reading and writing in the romanized script, and a smattering of literature suited to feminine sensibilities. Since middle-class women were heavily engaged in small-scale trading, they should also learn enough French to be able to deal with French customers or officials. As for upper-class girls, who would probably not have to do menial household work, their education should be aimed at turning them into talented and gracious hostesses for their husbands. But whereas traditional feminine accomplishments included music, chess, and poetry, Pham Quynh thought that the new Vietnamese woman should learn, in addition to literature, some geography, history, hygiene, and the natural sciences. If a student showed aptitude, she might learn Chinese and even French literature in translation, which he himself was busy promoting and interpreting in *Southern Wind*.[26] Pham Quynh envisaged the day when such a young woman would become the ideal wife for a modern man. He would be someone who had studied in France, and become a medical doctor, an extreme rarity in those days. Upon his return, he would practice medicine, then become involved in politics. As for his wife, aside from running her household and supervising the education of her children, she would involve herself in charitable work such as visiting hospitals, distributing relief, supporting kindergartens, and so forth. She would also become a celebrated hostess, maintaining a salon where she would welcome the flower of Vietnamese society. Then, coming down to earth, Pham Quynh conceded that such a dream would not materialize for another thirty or forty years.[27]

Although *Southern Wind* was the chief vehicle of neo-traditionalist thought, its position on the question of women was not without ambiguity. The overt message was clear enough: women must be taught how to be obedient daughters, supportive wives, and caring mothers for new generations of Vietnamese. But the subtext was open to different interpretations. In February 1922, *Southern Wind* ran a poetry contest to honor a Cochinchinese woman for contributing to AFIMA and to the building of a hospital in a Tonkinese village. Although her donation accorded with Pham Quynh's dictum on doing charitable work, it also underlined her financial success and independence, which went well beyond conventional ideas of household management. In that same issue ran an article proposing the casting of a bronze statue to the Trung queens.[28] In May 1924, *Southern Wind* ran a compilation of biographies of famous women by Ngo Huy Linh. Amid a gallery of women whose sole claim to fame was that they had married men of importance were three who were famous leaders in their own right, the Trung sisters and Lady Trieu, all heroines of rebellions against Chinese rule. Others had gained fame for their own literary accomplishments.[29] Thus, in its absorption in the topic, *Southern Wind* published a huge variety of articles on women, real and fictional, native and foreign. Not all of them were paragons of feminine decorum and meekness, and they had certainly not confined themselves to the kitchen hearth.

There was a barely concealed subtext to the discourse on women's rights: the question of political maturity and national independence. Among the cautiously progressive elements who dominated this discourse, the consensus was that education was the only way to attain the maturity necessary for national independence. This position united northern neo-traditionalists and southern Constitutionalists despite their differing educational philosophies. Debates on women's emancipation thus closely paralleled debates on political independence. By the mid-1920s, the idea that educating women was desirable had gained ground even among more conservative writers. Though hostility to New Women remained, the halo of the Traditional Ladies was dimming somewhat. Even their champions had to concede that the "true daughters of Confucius" were woefully ignorant, that they were ill prepared to face the rigors of modern life, to advance their husbands' careers, or even to defend themselves. They needed to trade some of their self-effacing ways for a modicum of the self-assurance which their modern sisters possessed in such overabundance. Even Nguyen Don Phuc thought that rustic virtue could be carried too far.[30] Though few girls were formally enrolled in schools, many more were being taught privately at home; their parents were fearful that in a more public setting their daughters might absorb immoral ideas along with the rudiments of math and geography. These numbers, however small, were gradually transforming elite and middle-class women into a distinctive social group. They also provided a ready-made readership for the fiction that was emerging as the most exciting literary trend of the decade. Indeed, fiction was the real arena in which the issue of women was debated most forcefully. As a result, northern individualism had a literary flavor quite lacking in its southern manifestation.

Fictional Emancipation

Here again, Pham Quynh played an important role. Passionately interested in developing a truly Vietnamese fiction, he wrote numerous articles explaining the nature, aims, and rules of this genre, buttressing his essays with profiles of authors he particularly liked and extracts from their works. He also did much to encourage the growth of native fiction; many of the contributors to *Southern Wind* tried their hand at writing short stories as well as essays. It was Pham Quynh's opinion, borrowed without acknowledgment from Liang Ch'i-ch'ao, that fiction should be rescued from its traditional ill-repute. Instead of being seen as immoral and of no educational value, it should enjoy the same prestige as scholarly essays. Fiction, he argued, possessed a didactic role and a high moral purpose.

But the fiction that captured the public imagination in the mid-1920s was of a heavily romantic sort. There had been many Western novels available in translation, including romantic ones, before. Some had been serialized in *Southern Wind*, others were published in book form. But, despite skillful translations, their Western origins were inescapable. To many readers, especially the conservative literati who formed an important proportion of the readership of *Southern Wind*, the psychology of Western characters, the problems they faced, the landscapes in which they moved, all remained alien. Even their style was criticized as lacking in poetry, for straight prose was still unfamiliar. Only with the appearance of native fiction in the early 1920s did literature truly become a vehicle of cultural discourse. Although clearly influenced by Western literature, its sensibilities owed a great deal to late Ch'ing fiction, in particular to the genre known as "mandarin ducks and butterflies." This was a type of popular literature, often with some obvious moral message, that appealed to a reading public caught, as the Vietnamese were, in the throes of cultural change.

A short story by Doan Ngoc Bich which appeared in *Southern Wind* in November 1922 illustrates the widespread distrust of women's education. The main character in this morality tale is the daughter of a rural scholar. Her father lets himself be persuaded, out of misguided paternal love, to send her to school instead of teaching her at home. She is sent to Haiphong, Tonkin's second-largest city, presumably to attend one of the new Franco-Annamite schools. But soon reports of her willful behavior reach her anxious parents. Called home, the young woman quickly becomes bored; she longs for the bright lights of Haiphong, the cinemas, theaters, hotels, and restaurants; she misses her fashionable clothes and shoes. Her mother worries that she has become bold, disobedient, and flirtatious. The good lady flies into a rage when she catches her daughter wearing make-up. Feeling misunderstood, the girl flees home and gradually sinks into vice and misery. She becomes addicted to gambling and has illicit affairs. She enters into a disastrous marriage with a wastrel who refuses to support her child, and is reduced to begging. Clearly, starting with innocuous adolescent rebelliousness and fascination with clothes and make-up, she has fallen beyond redemption. The whole tale is told with a heavily moralizing tone typical of the fiction of the period. There is no hint that the girl's parents may have erred by overreacting to her departures from conventional behavior. Although the author does not specifically lay the blame for her downfall on her schooling, the message is clear. A modern education for women promotes unfiliality, dishonesty, and promiscuity.[31]

Doan Ngoc Bich was not without sympathy toward women trapped into loveless, polygamous marriages. In another short story, entitled "The Daughter Sold in Marriage" *(Ga ban cho con),* which appeared only two issues later, he recounted the sorry tale of a young woman forced by her well-to-do but greedy parents to become the concubine of a married middle-aged man. Her marriage turned out badly. The more her husband showered unwelcome favors on her, the more his first wife victimized her. Eventually, she fled the conjugal home to extricate herself from this unbearable situation. For the next several years, she was able to support herself and was content with her life as an unattached woman. Her story, however, did not end there. Her creator, apparently, did not like to leave her in her single state and had her remarry. But her new husband turned out to be a wastrel and a gambler who spent all her hard-earned savings and beat her. The heroine fled again; and again, the author could not bear to let her live happily on her own. Although in the first half of the story he had heaped scorn on her greedy parents (who, among their sins, had reneged on their promise to give her in marriage to a poor student), at the end, he had her return to the bosom of her family, swearing to give up the idea of marital happiness and to live according to the dictates of filial piety. The story's improbable ending was in all likelihood the result of its author's difficulties in coming to terms with the contradictions of transitional morality.[32]

In a climate of opinion which prized filial obedience above all, it was considered *risqué* to advocate allowing young people to choose their own mates. Indeed, moralizing reformers preferred to preach obedience to the young while advising their elders to be thoughtful in choosing marriage partners for their children. But other aspects of marriage customs were coming under attack. In 1922, *Southern Wind* ran a series of articles by Tran Quan Chi on the need to reform customs, especially in rural areas, which were deemed more backward than the westernized urban centers (it was no coincidence that these articles ran together with a series on the need to overhaul village government). Early marriages were singled out as deleterious both to the health of the partners involved and to their chances of happiness. They were thought to be a contributing factor to polygamy, another custom which the author denounced. Among the reasons for arranging early marriages, the author cited a desire to acquire another pair of hands to work in the fields or in the house and the wish of one of the families involved to ally itself with a richer one in order to have access to new sources of money. The selling of young girls into marriage was also roundly condemned.[33] In these articles, a link was established between marriage customs and economic considerations; this would be an important theme of feminist rhetoric in later years. But, though the authors who wrote in *Southern Wind* occasionally showed an awareness of the economic plight of poor women, they were primarily interested in shaping a new elite. Therefore, when it came to discussing morality, most acted as if the typical Vietnamese woman never stepped outside the household compound or came into contact with males who were unrelated to her. And though polygamy was attacked, fidelity throughout marriage and even into widowhood, obedience, and meekness continued to be the ideals propounded for women.

A new development occurred in November 1923 when *Southern Wind* began to serialize the translation of a late Ch'ing novel, the *Chronicle of Great Tears of Bygone Days (Hsueh hung lei shih)*, by Hsu Cheng-ya. Its story, set in 1909 in the dying days of the Manchu dynasty, was one with which Vietnamese readers could easily empathize. Furthermore, it was written in the classical style, replete with poems whose absence in Western fiction the Vietnamese so deplored. The *Chronicle of Great Tears of Bygone Days* was originally written in 1915 in the form of a diary kept by one of its protagonists, Ho Meng-hsia. This was Hsu's attempt to improve on an earlier version, published in 1912 as a straightforward narrative under the title *Jade Pear Spirit (Yu li hun)*. In each format the novel was a phenomenal success, both in China and abroad.[34] Hsu Cheng-ya, who had been deeply influenced by Western classics such as Dumas' *La Dame aux camélias* and Goethe's *Young Werther,* skillfully blended Western romanticism with Chinese literary sensibilities.

In his introduction, the translator hailed the book for its newness, remarking that it was set in the last decade, not in some nebulous past, and that the story concerned a "talented and highly educated young man of our own epoch." Indeed, it represented a radical departure from the steady dose of historical novels which Nguyen An Khuong and others had offered to a Vietnamese reading public eager for literature in the new vernacular. The translator extravagantly praised it as being superior to the *Tale of Kieu,* considered the masterpiece of Vietnamese literature. Yet the classical style in which the story was written and its plot, centering on a love triangle involving two sisters, were familiar to readers of premodern literature, both Chinese and Vietnamese. The *Tale of Kieu* involved a young man of great talent and high birth who had to choose between two sisters; in the *Dream of the Red Chamber,* it was two cousins. In both cases, one was beautiful, talented, but also high-strung and overly romantic, the other more plodding though worthy. In both cases, the hero settled for the more prosaic one.

Essentially, the *Chronicle* concerns three young people: Ho Meng-hsia (Mong Ha in Vietnamese translation), an impoverished young man hired as tutor to the son of an attractive twenty-seven-year-old widow named Li Niang (Le Anh); Li Niang herself, the product of tradition; and her sixteen-year-old sister Yun-ch'ien (Van Kien), who attends a new type of school and typifies the modern young woman. Though Li Niang and Meng-hsia fall madly in love, Li Niang considers herself bound by the rules of chastity to remain faithful to her dead husband, and proposes to her father-in-law that a marriage be arranged between Meng-hsia and her sister. Meng-hsia reluctantly proposes to Yun-ch'ien, who, resenting its arranged character, is no more eager for the marriage than he is. But Li Niang remains afraid that Meng-hsia is still in love with her, and decides to set him free by taking to her bed and allowing herself to drift into death. Yun-ch'ien, who had been unaware of the attachment between her sister and her fiancé, comes across a farewell letter Li Niang had left for Meng-hsia. Shocked at Meng-hsia's duplicity toward herself and moved by her sister's purity and devotion, she falls ill, vowing to die. The Vietnamese translation of the novel stopped at this point in the June 1924 issue of *Southern Wind*. In the September issue, the translator reached into the earlier version to let his readers know what had happened to Meng-hsia. He had gone to Japan to study with the intent of serving his country. In 1911 he took part in the Wuchang Uprising, and, clutching a volume of his own poetry, died both for love and for country.[35] The combination of personal concerns and political engagement, the reference to Japan, and the death of Meng-hsia in an event so crucial to the overthrow of Manchu rule and the creation of Republican China all struck a deep chord in Vietnamese readers.

Still, the translator of the *Chronicle* seemed dubious about the moral content of the story and asked his readers to enjoy the novel without necessarily approving of the conduct of its characters. Despite this exercise in self-protection, the novel created a sensation. Emboldened, the translator changed its description from "a story of faithfulness" *(tieu thuyet chung tinh)* to "a love story" *(ai tinh tieu thuyet)*. The publication of the *Chronicle* seems to have given local authors the courage to publish romantic fiction of their own. One such effort is no longer extant, but an advertisement for it appeared in *Southern Wind* one month after the serialization of the *Chronicle* ended. Like the *Chronicle*, *The Tearful Story of Kim Anh (Kim Anh le su)* was described as a new novel, set in Tonkin within the last decade. The advertisement was followed by a highly favorable commentary from the newspaper *Cultural Overtures (Khai Hoa)*, which praised "its photographic portrait of northern society: ineffectual but greedy mandarins, treacherous masters, wrongdoings in high places, petty rivalry in villages."[36] Above all, it promised to show the tragedies caused by the institution of polygamy. The heroine was described as unusually beautiful and virtuous but burdened also by extraordinary sorrows. The novel was especially recommended to elite women who still lived behind "high walls and closed gates." Perhaps Kim Anh was too unbelievable a paragon of beauty and virtue to capture the imagination of modern readers, and therefore sank without a trace. But within months, a literary sensation occurred with the publication of *To Tam* by Hoang Ngoc Phach.[37]

Hoang Ngoc Phach, who had studied with a Chinese master, was familiar with late Ch'ing fiction as well as with the story of *La Dame aux camélias*. In 1921, he wrote a short story, "Tears from the Red District" *(Giot le hong lau)*, which fell within the late Ch'ing literary mainstream in its fascination with the lives of prostitutes.[38] He also began a longer story and sent it to the *Bulletin of the Alumni* of the Normal School where he was studying. But when the *Bulletin* stopped appearing, he set aside his novel. Then, in 1925, he went back to it, and published it under the title *To Tam*. The novel was an immediate success. A first printing of three thousand copies was sold in two weeks; a second printing of two thousand copies sold equally fast.[39]

Like the late Ch'ing novels from which Hoang Ngoc Phach drew inspiration, *To Tam* carried a preface in which its author set forth the salient moral points of the story. He explained that he had originally had qualms about publishing it, fearing the reception that would be accorded to it. But the highly favorable welcome received by the serialization of *The Chronicle of Great Tears of Bygone Days* may have changed his mind. Hoang Ngoc Phach's novel is also about two doomed young lovers, To Tam and Dam Thuy, a friend of her brother. When they meet, Dam Thuy, a writer, is already engaged to marry a young woman whom his mother has chosen for him. Despite his warning that he does not wish to go against his mother's wishes, To Tam is convinced that she can love for the sake of loving, that love and marriage are unrelated. To Tam herself had been resisting pressure from her mother to marry another young man. But when her mother falls ill, To Tam gives in to her mother's wishes and marries. But she cannot forget Dam Thuy and dies of a broken heart shortly after her wedding, leaving Dam Thuy (and presumably her husband) desolate. Romantic love, unsanctioned by family and existing outside the bonds of marriage, was thus portrayed as a recipe for disaster.

Hoang Ngoc Phach seems to have taken the didactic dimension of fiction seriously, even as he saw the danger of encouraging romantic self-indulgence in his readers. Before publishing the novel, he had sent to *Southern Wind* an article warning about the danger of fostering literary sensibilities among females.[40] In his preface to *To Tam*, written in August 1922, he stated:

> Sometimes, when I listen to my friends as they discuss modern culture, I hear of progressive young men with strong personalities, young men of culture and ideas, who abuse these gifts in the pursuit

of romance; they awaken the affections of young women in order to put to the test ideas they have read in books or thought up themselves. Sometimes, they do it on purpose, sometimes unconsciously; whatever the case, they find a good occasion to experiment and make someone fall in love with them; and thus, they provoke many a tragedy, bringing harm to themselves and misery to others, sowing turmoil in their families and in society.

This was no disingenuous disclaimer. Years later, after many more stories focusing on conflicts between duty and love had appeared, Hoang Ngoc Phach clung to his original, and totally unrevolutionary, belief in the virtue of resignation and self-abnegation: "The characters in my story know the meaning of sacrifice for the sake of their parents. That is as it should be. Only someone who can make sacrifices for his family can be faithful to his country."[41] But the young Vietnamese who clutched copies of his novel to their hearts and wept over the sorrows of its fictional characters had a very different interpretation of its message. They saw in its protagonists the embodiment of their own plight, and clung to the idea that To Tam and Dam Thuy were the victims of their respective families. In fact, the two mothers in the story were far from the tyrants who would later abound in similar novels. With the best intentions in the world, each had chosen for her child a highly suitable mate that the child could not love. To Tam and Dam Thuy were far too dutiful, filial, and perhaps far too weak to go against their mothers' wishes. Yet, for their youthful readers, it was enough that they gave voice to the individual's right to exist in the face of family pressure to conform.[42]

Contemporary commentators were divided on the merits of the novel. Literary critics expressed their fervent appreciation of its stylistic innovations, but moralists were loud in their condemnation of *To Tam*, seeing in it (as in *The Chronicle of Great Tears of Bygone Days*) a pernicious poison that would cause the downfall of Vietnam's youth.[43] Indeed, alarming stories began circulating after the publication of *To Tam* that young women who found themselves coerced by their parents into arranged marriages were seeking escape in death.[44] Much as the moralists might deplore the influence of romantic fiction over their delicate psyches, the fact remained that, by taking seriously their concerns rather than holding them up to ridicule, this fiction helped bury the idea that women should be kept cloistered behind "high walls and closed gates." It would be another decade before the next installment in the fictional war between the generations was published. Long before that, however, literature caused a political firestorm to erupt. It was not connected to the publication of a new novel attacking tradition and espousing alien principles. Instead, it erupted around the most beloved of traditional Vietnamese literature: the *Tale of Kieu*.

Patriots and Prostitutes

The *Tale of Kieu* contained the quintessential representation of woman-as-victim. In writing it, the nineteenth-century poet, Nguyen Du, had been inspired by an incident which took place in fifteenth-century China and had already been fictionalized in novels and plays before it reached him.[45] In Nguyen Du's reworking, the originally marginal figure of Kieu assumed a central role in the story. Ostensibly, it concerned a young woman of good birth, extraordinary beauty, and great talent. When her father was suddenly imprisoned on false charges, Kieu, anxious to rescue him, succumbed to the blandishments of a professional seducer, after which she fell into the *demimonde*. She endured many adventures, first in a brothel, then as the tyrannized concubine of a hen-pecked official, and later as the favorite of a bandit chief, before escaping from her life of degradation. She was eventually reunited in a platonic marriage with her first love, who by then had married her younger sister.

Originally written in the old demotic script rather than in Chinese, the *Tale of Kieu* was easily transliterated into modern Vietnamese. Its wonderful imagery, its music, its gallery of rogues and heroines, its psychological insights, and its Confucian ideals coupled with Buddhist philosophy all made it immensely popular with Vietnamese from every background, from scholars trained in Chinese classics to barely literate peasants who could remember only a few verses. It was the basis of countless pieces of popular theater and art songs; it was consulted by fortune-tellers; its rhyme schemes were used for poetry contests; its characters had become archetypes. But the *Tale of Kieu* also contained an autobiographical dimension which added a richness of meaning and poignancy lacking in the original. Born and educated under the Le dynasty, Nguyen Du had managed to avoid serving the Tay Son when they overthrew the Le. But when Gia Long in turn deposed the Tay Son and ascended the throne in 1802, he summoned Nguyen Du to his court. Nguyen Du went, in contravention of the dictates of dynastic loyalty, which called for him to serve only the Le. It was as an envoy of Gia Long to China that Nguyen Du had learned of the story of Kieu. Generations of poetry lovers, even illiterate ones, knew of Nguyen Du's personal dilemma, and saw in his verse-narrative more than the tragic story of a woman of beauty and talent of whom fate had been jealous. It was understood to be his *apologia pro vita sua* and a plea for compassion on behalf of all scholars trapped in the moral quicksands of political change.

Pham Quynh seized on the *Tale of Kieu* as the acme of Vietnam's literary heritage, the purest distillation of its national essence, but it was actually Nguyen van Vinh who had first become interested in making it the centerpiece of a new educational curriculum in the romanized script. Vinh began publishing an annotated translation of the *Tale of Kieu* in his *Indochina Review* in 1913. Pham Quynh published his first article on the *Tale of Kieu* in *Southern Wind* in December 1919; it was an essay intended to show how to apply the methods of literary criticism learned from the West. After his trip to France in 1922, where he lectured extensively on Kieu, this topic became a favorite theme of the journal. Beginning with the seventy-fifth issue (1923), a column entitled "Contributions to the *Tale of Kieu*" appeared regularly in *Southern Wind*, bringing forth comments from a variety of literary and cultural critics. Many who praised diverse aspects of the *Tale* nonetheless expressed reservations concerning its morality. Women had traditionally been forbidden to read her story for fear their moral fiber might be corrupted. Nguyen Don Phuc observed: "Few are those who read the *Tale of Kieu* to put literature and good conduct at the service of mankind; those who read it because they are seduced by passion and sexuality and thus poison society are far more numerous."[46] Until then, however, the debate had involved only contributors to *Southern Wind,* most of whom more or less espoused Pham Quynh's own political views. But in 1924, Pham Quynh decided to create a national cult to honor Kieu and to hold a solemn ceremony to commemorate her author. Pham Quynh's idolatrous admiration for the *Tale of Kieu* precipitated a debate in which literary aesthetics took second place to morality and politics, and in which the fictitious woman Kieu was used to articulate the conflicts of accommodation and resistance.

The ceremony was held on 8 September, the anniversary of Nguyen Du's death, under the auspices of AFIMA. It was a grand affair. *Southern Wind* jubilantly reported that "the audience was estimated at two thousand . . . In Hanoi, the only time a ceremony has attracted so many people was the reception for Governor-General Sarraut when he lectured at the Temple of Confucius in 1919."⁴⁷ The self-congratulatory tone of the article was not due entirely to the success of the event. In July, Pham Quynh had been asked to head the Chinese section of a new Indochina Normal School.⁴⁸ This new school was part of a set of educational reforms which had begun with the closing of the Faculty of Law and of hundreds of traditional schools as well as private Franco-Annamite institutions, but which included the establishment in Tonkin of a program of primary education in Vietnamese. Pham Quynh had long advocated such a program, so he could contemplate with satisfaction the realization of some of his most cherished ideas.

But Pham Quynh had chosen poorly in the timing of his grandiose ceremony. Pham Hong Thai's attempt to assassinate Governor-General Merlin in June had revived old tensions between upholders of the colonial order and advocates of revolutionary violence. To the latter, Pham Quynh's words rang like a challenge: "As long as the *Tale of Kieu* endures, so does our language, as long as our language endures, so does our country. As long as there are mountains and rivers, what is there to be afraid of?"⁴⁹ His solemn oath to "be faithful to the national language, the national soul, and the national institutions" sounded like an endorsement of the colonial status quo and an oath of collaboration. It provoked a backlash among those scholars of Tonkin and Annam who, unlike Nguyen Ba Hoc or Nguyen Don Phuc, combined cultural and moral conservatism with anticolonial politics. Some were newly released from the penal prisons into which they had been thrown in 1908. Though they were not able to set the terms of the discourse on culture and morality, their influence was not negligible, especially after they acquired a vehicle of their own. Their journal, *Friendship's Sound (Huu Thanh)*, had been launched in 1921 by the Commercial and Industrial Association of Tonkin (Hoi Tuong Te Thuong Mai va Ky Nghe Bac Ky) with subsidies from the Government-General, but soon its editor-in-chief, Ngo Duc Ke, had turned it into a platform for his own brand of cultural politics.⁵⁰ Ngo Duc Ke, a degree-holder who had once been a close associate of Phan Chu Trinh, was highly critical of Pham Quynh's accommodationist line. In April, he published an article which directly challenged Pham Quynh's argument. Starting from the same Social Darwinian premise as did Pham Quynh, Ke argued that the world had been formed at different times, and thus human beings had appeared in different places at different times. As a result, some people were civilized, others still barbaric. As the more advanced tried to conquer and exploit the less advanced, there ensued perpetual struggle and warfare. Therefore, he continued, "if a nation survives, so will its culture and language; if a country is exterminated, so will be its culture and language."[51]

After the ceremony, Ngo Duc Ke became vitriolic in his criticism. According to him, all the members of AFIMA, starting with Hoang Trong Phu, and all the contributors to *Southern Wind,* with Pham Quynh at their head, were people who "gave up their bodies and their good names into the keeping of brothels." They had allowed themselves to behave like girls "seduced by men so that they rejected their parents' teachings and now were prostitutes who let their bodies be used like those of horses or buffaloes."[52] Chagrined, Pham Quynh kept a dignified silence, but he stopped writing about Kieu. Contributions on the subject, however, continued to be printed in *Southern Wind,* and this was not the end of the controversy. Six years later, it erupted again, as virulently as before. Instead of embodying the survival of the Vietnamese language and culture, Kieu had become a symbol of the disintegration of the Vietnamese nation. Moreover, Kieu, the high-born girl whose love for her family had led her into prostitution, had become a symbol of elite collaborationism and treason. As the French authorities suspected, the patriarchal family often served as a stand-in for the colonial regime in contemporary fiction. On a superficial level, much of that fiction seemed to consist of fairly innocuous love stories; yet it could also be used to articulate critiques of colonial society.[53]

Although they chose to express their cultural anxieties through debates about women, conservative moralists were actually less concerned with issues of gender than of generations. Young Vietnamese looked upon the familial home not as a refuge from the storms of life but as a prison. It called forth visions not of the nurturing mother but of the domineering father. The degree to which their efforts to break free of familial ties and old-fashioned morality bred fear among their elders stands revealed in an apocryphal story recounted by Pham Quynh. As he told it, a modern young woman was refusing to let her husband send money to his aging parents on the ground that, according to Western ideas of marriage, she and her husband constituted a new family unit, distinct and separate from their parents, and owing nothing to them.[54] The intensely personal dimension of the effects of cultural change could not have been better underscored. But in advocating the retention of "tradition" and family morality while constantly reiterating their gratitude toward the French mother country, conservative accommodationists reinforced Sarraut's own efforts to put the family metaphor at the service of colonial rule. The perceived collusion between the family and the colonial state, and the parallelism between moralist conservatism and political collaboration explain why the first attempts at revolution seemed so much like a rebellion against familial authority, and why it seemed vitally necessary to emancipate women along with the nation.

4 Scandal Sheets

> Let us, joining hands, enter the battlefield
> And make known the men of talent in the Eastern seas.
> Who yet has won, that we should resign ourselves to defeat?
> Seizing men's rights, let's bring them back to the East.
> Only he who makes history deserves to be called a hero.
>
> *A Call to Youth*, anonymous, 1907

ALTHOUGH the controversies over culture were dominated by conservative writers with collaborationist tendencies, such disputes had allowed a spirit of iconoclasm to surface. But for this iconoclasm to assume political purpose and significance, it needed a catalyst. When a catalyst did emerge, it had nothing to do with youth, culture, or feminism. It did not even seem directly relevant to the controversies that surrounded collaboration. Its revolutionary potential was thus slow to be identified and exploited.

Few, in 1923, could have predicted that the scandals that began to roil Cochinchina that year would have such an effect. Compared with the impersonal forces that transformed Vietnamese society and economy, these scandals were mere epiphenomena. But they had names attached to them and belonged to the realm of conscious experience. For years, Vietnamese, and more particularly colonial civil servants and students enrolled in Franco-Annamite or French schools, had suffered under a daily staple of ill treatment and petty humiliations. But their stories had little journalistic value and no power to galvanize the public into action. By contrast, the scandals were exactly the sort of stories newspapers thrived on; they excited the interest of readers and provided a clear focus for popular outrage. Although only individual wrongdoers were ostensibly targeted for protests, the whole colonial system was also implicated. Sarraut, who served as Minister of Colonies until early 1924, liked to present the French colonial enterprise as a *mission civilisatrice* aimed at universalizing the ideals of the French Revolution. But the fallacy of his arguments was continually exposed by the tales of official misdeeds and miscarriages of justice which appeared with unrelieved regularity in newspapers that had once been launched with his blessings.

Considering where the verbal warfare provoked by the scandals eventually led, it is ironic that the first salvos were fired by Constitutionalists. Unlike the exiled revolutionaries and the still apolitical students, they were not interested in the pursuit of collective or individual liberty. But they were passionately conscious of the need to safeguard their hard-won economic and political gains. Yet, to their dismay, Sarraut's policy of aggressive economic development led to an influx of unscrupulous speculators into Indochina and to an unprecedented degree of corruption within the colonial administration. All this adversely affected both their social status and their purses, and, although they never repudiated their patron, nothing was more calculated to arouse their prickly sense of grievance than these direct threats to their interests. They protested loudly; in the end, however, they remained too fearful of unleashing the forces of disorder to mobilize the populace. But, although the Constitutionalists refused to abandon their collaborationist stance, to others, the scandals became symbols of the vacuity of the rhetoric of benevolent empire and the bankruptcy of Franco-Annamite collaboration. Spurred to action by a daily diet of diatribes, they began to transform their passive hostility toward the colonial regime into active rebellion.

The Economics of Corruption

Since the beginning of French rule, the perennially cash-starved Government-General of Indochina had relied on what seemed a sure-fire method of generating revenues: granting to specific companies the monopoly right to manufacture certain goods or deliver certain services in return for a guaranteed amount of taxes from the resulting profits.[1] But, since it was also a prime consumer of many of these goods and services, the Government-General suffered as much as it benefited from this practice; furthermore, in order to protect company profits and hence government revenues, the government was forced to spend huge sums to enforce the rights of the monopoly companies. These needs wiped out most of the benefits the government was supposed to derive from the arrangement, but this unhappy truth was obscured by prevailing accounting practices. What was clear was the precarious state of Indochinese finances and the continued need for infusions of cash from Paris.

Faced with chronic budget problems, Sarraut did not resist the lure of the monopolies. In 1913, he awarded the sole rights to manufacture and sell alcohol to the Fontaine Distillery. To maximize its profits, the Distillery imposed consumption quotas on the local population. The colonial administration enforced its monopoly by arresting those who dared brew their own alcohol at home, as was the popular practice, and penalized villages where alcohol purchases were deemed too low. Opium consumption was similarly encouraged.[2] But salt, the one commodity for which there was real demand, was sold at prohibitive prices. Fishermen were often forced to throw their catch back into the sea, within view of mounds of salt piled up along the waterfront, because they could not afford to buy the precious ingredient they needed to cure their fish. Not surprisingly, the monopolies became a focus of anticolonial sentiment, but the Government-General had become too dependent on the monopolies to disband them. The salt, opium, and alcohol monopolies were the most hated because they affected every Vietnamese on a direct and quotidian level, but practically the whole economic infrastructure of Indochina was built on and by monopolies.

Reliance on monopolies encouraged cronyism. Its restrictive practices also ran directly counter to the economic interests of the expanding Cochinchinese bourgeoisie. The ability of the Constitutionalists to maintain their claims of leadership among the natives and thus acquire some leverage in their dealings with the French settlers depended on their success in persuading their fellow Vietnamese to foreswear revolution. This in turn depended on their showing that a peaceful and gradual approach to change was more likely than revolutionary violence to lead to genuine progress. Unfortunately, such a strategy also depended on the cooperation of the colonial authorities and of the settlers.

The French community in Vietnam was by no means homogeneous or unanimous in its understanding of how best to respond to Vietnamese demands for concessions. The deep divisions of metropolitan politics were only partially submerged by colonialism. Virtually every political party that existed in France was represented in Indochina. There were Dreyfusards and anti-Dreyfusards, devout Catholics and freemasons, monarchists and republicans. There were settlers who had lived in Indochina for decades, others who had come for only as long as it took to make a killing in the overheated local economy; some were barely able to make ends meet, others enjoyed huge fortunes. Still others belonged to the vast bureaucratic army, whose members ranged from postal clerks to provincial administrators. But the single greatest source of conflict within the French community was ethnicity. In his book on nineteenth-century France, *Peasants into Frenchmen*, Eugen Weber speaks of "internal colonization," a process that closely parallels external colonization.[3] Colonization at home was achieved through universal education; colonization abroad through conquest, with Jules Ferry as chief architect of both. It was under Ferry that the conquest of Vietnam, suspended by the Franco-Prussian war, was resumed. The universalist impulses that underpinned his drive to expand public education at home could be detected in the assimilationist policies enacted in the early phase of colonial rule, though many were later rescinded. In the 1920s the process of internal colonization was far from complete (as indeed remains true today), and Vietnam, itself a colony, was also affected by the imperfect assimilation of Corsica into metropolitan France. No study has been made of the number of Corsicans who lived in Vietnam, but anecdotal evidence suggests that they were many. They resented the mainlanders, who did not bother to disguise their disdain for these recent and not entirely assimilated citizens. Reporting on the brutal behavior of a French soldier toward a street urchin who had been trying to sell copies of *Cloche Fêlée*, Werth mentioned his difficulty in understanding the soldier's thick Corsican accent.[4] Class animosities also abounded: visiting intellectuals often noted with distaste the uncouthness of some of their fellow countrymen. Higher officials also deplored "the sending of minor civil servants who are morally and intellectually ill-equipped for this delicate task [of being civil servants] and are completely ignorant about the country."[5]

The scandals which became an almost daily staple of Cochinchinese journalism in the early 1920s could be traced to a single source: the greed of the Governor of Cochinchina and of his cronies. That Maurice Cognacq owed his position as Governor to the support of the Constitutionalists was an additional source of bitterness to the latter. They had endorsed his candidacy in 1921 in the belief that, because he had been appointed by Sarraut to head the secondary education program, he would be a progressive governor amenable to their influence.[6] But, once he had realized his ambition, Cognacq felt able to dispense with their support and surrounded himself instead with some of the most unsavory characters in the whole of colonial history. Through them, he controlled all the important councils in

Cochinchina: the Colonial Council, the Chamber of Agriculture, the Chamber of Commerce, and the Saigon Municipal Council. Acting as his *éminence grise* was Darles, who, after 1917, was dubbed by the Vietnamese "the butcher of Thai Nguyen."[7] After his dismissal from the colonial civil service, he had been offered a lucrative job at the Fontaine Distillery; by the early 1920s, he was one of the most powerful men in Saigon. In 1924, Ernest Outrey, the Deputy for Cochinchina, admitted in the Chamber of Deputies that the accusations leveled against Darles were "unfortunately correct."[8] This did not prevent Darles from being named Chief of Police for Saigon.[9]

Outrey himself had been Governor of Cochinchina before becoming its Deputy, and was implacably opposed to Sarraut's idea of an Indochinese Constitution, which would have curtailed the power he had once wielded. When Sarraut launched *Tribune Indigène* in the South and *Southern Wind* in the North in 1917, Outrey decided that he needed a journalistic mouthpiece of his own. He bought *Impartial* in late 1917, and appointed Henry Chavigny de la Chevrotière as its editor-in-chief. *Impartial* became Cognacq's semi-official mouthpiece, and la Chevrotière one of his closest associates.

Despite his aristocratic-sounding name, which was in part his own invention (he added "de la Chevrotière"), la Chevrotière was only one-quarter French, his father being a Senegalese of mixed ancestry and his mother a Tonkinese. His complexion was described as "café au lait."[10] He had started out by working as a coolie recruiter and as a journalist assigned to cover insignificant events for various newspapers in Hanoi and Saigon. He also had a lucrative sideline as police informer and extorter. Under police rules, he was allowed to pocket half the bribe money he received from his victims. Operating on this principle, la Chevrotière would persuade people to give him money to bribe police officers on their behalf, then do an about-face and denounce them for attempted bribery. He eventually came to grief when he tried to incriminate an army officer. In 1916, a military tribunal sentenced him to spend three months in the Central Prison of Saigon. When he was freed, he had to contend with the possibility of being drafted to fight in Europe. Because a new regulation exempted men with large families, la Chevrotière filed an affidavit claiming that he was needed to support his six children. But his Vietnamese wife, whom he had long since abandoned together with their children, denied his claim in court. La Chevrotière was duly shipped to France in mid-1917 but feigned illness so convincingly that he was taken off at

Colombo to be sent back to Saigon. On 20 October, he was finally exempted from the draft. His escape from war service led to a miraculous recovery, and he was able to plunge into journalism. Acting on Outrey's behalf, he bought *Impartial* from its previous owners with funds he obtained from Outrey and possibly also from blackmail, which he had not entirely given up.[11]

By 1919, *Impartial* had established itself as the most vociferous of the settler papers, with la Chevrotière posing as the spokesman for French interests, the champion of morality, law, and order, and the scourge of all those he described as "anti-French," "revolutionaries," "anarchists," or "Bolsheviks."[12] Despite lack of proof, he had no qualms about accusing Nguyen Phu Khai and Bui Quang Chieu of distributing copies of *Paria*;[13] although it was a legal publication in France, *Paria* was not allowed to circulate in its colonies. His own mixed ancestry notwithstanding, he was a vocal defender of French prestige and liked to hold forth on the indisputable superiority of the French race in every sphere, and on the natural right of the French to rule over the benighted Annamites. Despite his criminal record, the head of the Cochinchinese Sûreté, another Cognacq intimate, routinely allowed him to consult police files so that he could muster ammunition against Cognacq's political enemies.[14] He also used the information to engage in blackmail on his own account.[15]

Later on, Cognacq would be officially accused of malfeasance and removed from his position.[16] But, even in the face of mounting evidence to the contrary, the Constitutionalists were slow to shed the illusion that Cognacq would be receptive to Vietnamese requests for concessions if these were not made too forcefully. They had sought to emphasize the nonviolent nature of their politics by adopting the name Jeune Annam, after Gandhi's Young India. But, having spearheaded a boycott of Chinese businesses in 1919 to protest Chinese dominance in the local economy, and having worked for the enlargement of native suffrage enacted in 1922, they were becoming more vocal in the defense of their interests. In late 1923, they found themselves at the head of a coalition that pitted itself against the Cochinchinese government and its supporters among the French settler community. The Constitutionalists, who had little taste for engaging in frontal combat with the French, made unlikely warriors. They certainly did not dream of advocating revolution when they began protesting the ratification of the Candelier Convention.

Candelier was a French financier who headed a consortium of European speculators. In the spring of 1923, this consortium proposed to the Cochinchinese Colonial Council that it be allowed to develop new facilities for the port of Saigon. The developers were to be given total control over access to the new facilities; Vietnamese businessmen suspected that their chance of being granted access was nil. Vietnamese members of the Council and their allies bitterly opposed the scheme, but they were in the minority, and were unable to prevent its ratification in November. But, instead of finishing off the affair, this became the prelude to a long series of confrontations which steadily politicized the Vietnamese reading public and mobilized opposition to colonial rule. As the author of a Sûreté report noted, the Convention seriously eroded the prestige of the Government: "I do not believe that there exist many villages near provincial capitals where this project has not been presented [by its opponents] as a government maneuver to raise taxes."[17] The Candelier affair led to such a deterioration of relations between the Constitutionalists and Cognacq that la Chevrotière accused them of promoting Bolshevism. Immediately on the defensive, Bui Quang Chieu protested that he believed in progress through education. Nguyen Phan Long also sought to reassure the French: "The Annamites possess too highly the sense of social hierarchy, they are too imbued with 'bourgeois prejudices' to allow themselves to be seduced by theories which inspire revulsion at first sight . . . So let us be reassured: the Annamites are not ripe for Bolshevism."[18] Yet, by year's end, *Tribune Indigène* and *Echo Annamite,* which both had been launched with government funds and had once enjoyed generous subsidies, were put on an official list of "revolutionary, anarchist, and Bolshevik publications." Civil servants were expressly forbidden to read them on pain of dismissal.[19]

Colonial Journalism

That the controversies which fed the Cochinchinese press were far less decorous affairs than the verbal jousts between Pham Quynh and his critics was no surprise. The journalistic scene in Cochinchina was much more lively than in Tonkin or in Annam, where a Vietnamese press was virtually nonexistent until 1927.

The law of 29 July 1881, which regulated the press in France, had been extended for a brief and heady period to its colonies, and covered publications in all languages. The law's extension to the colonies was rescinded, however, when the colonial government came under attack in the press during a particularly sensitive phase of the Tonkin campaign. The decree of 30 December 1898 once more extended the 1881 law to Cochinchina, but this time only with reference to French-language newspapers owned by French citizens. Vietnamese newspapers were considered part of the foreign-language press which, under the terms of the 1898 law, was subject to extremely stringent rules. Prior authorization to publish a new journal had to be obtained from the Governor-General. Each issue had to be submitted in French translation to the official censor 48 hours before going to print, and the discussion of politics was forbidden. Even so, the Governor-General seldom granted authorization unless it served his purpose. Such was the case for Pham Quynh's *Southern Wind,* whose first business manager (and de facto overseer) was Louis Marty, the head of the Indochinese Sûreté Générale and the real moving force behind AFIMA. *Southern Wind* received generous government subsidies and was distributed, at villagers' expense, not only in Tonkin but in Annam and Cochinchina as well.[20] The single largest Vietnamese-language newspaper was *News of Annam and Tonkin (Trung Bac Tan Van),* owned since 1915 by Alfred Schneider and edited by Nguyen van Vinh (who already directed *Indochina Review,* also owned by Schneider). According to Tessan, in the early 1920s, *News of Annam and Tonkin* had a circulation of six thousand.[21] In 1919, *Indochina Review* was turned into a scholarly journal, while *News of Annam and Tonkin* became a daily.[22]

The press regulations which prevailed in Tonkin and Annam made it impossible to use journalism as a tool for political discourse there. Besides having to placate French settlers and administrators, journalists had to be careful not to offend the sensibilities of the imperial court and its mandarins. Newspapers which circulated freely in Cochinchina could be banned in Tonkin and especially Annam if the slightest hint of lèse-majesté or disrespect toward either French or Vietnamese officials was detected.[23] If the author of the offending article was a subject of the emperor, his punishment would be entrusted to the imperial judicial system, which was much less particular about individuals' rights than French justice, even as meted out in a Cochinchinese court. Those who chose to stay in Annam and Tonkin could either write columns for southern newspapers under pseudonyms, advocate political reform under the guise of discussing culture, or turn to writing books, which were not subjected to prior censorship as were daily and periodical publications. But because books with a political message were usually confiscated and their authors imprisoned, writers in Tonkin and Annam concentrated on writing fiction or essays on culture. Northerners were thus driven to articulate fundamental disagreements over a whole range of issues through debates about women's education and the direction of Vietnamese culture.

Even the Vietnamese-language press in Cochinchina was freer than in the two protectorates, for southern journalists did not have to worry about the sensibilities of the court or its mandarins.[24] The most influential of the independent Vietnamese-language newspapers in Cochinchina was *Indochina Times (Dong Phap Thoi Bao)*, which was founded by the journalist Diep van Ky in 1923. Originally published three times a week, *Indochina Times* eventually expanded into a daily newspaper. Many on its staff were writers from Tonkin or Annam.[25] Like other Vietnamese-language publications, it operated under difficult conditions and often came close to being banned. In 1925, Tran Huy Lieu was fined for referring to "the bell which awakens," an oblique reference to Nguyen An Ninh's *Cloche Fêlée*.[26] Still, it was better off than the *Cochinchinese Economic Journal (Nam Ky Kinh Te Bao)*, which was closed down in 1923 for publishing a report on the Candelier Convention.[27]

Publication was relatively easy for French-language newspapers in Cochinchina: all that was required was an authorization from the Procureur de la République, the colonial government's top legal counsel. The business manager of the paper must be a French citizen over twenty-one years of age; he was held legally responsible for its contents, and his name had to appear on the back page. From 1922 on, one copy of each issue of every publication had to be sent to the depository at the Bibliothèque Nationale in Paris, and the signature of the business manager was required on this copy.[28] Censorship was on the whole retroactive rather than preventive. But newspapers which went too far in the eyes of the authorities could be suspended; their editors, publishers, business managers, and staff could be pursued under the various articles of the amended penal code designed to combat sedition and rebellion in Indochina.

Newspapers which represented the interests of the French settlers enjoyed a larger readership than those which belonged to Vietnamese publishers; with a circulation of ten thousand copies, *Impartial* was the most important of these French-owned dailies. There were other French newspapers with considerable circulation figures, but their ownership changed fairly frequently.[29] French newspapers in Tonkin also reflected the interests of business. *Courier d'Haiphong* was owned by the Fontaine Distillery, and *Avenir du Tonkin* belonged to the Société des Missions Etrangères.[30] Besides being well funded by their owners, some of these newspapers also benefited from government subsidies based on a system of readership quotas imposed on villages. Often, none of the villagers could read French, so the bundles of newspapers which were distributed to them remained unopened; nonetheless, they still had to be paid for out of village funds. In 1925, these forced subsidies amounted to 120,000 piasters.[31] Some of the settler newpapers appeared in a Vietnamese-language version as well. The native version of *Opinion, Cong Luan Bao,* had been in existence since 1916. In January 1924, la Chevrotière began publishing *Trung Lap Bao* as the Vietnamese counterpart of *Impartial;* it had a circulation figure of fifteen thousand.[32] In addition, there were two papers aimed at the small but economically important Indian minority in the colony, edited by the same man. As Camille Devilar, he edited *Temps d'Asie* (the French edition of *Asia Times*), and under the name of Edouard Marquis, he produced *Réveil Saigonnais.* Both were politically conservative and generally supported French interests.[33]

There were also newspapers published in French but whose owners were Vietnamese with French citizenship. Foremost in this group were the *Tribune Indigène* of Nguyen Phu Khai and Bui Quang Chieu and the *Echo Annamite* of Nguyen Phan Long. Besides appearing three times a week, *Tribune Indigène* also came out on Saturdays in condensed form under the name *Petite Tribune Indigène;* a Vietnamese-language version came out on Mondays as well. *Echo Annamite* was not as well endowed as *Tribune Indigène,* Nguyen Phan Long's finances being more modest than those of Nguyen Phu Khai and Bui Quang Chieu. Long took over as editor-in-chief of the paper in 1922, then closed down the paper temporarily while he sought additional funds. Even after he relaunched it, he still operated at a loss; the circulation of *Echo Annamite,* at two thousand copies per run, equaled only that of *Petite Tribune Indigène*. One Vietnamese-owned newspaper which did not prosper despite government subsidies was *Voix Annamite,* owned by Le Quang Trinh. The first Vietnamese to obtain a degree in medicine from a French university, Trinh had been an associate of Nguyen Phu Khai and Bui Quang Chieu in the Association Mutuelle des Indochinois en France. In 1923, he sat on the Colonial Council of Cochinchina and endorsed the Candelier Convention in a couple of articles that appeared in his newspaper, thereby earning the animosity of other Vietnamese. *Voix Annamite* folded soon after the Convention was passed, owing to lack of readers.[34]

Last, there was the gadfly press, papers owned by a handful of enlightened Frenchmen and run on a shoestring. J. A. Marx had set himself up as the voice of the colonial conscience since coming to Indochina in the 1890s, upbraiding Bui Quang Chieu in the pages of *Cochinchine Libérale* for his elitism during the debates on naturalization. Marx died in 1922, and with him, his newspaper. There was also *Voix Libre*, published by Edgar Ganofsky, who had been fired from his job as a teacher on Réunion Island because of his left-wing views. Absolutely destitute, he sometimes stayed with coolie families in suburban slums or found a place to sleep in opium dens, though he did not use the drug.[35] There were also a few other liberal papers, including *Libre Cochinchine* and *Argus Indochinois*, which was published in Tonkin. The most popular of the gadfly papers among the Vietnamese was *Vérité*, published by Paul Monin. Though Monin is little more than a footnote in biographies of André Malraux, he looms far larger in the history of the Vietnamese Revolution than his one-time colleague. Born in 1890 in the *haute bourgeoisie* of Lyons, he arrived in Cochinchina in the summer of 1919 with a law degree and an impressive war record just as Outrey was presenting himself for another term as Cochinchina's Deputy. The naturalized Vietnamese, and even some French settlers, were annoyed that Outrey had neglected Cochinchinese interests during the war, especially because the colony had done more than its share to assist the metropolis. The settlers, however, allowed themselves to be mollified by his lame excuses, for the election was shaping up as a referendum not only on Sarraut's proposed reforms but more specifically on the expansion of the native electorate. The southern reformist landowners, civil servants and businessmen who had recently announced themselves to be members of the Constitutionalist Party, decided to field their own candidate and asked Monin to stand. Outrey was backed by la Chevrotière, who lambasted the Constitutionalists for being "pro-Japanese" because they were then boycotting Chinese businesses.[36] He handily won the elections. Monin found that no law firm would take him on; so he opened a firm of his own which catered mostly to Chinese residents, many of whom turned out to have close links with the Chinese Kuomintang network in Cochinchina (Monin himself became a member of the KMT). With their financial assistance, he created his own journal, *Vérité*.

The gadfly press had a limited circulation and an equally limited influence on policy. Among the settlers, it had mostly irritation value. In the circles of the Cognacq administration, its publishers were variously castigated as "Annamite-lovers," "anarchists," and "Bolsheviks." Monin, a war hero, was excoriated by the draft-shirking la Chevrotière for being "anti-French."[37] In general, these journals did not attempt to mold Vietnamese public opinion; they sought to redress egregious wrongs by directing their editorials at the French authorities. Despite the name-calling to which they were subjected, their editors had little to fear personally, for they were protected by their Frenchness. Monin had friends in high places, among them the deputies Edouard Chavannes and Marius Moutet.[38] How much of an example the domestic gadfly press provided to radical journalists is unclear, since many also spent time in France and learned some of their skills there.

To a great extent, the journal *Cloche Fêlée* of Nguyen An Ninh resembled Monin's *Vérité* in both spirit and presentation. But Nguyen An Ninh, being Vietnamese, was in a very different situation from that of Monin. Lacking French citizenship or highly placed friends, he was vulnerable to retaliation by the authorities and the settlers, a fact that was not lost on his readers. He was also more interested in converting his readers to action than in engaging the authorities in dialogue. Thus, among the Vietnamese public, his words had an impact which none of the gadfly newspapers had had.

The Bell Which Awakens

Soon after Ninh gave his speech of 15 October 1923 entitled "The Aspirations of Annamite Youth," he was summoned by Cognacq to explain its anti-French tone. In the course of a heated exchange, the twenty-three-year-old Ninh could not resist flaunting his erudition before the man who had tried to dissuade him from going to France. Cognacq lost his temper and burst out: "There must not be intellectuals in this country. The country is too simple. If you want intellectuals, go to Moscow. Be assured that the seeds you are trying to sow will never bear fruit."[39]

Despite these threats, *Cloche Fêlée* appeared for the first time on 10 December 1923. Its business manager was Eugène Dejean de la Batie, who had just severed relations with *Voix Annamite* because of Le Quang Trinh's endorsement of the Candelier Convention. Dejean de la Batie was a *métis* of illegitimate birth who had grown up in Tonkin under the name of Eugène Lien.[40] His mother was a Vietnamese tradeswoman, his father a minister plenipotentiary who served for a long time in Latin America. During his childhood and adolescence, his father had ignored his existence, and Dejean de la Batie had grown up among Vietnamese. Belatedly, his father decided to acknowledge him and to take his education in hand. He was sent to the School of Public Works in Hanoi and later joined the Geographical Service of Cochinchina. This curious background produced a deep ambivalence in him. He looked very Vietnamese and spoke French even less fluently than Nguyen Phan Long, on whose journal he collaborated. He usually sided with the natives against the settlers. But at times, when his Vietnamese associates criticized his politics, he would take refuge behind his Frenchness.[41] During this period, when political positions had not yet solidified, he was an invaluable supporter of anticolonial activities. As a French citizen, he was able to lend his name to a number of journalistic ventures, including two French and two Vietnamese newspapers.

Cloche Fêlée was a far cry from *Tribune Indigène* or *Echo Annamite*. The measured, reasonable, conciliatory tone of the two Constitutionalist papers was not at all Ninh's style. *Cloche Fêlée*, he announced, would be fearlessly pamphleteering. Under its title, the journal featured a slogan, "We are French. All that is great, generous and noble is ours," alongside the announcement that the paper was an "Organ of propagation of French ideas." Taking his cue from the Parisian journal *L'Oeuvre*, Ninh featured quotations which changed with every issue. The first issue of *Cloche Fêlée* prominently featured an excerpt from the address in which Albert Sarraut had introduced his proposal for the economic exploitation of Indochina: "A great country like ours, wherever it might go, whatever it might do, must be able to say that it remains everywhere faithful unto itself. It must be able to look squarely even into its colonial policy as the mirror of its conscience."[42] Nguyen An Ninh merely held up French ideals and high-minded rhetoric like Sarraut's against the record of colonial rule in Vietnam. The more he juxtaposed lofty pronouncements and accounts of sordid colonial doings, the more clearly he showed that colonialism was antithetical to French ideals. However, Ninh's main purpose was not to irritate the authorities but to incite his readers to action. Although he would have preferred to reach as many Vietnamese as possible, he had to be content with publishing in French so as to benefit from the freedom accorded to the French-language press.

There are no records showing how *Cloche Fêlée* was financed, though as before, Nguyen An Khuong probably contributed to his son's political activities by raising funds himself and contacting old associates in the Reform Movement. Clara Malraux provides a vivid account of how funds were raised for *Indochine,* the paper which her husband and Paul Monin started a few months later; some of her information probably also applies to *Cloche Fêlée*. When Monin and Malraux were ready to start a newspaper of their own, Le The Vinh, a young protégé of Dejean de la Batie, was sent on a tour of the provinces. He returned with a considerable amount of money, which came from a wide variety of sources: poor peasants, small landowners, provincial civil servants, and even prosperous landowners who were willing enough to donate funds to a liberal newspaper as long as their identities remained secret.[43] Monin's Chinese acquaintances made a substantial contribution as well, so that *Indochine* was able to have a run of five thousand copies.[44] *Cloche Fêlée,* which did not enjoy this kind of support, did not run to more than fifteen hundred to two thousand copies per issue.

The first two issues of the paper were only two pages long, but with the third, *Cloche Fêlée* began to cover four pages. Even so, Ninh and Dejean de la Batie, who constituted the entire writing team (with occasional contributions from anonymous correspondents from Annam), had trouble filling the available space. It was just as well that *Cloche Fêlée* was a journal of opinion rather than of news since, owing to the hostility of the administration, it did not have good access to the semi-official news agency ARIP. News from abroad was available from the Associated Press at a cost which rendered it almost prohibitive, and therefore had to be used sparingly. Colonial and semi-colonial countries received the best coverage because of the inspirational value of reports on movements of independence. In the inside pages, readers were treated to authors such as Claudel and Lafcadio Hearn on Japanese culture, to Tolstoy's and Tagore's views on education, and Cooramaswamy's analysis of the situation of Indian women. Short quotations gave further clues about Ninh's politics. A flattering report by the journalist Charles Gide (not to be confused with André Gide) on the Soviet Union appeared in the issue of 21 January 1924. On 21 June, *Cloche Fêlée* printed excerpts from an article written by Nguyen The Truyen and originally published in *Paria* on 1 May 1924. The last page of the paper was filled with advertisements in very large type; they were offered at a discount, and probably did not contribute greatly to the newspaper's revenues. Only the hardiest souls dared to advertise in *Cloche Fêlée:* those who were already too well known to the Sûreté to have further cause to fear it. Above the ads was a column called "A Thought," which consisted of quotes culled from a wide variety of sources attesting to Ninh's erudition and philosophical leanings. Ninh's general message could be summed up in an editorial which appeared on 28 January 1924: "France has given you certain rights. Show her that you know how to guard them, and she will give you more . . . Compatriots, at least defend the rights you have obtained. Rebel against tyranny and despotism. Any concession you make today is binding on your heirs. Live in servitude and serfdom if you like, but you have no right to mortgage the liberty of your children." [45]

Ninh's arrival on the journalistic scene was greeted with enthusiasm by Bui Quang Chieu: "Since Monday evening, in the streets of Saigon could be heard Parisian accents advertising 'The Cracked Bell, organ of French and Annamite Interests! Ten Cents the issue!' This was Mr. Nguyen An Ninh, a student returned from Paris, licensed in law, founder of this new journal, who walked through Saigon selling his paper. Bravo dear compatriot, bravo and courage and success. Not all Annamites in Indochina can be muzzled for crying loudly their feelings on the affairs of their country." [46]

Chieu never cared for Ninh personally and considered him a hothead.[47] But, with the Candelier controversy still raging, Ninh's support was precious, and Chieu willingly set aside his disapproval of Ninh's impetuousness, intellectual arrogance, populist style, and utter disrespect toward his elders. So incensed were the Constitutionalists over the Candelier Convention that they refused to accept defeat after the Cochinchinese Colonial Council ratified it in November 1923. Monin left for Paris in December to lobby against it, after a big send-off which the Constitutionalists organized as much to keep public opinion in ferment as to honor him.[48] Two months later, *Cloche Fêlée* was able to report that the Candelier Convention was dead.[49]

This victory over Cognacq went almost unreported, because the colony was now gearing up for elections. Monin, who had returned in late March, decided to stand once more against Outrey at the May elections and resumed publication of *Vérité,* which had shut down during his absence. The Constitutionalists hoped that, since the Vietnamese electorate had been enlarged in 1922, they had a better chance of altering the composition of the Colonial Council.[50] But Monin was again defeated, though not so much by the size of the settler electorate as by the fraudulent practices that were an integral part of the Cochinchinese electoral process. At every election, Indians with French citizenship were routinely brought in from Pondicherry and Chandernagore by the boatload to cast their votes.[51]

Disappointed over the results of the local elections, angered by Merlin's closing of private Franco-Annamite schools that spring, yet at the same time heartened by their recent victory in the Candelier affair, the Constitutionalists maintained the belligerent tone they had adopted the previous year. Cognacq retaliated by launching a new offensive against them. In June, he delivered a stinging attack against members of Jeune Annam, whom he described as men "disappointed in their ambitions" who were "spreading their murderous venom" among the masses.[52] But in France, the elections had brought a left-wing government, the Cartel des Gauches, into office. It would be only a matter of time before Merlin was replaced by a more reform-minded Governor-General. Nguyen Phan Long made no secret of his expectations: "In the European governments where left-wing ideas are on the ascendant, a new conception of colonialism is emerging. Unless France wishes to be isolated, France can only follow this movement . . . which tends visibly toward the adoption of an increasingly liberal policy on the part of colonial powers vis-à-vis their overseas territories."[53]

Nguyen An Ninh, for one, did not believe that anything worth having could be obtained for free, and he harbored few illusions about the outcome of the elections: "Brothers, you had expected something from the latest elections. Do not expect anything anymore, except from yourselves. Devote yourself to the country, sacrifice yourselves if need be to save your race."[54] Ninh had not brought out his journal during the electoral campaign, explaining that he was sick with exhaustion and had had to go back home to recuperate. Unwell though he may have been, he still managed to escort Léon Werth through the provinces of the Mekong Delta.[55] Werth, who had come to Cochinchina in March in Monin's company, was a regular contributor to the left-wing review *Europe,* which was launched in January 1923 under the aegis of Romain Rolland to combat the French mistrust of everything foreign that had crystallized during the war.[56] During this trip through the Delta, Ninh also gathered information on corruption in Cochinchina for an article he had promised to write for the French review *Continents*, whose editor had contacted him through Werth's intermediary. Ninh resumed publication of *Cloche Fêlée* in May with a series of articles provocatively entitled "Is Revolution Possible?" But *Cloche Fêlée* was in terminal decline. It did not appear again on 9 June because of the Pentecost holiday, then reappeared the following week, only to close down for good on 14 July.

Only nineteen issues of the paper had been published since 10 December 1923. *Cloche Fêlée* had managed to attract six hundred subscribers, which was no mean feat, considering how dangerous it was to be known as one of its readers. But as Ninh pointed out in a bitter article, out of the six hundred subscribers, only two hundred had sent payment, and of these only half had paid in full. Ninh, who was proud of having rejected the offer of a magistrate's job and having resisted the bribe of one hundred hectares of land, believed that his subscribers' behavior betrayed an unwillingness to fight for their convictions which he had often noted among Vietnamese.[57] He ignored the possibility that they might prefer to use less cerebral weapons, especially if they could not read French. And since he wanted to shame his readers into action by pointing out what he saw as their cowardice, Ninh played down the role of the authorities in harassing them and him.

Cognacq had been unable to prevent *Cloche Fêlée* from being published, though he had tried to intimidate Dejean de la Batie by asking him to prove that he was French and thus had the right to act as its business manager. Cognacq had also turned the Sûreté on the printers; in the space of seven months, the paper had to change printers three times.[58] Eventually, Ninh's father sold another piece of land for two thousand piasters to enable him to buy his own printing press.[59] But there were never enough printers, for they and their families were subjected to constant harassment by Sûreté thugs. Ninh had to help out with the printing chores. When an issue was ready, he would take copies to hawk them in the streets of Saigon, often barefoot and clad in peasant clothes. He loved to mingle with ordinary people, although others, believing that a patriot should behave in a more sober manner and set an example to the populace, voiced their disapproval of his common touch.[60] Ninh often came across scenes in which settlers or Sûreté agents tried to prevent news vendors from selling his paper by overturning their stands and trampling on the journals. The street urchins who peddled *Cloche Fêlée* often came in for a roughing up as well.[61] Subscribers to *Cloche Fêlée* were also victimized. Every issue of the journal carried coupons which readers were urged to fill out and return to Ninh. Normally, it was possible to subscribe to a newspaper by filling out coupons available in every post office, but the postal service of Indochina had been turned into a weapon of repression against *Cloche Fêlée* and its readers. The post office did not deliver *Cloche Fêlée* to its subscribers because, it claimed, they refused to accept their copies. Readers reported that their mail was intercepted and that letters addressed to them arrived torn.[62] Others never even received theirs, for the Sûreté kept many letters addressed to Ninh.[63] This was done so openly that Ninh himself read a notice in the central post office in Saigon to the effect that all correspondence addressed to him must be handed to the postmaster for checking.

The Indochina Adventure of André Malraux

For a while, the more vocal opponents of Governor Cognacq were without a platform: beset by a similar combination of political and financial problems, *Vérité* had shut down in June 1924. Monin, casting about for another journalistic venue, teamed up with Camille Delong and Hippolyte Ardin to bring out *Saigon Républicain*. The two men belonged, as Monin did, to the local branch of the Radical/Radical-Socialist Party, but they proved a sad disappointment. Delong turned out to be an opium addict.[64] As for Ardin, who owned the biggest printing house in Saigon, Monin discovered that he had accepted bribes from the government to soften the attacks against corruption appearing in *Saigon Républicain*. Monin left the journal in great acrimony, and for good measure, also quit the Radical-Socialist Party.[65] He then went to France once more and did not return until October. On the boat which carried him back to Saigon, he struck up a friendship with Clara Malraux, who had gone to France a few months earlier to plead her husband's case.

André Malraux and his friend, Louis Chevasson, had been arrested the previous year for stealing Cambodian temple statues.[66] A few days after Clara's return to Vietnam, their sentences were reduced and they were given leave to appeal to the Cour de Cassation in Paris. Malraux and his wife immediately left for France. While there, Malraux conceived the idea of publishing a paper in Cochinchina. He made the rounds of French intellectual circles to raise funds and made contacts among writers, journalists, and news agencies to ensure a regular flow of high-quality items for the proposed paper. After successfully appealing the jail sentence, the Malraux returned to Saigon in February 1925 and immediately plunged into preparations for launching the paper, in collaboration with Monin. Their newspaper was called *Indochine*. The two men prevailed upon Dejean de la Batie to act as their business manager, despite his misgivings that Vietnamese friends and relatives would accuse him of going over to the "other side" in working for a paper belonging to a pair of Frenchmen. Malraux had no contacts among the local population, and Monin's tended to be highly visible political figures, such as Nguyen Phan Long, or shadowy ones, such as the Chinese members of the Kuomintang who gave him large sums of money but refused to appear at public functions honoring him. Thus it fell to Dejean to recruit the staff and locate a printer. He assembled a motley crew of eager, untrained, naive, and in some cases politically suspect young Vietnamese.

Apart from raising money for *Indochine*, Le The Vinh also acted as printer, and sometimes even contributed articles. For Monin and Malraux, he provided comic relief from the tension of publishing the newspaper in the face of government hostility. He would rather sleep in the newspaper's office than go home and tell his mother that he did not want to marry the bride she had chosen for him, a young woman she had adopted as a child and molded into a biddable wife and daughter-in-law.[67] Yet he could also be forceful enough to take the lead in political activities. He was assisted by Ho Dac Hien, the nephew of the Imperial Minister of Rites and one of the highest-ranking mandarins in Annam. Hien, who had been disowned by his uncle over their political differences, had made his way to Saigon, where he was registered as a student and eked out a meager living. "Swarthy, stocky, hard and violent ... Hien wanted to serve his people, but did not know how."[68] The proofreader was Nguyen Pho, a childhood friend of Dejean, who had quit his job at the Ecole Française d'Extrême-Orient in Hanoi with the hope of going to France, but had lacked the money to do so and had remained in Saigon.[69]

The first issue of *Indochine* appeared on 17 June 1925 with a run of five thousand copies and was an immediate success. It filled the vacuum left by the closings of *Cloche Fêlée* and *Tribune Indigène*, the latter folding in the wake of Bui Quang Chieu's transfer to Phnom Penh by a vengeful Cognacq. Much thought had been given to editorial policy. Clara Malraux had gone through every issue of *Cloche*

Fêlée for ideas.⁷⁰ But apart from appearing on a daily rather than weekly basis, and having a larger editorial staff, there was also a slight difference in the points of view expressed in the two papers. Under the masthead of *Indochine* was the legend "Journal of Franco-Annamite Reconciliation." Ninh was coming closer to the conclusion that revolution was inevitable, but the two Frenchmen shied away from advocating that their own compatriots be thrown out of Indochina.

Ninh was in France when *Indochine* was launched. He had remarried in late 1924, and, with funds his new wife gave him, had been able to take up Werth's invitation to come to Paris.⁷¹ In Vietnam, Ninh's politics were considered rash, and his demeanor eccentric. But in Paris, he was lionized as the courageous editor of *Cloche Fêlée*.⁷² He rejoined the group of radical expatriates who belonged to the Intercolonial Union.⁷³ During these months he devoted time to translating Rousseau's *Contrat Social* into Vietnamese and writing *La France en Indochine*, using material he had collected during his trip through the Mekong Delta with Léon Werth the previous year.

Ninh returned on 26 June 1925 in the company of Phan Chu Trinh. Phan had decided to come home after receiving assurances that he would be protected from the imperial wrath he had aroused in 1922 with his Seven Point Indictment of Khai Dinh. Pierre Pasquier, then Résident Supérieur in Annam, even proposed to give him personal financial support, and the Minister of Colonies, on the advice of the Governor-General, decided to pay for his voyage and give him the sum of five thousand francs to settle his debts in France.⁷⁴ When he disembarked Phan was met by a large delegation of Vietnamese, come to greet an old patriot who had returned home after a long exile. As for Ninh, he had discovered to his horror that the British authorities in Singapore had ransacked his luggage and had taken away the several hundred copies of *La France en Indochine* which he had brought back; two brochures authored and annotated by his hero, the Socialist leader Jean Jaurès; the translation of an anticolonial comedy, *Oxen and Buffaloes (Trau Bo)*; and texts from the League for the Rights of Man.⁷⁵ He eventually recovered his temper and was introduced to the Malraux, whose associate he quickly became. He agreed to write occasional articles for *Indochine* under his pen name Nguyen Tinh, though he ended up spending most of his time traveling through the Cochinchinese countryside to investigate peasant conditions.

More practical than Ninh had ever been, and less interested in inspirational journalism, Malraux and Monin focused on exposing colonial abuses and especially government corruption, of which there was plenty. Their timing was fortunate. Merlin had been recalled in April 1925; since the Cartel des Gauches would no doubt have a different colonial policy from that of the conservative Poincaré government which had appointed him, his replacement was awaited eagerly. Meanwhile, the acting Governor-General, Henri Monguillot, tried to stop the more egregious examples of fraud and corruption that Merlin had tolerated. One concerned the Khanh Hoi Realty Company, formed secretly in June 1923 to take advantage of the opportunities the Candelier Convention was expected to offer.[76] The Company bought nearly a square mile of land near the proposed dock facilities for 3,600 piasters. It then proposed to the Saigon Municipal Council that the city develop the area at its own expense in return for some parcels of land which could be used to build access roads and public buildings. The cost of this development was estimated at 300,000 piasters. Despite the lack of clear benefit to the city or people of Saigon, the Municipal Council, steered by Darles, approved the deal and work began immediately. But a new Municipal Council was elected in May 1925, along with a new mayor who was not part of Cognacq's circle. When the mayor realized how costly the project was for the city, he ordered all work on the site stopped and leaked the report of his investigation to Monin, who lost no time in publishing its findings in *Indochine*. It turned out that Cognacq and his cronies were shareholders of the Company and that its director was Eutrope, Cochinchina's Director of Public Security.

Almost immediately *Indochine* revealed another scandal, which involved no less than the president of the powerful Chamber of Agriculture, Eugène Labaste, who had been in office since 1908. When the unexpected death of one of his allies brought to light the fact that, over the years, he had defrauded the Chamber of half a million francs, his indignant colleagues demanded that he step down.[77] Despite Cognacq's threats of reprisal if they tried to replace Labaste, they elected a new president, taking the precaution of cabling his name to Monguillot. Yet after Indochina's Chambers of Agriculture were reorganized, Labaste, undeterred, ran for re-election in September. Owing to the extraordinary measures that Cognacq took to ensure his victory, Labaste returned to his old post and became the representative of the Chamber of Agriculture on the Cochinchinese Colonial Council. Cognacq also maneuvered for the presidency of the Colonial

Council for the session of 1925–1926 to be awarded to la Chevrotière despite fierce opposition from the Vietnamese Councillors.[78]

For the embattled crusaders at *Indochine,* such developments were dismal, but they were able to claim victory over Cognacq in one case. In July 1925, *Indochine* was approached by a group of peasants from Ca Mau who had been unable to persuade other newspapers to publicize their story.[79] The peasants had cleared large tracts of land in what had once been a vast saline marsh but had now become one of the most desirable agricultural regions of the country. It was customary when new land was cleared to wait to ascertain its viability before requesting title to it. When this was done, title to all or at least part of the land was usually granted. If the plots involved were very large, the government would hold an auction, following fixed rules to protect the rights of the original cultivators. The total area at stake in this case covered 26,000 hectares, of which more than three quarters were under cultivation. Some of the peasants who approached *Indochine* had worked on the land since 1913, and none had arrived later than 1920, but they stood to lose all of it to a shadowy financial consortium.

During an inspection tour in April, Cognacq had waxed lyrical about the economic prospects of Ca Mau. Shortly after his return to Saigon, it was announced that the twenty-six plots of land which made up the area would be auctioned off on 26 July under the chairmanship of Eutrope. Though Cognacq had assured the peasants of Ca Mau that their rights would be safeguarded, unusual conditions were to be applied to the auction. Those who wanted to take part in it were required to prove that they had enough cash to cover their bids, or to have certificates from the Governor indicating the extent of their solvency. These financial data were to be turned over to Eutrope, who was empowered to accept or refuse bids, and to exclude individuals from taking part in the auction without explanation. But to make absolutely sure that the plots fell into the right hands, Eutrope issued a further stipulation: contiguous plots whose surface area exceeded five hundred hectares could be put up for bidding together. Thus, "at the request of the buyers," fourteen of the twenty-six plots were to be auctioned together in this fashion. No single buyer could be expected to gather the two hundred thousand piasters needed to bid for the lot.[80]

The first article on the auction appeared in *Indochine* on 11 July 1925 and strongly implied that Cognacq's hand was recognizable in the scandalous proceedings. Immediately, the paper received letters from peasants, mandarins, and even settlers, who wrote in to add their weight to the original protest, along with copies of letters and telegrams they had sent to various members of the Cochinchinese administration, including Cognacq, and to the Minister of Colonies. Monguillot suddenly announced that he was coming to Saigon for an on-the-spot investigation. He arrived on 23 July and stayed for several days. On 26 July, Eutrope announced that the controversial rules had been withdrawn.

The constant harassment which dogged all those who worked for *Indochine* unhinged the not very bright Hien. One night, shortly before Monguillot was due to arrive in Saigon, members of the staff of the newspaper found themselves in the rooms of the Malraux seriously discussing the ramifications of Hien's plot to assassinate Cognacq. Cognacq planned to hold a welcoming procession in honor of Monguillot. Hien, who must have heard the story of Pham Hong Thai's bomb plot, proposed to pass himself off as a press photographer to get close enough to his target to shoot him. "The savage beast must be destroyed," he said. Malraux became lost in musings about the philosophical implications of political murder and the importance of free will; Monin and Dejean de la Batie argued that an assassination would change nothing but that, instead, it would give the authorities further pretext for repression. Someone pointed out that Hien had no organization behind him that "could take advantage of the ensuing disorder." One after the other, his friends pointed out the impracticality and the futility of his plan. "To hell with it all," shouted Hien.[81] In the end, Monguillot rejected Cognacq's proposal, the procession was canceled, and Hien lost his chance to put his plan into action. Thwarted in his desire to emulate Pham Hong Thai, Hien later achieved his own kind of immortality through Malraux' fiction as the model for Chen of *La Condition humaine* and Hong of *Les Conquérants*.

Indochine was paying dearly for inflicting so many blows to Cognacq's power and pocket. On 26 July, Monin complained to Marius Moutet: "My Annamite clients, and especially my Chinese clients, are constantly summoned and threatened by the Sûreté; they are forbidden to come to me under the threat of expulsion. The trick is to hit my very means of livelihood . . . My correspondence is routinely tampered with. Telegrams we send to France remain without answer;

probably, they do not get sent at all. Our newspaper does not reach our subscribers . . ."[82]

A Socialist Governor-General for Indochina

It was at this juncture, when tempers on all sides were still high, that the much-awaited name of the new Governor-General of Indochina was announced, sowing turmoil right and left. The left-wing coalition now in power had selected Alexandre Varenne, a lawyer and journalist who had been Deputy for the Puy de Dôme region since 1896. Varenne had served as Minister of Education in a previous cabinet and had gained considerable financial expertise in Algeria. In view of Indochina's tangled finances, this last qualification made him eminently suited for his new post. But the controversy over his appointment had nothing to do with his undoubted expertise. What rankled was the fact that he was a prominent member of the Socialist Party. At the Tours Congress, he had made an impassioned plea for the Socialists not to adhere to the Third International, but this did not prevent his detractors from raising the specter of Bolshevism. To counter their accusations, Varenne hinted that it was precisely because he wanted to maintain a French presence in the East that he had accepted the post. His declaration of support for imperialism backfired. At their annual congress on 15 August, his fellow Socialists voted by 2,113 votes to 381 to expel him from their ranks. This left him in a highly ambiguous position: disavowed by the left, including his own party, yet still suspect in the eyes of the right. It was not a propitious beginning for a new Governor-General whose task was to push through reforms for which the Vietnamese were clamoring, and which the metropolitan government recognized as necessary, but which the settlers were, as usual, determined to resist.[83]

The ambiguity of Varenne's position in the wake of the Socialist congress was echoed in the mixed reaction of the Vietnamese at home and in France. The anticolonial émigrés around Nguyen The Truyen had initially greeted the appointment with enthusiasm, seeing it as the harbinger of real reforms. But their enthusiasm cooled considerably when they realized that whatever reforms were enacted would be much more limited in scope and spread over a much longer period than they had hoped when Varenne's appointment was first made public. No such misgivings were entertained by the Constitutionalists. Bui Quang Chieu, who had managed to extricate himself from his Phnom Penh posting and had gone to France, was emphatic: "We are finished with regimes of exploitation and spoliation. Finished with grotesque policies and puerile assimilation. The people speak."[84] Always trying to walk a fine line down some imaginary political center, Chieu was attacking both those who had heeded too well Sarraut's call to exploit the riches of the French colonies, thereby coming into economic competition with the native bourgeoisie, and those who had proposed to reward Vietnamese war veterans with French citizenship, thereby seeking to undermine the native bourgeoisie's political position. Varenne's appointment seemed to herald the possibility that the bourgeoisie's political objectives were going to be realized. And with the change of personnel that was certain to take place, a brake would be put on the financial misdeeds of the Cognacq administration. Chieu declared: "We are going to find ourselves facing a man who represents neither party nor caste, nor any interest group, but France, the clear French spirit of good sense, reason, and solidarity."[85]

Cognacq reacted to the new appointment by intensifying his campaign against his political enemies. In August, the Sûreté discovered copies of an antimonarchical tract in the lodgings of Nguyen Pho. To their exasperation, the authorities found that he could not be deported to Annam, because he had been born in the French concession of Hanoi and was therefore not an imperial subject.[86] Yet soon after this episode, his Vietnamese colleagues on *Indochine* began to suspect that Nguyen Pho had hidden sources of income; he seemed to be living high on what were minuscule earnings. Had he been induced by the Sûreté to turn informer even though he was not going to be deported? His paranoid colleagues began to shadow him, and even succeeded in enlisting Dejean de la Batie in their surveillance. They could ascertain nothing, and Dejean became angry at their treatment of his friend.[87]

But the Sûreté found a way to silence *Indochine*. The paper was printed at a press owned by a *métis* with French citizenship, who, despite his good will, was not immune to the strongarm tactics of the Sûreté. Threatened with imprisonment if they continued to work for *Indochine,* his printers in turn threatened to stage a work stoppage that would have spelled financial ruin for him. After the issue of 14 August, he told Monin and Malraux to take their paper elsewhere. They spent most of the summer laboriously assembling makeshift equipment, no easy task since Cognacq had informed all potential suppliers that he did not wish their paper to reappear. Malraux made a special trip to Hong Kong to purchase printing type, but since it was designed for English-language newspapers, it lacked certain key letters, in particular the accented "e". Eventually, a group of Vietnamese arrived at the Malraux' quarters and handed the needed type to Clara.[88] The paper, retitled *Indochine Enchaînée,* was relaunched in November, shortly before Varenne's arrival.

Even when *Indochine* had been driven out of circulation, its offices had continued to act as a magnet for young journalists such as Trinh Hung Ngau of *Echo Annamite,* who had a special interest in labor problems, and Lam Hiep Chau and Tran Huy Lieu, both of *Indochina Times.* Ta Thu Thau, the future founder of the Trotskyist Party, gained prominence at these gatherings because of his keen intellect and a formidable gift for rousing others to action. The son of a poor carpenter, he had somehow managed to gain an education at the Lycée Chasseloup-Laubat and was then teaching at Nguyen Phan Long's school.[89] During Bui Quang Chieu's absence, Long, who had become the preeminent Constitutionalist in Saigon, moved closer to the young militants clustering around *Indochine.* The name Jeune Annam, which had hitherto applied to the Constitutionalists, began to refer more and more to them.

Cloche Fêlée also resumed publication one week after Varenne arrived, owing probably to an infusion of funds from a wealthy landowner named Ngo Trung Tinh. Tinh, a vocal opponent of colonial rule, reportedly gave two thousand piasters to Nguyen An Ninh with the comment: "If I find an Annamite courageous enough to fire a shot at the Governor's palace and say: 'I am shooting at France,' I will take it upon myself to subsidize his whole family."[90] *Cloche Fêlée,* however, now appeared under the editorship of Phan van Truong. Its tone was even more combative than before. It no longer bore the legend: "Organ of propagation of French ideas." Instead, it proclaimed itself an "organ of democratic propaganda." This motto was accompanied by Mencius' famous dictum, "The people is all, the state is secondary, the prince is as nothing," both in Chinese and in Vietnamese. Phan van Truong, who had left Vietnam soon after the end of the Reform Movement, may have remembered the charge contained in its Manifesto of 1904, that in Vietnam, the ruler was considered more important than the people. That incipient populism had awakened in him strong Socialist sympathies. He returned home so full of Marxist rhetoric that André Malraux, who was only just discovering politics and had little knowledge of ideology, took him for a Communist.[91] Truong wrote a hostile editorial on Varenne's appointment: "Socialism, at least in its pure doctrine, that is, shorn of all opportunistic ideas, must condemn colonial conquest and advocate the liberation of all subjugated peoples, in other words of the colonies . . . The day when the capitalist powers are deprived of their colonies—to be reconstituted into independent states—they will have been effectively defeated."[92]

The Trial of Phan Boi Chau

Almost immediately after Varenne arrived in Saigon on 18 November, he encountered a problem of major proportions. After nearly two decades of exile, Phan Boi Chau had been delivered into the hands of the Sûreté by an informer on 18 June and hauled back to Hanoi.[93] His trial began on 30 June, before Varenne was appointed. Approached on behalf of Phan while he was still in France, Varenne had refused to intervene: "What do you see in that business that might harm me?" he asked naively. "It is all strange to me; the Phan Boi Chau trial will certainly be finished in two months when I arrive in Indochina. There are laws there that should take care of things like that."[94] But if Varenne had hoped to avoid taking a stand on the matter, he was sadly mistaken. Colonna, the Corsican Procureur de la République and a staunch ally of Ernest Outrey, seems to have tried to conduct the trial in such a way as to cause the most embarrassment to the incoming Governor-General. He amply succeeded. Phan's trial was only winding down when Varenne disembarked. He was still in Saigon when Phan's sentence was announced on 23 November: hard labor for life. Protests erupted at once. Monin commented: "Already a hero, he will become a martyr."[95] Nguyen An Ninh wrote, "The only crime he can be accused of is to have loved his country too well."[96]

The Jeune Annam group was put in a delicate situation by the sentencing. Over the summer, Nguyen Phan Long had conceived a scheme to present to Varenne a pamphlet entitled *Cahier des voeux annamites,* which would be a compendium of urgently needed reforms. Ninh was later to claim that, until he personally advocated pushing for political freedoms, the Constitutionalists had not thought of including them in their list of demands.[97] The text of the *Cahier des voeux* would seem to bear him out, for its various clauses were unevenly presented. The most carefully written sections covered topics dear to the Constitutionalists: naturalization; education (a particularly sore point since Merlin's reforms of the previous year); reduction of military service for natives from four years to either twelve or eighteen months to bring it in line with what was required of Frenchmen; native representation in the various councils; reform of the administrative and judicial systems; government support of agriculture. The shorter sections, which seemed to have been lifted straight from the "Desiderata" drafted at a meeting which Ninh had attended in Paris on 25 May, dealt with political freedoms: freedom of the press (in particular the Vietnamese press), freedom of association, and freedom of assembly and travel.

It was deemed essential to present the *Cahier des voeux* as a distillation of the opinions and desires of Vietnamese from all walks of life. Nguyen Phan Long had taken the precaution of sending a cable to Varenne in Singapore to request an audience. Varenne accepted, and the date was fixed for 27 November. Editorials then appeared in *Echo Annamite*, calling on the population to turn out in force to welcome the new Governor-General and witness the presentation of the *Cahier des voeux*. The militants grouped around the resurrected *Indochine Enchaînée* and *Cloche Fêlée* had agreed to lend support to Long's campaign for his *Cahier des voeux*. There was now too little time to organize a separate protest on behalf of Phan Boi Chau. Thus *Cloche Fêlée* found itself urging Varenne to heed carefully the demands that were to be presented, while telling its readers to stay away from the audience as a protest against the sentencing of Phan Boi Chau. Presented with such conflicting advice, the populace decided to turn out in force. Six hundred people were on hand to see Nguyen Phan Long present the *Cahier des voeux* to Varenne. Fearful of arousing expectations that he might not be able to fulfill, Varenne chose to douse all their hopes. He warned that he would not expand personal liberties either in Indochina as a whole or even in Cochinchina in particular. Even if they had been included in the *Cahier des voeux* as an afterthought, their summary rejection by a supposedly liberal governor-general came as a rude shock. When Varenne left for Hanoi on the following day, there was only one Vietnamese among the crowd of well-wishers: Dr. Le Quang Trinh, in his capacity as vice-president of the Colonial Council.

As Varenne made his slow way up to Hanoi, he was able to assess the extent of Phan Boi Chau's popularity, even among those who deplored his advocacy of violent revolution. People turned out to line Varenne's path to present, on their knees, petitions asking for Phan's release. In July, the Hanoi branch of Phuc Viet had circulated leaflets on his behalf, and students in Tonkin and Annam were especially prominent in the crowds of petitioners. Varenne tried to obtain guidance from the Ministry of Colonies, but was told that he was better placed to judge the situation and act accordingly.[98] He meditated for a month before announcing on 25 December that Phan's sentence would be commuted to house arrest for an indefinite period. Phan was immediately moved to Hue, where he was allowed to live under loose surveillance. Though a gratifying number of scholars in Tonkin and Annam expressed their appreciation of Varenne's clemency, others dismissed it as inadequate. As *Cloche Fêlée* declared, what was needed was not clemency or generosity but justice and equity.[99]

Varenne's gesture had come too late to staunch the wave of disappointment. Malraux had earlier hoped that "the arrival of M. Varenne, of the Socialist M. Varenne, ought not only to mark the end of the period of administrative crimes, but also to toll the inescapable, necessary hour of retribution." By December, he commented: "Yesterday a Socialist, today an outstanding conservative among prominent conservatives: another conversion under the sign of the piaster."[100] *Cloche Fêlée* was equally scathing: "To believe that our present Governor-General will remain a militant Socialist is to believe in the sincerity of a wolf in sheep's clothing. From a militant Socialist, M. Varenne has been transformed into a colonialist pure and simple."[101] Militants and moderates alike were dismayed by Varenne's refusal to rescind the restrictive regulations governing Vietnamese-language newspapers on the ground that the Vietnamese had not yet reached sufficient maturity to be accorded freedom of the press. They were in no way mollified by the conciliatory noises which Varenne made in a speech to the Conseil de Gouvernement de l'Indochine (as the reorganized Conseil Supérieur was now called) on 21 December. Echoing Sarraut, he noted: "We do not pretend that the first French came to Indochina for the sole purpose of bettering the people ... However, in working for themselves, the French have also worked for the natives." He went on to exhort the Vietnamese to accept French guidance for the sake of creating a peaceful and prosperous country. That was the purpose of France in Vietnam, "and, her mission achieved, one can think that she will no longer claim to have a part to play in the life of the peninsula, neither to direct nor to advise, and that the peoples who have profited from her guidance will have no other links with France than those of gratitude and love."[102] Thus was perpetuated the metaphor of France as the mother country and Indochina as her immature child. As Varenne's speech carried few concrete proposals for reform, the Vietnamese press took scant notice of it, but the settlers were incensed that he had had the audacity to envisage an end to French rule in Indochina. Within the next few months, he was forced to retract most of the sentiments expressed in the speech.

The Constitutionalists had staked their political fortune on the idea that justice was compatible with colonial rule. Distrusting mob pressure, they believed they could rely on a handful of enlightened colonial officials to ensure that justice would eventually triumph, just as the Vietnamese masses ought to be able to trust their own elite to provide proper governance. But the scandals that had come to light over the last two years in the increasingly pugnacious press and Varenne's unwillingness to defy the settlers and implement reform seriously undermined that belief, to the extent that Nguyen Phan Long began adopting a more belligerent stance. Thus, although *exposé* journalism redressed very few of the wrongs visited on post-war Vietnam by settlers and officials determined to flout their own laws, it achieved other equally important results, in particular the radicalization of Cochinchinese politics.

On 30 November 1925, a fiery article by Nguyen An Ninh, entitled "Liberty Is Not to Be Begged For," appeared in *Cloche Fêlée:*

> Liberty is to be taken, it is not to be granted. To wrest it away from an organized power, we need to oppose to that power an organized force . . . When we ask for reforms, we acknowledge the authority of the established regime. But if they are refused to us, let us know how to organize ourselves. Let us not put any faith in the policy of association that is much talked about these days. To associate, at least there must be two sides, and only equals. Let us say to the government to wait until we have the same liberty and the same rights as those with which it wants us to associate.[103]

More and more Vietnamese were coming to agree with Ninh that without liberty there could be no real justice. The Sûreté noted that among the subscribers to *Cloche Fêlée* were a great many peasants and traders, rural teachers, paramedics, colonial civil servants, and students enrolled in secondary schools, many of whom had never before engaged in anticolonial action.[104]

One night in early December, Monin woke up with a start and saw a man hovering over his bed with a knife in his hand. Monin's awakening startled the intruder, who fled. For the Malraux, whose finances were drained and whose health had deteriorated in the tropical climate, this incident was the last straw.[105] They left the following month.[106] Throughout their collaboration, Malraux and Monin had tried to protect the rights of their fellow Frenchmen, taking literally Cochinchina's status as an overseas *département* of France while ignoring the existence of Tonkin and Annam (and neglecting to ask whether the Vietnamese wanted to be French). Wanting their country to behave honorably, they were outraged when confronted with the reality that laws mattered little when French interests or prestige weighed in the balance. But maintaining this sense of outrage in the face of continual rebuffs must have been exhausting, and for the Malraux at least, the excitement of tilting at the windmills of colonialism began to pall. They ended their Indochina adventure, leaving Monin to continue the good fight.[107]

André Malraux had come to Asia with no other aim than to steal a few statues and to sell them to art lovers in Paris. In Vietnam he discovered an aspect of life totally unknown to him—colonialism in all its corruption and sordidness. In working with Monin, he also discovered fraternity through political engagement. Changed forever by Indochina, Malraux wanted to leave his own mark on its history. In a letter he wrote to Edmund Wilson in 1933, he claimed to have founded and led a political party called Jeune Annam.[108] Thus, he averred, had he contributed to the Vietnamese Revolution. Looking back on this claim with the hindsight of several decades and a failed marriage, Clara Malraux observed acidly: "How heavy the White Man's burden! Ah Kipling, it has been necessary for decades to pass before we were able to reject the weight of fictitious responsibilities we had taken upon our shoulders."[109] As she observed, "the leaders of the Asiatics are Asiatic." But Malraux was right to claim his share of glory, for, though neither founder nor leader of Jeune Annam, he had played a part, however small, in its transformation from an accommodationist group to a more militant organization.

This transformation had only just begun when he left Vietnam.

Two years of incessant scandal had created a mood of general discontent which was heightened by the trial of Phan Boi Chau. It took the coincidental death of Phan Chu Trinh and the arrest of Nguyen An Ninh, however, to light the torch of patriotism. By then, it had passed into the hands of a new generation.

5   Prodigal Children

> Louis XVI: "C'est une grande révolte." Duc de la Rochefoucauld-Liancourt: "Non, Sire, c'est une grande révolution."
>
> A. Dreyfus, *La Rochefoucauld-Liancourt* (1903)

THE ARREST of Nguyen An Ninh on 24 March 1926 probably surprised no one, including Ninh, so assiduously had he tweaked the colonial authorities over the past two years. But the role of catalyst of revolution would have better suited Phan Boi Chau than the peace-loving Phan Chu Trinh. Time and exile having blurred their differences, Phan Boi Chau and Phan Chu Trinh had become linked together in the popular mind as the towering giants of scholarly patriotism, revered symbols of fortitude and continuity with the past. Phan Chu Trinh had always been eclipsed by the more flamboyant Phan Boi Chau, and the former's uneventful return in June 1925 was cast in the shade by the dramatic manner in which the latter was brought home one week later. In dying, however, Phan Chu Trinh managed finally to hold center stage. His death was not unexpected, for he had been ill for a long time. What was unanticipated was the intense popular emotion it released.

Opposition to colonial rule moved from the printed page and into the streets. Political radicalism and cultural iconoclasm fused together. Formerly apolitical youths seized the occasion to challenge the authority of their parents and teachers in a wave of strikes that gave them their first taste of control over their own lives. Most of those who took part in the protests of 1926 were born after the turn of the century; some were still in their teens when Phan Chu Trinh died. Unlike this classically trained scholar, they were the products of Sarraut's educational reforms.[1] This common educational background helped bridge some of the differences in political style among anticolonialists of the three regions.

Intellectuals from Tonkin and Annam, especially those inclined toward a career in journalism, came to Cochinchina to take advantage of the more liberal atmosphere there; in turn, there was a considerable readership for southern publications in Annam and Tonkin. When students in Annam faced expulsion from school, it was to southern newspapers that they told their story. Exile was another means of overcoming the parochialism so carefully nurtured by the colonial authorities. In foreign lands, regional differences mattered less than national commonalities. Nonetheless, such differences were not completely obliterated. The fragmentation of the political scene prior to Phan Chu Trinh's death attested to the success of the colonial policy of divide and rule.

Whether they were classically educated literati or graduates of Franco-Annamite schools, anticolonial activists from Annam and Tonkin still derived their inspiration from China. But emulating organizational models was easier than absorbing strange ideas, especially since the need for secrecy put a premium on organizational minutiae and discouraged vigorous and informed debate. The groups that did exist were not without access to information about foreign ideological currents, but this information was limited; censorship and repression prevented it from being easily shared and properly evaluated.

The arrest of Phan Boi Chau roused the Annam-based Phuc Viet group from the somnolence into which it had fallen after its reorganization in 1924 as a result of its inability to choose between direct action and nonviolent means. But when it convened in July 1925, its adherents still had not resolved their disagreement over fundamental goals and tactics.[2] They decided to study the political situation further before deciding on a strategy, to forge links with émigrés in China and Siam in order to learn more about their situation and their plans, and to do more recruiting. Ton Quang Phiet, who had resumed his studies at the University of Hanoi, was given the task of creating a new section in Tonkin; Tran Mong Bach and Tran Phu took on the responsibility for propaganda work. Bach organized a clandestine Self-Cultivation League (Tu Than Hoi) among older students of the Collège de Vinh, where he was employed and where he also taught adult education courses with another teacher, Ha Huy Tap.[3] The two men enlisted several colleagues in northern Annam, who, in turn, proselytized among their own students. The Phuc Viet party was thus making progress. But after the Tonkinese section formed by Ton Quang Phiet distributed leaflets demanding the release of Phan Boi Chau, Tran Mong Bach became so disturbed by the unwelcome publicity that he decided to change the name of the party to Hung Nam. (This appellation never stuck, and the group went through two further name changes before finally being absorbed into the Indochinese Communist Party in 1930.)[4]

Bach also elaborated an organizational structure and a political program. Each candidate for membership had to be at least twenty years old and to have reached a certain level of education. Members were to behave at all times like sober patriots and provide to the people examples of modesty, altruism, thrift, hard work, prudence, and courage.[5] The goal of the party was to wage a peaceful revolution in order to bring about national independence. To achieve this, the party would first work toward the moral, intellectual, and economic restoration of the country; this translated into promoting fundamental reforms in the organization of the family and the village and combating superstition and antiquated customs. The party would encourage studies in Franco-Annamite schools and the translating and distributing of books and journals. On the economic front, it would seek to develop commerce, industry, and agriculture by creating large businesses and reclaiming uncultivated land. Upon independence, the country would become a republic. Vaguely aware of the growing influence of Marxism among émigré organizations, the Phuc Viet also anticipated that once independent, Vietnam would adopt Communist theories, but only after they had been adopted by the great powers. Unable to choose among different options, the Phuc Viet thus tried to be everything at once, nodding in the direction of Marxism for the sake of appearing in tune with the times, but also espousing essentially neo-traditionalist ideas of progress.

At around that time, a group of low-level civil servants and teachers launched the Nam Dong Publishing Society in Hanoi with the aim of raising money and producing patriotic propaganda. Unlike the periodic and daily press, occasional publications were not subjected to prior censorship, and thus pamphlets seemed an ideal way of reaching a mass audience. The author of many of the pamphlets was a teacher named Pham Tuan Tai, who used them to tell the story of the Chinese Revolution, explain the meaning of nationalism, and spread the ideas of Sun Yat-sen.[6] The authorities found out about the pamphlets and ordered the publishing house closed. But the Society did not disband even after Tai's transfer to a provincial teaching post; gradually, it turned its attention from propaganda to organizational problems, including the problem of expansion and merger with other groups.

Unlike the Phuc Viet and the Nam Dong Publishing Society, the Constitutionalists, who were the only organized political group in Cochinchina at the time, did not try to work for the demise of colonialism. They wanted only to be recognized as legitimate participants in the existing political system. To do so, they had to transform themselves from a loosely constituted interest group with no formal standing into a party enjoying official recognition. Such recognition was unlikely to be granted by the colonial authorities, especially in the worsening political climate, but it was possible to open a local branch of a political party already operating in metropolitan France. This consideration dictated the strategy Bui Quang Chieu decided to pursue. Chieu went to France in late spring 1925, before the name of the new Governor-General was announced. He maintained a high profile, publishing articles, writing to the Minister of Colonies, and making public appearances in Paris and the provinces. In June, he published a pamphlet entitled *France d'Asie,* in which he advocated a gradual process of decolonization and the granting of dominion status to Indochina. His nephew, Duong van Giao, produced a thesis outlining the contributions to the recent war effort made by the Vietnamese, and by the bourgeoisie more particularly, in order to argue for increased native representation.

One of Chieu's aims undoubtedly was to create the impression at home that he had entrée to the highest governing circles in metropolitan France as well as the backing of the Vietnamese émigrés. But Chieu declined to be associated with the Intercolonial Union on the ground that he was not a Communist.[7] That he was even invited to join it showed the disarray into which the Intercolonial Union had fallen after Nguyen Ai Quoc's departure for Moscow in 1923. Nguyen The Truyen tried in mid-1925 to promote a merger with Chinese expatriate organizations, but the latter gave him a cool reception.[8] A Constitutionalist Association was created in Paris on 15 November 1925.[9] Bui Quang Chieu was thus away from Vietnam when Phan Boi Chau was sentenced, leaving more radical figures free to shape and mobilize popular opinion.

The Truong Cao Dong Affair

Varenne's delay in deciding to commute Phan Boi Chau's sentence kept tensions so high that Phan Boi Chau under house arrest in Hue posed a greater threat to the authorities than when he had been free in South China. When, in mid-January, it became known that he was living in penury, the reformist press in Cochinchina launched a fund-raising campaign in his behalf, thus keeping his name in the news more effectively than Phan himself had done during his long exile, and providing a focus for resurgent anticolonial feelings.[10] It was during this period of heightened political awareness that yet another controversy erupted in Cochinchina.

On 8 January 1926, *Echo Annamite* published letters from a journalist named Truong Cao Dong about the ill-treatment of coolies sent to Cochinchina from Tonkin and Annam. The fraudulent recruitment of coolie labor had, until then, brought only occasional protests in the Cochinchinese press, usually about the sending of Vietnamese workers to the New Hebrides or New Caledonia. Less attention was paid to the plight of coolies working in the rubber or rice plantations of Cochinchina, possibly because they were not of local origin, or perhaps because agrarian issues had not yet become a major concern of the largely urban readership of the press. Recently, however, interest in trade unions and labor-related issues had increased, especially among journalists who came from Tonkin or Annam. To punish Truong Cao Dong for denouncing the appalling conditions in the plantations, the Cochinchinese authorities began proceedings to have him expelled to his native Annam. When Dong claimed that he had been the target of an assassination attempt, Dejean de la Batie introduced him to Monin, who gave him shelter.[11]

The timing of Truong Cao Dong's deportation could not have been more fortuitous, for freedom of travel was one of the political freedoms that had just been rejected by Varenne. To the Vietnamese, this underlined the fact that they could be treated like unwanted aliens on their own soil. The Jeune Annam militants, whose appetite for action had been whetted by previous scandals, seized the deportation order as the pretext for their first foray into popular mobilization. On 25 January, Cao Chanh, who edited the journal *New Century (Tan The Ky)*, and Nguyen Pho, the proofreader for *Indochine,* went to a theater to urge the audience to protest the expulsion of Truong Cao Dong. Dejean de la Batie, Monin, and others from Jeune Annam made similar speeches to audiences ranging in size from several hundred to two thousand.[12]

Things cooled down in February, but a harbinger of a new type of trouble appeared when a strike erupted at the Collège de Vinh Long. After a dispute with a circus owner, some students at the Collège were severely beaten by the police; instead of siding with his charges, the director expelled a dozen students who were accused of being ringleaders in the dispute. Their classmates, who already resented the director's frequent displays of racial insensitivity, reacted by going on strike.[13] Rebelliousness was also spreading in Annam. In March 1926, a strike took place at the School of Applied Industry in Hue, one of several vocational schools in Indochina. Students complained that the school used them as unpaid coolie labor instead of providing them with proper technical training; as a result, they charged, a graduate would be unfit to earn a living as a driver, let alone as a skilled worker. The immediate cause of the strikes was ill-treatment. On 3 March, a third-year student who had refused to perform *corvée* work was severely caned by the director. At a meeting, his schoolmates agreed that only by staying united could they win concessions. One of them took out a packet of cigarettes and said: "Remember, this cigarette represents our oath and the bond that unites us." They drew up a list of demands: the director must be replaced, *corvée* abolished, and the curriculum revised. When they presented these demands to the Résident Supérieur, he dismissed them with a curse. Back in school, they were ordered to perform *corvée* as before; they reacted by going on strike. Response was swift: the authorities arrested nine students and announced that they would be deported forthwith to the penal island of Con Son. Stranded far from home and lacking funds to live on their own, the remaining two hundred and fifteen students sent a letter to *Echo Annamite* appealing for understanding and support.[14] The letter, published on 18 March (and also reprinted in *Cloche Fêlée*), added to the general mood of restiveness and expectancy that had been growing since Bui Quang Chieu's imminent return from France had been announced.

Meanwhile, on 5 March, *Echo Annamite* published the text of "Les Revendications du Peuple Annamite," a resolution which had been voted by expatriates in France on 17 December 1925. The "Revendications" were an enlargement of the *Cahier des voeux* that Nguyen Phan Long had presented to Varenne in November. Their very name—demands rather than wishes—signified a hardening of position.[15] On 11 March, *Echo Annamite* announced that a formal garden party was being planned in honor of Bui Quang Chieu and called on the public to send donations to defray its costs. Similar announcements appeared in every issue of the liberal press for the next two weeks. Members of Jeune Annam decided to make use of the opportunity to engage in direct competition for public influence with the Constitutionalists.[16] They threw themselves into a flurry of activity in support of the planned reception. They sold copies of Nguyen An Ninh's speech "The Aspirations of Annamite Youth" to raise funds and even made plans to bring eight hundred workers from the Saigon Arsenal to serve as marshals.[17] This resurgence of activity coincided with the resumption of Dejean de la Batie's campaign in favor of Truong Cao Dong. When the authorities refused to rescind the deportation order, members of Jeune Annam decided to escalate their tactics. They also decided to form a political party. On 19 March, seventy people met at the house of Le The Vinh to hammer out a program of action. They did not reach any concrete decision, though they rejected Lam Hiep Chau's suggestion that they should provoke the authorities into acts of repression that would show their true colors.[18]

Nguyen An Ninh was offered the leadership of the new party but declined it. Much to the displeasure of Dejean de la Batie and of Phan van Truong, he had largely given up journalism. Ninh was going through a difficult period in his life. He was about to become a father, but was increasingly tempted by the religious life.[19] Having all along advocated action as the key to self-knowledge, he now faced the necessity of choosing how to act. Ninh had identified the problem facing Vietnamese youth as the absence of a moral basis for action, but what he lacked was an ideological foundation. At a loss, he decided to retire for the time being from the political stage. But for all his inner disarray, Ninh was incapable of half-measures. At the meeting, he announced that he was planning to bring out a paper devoted to promoting revolution, through violence if necessary.[20] He decided to distribute six thousand tracts calling on the population in and around Saigon to attend a rally on 21 March to discuss the deportation of Truong Cao Dong. Ninh, who was the best orator, had been asked to be the main speaker at the rally. Dejean agreed to let his name be used in the tract, but did not bother to check the wording. Dejean later regretted his failure to do so, for the tone was more virulent than anything that had circulated in Vietnam in a long time.

> Brothers! We have been slaves for seventy years. During this time, a tyrannical government has oppressed us. Today, it asks us to love it and actually pretends to carry us toward a better civilization. It preaches accord between conqueror and conquered . . . If we do not

care for our own fate, no one else will. The Sage Tagore has said: "Asiatics are not beggars. Why should they hold out their hands to the Europeans?" But we are impotent and unable to accomplish anything against the government. However, we can unite, and demonstrate that we have a despotic ruler above us. The most brilliant of our comrades have been repressed by this government. For seventy years, they have been killed, or condemned to exile and martyrdom. Will you always accept the role of beasts? If you had human blood in your veins, you would rebel.

Here we stand on the soil of our ancestors. We should march from north to south. If the government asks local officials where to expel us, we reply—To Moscow . . . The people of Annam should take up arms and drive the invaders from our land. Why do we hesitate? Under the pretext of accomplishing a civilizing mission, France has reduced us to slavery. Let us unite, for numbers make strength, and we are millions against a few thousand Frenchmen.[21]

The words had an electrifying effect. A crowd of three thousand came to the meeting, including six hundred workers and an equal number of students enrolled in schools in and around Saigon. The meeting turned out to be an almost exclusively Jeune Annam event, for Nguyen Phan Long, sensing trouble, had refused to come. Dejean de la Batie, who had no inkling of the contents of the tract, and a member of the Colonial Council, Le Quang Liem, were chairing the meeting; Monin, newly returned from China, lent his presence. After speeches by several members of Jeune Annam, it was Ninh's turn to speak. Greeted with thunderous applause, he repeated what he had said in the tract: "We are being preached Franco-Annamite collaboration but we are treated like cattle." The meeting voted to demand concessions that by now outstripped the original request that Truong Cao Dong be allowed to stay in Cochinchina. They included the demand that the Rights of Man and the Citizen be observed in Cochinchina as they were in France and demands for freedom of education, assembly and movement, and the cessation of detention for people involved in civil and commercial cases. One thousand people were bold enough to sign the petition, despite the risk of reprisals.[22]

Concerned by the growing militancy of the Vietnamese, and especially alarmed by the formation of Jeune Annam, Varenne had ordered that measures be taken to halt its growth. With his tract, the impulsive Ninh had handed the authorities an ideal pretext for a crackdown. Ninh was arrested immediately after the meeting, together with Dejean de la Batie. Meanwhile, the sudden upsurge of militancy produced cracks in the ranks of the Jeune Annam group, which was already beset by personal jealousy and suspicions. Lam Hiep Chau's suggestion that Jeune Annam provoke the authorities into repression had aroused suspicions that he might be an *agent provocateur*.[23] On 23 March, *Echo Annamite* reproduced a letter from Le The Vinh on behalf of the "Provisional Council of the Jeune Annam Party," stating that the newspaper called *Jeune Annam*, which Lam Hiep Chau was bringing out that very day, was not the Party's official organ. After it appeared, Lam Hiep Chau was arrested for making fraudulent representations to obtain a publishing permit, since, being only twenty, Chau was not of legal age. It was, however, believed that the real reason for his arrest was that he had reprinted an article from *Paria* and one from the liberal *Argus Indochinois*.

News that Nguyen An Ninh, Dejean de la Batie, and Lam Hiep Chau had been arrested reached the public on 24 March. The following day came the announcement that Phan Chu Trinh had died during the night.

Death and Transfiguration of a Patriot

Phan Chu Trinh's deteriorating health had made it impossible for him to travel north to his village or to visit his old friend Phan Boi Chau. Forced to remain in Cochinchina, he had kept occupied by preparing and giving lectures. During his long years of exile, he had refined his position on issues that had been hotly debated during the heyday of the Reform Movement but in which the public seemed to have lost interest. Two major lectures he gave in October and November 1925, "Morality and Ethics, East and West" and "Monarchism and Republicanism," were accorded the deferential hearing owed an elder statesman, but generated little excitement.[24] He remained, as ever, bitterly opposed to the monarchy, but it no longer constituted a worthy target. As if to show how little it had come to matter, the death on 6 November 1925 of his old nemesis, Emperor Khai Dinh, passed virtually unnoticed in the press and unmourned by the general public. The trial of Phan Boi Chau and Varenne's refusal to introduce reforms commanded far more attention. Even Pham Quynh, Khai Dinh's defender, produced an ambiguously worded obituary: "Now that the emperor has passed away, it does not behoove us to discuss his ten-year reign; it is history's place to pass judgment on its achievements and shortcomings." [25]

Phan Chu Trinh fell terminally ill in December. He was taken to the home of Nguyen An Ninh's uncle, where he was attended by relays of friends and admirers. When his condition worsened, he was transferred to a hospital in Saigon, where he died on 23 March. Knowledge that his end was approaching provoked speculations about the proper way of mourning him. In the one and only issue of *Jeune Annam,* which came out the day before his death, Lam Hiep Chau asked: "What is your duty toward a great patriot, a martyr for a cause common to us all? Young China, for whom Sun Yat-sen freed [his country] from Western imperialism, transformed his death into an event of national mourning. And what is going to come of the death of our own Phan Chu Trinh? Will it be an event of national mourning for us? . . . Readers, compatriots, what do you think?"

Whether or not they were inspired by Lam Hiep Chau's suggestion, the progressive papers combined the announcement of Phan's death with an appeal for funds to organize a grandiose funeral. Nothing, however, happened immediately: all were anxiously waiting for Bui Quang Chieu to return, hoping he would provide the sorely needed leadership to deal with the situation that had so unexpectedly arisen.

When Chieu stepped off the boat on 26 March, a crowd of several thousand well-wishers was on hand to greet him; its size was clearly owing to the climate of expectancy generated by Nguyen An Ninh's arrest and Phan Chu Trinh's death.[26] Present also were about fifty Frenchmen, led by la Chevrotière and bent on creating trouble. All the police of Saigon had been mobilized, but did nothing to keep the two sides apart. Into this tense situation walked Chieu, who had been informed of the events that had taken place in his absence only moments earlier.[27] Always distrustful of mobs, Chieu made his way through the crowd, preaching, "Keep cool, keep cool." But, as he wrote in a private letter the following day, he was "in a cold sweat." [28] La Chevrotière, who had been hurling invectives at the Vietnamese, lunged forward; pandemonium broke out. Chieu was whisked away to a reception, leaving his well-wishers at the mercy of the settlers and the police, nursing a strong sense of anticlimax. The next day, Chieu made a speech that was intended as the high point of his domestic campaign to launch the party he had been at such pains to establish in France. He preached patience and reiterated his faith in total assimilation, which he argued would lead to equal rights and equal opportunities for people of all races in Indochina. In the explosive mood of the moment, Chieu's speech misfired. The majority of Vietnamese had no wish to become French; many were running out of patience with unfulfilled promises. After three months of mounting agitation, Bui Quang Chieu's long-planned triumphal homecoming had somehow fizzled. But the dimming of his political star was only a sideshow in the growing pressure to mount a national funeral for Phan Chu Trinh.

Coming so soon after the sentencing of Phan Boi Chau to life imprisonment, and amid evidence that the Constitutionalists were unwilling to carry the patriotic struggle forward, the death of Phan Chu Trinh assumed symbolic meaning as the signal that the new generation must take over from the old. Nowhere was this more keenly understood than within the Jeune Annam group, which decided to turn his funeral, scheduled for 4 April, into a national event similar to what had been done in China for Sun Yat-sen. A committee to organize the funeral had been established the night of Phan's death; aside from a few natives of Annam where Phan was born, it included all the major Constitutionalist leaders, but also a good sprinkling of Jeune Annam adherents. They were eager to exploit the event to the full and had managed to raise thirteen thousand piasters to mount the funeral.[29] They were unwittingly assisted in their efforts to mobilize public opinion by the authorities' own attempts to thwart them. The authorities feared that large groups of mourners might turn into angry mobs demanding political concessions. But police bans against funeral processions merely angered the population and helped swell the ranks of mourners in all parts of the country. Funeral processions or commemorative rites were held in every province in spite of official prohibitions.[30]

During the eleven days that elapsed between Phan's death and his funeral, mourners came from all corners of the country to the hotel owned by one of the men who had cared for Phan during his last months of life. When the funeral procession assembled on 4 April, a conservative estimate put the number of participants at fifteen thousand.[31] Others spoke of several tens of thousands. They were shepherded by members of Jeune Annam, recognizable by their yellow armbands (other mourners wore either black or white armbands). First came students from various schools of the capital, both public and private, student teachers from the Normal School, and representatives of provincial schools. Then came workers from the Kroff (Ba

Son) Factory, followed by a women's delegation, and last, a delegation of Jeune Annam adherents. Each group marched behind a little portable altar decorated with lilies and banners bearing the customary parallel sentences commemorating the deceased. Hundreds more banners and parallel sentences sent from all over the country flew overhead. They came from old associates of Phan Chu Trinh, from individuals who had never met him, from employees of Vietnamese enterprises as well as of French businesses and factories, and from students and alumni of various schools; from monks residing in pagodas, and hermits in the mountains. There were banners from associations of natives of Annam residing in Cochinchina, and even from members of the local Kuomintang and from Vietnamese émigrés in Phnom Penh. From prison, Nguyen An Ninh had sent a couple of parallel sentences written in impeccable Chinese, as custom demanded, in which he recalled their trip home together.

Behind one altar marched a group of women led by the wives of Tran Huy Lieu and Nguyen Kim Dinh of *Indochina Times*. Women had long been involved in anticolonial activities; this constituted one of their first public acts in the name of patriotism. Its altar featured a poem in the vernacular that closed with the lines: "Your mission is not yet achieved, but your spirit has not diminished. If your soul watches over us, please agree that the duty to defend our mountains and rivers is as much a woman's job as it is a man's."[32] Patriotic fervor not being exclusive to the elite, a group of female stall-holders in Saigon had also sent a banner. The prevailing mood was best summed up by the pair of sentences written by the scholar Mai Dang De:

> One Phan is dead and gone, one is living a half death, woe is our country;
> Immortal words versus immortal deeds, who can say who was the superior man.[33]

Mai Dang De seemed to imply that neither Phan Chu Trinh nor Phan Boi Chau knew which was the best method of winning independence for the country—cultural transformation or political activism. And yet, though the funeral was for Phan Chu Trinh, who had always abhorred violence, the mood was pure Phan Boi Chau–style activism. Phan Chu Trinh's death touched off a wave of strikes that engulfed the nation for the next two years. Strikes occurred in various factories and businesses owned by French interests, in particular the Banque d'Indochine, but it was the schools which were the hardest hit.

Schools for Rebels

Young Vietnamese had suddenly sloughed off the apathy with which their elders had so often taxed them and had become activists with a vengeance. For many, the desire to defy authority was as potent a motive as the expression of patriotic sentiment. Those who marched behind Phan's coffin were the hardiest among their peers. In most schools, students who had asked for permission to absent themselves for the occasion had been rebuffed, and those who sported black armbands in class were disciplined, thus provoking further unrest. As in the past, strikes were often sparked by trivial incidents. But there was now more contact between students and outside activists. With the overt or covert advice of Dejean de la Batie (released from prison on 1 April) and Phan van Truong, and under the prodding of Jeune Annam, the strikes became more coordinated and more politicized.

At the Institution Taberd, where students had been refused leave to attend the funerals, a French supervisor tore off the black armbands which some insisted on wearing on their sleeves as a sign of mourning; on 3 April, ninety students went on strike in protest. At the Lycée Chasseloup-Laubat, students' anger had already been triggered by the director's decree that teachers and staff were entitled to beat the students without giving a reason; on the advice of Jeune Annam leaders, the students planned to hold a strike on 16 April. But a similar refusal by the administration to allow them to wear armbands or attend the funeral provoked them into a premature strike, which robbed them of the chance to become better organized.[34] Other students wanted to strike to show support for Nguyen An Ninh, but Dejean de la Batie told them to wait and see, while Nguyen Phan Long declared that, although he sympathized with Ninh, he had faith in French justice.[35] At a banquet held in his honor by the Association of Annamite Businessmen and Industrialists, Bui Quang Chieu was publicly taken to task by two women for not lending support to Ninh; he responded by preaching on the need for discipline in politics.[36]

The two women were dismissed by the authorities as "disreputable," presumably because they had dared to speak in public.[37] It was more difficult to so describe the young girls who, that same day, began to defy their teachers and administrators at the School for Native Young Ladies. The confrontation was the result of a simmering dispute which had begun on 28 March, when a supervisor scolded a student for talking too loudly during study hours. The scolded girl protested her innocence but was told to go and sit at the back of the class anyway; she refused. "Impolite, dishonest girl!" cried the supervisor. "Not more than you, miss!" retorted the girl. The director and head supervisor were sent for and, to the dismay of the students, took the side of the supervisor. The mutinous girl was sent to the infirmary until she agreed to apologize. Her fellow students threatened to quit school as a gesture of solidarity. The supervisor, who was heartily disliked for using abusive language toward the Vietnamese and for causing the withdrawal of a scholarship from one student and the expulsion of another the previous year, taunted the protesters: "I will crush all the Vietnamese under my feet. Ah, you want me to leave? But know well that I will leave only when there is no Annamite left in Cochinchina."[38] Calm was temporarily restored after the director called a meeting between the school staff and the children's parents. It was shattered again when the girl's uncle, a municipal councillor, decided to accompany his niece to school and force her to apologize. He presented his excuses to the staff for his niece's behavior, which he blamed on "external influences." But when he began preaching obedience and respect to the assembled students, his little homily was interrupted by shrieks, foot-stomping, and tears. Emboldened by the political storm brewing outside the school walls, the girls loudly proclaimed their disgust with both their teachers and their parents. The Director of Cochinchinese Education, Georges Taboulet, was called in. He received a delegation of students who presented their complaints: the supervisor had insulted the Vietnamese, and they wanted her transferred. Taboulet decided that her remarks, regrettable though they were, did not warrant her transfer. But he extended no such leniency to the student delegates and told them that they would be expelled forthwith. This so outraged their schoolmates that they all decided to go on strike.[39]

Varenne, alarmed by the sudent unrest, ordered a severe crackdown.[40] But strikes were spreading to the provinces, where local attempts to hold funeral processions ran up against the opposition of the authorities. In Tonkin, students at several institutions, including the Girls' School in Hanoi, went on strike, as did their teachers. In My Tho, students from the local Collège picketed a theatrical troop owned by Luong Khac Ninh, a well-known collaborator, who was the editor-in-chief of *Trung Lap*, the Vietnamese version of *Impartial*. The newspaper, previously owned by la Chevrotière, now belonged to the Banque d'Indochine, where the Vietnamese staff had gone on strike. The students' boycott was provoked by their wish to show support for the staff of the Banque d'Indochine, their distaste for Luong Khac Ninh's financial dependence on la Chevrotière, and anger at disparaging remarks he had made in public about Phan Chu Trinh.[41] It brought the students into conflict first with the police, then with the school authorities, and escalated into a full-blown strike on 24 April. In the Collège de Can Tho, a group of students, already in trouble for having protested that the sugar they were given came mixed with coal and their rice with dirt, were expelled for producing a clandestine paper that took its tone from *Indochina Times*.[42] Strikes also occurred in Hue, Hanoi, Nam Dinh, Phu Lam, and elsewhere during the month of April. But it was in Cochinchina, where the combination of Phan Chu Trinh's death, the rise of Jeune Annam, the arrest of Nguyen An Ninh, and the return of Bui Quang Chieu had produced a sharp swing to the left, that most of the unrest took place. An indication of how far things had suddenly gone was the serialization in *Cloche Fêlée*, beginning on 30 March 1926, of the *Communist Manifesto*.

Fall of a Hero

Nguyen An Ninh was brought to trial on 24 April in front of a packed audience.[43] It was clear that Ninh had been found guilty beforehand. His ingratitude toward the mother country was mentioned at length. Speeches he had made in Paris were used against him, in particular one in which he had predicted the inevitability of violent revolution. Even his translation of Rousseau's *Contrat social* was offered as evidence of his seditious intentions. The prosecutor demanded two years of prison without reprieve, and the withdrawal of his civic rights.[44]

Nguyen An Ninh was later to quote Chamfort's epigram: *En prison, le coeur se brise ou se bronze* (In prison, the heart either breaks or becomes as hard as bronze). He would be imprisoned another four times, and die in 1943 after four long years of incarceration. But this was the first time he had lost his freedom. When sentenced, he had already spent one month in jail; during that time, his wife had given birth to their first child, increasing his state of anxiety. Nguyen An Ninh lacked neither physical nor moral courage. Frail and prone to minor ailments, he pushed his body to the limit. But as someone who loved the open air and to whom a house could seem as constraining as a cage, he found the prospect of spending two years in prison unbearable.

Cognacq had left Cochinchina in April, so quietly that it was not immediately apparent that he had been forced out by Varenne.[45] He had been replaced by Le Fol, whom Ninh had gotten to know while in Paris. Relying on this personal connection, Ninh made a catastrophic blunder. The day after his sentence was passed, he wrote to Le Fol pleading for mercy, and promising to abjure politics: "What I am looking for is not in politics. Return me to the countryside, to trees, to life itself." He also addressed a letter to the Procureur de la République, in which he minimized his role in fostering the unrest that had overtaken Cochinchina since the beginning of the year. In recent months, he explained, he had not engaged in political action; he had had to be persuaded to take part in organizing the meeting of 21 March. The reason was that he had been in the throes of a spiritual crisis: "Since the age of eighteen, I have been tormented by a spiritual evolution which gnaws at me ceaselessly and often makes me doubt myself, my ideas, and the usefulness of my actions. I have many times been tempted by religion. This anguish explains my abrupt decision to abandon everything in order to rest."[46]

Varenne favored clemency, but the Procureur opposed it.[47] Colonna, who had already embarrassed Varenne over Phan Boi Chau's sentencing, leaked to the press Ninh's letters, one of which was addressed to him.[48] When their contents became known, the settlers were delighted, the advocates of Franco-Annamite collaboration scornful, and the radicals stunned. Young people had put Ninh on a pedestal, displaying his photograph as their parents did portraits of their ancestors. What they had admired in Ninh most of all was his personal courage. He represented the triumph of human will over adversity. It was Ninh who had introduced them to Nietzsche and to the idea of the Superman which he had seemed to embody. His supporters even accused Nguyen Phan Long of fabricating the letters. Still angry with Ninh for implicating him in the business of the tracts, Dejean de la Batie forgot he was half-Vietnamese: "I have never asked for favors from the authorities. Since I am French, kowtowing is not in my blood."[49] Bui Quang Chieu let it be known that he had advised against a general strike in support of Ninh.[50] In the uproar that had broken out over Ninh's fall from grace, little attention was paid to the news that Truong Cao Dong, in whose cause so much energy had been spent, had received a pardon from Varenne shortly after being condemned to two years' imprisonment.⁵¹

The radicals tried to persuade Phan van Truong to substitute as a role model and asked him to take the lead of Jeune Annam. Truong declined the honor, though he continued his journalistic efforts.⁵² *Cloche Fêlée* closed down on 5 May 1926, but was immediately replaced by *Annam,* under the editorship of Phan van Truong, with Dejean as its business manager. This new journal had the same format as *Cloche Fêlée* and, like it, appeared twice a week on Mondays and Thursdays. Less inspirational than *Cloche Fêlée,* less concerned with youthful idealism and the need for a new culture than with social justice, *Annam* was also more openly hostile to the colonial regime. On 19 August 1926, it dared publish photographs of a torture session conducted by Sûreté agents in My Tho. It was in regular correspondence with writers from Tonkin, Annam, and especially from France and often reprinted articles from *Humanité.* It thus served as a link in the chain of communications between different groups of activists at home and abroad. It also acted as a mouthpiece for students who complained that during the strikes, only Phan van Truong had lent them support.⁵³

The continued prominence of Jeune Annam after Phan Chu Trinh's funeral increased Bui Quang Chieu's desire to organize a formal Constitutionalist party.⁵⁴ In August, Chieu launched a new newspaper, *Tribune Indochinoise,* to replace *Tribune Indigène,* which had folded one year earlier. In October 1926, the French-based Constitutionalist Association transformed itself into the Constitutionalist Party, allowing Chieu to open a Cochinchinese branch. Chieu's distrust of the masses had not abated; if anything, the tense mobs which had welcomed him home had intensified his fears.⁵⁵ The Constitutionalist Party never had more than thirty members.⁵⁶

Pham Quynh, who had been closely following Chieu's progress, was inspired by his example to attempt to form his own party. When the student strikes waned with the coming of the summer vacations, Quynh found reinforcement for his belief in culturalism, and disdainfully described the strikes as "childish."⁵⁷ Ninh's tragedy, Pham Quynh commented, was that he had plunged into action without having a clear idea of what he wanted to achieve. Ninh's apparent apostasy gave him the pretext to return to one of his favorite topics, the "moral malaise" that afflicted the country, and to redouble his calls for cultural renovation. The students had shown themselves to be politically immature and incapable of sustained action. It was useless to grant political concessions to the Vietnamese, Pham Quynh argued, as long as they did not yet possess the appropriate mentality to deserve them. Borrowing the words of the colonial writer Albert de Pourvourville, Pham Quynh contemptuously characterized Vietnam's youth as still lacking in the "'personal power,' strength and force of will, spiritual vigor and moral virility, which, even more than intelligence or knowledge, are the hallmark of real men . . ."[58] Instead of striving for maturity, they had allowed themselves to become social misfits *(désencadrés sociaux)*. Pham Quynh allied this indictment of youth with a political program of his own. He argued that Varenne's failure to implement reforms was due to the continuing pressure exercized by the settlers and by their champions, Outrey and Colonna, whereas the Vietnamese elite, who represented the majority of his constituents, lacked the ability to act as a counterweight and give him adequate support for his reformist program because they were unorganized.[59]

The party he proposed to create was to be called the Vietnamese People's Progressive League (Viet Nam Tan Bo Dan Hoi). Its purpose was twofold: while marshaling Vietnamese support for reforms, it would also strive to stem the rising tide of radicalism by raising the moral, intellectual, and economic standards of the country in close collaboration with the colonial regime. Despite that reactionary aim, the cultural agenda of the party attracted a large number of people suspected by the authorities of anticolonial activism. Among those who flocked to support Pham Quynh were members of the Phuc Viet who discerned similarities between his ideas and their own program of peaceful revolution. Tran Mong Bach and others wrote numerous press articles favoring the creation of the Vietnamese People's Progressive League and took part in an organizational meeting on 10 September 1926 to draft a program for submission to the Governor-General. But although this was a blatant attempt by Pham Quynh to court Varenne's favor, the latter, aware that behind Quynh's proposed party were numerous anticolonial activists, refused to give it his official blessing; and so the Vietnamese People's Progressive League died aborning.[60]

In 1924, *Southern Wind* had translated an article which had originally appeared in *Revue Mondiale*. Its title was "Two Movements of Reform in the World Today, Wilson and Lenin." The gist of the article was that "if the Wilsonian strategy does not succeed, then Leninism will spread throughout the world." [61] Whatever motive had led Pham Quynh to publish that article in 1924, two years later, in his disappointment, he dared not even threaten the colonial authorities with the specter of revolution. When he was refused permission to launch the Vietnamese People's Progressive League, he contented himself with observing that "Franco-Annamite collaboration founded on true equality and justice has not yet found a satisfactory formula in governmental projects, and even less, in administrative acts." [62]

Not all young Vietnamese accepted Pham Quynh's assumption that maturity consisted of adapting to the status quo; the failure of his political plans pushed the Cochinchinese radicals further to the left. When Le The Vinh set forth the manifesto of Jeune Annam on 20 May 1926, he was still hoping that concessions could be won by legal methods and therefore described the goal of the party as follows: "to closely unite young Annamites of all social classes above the age of twenty-one and to demand by all legal means the Rights of Man and the Citizen." Vinh shied away from clandestine action because "Annam does not yet possess a revolutionary elite capable of launching and leading a revolution . . . Any revolutionary action therefore could only be disastrous for its authors." [63] But Varenne's refusal to allow Pham Quynh to form a political party, even one dedicated to combating radicalism, showed how useless it was to hope that political concessions could be obtained by legal means. *Annam* commented: "French liberalism is always translated into words, never into action." [64] Such experiences led the radicals to think of ways to replace words with action.[65]

The politicization of Vietnamese youth had happened too quickly for them to have acquired an ideological framework for their activities. The growing organizational effort that spawned groups as diverse as Jeune Annam in Cochinchina, Phuc Viet in Annam, and the Nam Dong Publishing Society in Tonkin was characterized by a confusion of objectives. All three groups, for example, were hostile to colonial rule, but none had yet made a clear choice between reformism or revolution. Although they were essentially political and goal oriented, they shared a characteristic with many other apolitical groups which sprang up around that time: their existence was to some extent their *raison d'être*. They were as much a means of self-realization as an instrument of political action.

There was an explosive growth of new types of organizations in 1925–1926. Some were ephemeral, others more permanent; all, in their way, reflected the breakdown of old bases of community and the atomization of society since colonial conquest. Under the assault of long-term socioeconomic trends, colonial policies, and reformist zeal, old social structures had undergone dramatic change. The perception of their true nature had changed even more radically. Institutions that had formerly promoted social cohesion and harmony, such as the family and the village, now seemed to be sources of oppression and conflict. The primary reason for this changed perception was the old institutions' largely ascriptive and nonegalitarian nature. The new organizations emphasized voluntary membership and shared purpose. They took a multitude of forms, ranging from publishing houses, theatrical troops, educational organizations, women's associations, and mutual-help societies to trade unions and political parties. Although not all were political in origin, they were quickly caught up in the ferment of the times; they were politicized by the exercise of free choice and the stress on shared commitment among their members as well as by the hostile attitude of the colonial authorities, who viewed with suspicion any effort at organized behavior.[66] Though the efforts of young radicals to organize themselves lacked momentum and direction, they were more sustained than Pham Quynh realized.

Varenne, too, underestimated their staying power when, contemplating the end of his turbulent first year in office, he congratulated himself that the country was "perfectly calm."[67] He had spoken too soon, for a new school year had just begun, and the students had not yet had time to organize themselves. Two months later, the schools were in an uproar again. This time, the strikes had spread to Tonkin and Annam.

Having moved leftward again after the rebuff to Pham Quynh, the Phuc Viet, now renamed the Vietnamese Revolutionary Party, had made further inroads among teachers and students. On 20 January 1927, Ha Huy Tap was dismissed from his job at the Collège de Vinh for sending seditious articles to *Annam*.[68] His firing prompted his students to stage a sympathy strike. At the prestigious Imperial College, a strike began on 6 April after a French teacher accused one of his students, a member of the imperial clan, of cheating, and slapped him across the face. Those among his classmates who raised their voice to protest were summarily expelled. Scuffles broke out between students and staff. The school director brought in a bevy of mandarins in full court dress to address the students on the subject of obedience and humility. The mandarins chose to illustrate what they had been brought in to preach by prostrating themselves in front of the director. Far from having the wished-for result, this display of self-abasement enraged the students: "They threw themselves on the cowards who dishonored the Vietnamese race by prostrating themselves as in adoration in front of men who oppressed them."[69] When, attracted by all the noise, the police arrived, the students fought them before marching out of the College. They were joined by the female students of Dong Khanh School. These two strikes unleashed others that lasted through the month of April.[70] Expulsions no longer held any terror for the increasingly combative students. Strikes succeeded one another throughout the months of September and October. Students struck when they were served bad food, when they were ill treated, or when they wanted to show sympathy with fellow students.[71]

A Patriotic Emigration

The radicalization of Vietnamese youth was deeply worrying to the advocates of Franco-Annamite collaboration. The strikes discredited one of the most cherished beliefs of the Constitutionalists and neo-traditionalists: that it was possible to bring about real progress in a gradual, peaceful fashion by relying on education rather than on political confrontation. More worried about adverse reaction from the French than from their compatriots, the Constitutionalists had argued that education would induce the natives to better appreciate the aims of French rule, and hence foster political stability. To the Vietnamese, the Constitutionalists had held out promises of increased participation in the administrative and political processes of the colony and the security and prestige of better jobs in the civil service or in business. But neither the Constitutionalists nor the neo-traditionalists understood how much their ability to present themselves as effective champions of gradual reform was being undermined by Varenne himself. After one year in office, Varenne had renounced his earlier vision of an eventual end to French rule in Vietnam. The Minister of Colonies made it clear that, as far as he was concerned, the accommodationists were as dangerous as the most extreme radicals: "The goal is the same, only the deadlines vary, and perhaps the means."[72]

It had been fashionable to bemoan the lack of public spirit in the younger generation; now, older Vietnamese were aghast at their sudden interest in politics. Since only about 10 percent of the school-age population was actually able to attend school, education, especially at the post-primary level, tended to be regarded as a privilege for which parents schemed and made sacrifices. They were dismayed to learn that their children saw themselves as victims rather than beneficiaries of colonial education. Bui Quang Chieu spoke for many when, at the height of the first wave of strikes, he wrote an article upbraiding the students for "their sudden infatuation with politics" and reiterated his position "that the first duty of children is to obey their parents and their teachers."[73] Many patriotic literati found student unrest just as discomfiting, for they had been schooled at a time when respect for teachers had been an unquestioned norm and racism had not tainted the relationship between ruler and ruled or between teacher and student. Even Phan Boi Chau, who had always counseled rebellion, shied away from advocating that it be waged in the schoolroom. This led Tran Lanh Sieu, who had been expelled from Chasseloup-Laubat, to comment bitterly:

> Phan Boi Chau tells us to endure without a murmur the bullying that they inflict on us in the colleges. We don't want to displease you, eminent compatriot, but suppose you became suddenly at the stroke of a magic wand, young like us for a short while, and with a spirit like ours, and took our place as the object of harassment and bullying by our directing personnel. I would like to know how you would respond to a supervisor pulling off your armband of mourning to crush it under his feet. But the root of this year's strike is earlier and (accumulated) discontent that is merely being poured out now. You must not believe that these arbitrary acts by our educators have not been perpetrated in the past.[74]

The almost universal lack of support students encountered helped produce a decisive split along generational lines. Among the new adherents of Jeune Annam was Nguyen Khanh Toan, who had been dismissed from the Normal School in Hanoi as a result of the strikes of April 1926.[75] In the lone issue of the journal *Peasant (Nha Que)* which he managed to bring out before he was arrested, he asked, "What does Annamite youth want?" He answered: "At a time when, in politics, impatience alone is the surest guarantee of success, it is more than just stupid to subordinate the liberation of an oppressed people to patience ... Those who are supposed to be leading the masses like moderation and even quiet. To the gibberish of our elders—elders in age but not in reason—we will from now on turn a deaf ear. By freeing ourselves from their tutelage, we will do our duty, all our duty."[76]

The strikes had the effect of cutting the umbilical cord that had tied Vietnamese youth to home and family. Like the prodigal children that Nguyen An Ninh had exhorted them to become, they were leaving the house of their fathers to go into exile. Expelled from their schools, kept at arm's length by their disappointed and fearful parents, shadowed by the Sûreté, most had little choice but to leave the country.[77] Not all those who went abroad were forced into exile. Some went to France merely to obtain a degree that could be parlayed into a comfortable job and a prominent social position back home. Others were motivated by the idle curiosity which Nguyen Ai Quoc had deplored only the year before. Some went in style; others were able to scrape together just enough money for their boat fare. Still others went as stowaways; these included Nguyen van Tao, who was expelled from Chasseloup-Laubat in April 1926. But whatever their motive or the manner of their going, they were leaving in such numbers that by the end of 1926, the colonial authorities no longer exerted themselves to prevent their departure. Soon, advice began pouring back on how to obtain permission to go to France, and what to do once there.[78] Although the departures for France were the more visible, even more young Vietnamese made their way clandestinely to China, where Nguyen Ai Quoc's newly formed Vietnamese Youth League was waiting for them with open arms.[79]

Leaving home was a sea-change figuratively as well as literally, as Nhat Linh observed during his trip to France in 1927. He was then twenty-four years old and had recently married, but he seemed unable to settle into a career or to accept the responsibilities of married life. He had begun training in medicine and tried his hand at writing in his spare time. In 1925, he transferred to the newly opened School of Fine Arts, where he showed considerable promise. But the strikes of 1926–1927 so thoroughly unsettled him that he found himself unable to pursue his studies, and he hit upon the idea of applying to go to France to learn photography. During the month-long voyage he noticed:

> The farther the ship got from Vietnam and the closer it got to France, to the same degree the more decently the people aboard the ship treated me. In the China sea they did not care to look at me. By

the Gulf of Siam they were looking at me with scornful apprehension, the way they would look at a mosquito carrying malaria germs to Europe. When we entered the Indian Ocean, their eyes began to become infected with expressions of gentleness and compassion . . . and when we crossed the Mediterranean, suddenly they viewed me as being civilized like themselves, and began to entertain ideas of respecting me. At that time, I was very elated. But I worried about the time when I would be returning home.[80]

Nhat Linh had discovered one of the ironies of colonialism: to be treated like a human being, it was better to be on foreign soil than in one's native land. In France, Vietnamese students, no matter how straitened their circumstances, could feel that they were the equal of any Frenchman, not second-class citizens to be browbeaten in their own homes. For young people who had been sickened at the sight of court mandarins prostrating themselves in front of French officials, it was a revelation to be granted ordinary courtesies, to be free to come and go as they pleased, to read whatever they liked, to attend lectures and meetings, and to be able to express their opinion in public, even though they were often shadowed by the Sûreté. Recounting her interview with Ta Thu Thau, Nguyen An Ninh, and Phan van Chanh in 1931, Andrée Viollis captured the heady sense of freedom and personal dignity which they had taken back from France: "They lived in the Latin Quarter, they became friends with French students; they were warmly welcomed into French families . . . their professors invited them to their homes and took their opinions seriously. They bought newspapers and books as they pleased; they frequented advanced circles, they attended discussions, meetings. Sometimes, they even spoke up."[81]

Nhat Linh spent three idyllic years in France, living a hand-to-mouth existence but free of responsibilities to either parents or wife, and free most of all of the duty to decide upon a career. For him, liberation came in a literary guise: he fell in love with André Gide's style. But though he resolutely shunned politics, he could not avoid meeting political activists, since so many had made their way to France. In the end, Nhat Linh was abruptly deported after a Sûreté agent spotted him lending money to a chance acquaintance whom he did not know to be a radical.[82] But for the politically minded, emigration was a consciously patriotic odyssey. On his way to France in October 1927, Ta Thu Thau told his fellow passengers: "We students must amass and conquer the education that they deny us in our country ... Do you know, my dear comrades, that at each ship's departure, some young Vietnamese who have neither relatives nor friends aboard abandon work in order to be present at the pier? ... They find out how many people are leaving and their joy rises with the number of emigrants. These compatriots who thus come to see us off represent for us Vietnam, and their hopes are those of the fatherland." [83]

Another student wrote: "The young generation to which we belong has the duty to seek by every available way to escape from the Indochinese prison, to exile itself in foreign lands in order to find the means to overthrow the colonial regime." [84] The *Courrier Saigonnais* warned that "the path to France is the path to anti-France." [85] But Varenne was relieved to see the students go, for he considered it "preferable that Annamite revolutionaries pursue their activities in France rather than in Indochina." [86]

Superficially, though the numbers involved were far larger, this wave of student travel was reminiscent of the Eastern Travel Movement organized by Phan Boi Chau in 1905. But the students brought by Phan to China or Japan had conceived of Western learning essentially as a technique to fight colonialism; they sought to contain new ideas in a strictly functionalist framework, leaving intact their fundamental values and sense of self. By contrast, the students now leaving home were not just trying to make up for the inferior education they had been receiving in Franco-Annamite schools. They had become conscious that they needed a new map of the world, a new conceptual framework to help them analyze the present and imagine the future.

6   Organizing Revolution

> Where do you keep your armies, O Wind God?
> Unleash your power and tumble ocean waves.
> Whip, whip—blow off all temples and all shrines.
> Roar, roar—bring down all forests and all hills . . .
> May Heaven storm and sweep our kingdom clean, then put it back within its rightful bounds.
>
> Nguyen Dinh Chieu (1822–1888)

THE REVOLUTION, having begun, needed ever more recruits; but most Vietnamese still did not understand what it meant. Even those who longed for a better world and who had convinced themselves of its necessity had not worked out how society, culture, and politics should be transformed and what roles to assign to the individual and the family in the new order. Nor did they know how to go about waging revolution. They were about to serve an arduous apprenticeship.

In Tonkin and Annam, where politics was a forbidden topic, revolution lay outside the bounds of legitimate public discourse. The word "revolution" had only recently been introduced into the Vietnamese language, probably through the writings of Liang Ch'i-ch'ao (who had probably encountered the word as a Japanese neologism). But the meaning of the term that had been adopted, "changing the Mandate of Heaven" *(cach mang)*, could not be explored in an open and systematic way. Little literature was available on the subject; French-language materials did not circulate as freely as in Cochinchina, and Chinese materials were usually confiscated at the border. When it came to defining revolution, local Vietnamese were thus left to their own devices. The notion of changing the Mandate of Heaven, redolent as it was of classical connotations, could be interpreted in any number of ways without recourse to historical experience, opening the way to misunderstandings.

The ignorance prevalent among old-style literati on the subject is amply illustrated in a thirty-two-page tract by Nguyen Thuong

Huyen entitled "On Revolution" *(Luan cach mang)*.[1] Huyen had fled to China after the Sûreté discovered he had written anonymous letters criticizing Vietnamese mandarins for their servility and French officials for their cruelty.[2] Freed by exile from censorship, he tried to wrestle with the topic of revolution. Huyen was more comfortable using a classical style, and even in dating the pamphlet, he had used an old-fashioned form: the nineteenth of the twelfth month of the year Giap Ty (3 January 1925). A misguided attempt at definition through etymology led him to conclude that the idea of changing the Mandate of Heaven originally came from the Book of Changes, where it was symbolized by the trigram meaning "fire in the lake." Having thus domesticated the alien concept and equated it with dynastic change, he went on to claim that brutal repression by the French was responsible for revolution's failure in Vietnam. Nonetheless, he concluded, it was possible to wage a peaceful and bloodless revolution; he therefore advocated a boycott movement similar to Gandhi's in India. Throughout the tract, Nguyen Thuong Huyen defined neither the process nor the goal of revolution.

Despite the evident constraints under which Tonkin and Annam-based anticolonial activists were forced to labor, there was some benefit from their earnest attempts to domesticate foreign ideas. Compelled to learn about revolution the hard way and in their mother tongue, they acquired valuable experience in explaining what it meant to themselves and to others; this eventually allowed them to bridge the gap between elite and mass politics. By contrast, in Cochinchina, the motto of the French Revolution had become an integral part of public discourse, used as a rationalization of the French *mission civilisatrice* and a yardstick with which to assess the colonial record. Both opponents and proponents of revolution were able to argue their case with reference to key documents of the French Enlightenment, and even to Marxist doctrine, but there was a negative side to this freedom of expression. Materials that were easily accessible in French were not allowed to circulate in Vietnamese. This tended to reinforce elitist tendencies among the French-educated urban elements, who thought of revolution as something to be done for the people rather than by the masses. Unconscious yet of the need to reach out to the populace, they were content to dispute the meaning of revolution among themselves in a language that shut out most of their compatriots. Moreover, their interest in discussion was not matched by an equal interest in organization-building. The individualist orientation of Cochinchinese political culture, so powerfully symbolized by Nguyen An Ninh, made revolution as much a vehicle of self-expression as a means of overthrowing colonial rule. Although there were plenty of revolutionaries in the South, there was no single effective revolutionary organization. Thus, though the revolutionary tide swept through all three regions of Vietnam at the same time, its effect on the local political landscapes was very different.

Would-be revolutionaries with a better grasp of ideology than Nguyen Thuong Huyen were drawn to variants of socialist and anarchist thought. By the 1920s, these two ideological currents, which Phan Boi Chau had earlier encountered in a single hyphenated form, had become antagonistic, forcing adherents of revolution to choose between them. Both presented politics as a moral enterprise, but pitched at different levels. Anarchism, especially in its libertarian strain, responded to the interest of the young in marrying the emancipation of the individual from social constraints with the liberation of the nation from foreign rule. Its iconoclastic disdain of authority appealed particularly to radicals whose first taste of politics had consisted of insurrection in the classroom. In contrast to this emergent individualism, socialism, as it came to Vietnam through Lenin's works, resonated with the long-standing collectivist orientation of Vietnamese public life. At the beginning, the chief appeal of socialism lay in the Leninist organizational doctrine, which directly addressed the quest for an effective movement of opposition to French rule; interest in the Marxist theory of history came later.

To which ideological current would the neophyte revolutionaries be drawn? Apart from quirks of personal predilection, there was a certain degree of serendipity at work: where they came from, who their friends and relatives were, where they went, all this influenced their ideological choices. The experiences of Vietnamese émigrés in their two countries of exile, China and France, varied considerably.

In China, socialism had definitely triumphed over anarchism. The leadership of the Kuomintang was no longer as helpful as in the days when Phan Boi Chau had been active, but the Chinese Communist Party (CCP) was able to provide considerable assistance to the revolutionaries in exile. This assistance, which operated at both the ideological and the organizational levels, had the effect of shielding the Vietnamese who migrated into the orbit of the CCP from competing influences.

The émigrés in France were less directly involved in organized politics than their counterparts in China. The involvement of the French Communist Party in anticolonial issues had declined since the departure of Nguyen Ai Quoc for the Soviet Union. Furthermore, the French Communist Party was a marginal force in French politics, and by no means the only one on the left. Since the repression of the Kronstadt Uprising, hostility between anarchists and supporters of the Soviet Union had increased. The loose relationship between French Communists and Vietnamese émigrés allowed the latter greater exposure to the major ideological currents of the times; but it gave them little direct experience of political organization and exacerbated individualistic tendencies among them.

Finally, those who stayed at home came across forbidden political knowledge in haphazard fashion by reading smuggled materials or coming into contact with returnees. Whatever they did, they were greatly circumscribed by the need to operate clandestinely and by their imperfect understanding of events and trends outside Vietnam's borders. After the onset of student strikes, increased contacts with anticolonial activists abroad considerably lessened the isolation of those in Vietnam, and Vietnamese revolutionary culture became somewhat more integrated.

The Vietnamese Youth League

Nguyen Thuong Huyen had sent a copy of "On Revolution" to Nguyen Ai Quoc. Although Nguyen Ai Quoc had arrived in China from the Soviet Union only a few months earlier, he was already emerging as the leading figure in the Vietnamese anticolonial community there, eclipsing Phan Boi Chau, whose secretary Nguyen Thuong Huyen had become. Using the flowery language of the Confucian scholar, Huyen respectfully solicited Nguyen Ai Quoc's comments on his efforts.

Literally and figuratively, Nguyen Ai Quoc had traveled a long way in the eight years since he had arrived in France, full of enthusiasm for Wilson's advocacy of self-determination for colonial peoples. Until he showed up in Moscow in early 1924, the Comintern had paid no attention to Vietnam, seeing it largely as an appendage of China. But two tracts in Vietnamese, probably written by Nguyen Ai Quoc, were published during his stay in the Soviet Union.[3] At the Fifth Congress, he demanded that more attention be paid to colonial matters, arguing that revolution in Europe would succeed only after it had taken place in the colonies.⁴ Shortly after the Fifth Congress, Nguyen Ai Quoc followed Mikhail Borodin to Canton, ostensibly as an interpreter, but in reality to promote communism in Indochina and in the rest of Southeast Asia as well.⁵

Nguyen Ai Quoc decided that there was little possibility of launching a full-fledged, openly Communist movement among the expatriates in China, since "no one yet understood the meaning of the word communism."⁶ After talking to a wide range of émigrés, in particular members of the Society of Like Hearts, he concluded that the Society and other émigré organizations "knew nothing about politics and much less about organizing the masses."⁷ Nguyen Thuong Huyen's tract, which he received soon afterward, confirmed his worst suspicions about the political naiveté of the Vietnamese expatriates in China. Using the pseudonym of Ly Thuy, Nguyen Ai Quoc fired back a reply that was nearly as long as Huyen's pamphlet, and in which he barely contained his exasperation with Huyen's muddle-headed thinking.⁸ He scoffed at the notion that the term *cach mang* might have been taken from the Book of Changes, and insisted on the need to differentiate between "reform," "evolution," and "revolution." He rejected reformism on the ground that "even after reforms, there would always remain something of the original order," and explained that "revolution is the total replacement of an *ancien régime* by a new one." Criticizing Nguyen Thuong Huyen's scholarly obsession with education and censorship, he enumerated the many other domains in which the French were trampling over the rights of the Vietnamese. He berated him for confusing boycott movements with revolution, ends with means. When Huyen wailed over French brutality, he answered rudely: "What do you want? That they should give us full freedom to do everything we like, to seek every means to challenge them? You want them to do nothing to prevent us from harming their interests? Instead of blaming others, it is much more reasonable to blame ourselves. We must ask ourselves: Why are the French able to oppress us? Why is our people so ignorant? Why have we not been able to successfully wage revolution? What must be done?" He concluded: "You have expended twenty pages on a discussion of revolution, but you have not said: what must be done before revolution; what must be done during revolution; what must be done after revolution."

Nguyen Ai Quoc had given much thought to those questions. In February 1925, he created the League of Oppressed People of the

East, an internationalist organization similar to the Intercolonial Union, which included Koreans, Taiwanese, Indians, Vietnamese, Chinese, Malays, and Indonesians. He then turned his attention to creating an exclusively Vietnamese organization.[9] Though dismayed by the lack of political sophistication of the adherents of the Society of Like Hearts, Nguyen Ai Quoc had been impressed by their patriotism. He found enough suitable recruits among them to establish a secret organization called the Communist Youth Corps (Thanh Nien Cong San Doan), which initially had nine members.[10] Except for the Tonkin-born Lam Duc Thu, all came from his own native province of Nghe An in Annam. Some, like Thu, had previously belonged to Phan Boi Chau's Restoration League.[11]

The Communist Youth Corps formed the secret nucleus of a larger, public organization which presented itself as an essentially nationalist and unitary movement, in the spirit of the Comintern's United Front policy in China. In setting up this public organization, Nguyen Ai Quoc cast his net as wide as possible, lamenting that "because there is no spirit of solidarity among our compatriots, barely two hundred thousand Frenchmen are able to dominate a population of twenty million inhabitants."[12] He declared: "Our goal is as follows: To unite all our compatriots so as to bring about the triumph of political, judicial, administrative and economic sovereignty for the people, for the people is all."[13] He went on: "Revolution can be compared to climbing a mountain. The stronger make it to the top, the weaker remain half-way; everyone climbs according to his strength. If we compelled everybody to climb all the way up to the top, many people would refuse to accompany us." The organization was deliberately aimed at young people whose political ideas were still unformed despite their growing disaffection; it was publicly called Vietnamese Revolutionary Youth (Viet Nam Kach Menh Thanh Nien). To initiates, however, it was known as Vietnamese Revolutionary League (Viet Nam Kach Menh Dong Chi; hereinafter, it will be referred to as the Vietnamese Youth League or the Youth League).[14]

The Vietnamese Youth League was formally launched on 21 June 1925 with the publication of the first issue of its journal, *Youth (Thanh Nien)*. Nguyen Ai Quoc's efforts to set up a new revolutionary organization may have benefited from the removal of Phan Boi Chau from the scene three days earlier. The Youth League set up recruiting points in ports and on the Chinese border to facilitate the sending of materials into the country and bringing out new trainees.[15] One of its earliest recruits was Nguyen Luong Bang, who was introduced into the Youth League in late 1925. Bang was working on a French ship near Canton when he was befriended by a Chinese sailor who later turned out to be a member of the Seamen's Union of the Chinese Communist Party. Having ascertained that Bang hated the French, the Chinese sailor took him on a pilgrimage to the tomb of Pham Hong Thai and introduced him to Ho Tung Mau, who in turn led him to Nguyen Ai Quoc.[16]

The League expanded rather slowly in its first year of existence, and picked up momentum only with the student strikes. In September 1926, Bang volunteered to return home to recruit new adherents. He left Canton, armed with detailed instructions from Nguyen Ai Quoc. Bang was to seek out old friends in his native village or in the city. In every conversation, he should bring up the subject of colonial oppression:

> If my interlocutor seemed to agree I would then ask: "Will we let them oppress us like this forever?" In turn, I would be asked: "Where is the strength to do otherwise?" I would then reply: "Strength is in unity; if we are united, then the guns of the enemy become our guns." Little by little, I would lead friends and relatives into mutual-help associations, fraternal associations, and so forth. I would recruit the more active ones into the Youth League. The good recruits would then go on to recruit more. In this way, I would expand the movement.[17]

The League had additional ways of promoting its ideas and recruiting members. During its lifetime, it published four periodicals, each aimed at a slightly different audience. *Youth,* which appeared on a weekly basis between 21 June 1925 and May 1930, had the widest audience.[18] It was the League's public platform, although it circulated clandestinely in Vietnam. Only one hundred copies of each issue of *Youth* were printed, but it was required reading for the whole membership. As a result, each printed version was handcopied many times and passed on to others.[19]

Youth was not strong on theory; it did not aim to present reasoned arguments, merely ones that would sound persuasive to youths eager for action but lacking ideological direction. Its purpose was to promote adherence to the Youth League by showing the importance of collective action to the success of revolution. Since it consisted of only a couple of sheets, a single article was often spread over several issues.

A favorite technique was the question and answer format. Questions served as a pretext for proselytism and were not always fully answered; sometimes they were sidestepped altogether when they would have taken the editor too far from the position he wished to promote. Although the journal's thrust was unmistakably left-wing, its ideological underpinnings during the first year were not clearly discernible. On 19 July 1925, Nguyen Ai Quoc explained: "If the people wishes to claim its rights, it needs political parties. In order to have them, it must unite" (no. 5). For the next fifty-five issues, he concentrated on explaining basic political concepts and refuting rival ideologies. On 22 August 1926, he asked his readers: "To which party should we adhere?" By then, he had sufficiently undermined the plausibility of most parties to confine himself to only a few: syndicalism, socialist-associationism, state socialism, anarchism, and finally communism. Two issues later, after having prepared the ground for more than a year, he urged his readers to choose communism.

With *Cloche Fêlée,* Nguyen An Ninh had achieved a bigger readership, but he had never converted it into an organized political party, and had seen his following disintegrate in the wake of his imprisonment. Nguyen Ai Quoc, however, was fully conscious of the importance of organized collective action. To Nguyen Thuong Huyen, who had written admiringly of the independence movements of Egypt and India, Nguyen Ai Quoc had replied:

> In India and Egypt, the different political parties number many adherents, some of whom are in charge of propaganda, others of organizing clubs. There are organizations among students, farmers, workers, civil servants. All obey blindly the orders of their party. The propagandists are in charge of awakening their people. Everyone knows how to love his fatherland, everyone knows what revolution is about. The programs of each party have all been carefully studied; the implementation of every project has been mapped out down to the last step. The affiliates are numerous; the regulations that control their actions are very strict.

New members no longer trickled in one by one. Those who managed to elude arrest arrived in China in groups of ten or twenty at a time. They were students expelled from school for taking part in strikes, or others made restless by the political ferment. Recruiters in Vietnam would play on their thirst for knowledge and their hatred of the French, suggest that they could resume their studies abroad, and say nothing of the political character of the League until they had arrived in China. One of the most fertile recruiting grounds was the prestigious Lycée Albert Sarraut in Hanoi. From its ranks emerged a number of prominent leaders of the Vietnamese Communist movement, including Pham van Dong, a court mandarin's son who joined the League in late 1927. The Franco-Annamite school of Nam Dinh, also hit by strikes in 1927, produced its share of recruits; among them was Dang Xuan Khu, who later adopted the pseudonym Truong Chinh ("Long March"). Most of these recruits were very young. Members of the Youth League ranged in age from seventeen to twenty-five. Of a group of nine who traveled together to Canton in 1927, none was yet twenty years old.[20]

Criteria for admission into the League were rigorous. Membership was open to men and women over seventeen years of age who accepted the aims of the League and were sponsored by two members of good standing. Gamblers, opium-smokers, criminals, and other undesirables were excluded. To make sure that recruits were properly screened, sponsors were held responsible for the crimes committed by their protégés. Punishments for infractions of the rules were decided by majority vote at the appropriate level. Before being admitted to full membership, a new recruit underwent a training seminar lasting from three weeks to four months. Trainees often went to the headquarters of the Chinese Communist Peasants' Union to take their meals and listen to lectures by CCP cadres or Comintern agents.[21] Between 1925 and 1927, some two hundred students attended the training seminar at 13 Wen Ming Street.[22] Hong Son and Ho Tung Mau assisted Nguyen Ai Quoc by conducting sessions at which students made reports and speeches and answered hostile questions from their fellow students. This was meant to simulate the kind of experience they would face when trying to make new converts and explain the program of the Youth League.[23] The most promising recruits were sent to Whampoa Military Academy for further training. A few went on to Moscow to attend the Workers' University of the East. Le Hong Phong was the first to go from Canton to Moscow in early 1927; by autumn, fifty Vietnamese were registered at the Workers' University.[24] The rest were sent back to Vietnam.[25]

In 1927, Nguyen Ai Quoc gathered the text of the lectures he had been giving in the seminar into a pamphlet, published by the propaganda branch of the League of Oppressed People under the title *The Road to Revolution (Con duong kach menh)*. The cover of the pamphlet was adorned with a picture of a man in fetters; underneath was a quotation from Lenin's *What Is to Be Done:* "Without revolutionary reasoning there can be no revolutionary mobilization. Only by following the most advanced revolutionary reasoning can the revolutionary party fulfill its responsibility as revolutionary vanguard."[26] In the preface, Nguyen Ai Quoc explained why he wrote the pamphlet: "It is to explain to our people why we must wage revolution in order to survive; why revolution is a common enterprise, and not the work of one or two people; to use the history of other countries' revolutions to serve as examples for us; to teach the people about international movements; to discuss who is our friend; who is our enemy? What is to be done in order to wage revolution?"

The Road to Revolution contained a long analysis of the differences between the First, Second, and Third Internationals, followed by a discussion of the various bureaus of the Third International, and the kinds of organizations the Youth League should create. After explaining the various meanings of revolution, he went on to discuss the differences between capitalist, nationalist, and class revolutions, itemizing the lessons to be drawn from each type. The American Revolution, he explained, had been a bourgeois revolution, and therefore an unfinished one. British colonial rule had been overthrown, but the American government was profoundly reactionary; as a result, American farmers and workers were miserable and still dreamed of revolution. The French Revolution and the Paris Commune taught that "it is necessary to have a very strong organization to wage revolution; that women and children can be helpful; that the French Revolution has sacrificed many people without flinching. If we want to wage revolution, we must not be afraid of sacrifices either."

Despite his endorsement of revolutionary violence, Nguyen Ai Quoc discouraged the use of the terrorist tactics favored by the anarchist Society of Like Hearts, from which the founders of the Vietnamese Youth League had come. Hong Son, who helped conduct the training seminar, had assassinated Phan Ba Ngoc and had taken part in the attempt against Merlin. But Nguyen Ai Quoc emphasized: "Assassination is reckless, and yields little result, because if you kill someone, there is always someone else, how can you get rid of them all? Revolution means uniting all the oppressed people to overthrow the oppressing class, it does not consist of asking a couple of people to assassinate two or three kings, nine or ten officials."[27] New recruits were taken to pledge allegiance to the League in front of the tomb of

Pham Hong Thai; but, though they were supposed to keep alive his patriotic spirit, they were also taught to eschew his tactics.

Each returnee was considered the nucleus of a new cell and was responsible for finding new adherents. Since the League's core was made up of the Nghe An–born members of the Society of Like Hearts, its membership reflected this regional strength. Hundreds of recruits were trained on the spot in the country, including two hundred in northern Annam alone. With an expanding membership, regional committees were set up in 1927 for each of Vietnam's three regions; below were provincial, district, municipal, and village committees. Control of the Youth League remained with the China-based Central Committee. Although its organizational structure was remarkably similar to the one drawn (on paper) by the Society of Like Hearts, there was a fundamental difference in that the Youth League, following guidelines established by the Comintern in 1924, emphasized the formation of cells by place of work and occupation.[28] Auxiliary associations were created to organize sympathizers not deemed suited for full membership. Into these went workers and peasants whom the League began to recruit in 1928.

But the explosive domestic growth of the League took place without strong guidance from the Central Committee for, beginning in 1927, it fell victim to successive waves of anti-Communist repression in China. The United Front that had existed between the CCP and the KMT since 1923 came to an abrupt end in April 1927 when the KMT raided the Soviet embassy in Peking. Nguyen Ai Quoc had been tipped off about the impending raid by a League member who served in the Canton police. He was able to go into hiding in Hankow, eventually resurfacing in Moscow.[29] Most Youth League members who had been arrested were released when the anti-Communist campaign subsided a few weeks later, except for Hong Son, who had joined the CCP at Nguyen Ai Quoc's behest in August 1925.[30] Because the KMT preferred to ignore the Vietnamese émigrés' anti-French activities so long as they did not meddle in Chinese domestic politics, the Youth League was largely unscathed by the second anti-Communist wave of December 1927. But Ho Tung Mau, who had joined the CCP in March 1926, was arrested in December 1928 during the third anti-Communist wave. Fortunately for the organization, Hong Son was released from jail at about that time and was able to take over the reins of the Youth League. Although the Central Committee remained under the leadership of its most experienced members, the League's activities were greatly disrupted nevertheless, especially when it was forced to move from Canton to Hankow and later to Hong Kong. Communications between the Central Committee and the domestic branches of the League suffered considerably.

Epigones of the Youth League

The travails of the Central Committee in China coincided with the growing success of its propaganda work at home. By 1928, materials produced by the League were being spread by groups with no overt connection with it. The Bao Ton publishing house was created in Saigon to publish anticolonial propaganda, some of which came straight from the League. Diep van Ky, the publisher of a Cochinchinese newspaper called *Morning Bell (Than Chung)*, brought out a *History of Revolution* which turned out to be a collection of lectures given at Whampoa.[31] Children in Annam sang revolutionary jingles.[32] The influence of the League was reflected in the changing orientation of anticolonial organizations operating within the country. Many were composed of intellectuals, including some Confucian literati but mostly students and teachers at Franco-Annamite schools or employees in the colonial bureaucracy. They tended to emphasize propaganda and advocacy, pinning their hopes on appeals to reason. While émigrés were already talking openly of the inevitability of a bloody revolution, Vietnam-based groups still shied away from embracing terrorist tactics. But, although they did not fully accept the idea of violent revolution, two of these groups adopted the organizational model provided by the League. They were the Phuc Viet, based in Annam, and the Vietnamese Nationalist Party, which had developed from the Nam Dong Publishing Society.

The Phuc Viet had decided in the summer of 1925 to make contact with émigrés in China and Siam. Le Duy Diem (also known as Le Loi), who spoke fluent Chinese, was chosen to carry out this mission. After a short stay in Siam, Diem arrived in Canton in late 1925. He found himself shunned by some exiles who suspected him of being a Sûreté informer because he lacked letters of introduction; but he was warmly welcomed by the Youth League.[33] Coming from Annam, where discourse of almost any kind was heavily circumscribed, Le Duy Diem was amazed at how active the League was: its members discussed politics every day; they held seminars and conferences; Vietnamese and Chinese newspapers were openly distributed.[34] Diem was told to obtain proof that he was the representative of a truly revolutionary party. He was asked to outline his party's political program more fully and to bring along some students on his next trip. Diem arrived back in Vinh in June 1926, just as the first wave of student strikes peaked. After hearing his report, the Phuc Viet decided to explore further the possibility of an alliance and even fusion with the Youth League. At Diem's suggestion, the party's name was changed to the Vietnamese Revolutionary Party (Viet Nam Cach Mang Dang) in order to convince the Youth League that it was committed to revolution and not merely reform.[35] Diem then returned to Canton at the head of his party's delegation and with five recruits for the League. Not only did they join the League, but so did all of the delegates. Thus, in the summer of 1926, even as some of its members toyed with the idea of Franco-Annamite collaboration, the Vietnamese Revolutionary Party became a channel of recruitment into the Youth League. This gradual political reorientation angered some of its original members (one of them, Hoang Duc Thi, eventually wrote a history of the group for the Sûreté). The resulting friction among its leaders prevented it from coalescing into a tight-knit organization, a problem made more acute by the systematic drain of its best and most energetic adherents into the Youth League.

The Nam Dong Publishing Society was also affected by the radicalization of domestic politics and the effects of Youth League propaganda, but with very different results. At the time, Tonkin fairly bristled with small, localized groups, made up of Western-educated youths eager to do something "for the revolution."[36] In one such group was Nguyen Thai Hoc, a twenty-seven-year-old former student at the School of Commerce. Hoc was already known to the Sûreté, for, since 1925, he had submitted proposal after proposal to improve the condition of the Vietnamese people.[37] He had first advocated that the colonial regime protect Vietnamese economic interests by establishing a School of Industry; he had called for the freedom to create popular libraries in all villages and industrial towns. On another occasion, he proposed reforms to improve the living conditions of the poor. Finally, he requested permission to found a journal dedicated to the protection and promotion of native economic interests. None of the requests was granted. Meeting only with rebuffs, Nguyen Thai Hoc progressed steadily leftward.

"You listen to Gandhi spouting about peaceful revolution. But ask yourself, what has Gandhi managed to accomplish for India?" demanded Hoc of a friend in the Nam Dong Publishing Society in 1927.[38] The setting was an organizational meeting at which the Society fused with various provincial groups to found the Vietnamese Nationalist Party (Viet Nam Quoc Dan Dang, or VNQDD). At that meeting, held on 25 December 1927, Nguyen Thai Hoc was chosen as chairman of the VNQDD for a six-month term. With his ascendancy, the Party committed itself decisively to the principle of violent revolution. The VNQDD envisaged a revolution in three stages. The first would be an entirely clandestine party-building period, when recruitment would be emphasized. The second stage would be a semipublic, semi-clandestine period of preparing for revolution through stepped-up propaganda and the creation of organizations: workers', peasants', and soldiers' syndicates, students' associations, and so forth. Then would come a period of destruction of the enemy and the "establishment of a democratic republic in order to bring independence and freedom to the fatherland, happiness and progress to the people."[39] The immediate post-revolutionary period was further divided into three phases. The first would consist of establishing local revolutionary governments as the enemy was destroyed. The second would focus on education. The Party would govern the country, and teach the population about the rights and responsibilities of democratic government. The last stage would consist of national elections, the establishment of a constitution, and the return of sovereignty to the people.[40]

The VNQDD resembled other anticolonial groups in its combination of a vaguely defined program of social transformation with the notion of unitary national liberation. Equally important was the fact that it drew both its name and its ideological inspiration from the Kuomintang as it existed prior to the collapse of the United Front. As a result, traces of Communist influence could be found in both its political program and its organizational structure. Its ideology was an amalgamation of the ideals of the French Revolution and of Sun Yat-sen's Three People's Principles.[41] The Party's ultimate goal was summed up in the slogan "democracy, nation, society." The VNQDD adopted the principle of working for "national revolution" for the "recovery of independence" and pledged itself to help "small and weak nations to liberate themselves from enslavement." It pledged to work for the liberation of all from every kind of oppression, but refused to consider support for world revolution, on the grounds that this smacked of communism and divisive class struggle.[42] Though the

VNQDD had a more fully articulated program than most other parties, there remained large gaps caused by its refusal to disaggregate the concept of nation into its various components with potentially conflicting interests.

Organizationally, the VNQDD was a close copy of the Youth League. This was not surprising since Hoang van Tung, head of a small anticolonial group which merged with the Nam Dong Publishing Society, and a friend of Ton Quang Phiet, proposed that the VNQDD adopt the organizational structure of the Revolutionary Party, a structure that was inspired by the Youth League.[43] In time-honored fashion, the Party opened a hotel to serve as a meeting point and raise funds. Thanks to the assistance of a Vietnamese financier, the party was able to conduct an active propaganda campaign among young civil servants, and especially among teachers and students. A special effort to recruit colonial troops into the Party was also highly successful. Following the KMT model, the VNQDD created a women's branch, in which the wives of several leaders of the party became involved. And, despite the overwhelming preponderance of intellectuals in the party, there was also a small but active workers' section. Thus, unlike the Vietnamese Revolutionary Party, the VNQDD managed to spell out a political program and a strategy of revolution which it could call its own, however striking the ideological and organizational similarities with the Youth League. This fact alone made its members less receptive to the blandishments of Youth League recruiters. Instead of fusing, the two organizations were soon engaged in competing recruitment drives that targeted essentially the same strata of the population and made use of similar rhetoric. Sooner or later, the VNQDD and the Youth League were bound to collide.

Ultimately, revolutionaries in Annam and Tonkin were divided into three groups—the Youth League, the Vietnamese Revolutionary Party, and the VNQDD—that shared a common orientation and competed for the same membership. They all looked to China rather than to France for inspiration. They had the same preoccupation with the political and the social above the cultural and the moral. For them, freedom was a collective rather than an individual issue. Consciously in the case of the Youth League, and less so in the case of the other two groups, they were gravitating toward a Leninist organizational model. Their interchangeability was a source of intense competition but also of constant fluidity.

No such unity characterized Cochinchinese politics. The Youth

League was making as many converts in Cochinchina as it did in Tonkin and Annam, but it also had to contend with more serious ideological competition as well. With their political visibility and economic resources, the Constitutionalists presented a plausible alternative to advocates of revolution. But by far the greatest challenge came from anarchism. It appealed to the very same potential recruits as the Youth League, and it had a formidable champion in the person of Nguyen An Ninh.

The Limits of Populism

Nguyen Ai Quoc was well aware of the seductive appeal of anarchism, especially of its French strain, which Cochinchina-born Vietnamese would most likely encounter. With its exaltation of the individual as the primary locus of revolution, its emphasis on moral transformation, its rejection of authority, and its faith in populism, anarchism was anathema to the creation of a Leninist party. Nguyen Ai Quoc did his best to combat it. In the sixth issue of *Youth* on 26 July 1925, he offered a cursory survey of different types of political movements, including anarchists, Communists, conservatives, laborites, the Ku Klux Klan, fascists, democrats, liberals, nationalists, republicans, royalists, and Socialists; then, two issues later, he presented his own analysis of anarchism:

> This party knows no unity, no friends, no rules, no program, no government. Everybody must be free and must have no masters. This leads us to think that its goal is noble and exalted. But we cannot apply these principles. Why? In order that everyone be free, every single government would have to be overthrown to begin with. Then every single person would have to be virtuous and without weakness, free of every ambition and of every self-serving feeling. Only on this condition could we do without rules. But people are far from perfect. Out of every hundred people, ninety-nine are ignorant, greedy, mean. Everyone wants to dominate everyone else. Nowadays, anarchism is nonsense; to spread anarchism is as stupid as proposing to a dying man that he should fight in hand-to-hand combat, or run a race.

On 14 August 1926, in an article entitled "Freedom and Laws," Nguyen Ai Quoc returned to the topic:

Nowadays, Peter [Kropotkin] advocates anarcho-communism, that is, the redistribution of riches and the suppression of laws. In our opinion, this doctrine is still unfeasible. We must first wrest economic power from capitalist hands then use laws to punish those guilty of crimes against society. Peter's supporters claim that all laws are tyrannical in character; they ignore the fact that people are still corrupt, mean, ignorant, and that they would transgress against the freedom of others and would neglect to fulfill their duties if their passions, their hatreds, were not reined in by laws. In sum, if we reform the mode of wealth distribution, and if we reeducate the people, then we will be able to envisage the suppression of laws.[44]

At first, Nguyen Ai Quoc prudently conceded that, although unrealizable in the present, achieving a society without laws was nonetheless an admirable ideal. But as time went by, he became more strident. On 22 August 1926, just before advocating communism, he again marshaled his arguments against anarchism and concluded: "In reality, anarchist theories dupe the weak and sow disorder in society." Nguyen Ai Quoc wished to refute not so much the anarchist vision of post-revolutionary society as the anarchist critique of political parties and authority, which undermined his efforts to build a strong Leninist party. In his seminar, new adherents of the Youth League were guided through further critiques of anarchism as well as of Sun Yat-sen's Three People's Principles, the only two ideologies that posed enough of a threat to communism to merit discussion in the seminar.[45]

Both the potency and the limits of the anarchist vision were amply illustrated by Nguyen An Ninh's attempt to build a revolutionary populist movement, which became known as the Nguyen An Ninh Secret Society. Ninh showed his future wife a picture of Lenin; but the man he admired was the benevolent leader of the Soviet Union, of which he maintained an extremely flattering view, not the ruthless builder of a revolutionary vanguard. For a long time, Ninh had recoiled at the human price of a Bolshevik-style revolution, but he had come to believe in its inevitability. When he was in Paris in the spring of 1925, Ninh, speaking more freely than he dared at home, had warned: "Oppression must be met by violence and rebellion ... In four years, revolt will break out and catastrophe will thunder through Indochina."[46]

Before his incarceration, Ninh had talked of the need for a new elite. He had not actually envisaged it as an organized party, but more as a loose movement resulting from the moral and intellectual transformation of a few individuals. Like the European anarchists from whom he drew inspiration, he was uncomfortable with the inherently authoritarian nature of political parties. He had also been deeply disappointed by the swift disintegration of Jeune Annam, most of whose leaders were now abroad, and by the erosion of his own popular support. Ninh was growing more hostile toward the bourgeoisie, but was also loath to abandon the notion of classless revolution. Disenchantment with youth-oriented politics and an inbred dislike of authority led the incurably romantic Ninh from one pole of anarchist thought to the other. He thought that the key to creating a nonauthoritarian liberation movement could be found in anarchist populism. He embraced the notion of popular spontaneity as the wellspring of revolution. As the Nietzschean language of his play on the Trung sisters, which he wrote in 1928, attests, his libertarian streak did not become submerged altogether.[47] Like Tolstoy in his *Narodnaya polyana,* "he wanted to give the example of a revolutionary, free but laborious like the people, at home anywhere in simple cotton pyjamas and a straw hat and carrying only a jug of water."[48]

Herzen's famous dictum, "Go to the people," had been taken up by other Russian anarchists, in particular Bakunin. But who were the people? Bakunin disagreed with Marx and Engels on the historical role of the *lumpenproletariat:* "It is in it and in it alone and not in the middle-class stratum of the working masses that the spirit and the strength of the future social revolution reside."[49] Before converting to anarchism, Bakunin had been a keen student of secret societies and social bandits. Whether consciously or not, Ninh followed Bakunin's intellectual trajectory. Nguyen An Ninh had grown up in Hoc Mon; it was his "territory" and would so remain throughout the rest of his career, the area of his greatest popularity and influence, which other revolutionaries automatically conceded to him.[50] Hoc Mon was a suburb of Saigon whose chief claim to fame was that a band of adherents of a secret group, the Heaven and Earth Society, had assassinated an infamous collaborator there in 1884. To Ninh, therefore, the "people" included members of the Saigon underclass whose ethos resonated with his own: "All men of the four seas are brothers. Assist one another in times of trouble; in life or in death we shall not be parted."[51] In 1925, when considering possible bases for his notion of a modern organization of resistance, Ninh had already thought of Phan Xich Long, a leader of the Saigon underworld who had been involved in not only the Heaven and Earth Society but also millenarian sects of the Mekong Delta in the riots of 1913 and 1916. Although Ninh's references to Phan Xich Long were rather patronizing, the publication in Saigon in 1926 of Georges Coulet's *Sociétés secrètes en terre d'Annam* may have given him a different perspective on secret societies.[52] Basing his analysis almost entirely on police data about the riots of 1913 and 1916, Coulet implied that secret societies and religious sects were the natural, indigenous modes of organization of the Vietnamese, that they were everywhere, and moreover, that they could be coopted by revolutionaries as had been done by Phan Boi Chau. In other words, they lent credence to Bakunin's description of social bandits as "instinctive revolutionaries."

Nguyen An Ninh was released in December 1926 on the condition that he forsake politics, and he arrived in France in August 1927.[53] He took part in meetings but seems to have been uncharacteristically subdued. Upon returning home in January 1928, he headed straight to his village of My Hoa in the suburbs of Saigon. Although the Sûreté kept watch on his movements, it was unable at first to detect signs of political activity. To all who cared to listen, Ninh declared that he had decided to embrace religion, an assertion which seemed quite plausible in view of his spiritual crisis of 1926, and his current fascination with the Cao Dai sect.

Founded in September 1926, the sect was the most important sign of the revival of religious sectarianism after a decade of comparative quiet caused by the repression of 1916–1917. Its founders, a group of Cochinchinese businessmen, landowners, and civil servants, all had, in one way or another, direct exposure to the Westernized urban culture that had emerged under colonial rule. But their intellectual roots were firmly embedded in popular culture rather than in the elite culture from which political figures as diverse as Pham Quynh, Bui Quang Chieu, and Nguyen An Ninh had come. The Cao Dai sect was their antidote to the anomie that preoccupied members of the intelligentsia. It consisted of mixing nativism and universalism in almost equal parts, by incorporating references to every religious current known to the sect founders into a single doctrine which remained firmly based in Sino-Vietnamese popular religion. A prolix hierarchical structure was their answer to the loss of social cohesion and the perceived organizational superiority of the West.[54] Before establishing the Cao Dai sect, its founders had been part of a spirit-medium cult; spiritism remained the foundation of Cao Dai religion. Teen-age mediums churned out messages from the Supreme Being which blended advice on cultic and moral practices with the familiar apocalyptic rhetoric of Vietnamese millenarianism. The Social Darwinian vision of perpetual struggle for survival had by then percolated into popular culture and was incorporated into the millenarian rhetoric of the Cao Dai sect, but with a twist. It was presented, not as an eternal law, but as a world-historical stage: in the new millennium, competition over limited resources would be rendered unnecessary by unbounded prosperity.

Most young revolutionaries had become too Westernized to be attracted to this religious hodgepodge of East and West. But Nguyen An Ninh, the populist rediscovering his roots while searching for a new culture, was impressed by the sect's ability to tap into Vietnamese popular culture and to attract members by the thousands. There were rumors that the Cao Dai sect had financed Ninh's trip to France in 1927, though his supporters claimed that the funds had come from the sale of his printing press and of various pamphlets he had authored.[55] Fascinated though he was by Caodaism, Ninh did not join the sect. But he gave every sign of having embraced the religious life: he shaved his head and became a strict vegetarian; his house now displayed an altar dedicated to the God of War, and he spoke constantly of Gandhi and Tagore.

Although his interest in religion and mysticism was real, so was his streak of populism. Within months, the Sûreté began to pick up rumors that Ninh was agitating among workers and peasants around the Saigon area, using techniques traditionally associated with the Heaven and Earth Society. Ninh always traveled a great deal on his bicycle, purportedly to sell balms and other medicinal concoctions fabricated by his uncle. Eventually, it became common knowledge that whenever he stopped by a pagoda to rest, "monks would come out to greet him in their ceremonial robes, and light incense sticks in his honor, while peasants gave him money as reimbursement for his travel expenses."[56] That the Sûreté did not fathom the additional purpose of his trips sooner was a sign that he had absorbed a few basic lessons about clandestine work. Ninh's two closest associates were Pham van Chieu, a working-class organizer and a leader in the Saigon underworld, and Phan van Hum, a former student of Georges Coulet who had written a fan letter to Ninh in 1924.[57] Phan van Hum was a rarity among young southerners, for he was versed in classical scholarship. At the School of Public Works in Hanoi, he had amused himself by producing a handwritten weekly devoted to correcting the stylistic errors committed by Pham Quynh in both French and Chinese.⁵⁸ Hubris indeed, since Pham Quynh's reputation rested largely on his mastery of both languages. After graduating, Hum had become a technical agent of the Public Works Bureau in Hue. He first drew attention to himself by donating part of his salary to Phan Boi Chau. He was asked to resign after he gave assistance to striking students from Dong Khanh School.⁵⁹ He returned home in Dong Nai province, shaved his head, and, equipped with an umbrella, went from pagoda to pagoda in search of monks with whom to discuss Buddhist dogma. It was on one such trip that he met Nguyen An Ninh. Coincidence or prearranged meeting? Despite all their precautions, the existence of a Nguyen An Ninh Secret Society (Hoi Kin Nguyen An Ninh) became known to the Sûreté by March 1928.⁶⁰ Details piled up little by little: the Society was also known as the Aspirations of Youth Party (Cao Vong Thanh Nien Dang) after Ninh's famous speech, "The Aspirations of Annamite Youth," and less commonly as the Youth Party (Thanh Nien Dang); it had a sketchy organization seemingly inspired by the Heaven and Earth Society:

> People went through villages, recruiting for membership into mutual friendship *(luong huu)* or mutual aid *(tuong te)* associations, so that in case of poverty, ill-health, or death, financial assistance would be provided to one's family. Upon entering the Society, people had to pay a fee of 1.50 piasters, or 5 piasters or only 30 cents, depending on their financial circumstances. They met to hold ceremonies to heaven and earth, to the spirits and genii, and to hold initiation rites. They swore on their lives not to separate, to help each other in times of hardships and to forever be friends.⁶¹

A description of the initiation rites undergone by thirty-three recruits appeared in the press during Ninh's trial the following year: "Strangest is the initiation rite. It is always held in a pagoda. Each pagoda entrance is guarded by two men armed with swords. A new recruit chooses a door through which to enter but the guards prevent him from entering by crossing their swords and asking: Where are you going? He answers: I am going to sacrifice myself for the defense of the fatherland. Similar answers are given at each place. Finally, once he has entered the pagoda, he is welcomed by the leaders. Then he must give an oath before he can be accepted as a soldier."⁶²

The initiation over, recruits were told they had joined the Nguyen

An Ninh Secret Society.⁶³ According to internal documents seized by the Sûreté, the Society supposedly included a quasi-military structure organized by villages, to which were added three sections recognizable by the color of their banners: a yellow banner for the section led by Nguyen An Ninh himself, a white banner for the women's section headed by his wife, and a blue banner for a section headed by one of his lieutenants in Vinh Long.⁶⁴ In traditional secret society fashion, the connection between various groups of members was extremely loose. How much responsibility Ninh bore for the secret society trappings of his movement is unclear, since he was not directly involved in recruiting and traveled only to make speeches after the groundwork had been laid by his lieutenants. It is conceivable that members of pre-existing secret societies had been roused from their lethargy by the activities of his allies and, in reorganizing themselves, were claiming, rightly or wrongly, affiliation with the Nguyen An Ninh Secret Society.

Through a combination of persuasion and intimidation, Ninh's associates were able to recruit seven hundred to eight hundred members, mostly among workers and peasants of the Saigon suburbs. Large numbers of people who joined the Nguyen An Ninh Secret Society also joined the Cao Dai sect under the influence of the apocalyptic warnings coming out of the Cao Dai temples.⁶⁵ With its network of temples, the sect constituted a formidable propaganda machine and became an important factor in Cochinchinese politics. Its leaders advised accommodationists such as Bui Quang Chieu to take their lead from more radical figures. This cannot have been pleasant for Chieu, who, for all his snobbery, also craved popularity. But, with another election looming, the Constitutionalists decided to mend fences with the radicals; Chieu had to swallow his pride. Duong van Giao, home from France, managed briefly to repair the relations between the "older moderates" and the "young extremists," strained since Chieu had earlier refused to support student strikes. On 25 December 1927, Giao declared that for neither Bui Quang Chieu nor Nguyen Phan Long was the policy of Franco-Annamite collaboration more than a tactic; it was never an article of faith. He counseled the radicals gathered at that meeting to ally themselves with older politicians "to profit from their experience and their social situation" and promised that he would work to persuade the moderates to abandon the policy of Franco-Annamite collaboration in favor of independence if the radicals would present their claims in less strident terms.⁶⁶

But the reconciliation was short-lived. In the spring of 1928, a squabble erupted between peasants and landowners in a village in Hoc Mon which included a sizable number of workers, many of whom were organized in gangs. The landowner-dominated village council had established a Society for the Encouragement of Learning (Khuyen Hoc Hoi), which enjoyed the support of Bui Quang Chieu. Prodded by the workers, the peasants in the village accused the councillors of exploiting this support to legitimate their intolerable oppression. Calling themselves the "Nguyen An Ninh side," the peasants declared: "How can Bui Quang Chieu be a match for Nguyen An Ninh?" Chieu's newspaper, *Tribune Indochinoise*, went to investigate and Chieu helped the council draw up a suit against the villagers. The Hoc Mon district police were also called in, but nothing came of their inquiries, the villagers having turned belatedly discreet.[67] But the existence of the Nguyen An Ninh Society was no longer a Sûreté secret.

On 28 September 1928, as Ninh and Hum returned from a speaking engagement, Ninh became involved in an altercation with a policeman. When the two men began exchanging blows, Hum went to his friend's assistance. Ninh and Hum were promptly arrested. The Sûreté took advantage of the incident to expose the Nguyen An Ninh Secret Society. Five hundred of Ninh's followers were detained for questioning and one hundred and fifteen stood trial with him the following year. Phan van Hum was given an eight-month prison sentence for crimes ranging from hitting a policeman—which Hum admitted—to borrowing from Ninh a copy of *The Brothers Karamazov*. The prosecution took his interest in the novel as a sign of his subversive intentions; Dostoevsky was "the father of the Russian Revolution because he depicted the beginning of social disintegration."[68] Hum went immediately to France upon his release. But Ninh served three years in jail, and was freed only in October 1931.

Shortly before his arrest, Ninh had proposed a merger to the leaders of the Vietnamese Revolutionary Party. The latter found the idea tempting, for Ninh's following was larger than theirs, but in the end, they turned down the proposal, "preferring to a large number of adherents without conviction a smaller number of true affiliates."[69] The VNQDD also rejected a merger, but on more ideological grounds, for it found Ninh's politics too extreme. At any rate, by the time it began considering that option, Ninh had already been arrested.[70]

The case of the Nguyen An Ninh Secret Society provided an insight into the difficulties of building a "modern organization of resistance" out of the lumpenproletariat of Saigon. A village teacher remembered a lecture by Ninh: "In the eighty years since independence was lost, the people of Annam have been treated like cattle. Now, we must unite to demand that the government give us back our country. If, within three years, they do not do away with taxes and return our country to us, then the people of Annam will take up arms." [71] But the only concrete piece of advice was that recruits should not pay personal taxes or land taxes, but contribute to common funds instead. Ninh failed to communicate his larger vision, so that "those who had met Ninh, talked to Ninh and would have followed him anywhere were many. But besides knowing that they followed Ninh because he was a revolutionary, they really did not know which path they were following and where it led." [72] Nguyen An Ninh had striven to achieve his anarcho-socialist utopia by combining an individualistic, heroic approach to revolution with a naive belief both in the essential goodness of the people and in the people's potential for spontaneous collective action. In so doing, he had tried to avoid creating a centralized and authoritarian structure of command; but his attempt had foundered on the shoals of ideological incoherence and organizational laxity. Whether they had opted to join him because they admired his reputed revolutionary spirit or because they had been intimidated by his lieutenants into becoming members of the Nguyen An Ninh Secret Society, his followers remained undisciplined and uncoordinated, and largely in the dark as to his ultimate purpose. Ninh, however, had not misjudged the revolutionary potential of uneducated peasants. Pham van Chieu and Truong thi Sau managed to keep the Secret Society going during his term in jail. When mass protests erupted in the countryside in 1930, Chieu led most of Ninh's erstwhile followers into the newly formed Indochinese Communist Party.

Still, the most obvious lesson of the Nguyen An Ninh Secret Society was that revolution could not be left to the masses alone. Nguyen Ai Quoc, who dismissed 99 percent of people as "ignorant, greedy and mean," had no faith in popular spontaneity. As he made clear in *The Road to Revolution*, he firmly believed in the need for a revolutionary vanguard, a Leninist party. He tried to construct one out of the only human resources available to him in the mid-1920s: young Vietnamese looking for an appropriate venue for their idealism and yearning for emancipation. Their sudden shift from passive disaffection to active confrontation gave revolutionary parties an unexpected opportunity to enlarge their membership but little time to properly indoctrinate new recruits. The Youth League, coming under KMT fire just at that time, labored under the added burden of being unable to adjust its strategy to post–United Front realities.

Earlier anticolonial activists had opted for cultural and social reform because they were committed to the goal of national liberation. The youth of the 1920s traveled the same road, but in reverse. They began by rebelling against those they held responsible for their personal alienation, their teachers and parents. Only later did their rebelliousness take on political overtones and their target include the colonial state. The primary concern of their predecessors—the political and cultural survival of the nation—was, temporarily at least, pushed from the forefront of the students' consciousness as they viewed the making of revolution as an exercise in self-realization.

Voluntary bonds of brotherhood were held up as the antidote to unwilling submission to hierarchical rule, but this created a contradictory role for the family. The patriarchal family was made to stand for everything that was wrong with Vietnamese society even as it provided a steady channel of recruitment into revolutionary parties; new recruits, having left their real families behind, tried to find emotional comfort in revolutionary fraternity. The consequence of this contradictory symbolism was to turn would-be Leninist revolutionary parties into new arenas for contesting not only kinship—both real and symbolic—but gender roles as well.

7   Freedom and Discipline

> To roam the universe in length and breadth
> To pay a man's full dues and be a man
> To work one's will north and south, east and west
> To struggle one's own way across the seas!
> Who lacks a trade on earth? But how to live
> and leave on history a heart's red stamp?
> Who yet can tell true glory from crass fame?
> How many see a hero still unsung?
> The time will come when, fighting mists and waves
> his hand will steer the vessel through a storm
> He will fill rivers up, cut mountains down,
> and all the world shall know of his high deeds.
>
> Nguyen Cong Tru (1778–1858),
"A Hero's Will"

> Brothers and sisters are like the limbs of the body
> But husbands and wives are like shirts that can be discarded.
>
> Vietnamese popular saying

ALTHOUGH Nguyen An Ninh may have overestimated the revolutionary potential of the populace, he was not the only romantic of his generation. The sudden onslaught of strikes led to the rapid expansion of revolutionary organizations, but new members were often admitted without proper discrimination and inadequately indoctrinated by novice recruiters. Both the Youth League and its chief rival, the Vietnamese Nationalist Party (or VNQDD), having adopted a Leninist party structure, suffered from the collision between the individualistic spirit which had driven their adherents into rebellion in the first place and the need to enforce a code of discipline more ruthless than anything they had experienced before.

New recruits took seriously the slogans of liberty, equality, fraternity, not just as goals to be striven for, but as rules to live by in the here and now. They tried to turn their parties into the embodiment of these ideals. Many looked upon their membership in a revolutionary organization as an expression of their capacity to act as autonomous individuals rather than as cogs in the family unit. But the release of their individuality also increased their desire for compensatory solidarity. Wanting both freedom and solidarity, and rejecting the traditional family as oppressive, they found irresistible the idea of the party as a quasi-family more egalitarian and nurturing than their own. The revolutionary community became the new focus of their allegiance and their source of emotional support. Often related to one another by ties of real kinship or affection, they aspired to become, like Henry V and his men, "we few, we happy few, we band of brothers."

The language of family has so often been invoked by revolutionaries as to seem the natural idiom of revolutionary rhetoric. Such language is an attempt to reinvent the idea of nation and community, to redraw social, ethnic, and cultural boundaries or even to obliterate them. In the early stage of the Vietnamese Revolution, it was also an essay in redefining the self in relation to others. Equality was not yet understood in class terms; it was sought between individuals. This was reinforced by the peculiarities of the Vietnamese language, in which nearly all social relationships are encompassed in the vocabulary of kinship. Only a few terms convey total equality; they are limited in their applicability and suggest formality and unconnectedness. Kin terminology, however, when applied to non-kin, tends to underline the hierarchical arrangements of social classes along generational lines. Servants used to refer to themselves as children when addressing their masters. Mandarins, who were the "fathers and mothers of the people," and even members of the royal family often used this servile self-designation in their dealings with French officials. Young iconoclasts preferred to think of themselves as siblings, which was particularly apt because they tended to seek converts among their relatives and friends. Older brother and older sister *(anh, chi)* became their preferred terms of address, strengthening their sense of generational solidarity and individual autonomy.

At least a decade older than the majority of the recruits, Nguyen Ai Quoc played the role of older brother to perfection. To the twenty-two-year-old Nguyen Luong Bang, he appeared like "an elder brother who was concerned with the minutest details of my welfare."[1] The rules of the Youth League reinforced the image of party-as-family while stressing the primacy of the party: "Adherents must keep absolutely secret all party matters and never reveal them to their parents, their friends and acquaintances. Adherents must consider themselves as members of the same family; they must set aside their own ideas and personal feelings and devote themselves entirely to the revolution."[2] But no rule succeeded in turning strangers into brothers or in preventing Sûreté informers from infiltrating the ranks of revolutionary parties. Fictive kinship turned out to be as demanding as real kinship; it also brought with it the problems inherent in social experiments when new rules of behavior are made up along the way and clash with established norms. Not only was the Youth League faced with the problem of steering a middle course between adequate discipline and excessive authoritarianism; it also had to find a way of mediating the conflicting demands of familial obligations and party loyalty, and of individual and collective goals.

To add to the confusion, revolutionary organizations became arenas for redefining women's roles. Young women were flocking to revolutionary organizations, attracted by a rhetoric that married national liberation with individual emancipation. The Vietnamese Nationalist Party actively recruited women into its ranks, often in competition with the Youth League, but it was the latter which produced most of the feminist rhetoric. In the revolutionary propaganda of 1926, young women were used as stand-ins for the rest of their generation, which believed itself victimized by parental tyranny. The dominant theme was not economic exploitation in the marketplace but domestic oppression. It was this theme that was used to persuade young women to leave their patriarchal families and join the fraternal revolutionary parties.

The Feminization of Revolution

To neo-traditionalists, women, whose traditional status had been that of perpetual minors, represented the immaturity and ignorance of the Vietnamese populace. Educating them would be the first step toward emancipating them. Others, however, believed that the explanation for women's bondage was to be found not in the victims but in their unequal relationships with their oppressors. For them, women were symbols not of popular ignorance but of national enslavement. In *Le Procès de la colonisation française,* Nguyen Ai Quoc devoted one chapter to describing the impact of colonialism on women. Like the rest of the book, it consisted largely of sensational stories illustrating the ill-treatment of Vietnamese women by French settlers. Tales of rape, murder, bestiality, beatings, and common exploitation were strung together to provoke indignation and shame among the French readers at whom the book was aimed. The victimization of women was presented as one more aspect of the unequal relationship that existed between colonial masters and enslaved natives. There was no recognition that women had been victimized before colonialism and that they continued to be oppressed by their own menfolk, just as there was no acknowledgment in Pham Quynh's speech at AFIMA one year earlier that tradition alone did not account for all their sufferings. Over the next few years, debates on women would unfold along these two themes: on the one hand, the emancipation of elite women from the burden of tradition and the training they should receive in order to fulfill their changing roles as wives and mothers; and on the other hand, the liberation of working women from the brutalities and exploitation of colonial capitalism. In a certain sense, these two views of women's roles, as either wives and mothers or comrades and workers, were irreconcilable.

The first women's organization came into being in 1926 in the midst of student strikes. Ostensibly apolitical and devoted solely to improving women's education, it was the creation of Mme. Dam Phuong, a member of the imperial clan who had married a journalist. While raising eleven children, she managed to make a name for herself as a woman of letters.[3] Her organization, which was based in the imperial capital, was called Association for the Study of Domestic Arts (Nu Cong Hoc Hoi). According to the warmly supportive notice which appeared in *Southern Wind,* its goal was to "teach practical women's skills; to teach about the duties and responsibilities of women; to improve the intellect and morals of women and girls."[4] This would be done through classes in cooking and sewing, embroidery, mulberry-growing and silk-weaving; family management and hygiene; child-rearing; literature; and morality instruction. It was an unexceptionable program of education for middle-class women, which Pham Quynh himself could have advocated. But the avowedly apolitical program of the Association was belied by the choice of Phan Boi Chau as keynote speaker for its inaugural ceremony on 28 June 1926.[5] Phan's ideas about the proper role of women had not altered since 1913, even though in China and Vietnam, new views of women's rights were being voiced.[6] Phan reminded women of their responsibilities as daughters, wives, and mothers, and criticized the fascination of the modern woman with physical adornment, thus coming close to the position adopted by Pham Quynh. Where he parted company with Pham Quynh was in his carefully worded encouragement to women to become involved in the anticolonial struggle and to subordinate their own wishes for sexual equality to this higher goal.[7]

At the time when the Association for the Study of Domestic Arts was founded, young people of both sexes were caught up in the excitement of defying their elders and being expelled from school. To young women who, only two months earlier, had taken part in demonstrations and marched in Phan Chu Trinh's funeral procession, the Association's curriculum of lessons in cooking and sewing, domestic hygiene, and child-rearing methods seemed not only tame but even reactionary. A young woman wrote to *Youth:* "In Hue, there is a society which supposedly has as its goal the expansion and development of women's education. Yet, there is only one working woman among the members of this society. The women of the Society are all socialites who don't know what to do other than strictly observe the Three Submissions and the Four Virtues, these Seven Bonds which have kept Vietnamese women enslaved since high antiquity."[8]

The column in which this letter appeared was a new one, inaugurated on 24 March 1926, nine months after *Youth* was first published. Originally called "The Ladies' Mail," its name was changed shortly thereafter to "The Ladies' Forum." Until then, Nguyen Ai Quoc had not paid much attention to what the Vietnamese called the "family system" *(che do gia dinh)*. The column reflected his new awareness of the potency of the question of women and his eagerness to harness it to the cause of revolution. In the column were queries and comments addressed to the journal by female readers, replies to these letters, articles analyzing the status of women throughout history, and accounts of women's efforts to emancipate themselves in other countries, often in a colonial setting. The technique was familiar: to shame Vietnamese readers into fighting for their own liberation. Women from Japan, India, the Muslim world, and Ireland were described in highly tendentious articles as being more fearless in their fight for political and economic rights and equality with men. On the basis of these articles, a reader would easily conclude that Vietnamese women were more backward and more supine than any other women in the world. Inspirational articles appeared occasionally, depicting the Soviet Union as a paradise for women at home and in the workplace. More interesting were letters from readers (though some may have been apocryphal) and the replies from the editors, who used them as pretexts for more pointed advocacy than they employed in journalistic accounts. An analysis of this dialogue and of its importance in the cultural universe of the Youth League must be set in the context of an evolving climate of opinion on the issue of women within Vietnam and among émigré groups. That women should be emancipated was clear; but from what? Neither readers nor editors were clear on the subject. There was inconsistency from column to column about the relationship between education and revolution. The reasoning of both readers and editors was often flawed. The first column consisted of a letter from women who asked men in the most humble terms to give them their freedom: "Until now, we have toiled in obscurity to earn our living and fulfill our duty toward our parents. But now, the bell of liberty has sounded in our ears and has suddenly awakened us. It seems to us a propitious occasion to put into your hands the task of protecting our rights, of emancipating us and reforming our customs. Have pity on us. Exert yourselves to improve our lot, and we promise to follow you wherever you wish." [9]

Despite the denigrating tone of the letter concerning the Association for the Study of the Domestic Arts, on the whole, the women who wrote to *Youth* seemed more interested in gaining greater access to formal education and improving their positions within the family than in overthrowing the French. A thread which ran through the correspondence was women's lack of education and abysmal ignorance. Nguyen Ai Quoc tried to turn this concern into an anticapitalist propaganda point: "In order to work, one must be educated or strong. But women are ignorant, weak, and often immobilized by pregnancy. They will never be able to earn their living like men, whose slaves they are, so long as proletarians must work for capitalists. If we wish men and women to enjoy the same rights and advantages, we must totally reform customs, education, and the method of distributing wealth." [10]

But could ignorant and weak women be of use to the revolution? Should they not become educated before thinking of participating in the struggle for independence? To that line of argument Nguyen Ai Quoc and subsequent editors of *Youth* replied that, since the colonial regime pursued a policy of obscurantism, real education was out of the reach of both sexes. Only when the revolution was successful would it become available; it was therefore in women's interest to join the revolutionary movement. Such arguments did not fully convince female readers of *Youth*. A cynical reader evinced skepticism that women would benefit from delaying their drive for education and subordinating their own interests to the larger cause:

> In *Youth*, there is much talk of emancipation, of revolution, of the organization of women. These are truly interesting topics for us women, for we are oppressed and deprived of every advantage enjoyed by men. But theory is easy, practice is more difficult. And so we fear that the principles formulated by *Youth* on women's emancipation, on women's organization, on equality of the sexes may turn out to be as fragile as the policy of cooperation between French and Annamites. No need to tell you for whom this policy is most advantageous; you know perfectly well. Since Annamite women are ignorant, how will they achieve emancipation and how will they obtain the help of the stronger sex, which has not yet been able to obtain its own emancipation [from colonial rule]?[11]

The editor who took over *Youth* after Nguyen Ai Quoc fled from Canton replied: "If you want to learn, you must first be free, and if you want to be free, you must make revolution together with your brothers." He rejected the reader's "fears that cooperation between the sexes might be a repeat of the Franco-Annamite cooperation" as unfounded.[12] A week later, in tones reminiscent of Phan Boi Chau, he went on: "Women constitute one part of the revolutionary forces. If they neglected their duties and abandoned their brothers, they would delay the triumph of the revolution and their own access to political, administrative and economic rights. This is why I tell them: 'Sisters, struggle to achieve your own emancipation.'"[13]

But even if women could free themselves from ignorance, what about their subjugation by men? In the early correspondence, this was seen as a generational issue: "My parents have taught me my duties as a daughter, a wife, and mother. But they always forbade me to speak out or leave the house. O sisters of Annam, if we are drugged, slaves, and criminals, it is the fault of our parents. But now that our brothers have sounded the awakening, and have shown the road to follow, let us quickly rise up."[14] A few months later, the rhetoric escalated and incorporated more fully Engels' analysis of the condition of women. "Women are considered as chattel. Marriage and prostitution are the results of the same cause, namely private property and commerce. Sisters of Annam, if you want to obtain your emancipation, make revolution."[15] On 12 December 1927 appeared this statement: "So long as private property is not destroyed, the patriarchal system will endure and women will be constrained to breastfeed their babies, prepare food, wash the laundry, darn their clothes; they will be ruled by others, they will depend on others, and will have neither the time to educate themselves, nor the possibility to take part in administrative or governmental affairs." [16]

This hardening in the line of argument was caused not only by a slide to the left on the part of the Youth League but also by the fact that improved conditions for women had become a universal demand. Even the Constitutionalists were getting into the act.

When he attended the Brussels conference against imperialism in February 1927, the Constitutionalist Duong van Giao met two representatives of the International Women's League for Peace and Freedom, a left-wing organization founded in 1915, and invited them to stop by Saigon on their proposed trip to Asia.[17] Edith Pye and Camille Devret sailed from Marseilles on 28 October in the company of Duong van Giao. They arrived four weeks later in Saigon without much fanfare, the authorities having refused permission to hold a quayside reception. During their three weeks in Vietnam, the two women gave a series of lectures in which they expounded on the need to combat fascism and dwelt at length on the subject of women's rights. But they left for China convinced that in Vietnam emancipation was a more urgent issue in the minds of the men than of the women. Compared with their Chinese sisters, the Vietnamese women were quite backward: they had no group representing their interests, no mouthpiece of their own.[18]

In fact, their Constitutionalist hosts had been more interested in using their visit to put pressure on the authorities for political reform and to increase their stature among their compatriots than to promote feminism. Indeed, they were the most unlikely advocates of women's rights. Ever the elitist, Bui Quang Chieu opposed equal rights for women on the ground that it would only make them more eager to oppose men on every issue at home and abroad. Chieu drew a parallel between women's enfranchisement and male universal suffrage. In 1929, responding to a poll taken by *Ladies' News* on the subject of women's emancipation, Chieu suggested that men had enough troubles already without having to deal with contentious women, just as property owners were busy enough trying to win power from the settlers and running the country without having to fend off peasants who would be made bolder if they received the right to vote.¹⁹ For his part, Nguyen Phan Long joked that women did not need to be set free: "I don't understand why people deplore the conditions of Vietnamese women. They proclaim: liberate women, but are women really enslaved by men? I see that in many households, women hold all the power." ²⁰ Despite the Constitutionalists' hostility, their sponsorship of the two IWLPF representatives nevertheless gave feminism an added boost in the South.

Meanwhile, Dam Phuong's Association for the Study of Domestic Arts was expanding, gaining new members in both Cochinchina and Tonkin.²¹ It closely reflected Phan Boi Chau's vision of an organization combining the improvement of women's conditions with a patriotic orientation, though its patriotism was unfocused and its efforts to improve the conditions of women centered largely on teaching them domestic skills. Still, it was precisely this unthreatening aspect of the Association's program that made it widely acceptable, and therefore a formidable source of competition for the Youth League in its efforts to win the allegiance of women. On 4 March 1928, Tran thi Nhu Man, vice-president of the Association for the Study of Domestic Arts, organized a highly successful Women's Fair in Hanoi. Because she had been fired from her teaching job for organizing strikes in 1926, the event was seen by all as a sort of patriotic rally.²² The VNQDD also had a very active women's section in many of the provinces in which the Youth League was active; the wife of one of its leaders ran a Women's Publishing Society, the Nu Luu Thu Xa.²³

This climate of competition led *Youth* to adopt a two-pronged strategy. First, it adopted a dismissive tone toward "bourgeois" notions of women's emancipation, and second, its antifamily rhetoric became more strident. Elite women were described as parasites, puppets whose happiness depended on the will of others. Bourgeois women were deemed "less frivolous; but they are still the slaves of their husbands. To this unique tyranny, this monstrous domination of the male, they submit themselves with joy, for they believe, like all the rotten philosophers of antiquity, that submission is the greatest duty of women." ²⁴

> Some believe, erroneously, that emancipated women are the social butterflies who haunt shops in Saigon and Hanoi, their bodies molded in pink or blue dresses; or flirts who yearn for free love, and flaunt themselves in the streets, in theaters, in cinemas, and hotels, holding their boyfriends by the waist or by the arm; or intellectuals who, in order to attract attention to themselves, write in journals and make public speeches on every topic, political or social, and

dream of turning their husbands into crowd leaders or generals such as Tran Hung Dao or Chiang Kai-shek.[25]

Thus was the neo-traditionalist vision of the New Woman disposed of, and so was Dam Phuong. Romantic fiction, which was popular among middle-class women, was also attacked for providing false values and models: "As soon as some of our sisters were able to read, the French had translated French and Chinese romances such as *Manon Lescaut, Paul et Virginie, Hsueh Hung Lei Shih, To Tam* [sic], etc. . . . These works, which are sold cheaply in all the big cities, have caused the corruption of mores and the ruin of our women."[26] In comparison with some, the editors of *Youth*, even when speaking of marriage as prostitution and families as agents of enslavement, were models of restraint. Radical exiles in Siam had organized a branch of the Youth League and published a biweekly newsletter called *Unison (Dong Thanh)*, which, like *Youth,* contained a regular column called "The Ladies' Forum." The columns of 15 October and 1 November 1927 (*Dong Thanh* 13 and 14) were entitled "Mea Culpa":

For a long time we have rotted in ignorance, ears shut, knees bent, and arms crossed. But now, the international feminist movement draws us out of our lethargy little by little; it makes us conscious of the oppression of which we are the victims and it makes us hate society and especially philosophers such as Confucius and Rousseau who committed the evil of writing: "It is difficult to educate women. Women are the natural servants of men. The husband commands, the wife obeys, etc. . . ."

Sisters, I confess that my musings make me mad with anger. I recognize that ancient institutions have been the cause of all the ills which our sisters have endured. But I could not pretend to ignore that they also gave rise to admirable women such as Louise Michel, Charlotte Corday, the mother of King Wen, the mother of Mencius, the Trung sisters who perished while defending their country against the Chinese invaders.

Sisters! Think that all these heroines lived at times when the subjugation of the weaker sex was more tyrannical than today, and yet, they accomplished magnificent exploits which we still laud today. And meanwhile, what do you do? You buzz like greenflies around latrines, you joyfully speculate on your emancipation and your freedom, but you make no effort whatsoever to free yourselves from the domination of your husbands and mothers-in-law. If you suffer this state of subjection, it is because you are ignorant and stupid. You must shake off this lethargy, educate yourselves, correct yourselves, for you must work like our brothers for the conquest of our rights and the independence of our country.

The next issue of *Unison* argued that "at birth, boys and girls receive of Heaven the same physical and intellectual gifts. The two sexes are therefore naturally equal. But they receive unequal education." The article went on to propose that women perfect themselves physically and intellectually in order to fulfill their duties as citizens and to contribute to revolution. But it also called for freedom of marriage, equal rights to inheritance, equal access to education, equal access to work, and the same political and social rights for women as for men.[27] But *Unison* did not have as wide an audience, nor was it part of a larger effort to win recruits, as was *Youth*.[28]

But it was the middle-class journal, *Ladies' News (Phu Nu Tan Van)*, which presented the greatest challenge to *Youth* when it began appearing in Saigon on 2 May 1929, for it was a legal publication with a wide circulation. Its publishers were a husband and wife team who owned a prosperous textile business. Of no little importance to the success of *Ladies' News* was the perceived patriotism of its publishers, all the greater since they claimed not to be affiliated with any political party. Politically, they were to the left of Bui Quang Chieu and Nguyen Phan Long; they did not hesitate to engage in an acrimonious exchange with them when it was learned that Chieu had received a monthly retainer from one of the most reactionary figures in Cochinchinese politics, and had agreed to participate in some highly questionable land deals.[29] Under their guiding hand, the journal became perhaps the most important vehicle of non-Communist progressive *(cap tien)* ideas in the South. Since it was widely understood that debates on women had wider implications, the influence of *Ladies' News* extended far beyond the confines of traditional women's issues. Within months of its launching, the authorities were dubbing it the "organ of feminism and nationalism."[30]

Numerous pamphlets and articles had been published after the visit by Camille Devret and Edith Pye. Many of these, like the play on the Trung queens which Nguyen An Ninh published in October 1928, openly linked women's rights to the struggle for national salvation. The launching of *Ladies' News* in 1929 showed that the issue of women's emancipation and sexual equality had finally stirred the interest of the Cochinchinese public. *Ladies' News* was typically southern in its pragmatic, even consumerist, approach to journalism. It succeeded, where *Women's Bell* had failed ten years earlier, in striking the right balance in its combination of advocacy journalism, recipes, advice on health and child-rearing, literary essays, fiction, and social reportage. Even more than the poll which *Ladies' News* conducted among well-known personalities on the issue of women's rights, its contents demonstrated how far the debate on women had progressed since Pham Quynh's speech of 1924.

Like Pham Quynh, the editors of *Ladies' News* were chiefly concerned with women of the elite, who provided its readership. But instead of the "true daughters of Confucius," these were middle-class women from the South. The "New Woman," once denounced by old-time moralists and lampooned by Pham Quynh, was dear to the editors of *Ladies' News*. The journal was an ardent proponent of education for women, but not of the type proposed by Pham Quynh. Its publishers wanted to create a new kind of woman, no longer the timid kitchen mouse of tradition, but an educated, self-confident woman capable of discoursing with men intelligently and active in the world outside the "high walls and closed gates" of home. In the first issue, the editors argued that the time had passed for women to live only in the "family prison." Using the rhetoric of Social Darwinism, they explained that "in order to survive in these times, you must find ways to be self-reliant; you must study, you must compete, you must progress." Women should stop being dependent on their menfolk. "In life, if you depend on others, then you are beholden to others; if you are beholden to others, you are enslaved by others; what becomes of freedom and equality then?"[31] By now, the activities and propaganda of both the Youth League and the VNQDD were common knowledge; it was thus inevitable that the *Ladies' News* borrowed their feminist rhetoric. If women were unable to fend for themselves and participate in public affairs more fully, it was because of their lack of education. This was not the result of some inborn deficiency on their part, but merely the result of social circumstances. Women were entitled to exactly the same education as men. Such was the message of *Ladies' News*.

Phan Khoi, a failed degree candidate who was one of the journal's star columnists, had no qualms about attributing the oppression of women to Confucianism. On 17 October 1929, he published an article entitled "A Bill of Accusation against the Annamite Family System."[32] After describing how his great-grandmother had been ostracized for remarrying after the death of her first husband, he argued that the remarriage of widows should be allowed and attacked the Sung philosopher Cheng Hsi for declaring, "Starving to death is a minor issue; loss of chastity is a grave matter." Ever provocative, Phan Khoi argued a few months later in a series of articles on Empress Wu that, in fairness to women, they should be allowed to practice polyandry.[33] But the more sober publishers of *Ladies' News* deplored the loose behavior of Westernized young women almost as strongly as did Pham Quynh or Nguyen Don Phuc. Though they spoke of the family as a prison and exhorted women to be self-sufficient and earn their own living, they also insisted on the importance of women as mothers and wives. But here, too, they were able to inject a new theme into the discourse by highlighting the conflict between mothers-in-law and daughters-in-law that was so often found in multigenerational families. Though the problem was not unknown in the South, it was more widespread in the North. Phan van Truong, a transplanted northerner, explained the process that turned former victims into oppressors: "Why is that so? I think it is because they are ignorant and therefore small-minded; since they cannot lord it over anyone else, they lord it at home and ill-treat their daughters-in-law. And thus, this cruel custom is transmitted from generation to generation. A woman who has been oppressed and humiliated as a daughter-in-law revenges herself by oppressing and humiliating her own daughter-in-law."[34]

Reporting on the suicide of a young woman whose life had been turned into a living hell by her in-laws, the journal proposed that the solution to family conflict was to establish nuclear families.[35] *Ladies' News* thus provided a contrast with the more traditionalist views of Pham Quynh on the subject of intergenerational relationships and set the theme for the romantic fiction of the 1930s.

The debate on women also fed on the Vietnamese fascination with international events. *Youth* tried to inspire its readers with accounts of women of other countries uniting to struggle for greater rights. So did *Ladies' News;* in addition, it offered its readers individual and concrete examples, taking sisterly pride in the achievements of women in every field. Reporting on Marie Curie's Nobel prize, it speculated wistfully on the likelihood that a Vietnamese woman would ever receive such an accolade. It followed faithfully the progress of female pilots and exhorted its readers to learn to swim and play tennis. Thus *Ladies' News* gave its readers a gallery of role models that was radically different from the long-dead paragons of feminine virtue once found in the pages of *Southern Wind*. The doings of these new role models, as chronicled by *Ladies' News,* were at variance with its unexceptionable philosophy. Its editorial stance, too, was not always consistent. The journal argued that women should not participate in what it called "affairs of state" *(quoc su)* because they were not yet educated enough or disciplined enough to do so.[36] Yet, it encouraged women to become involved in public oratory. It also listed countries in which women had won the right to vote and ran admiring profiles of politically active women from the United States to the Soviet Union. The photograph of Alexandra Kollontai, the prominent feminist and Soviet Foreign Minister, appeared several times in the journal. When the journal reported the arrests of adherents of the VNQDD and the Youth League, it could not refrain from noting with a sort of perverse pride the presence of women in these two organizations: "When it comes to being arrested, men and women have equal rights."[37]

The publishers of *Ladies' News* exerted strong editorial control over what was printed in their journal, but did not try to use it to further a political career as had so many other publishers. *Ladies' News* was a business venture, and therefore sensitive to shifts in public opinion. Nevertheless, its publishers did not hesitate to introduce into the mainstream of public discourse ideas that had first been printed abroad or in clandestine revolutionary publications. *Ladies' News* seemed at times to be full of Marxist rhetoric. Its second issue contained a vigorous attack on prevailing labor conditions in Indochina, in which the author did not flinch from drawing comparisons with the Soviet Union:

> Those inhumane capitalists are exploiting the sweat and tears of our sisters. We have seen many factories in the North where they employ women at the rate of only twenty-five cents a day for a ten-hour day. They even hire children of ten for less than ten cents a day. We have even seen women recruited to work in the rubber plantations of New Caledonia at starvation wages. Their weak bodies cannot stand the climate. How many come back, their health destroyed, unable to earn their living and to bear children? How many factories have we seen where women are forced to perform heavy tasks beyond their strength . . . But to whom can we complain? If we complain to the administration, it says it is concerned, but we know that our government is not the Soviet government *(The Soviet Union is the worker's government in Russia)* . . . If we want to defend our

rights, we must have organizations, we must have strong syndicates, but who will allow us to organize syndicates?[38]

The journal also used its regular column "Letter to a Friend" to report on the oppression of Cochinchinese peasants by landowners.[39] Debates on oppression were thus gradually moving from the domestic sphere to the workplace, as was the debate on women.

Youth tried to come up with a profile of the female population by class: it estimated this population at "12,500,000 women; of these, 10,625,000 were rice planters; 5,626,000 were workers; 250,000 were traders; 725,000 were housewives; 125,000 were servants; 62,500 were prostitutes; 31,250 were students; 31,250 were unemployed; and 62,500 were bourgeois women (and therefore idle)."[40] The numbers seemed promising (though highly suspect since the total population in 1925 was only seventeen million). With so many working women, the potential for recruitment was deemed great. The journal therefore concluded: "In Annam, women constitute the most important segment of the popular forces. Rural women, dispossessed of their land by our tyrants, leave to hire themselves out in the plantations of Cochinchina or southern Annam. Their situation is identical to that of the proletarians of the great capitalist powers. Being numerous, and, in a manner of speaking, organized, they constitute the core of the feminine revolutionary forces, the avant-garde of the popular army which will soon exterminate the French imperialists and the enemies of our revolution."[41]

But did women really constitute the vanguard of revolution? Articles suggesting that the issue of women's emancipation be analyzed from a class perspective were few. More familiar were unconsciously patronizing appeals to supposed feminine skills. When a group of street vendors in Nam Dinh humbly asked, "What can women do to help the revolution?," the editors of *Youth* replied: "(1) They can go among their sisters to interest them in the revolutionary cause and organize them. It goes without saying that they are much more skillful propagandists than male revolutionaries. (2) They are much better at propaganda than men because they move their listeners more easily. (3) Women have special ways of initiating their listeners (such as young boys) into revolutionary theories and organizing them. Young men are happy to be stopped by them and to listen to their talks. (4) No one can surpass women as couriers."[42]

Even in revolution, women were thus cast in the traditional roles of seductresses and helpmeets. Leaders of the Youth League often complained at how arduous it was to mobilize women: "Some of our awakened sisters are truly our friends and our support. They do not hesitate to join us and to lead our countrymen onto the revolutionary path. But I must confess that they still lack many qualities that would enable them to merit the name of 'true revolutionaries' and to be given as examples to their sisters. They are not filled with the spirit of sacrifice; some embrace the revolutionary cause, but unfortunately, they do not stop thinking about their parents, their husbands, their children. Others complain because, now that they are revolutionaries, they can no longer dress and eat well."[43]

But such arguments left women unmoved. They wanted to know how to address the practical problems caused by unchallenged assumptions that they were solely responsible for performing household chores and other familial duties: "(1) If we were to work for the revolution, who would take care of our housework? (2) Since we have to work to earn our living, can we afford the time to work for the revolution? (3) If we embraced the revolutionary cause, we would of necessity come into contact with men. In that case, would people not consider us women of little virtue?"[44]

The editors of *Youth* could not hide their exasperation at women's concern over their good names, but could not dismiss it altogether. Most of the women likely to join the Youth League had grown up in households where the segregation of the sexes was rigidly enforced. Much as they might resent parental authority and yearn for the right to choose their own husbands (for such, essentially, was the meaning of the call for free love), they feared that others, both within and without the revolutionary movement, might denigrate them because of their willingness to emerge from behind their "high walls and closed gates" to work alongside men. The editors therefore suggested: "If you worry so much about your good name, have contacts only with other women; awaken them and lead them into the revolutionary road."[45] Some female adherents of the League did just that, starting their own chapters of the Association for the Study of Domestic Arts in several northern provinces.[46] Their Association compromised by these more radical elements, Dam Phuong and Tran thi Nhu Man were arrested in September 1929.

Regarding women's other practical questions, *Youth* provided no answer. Though women continued to be chided for letting their domestic chores and their responsibilities to their husbands, children, parents, and in-laws get in the way of involvement in revolutionary activities, nowhere was it suggested that any of these duties be neglected, or that men might perform some of them. As was so often the case, the editors of *Youth* sidestepped difficult questions. The general theme of "The Ladies' Forum" in *Youth* was succinctly summed up in the title of the article which appeared on International Women's Day in 1929: "Sisters of Annam! Unite to Fight Imperialism and Destroy Ancestral Society." But the destruction of "ancestral society" would have necessitated a fundamental restructuring of gender roles and family relationships, which, for all their fiery rhetoric about total transformation, the male leaders of the League were not ready to contemplate. The result was that women who decided to join the League and "devote themselves to the revolution" often did so at the expense of marriage and family life. This was also true of men, but they, at least, could live on their own without arousing comment, whereas women who chose to live away from their families put their reputation at risk. The women who were active in politics tended to come from families which were already devoted to the anticolonial cause and fully supported their activities or to be married to like-minded men. A handful were single.[47] But it seems to have been married women who were behind the creation of chapters of the Association for the Study of Domestic Arts, weaving factories, bookstores, and shops which served as meeting points for other adherents of the Youth League.[48]

Despite all their arguments to show women why it was not only their patriotic duty but also in their interest to become involved in revolutionary work, the editors of *Youth*, starting with Nguyen Ai Quoc, never truly addressed the question of whether women would be better off if they subsumed their fight for sexual equality to the fight for national independence. In stressing the need for solidarity, they ignored what women knew too well: that the oppression of women started at home, and that the oppression was the work of the men with whom they were supposed to join forces in the struggle against the French. As four Hanoi students wrote to the writers of *Youth:* "We have noticed that, contrary to your assertions, the French are not the authors of all our ills. If Annamite women are miserable, the cause of their misery is the family education system. Only Annamite males suffer under the yoke of French colonialism, by having to pay taxes, and being liable for military service."[49] Theirs was a common argument: that the struggle for independence was essentially a men's fight that had nothing to offer women, because women were the victims of entirely indigenous forces, namely, tradition and their own families. In response, the editors of *Youth* acknowledged that women were victims both at home and outside it.[50] The journal *Worker, Peasant, and Soldier (Cong Nong Binh)*, another organ of the Youth League with a more limited readership, was even more blunt: "Women represent half of the population. Not only are they victims of all kinds of oppression and as exploited as men, but they are also oppressed in society, in their homes, in family instruction, in rules of decorum, and in marriage. During the whole of their lives, they serve as instruments, as playthings for men."[51]

At first glance, the rhetoric of women's emancipation was only a variant of the discourse on freedom, whose theme was the emergence of the autonomous individual. Revolution was still cast in generational terms, and the party was still conceived of as a band of siblings. It seemed perfectly reasonable to the editors of *Youth* to exhort women to ally with their brothers in rebelling against their fathers. Although the wave of student migration had been triggered by the strikes and subsequent expulsions, not all the exiles had left home under pressure. Even those who were denied readmission in school and had come to the attention of the colonial authorities often recast their experience as quest rather than flight. From their place of exile, the editors of *Youth* wrote of emancipation as a literal process of leaving home, casting off the shackles of parental authority and finding oneself. Women, however, had greater difficulties imagining themselves outside the familial context; for them, emancipation did not entail physical movement so much as a restructuring of gender roles and a redistribution of familial obligations and authority. This divergent conception of emancipation was related to the different view of the relationship between men and women held by the female readers of *Youth* and its male editors. Female readers regarded men essentially as fathers or husbands, as actual or potential oppressors. The male editors of *Youth*, however, regarded themselves as their brothers: related but more or less equal. They were thus less concerned with the issue of male domination than with the problem of persuading women to unite with them in the anticolonial struggle.

Passion and Politics

The advice that readers concerned with their reputation should work exclusively with other women was the last installment in the correspondence that appeared in "The Ladies' Forum." Caught between

Kuomintang repression and the ideological discord within its ranks, the leadership of the League was no longer able to give its full attention to the editorial policy presented in *Youth*. Articles continued to be published regularly on the subject of women, but they consisted mostly of descriptions of foreign movements of emancipation rather than an exchange of views.

Disarray among the top leadership in China led to disarray inside Vietnam. At the time the Central Committee was hit by the third anti-Communist repression in December 1928, the Cochinchinese section of the League came close to destroying itself. In many ways, that section was the weakest of the three regional branches. Not only was there no southern-born representative on the Central Committee but the structures of communication and authority between the China-based leadership and the section were weak, for the more sophisticated activists from Cochinchina preferred to go to France. The difficulties were compounded by the policy of sending back second-rate recruits to Vietnam while the more promising ones were enrolled in the Chinese Communist Party or sent to Moscow. Thus men with very little prior training and incomplete indoctrination were suddenly thrust in positions of responsibility. They lacked experience, and were impatient with the unfamiliar and painstaking work of party-building. Despite the careful organizational charts, there was confusion as to the relationship between different echelons of the League. In addition, the Cochinchinese Regional Committee suffered simultaneously from both insufficient party loyalty and excessive authoritarianism.

What happened to the Cochinchinese Regional Committee in late 1928 is a mere footnote in the history of the transition from the Youth League to the Indochinese Communist Party. But it remains a poignant illustration of the ambiguous meaning of the family metaphor and the inability of revolutionary discipline to contain human foibles. Among Vietnamese of the three regions, southerners were the least influenced by Confucian familial ideology; they also had a less rooted sense of community.

Until early 1928, the Regional Committee of Cochinchina had been headed by Ton Duc Thang. During World War I, Thang had served at the Toulon Arsenal as a volunteer specialist worker.[52] While there, he became interested in politics and began to read *Humanité*. He returned to Vietnam in January 1919 with the rank of corporal and was awarded the medal of the Dragon of Annam for his war service.

He joined the Kroff (Ba Son) Company, which specialized in land drainage and reclamation, and became a foreman. At work, he made the acquaintance of Ngo Thiem (alias Hue), who had been born in Nghe An. Thiem was barely out of his teens but had already attended Nguyen Ai Quoc's training seminar in Canton and was now busily expanding the membership of the Youth League in Cochinchina. At Thiem's urging, Ton Duc Thang joined the League in 1927 and went to Canton for two months of further training. Meanwhile, Thiem turned Thang's household into a center of recruitment into the Youth League. He enlisted Thang's lodger and fellow worker, Tran Truong, and Truong's distant cousin, Nguyen Trung Nguyet, who had joined the household in late 1927. Playing on Nguyen Trung Nguyet's thirst for education, Thiem persuaded her to go to Canton as well. When she was judged ready for induction into the Youth League, she was taken to the tomb of Pham Hong Thai to swear allegiance before sailing home in November with the special mission of recruiting more women. Ton Duc Thang, then in his mid-thirties, was thus at the center of a highly successful recruitment drive. His rapid rise to power after he returned to Vietnam from Canton was probably due to this overall success but also shows how hastily the Cochinchinese section was being organized. Only two or three months after his entry into the League, he found himself, somewhat to his surprise, the representative of the Central Committee to the Cochinchinese Regional Committee.

Things changed, however, in early 1928, when the Central Committee appointed Le van Phat as head of the Regional Committee, a post which ranked higher than Thang's. In his late twenties, Phat was, like Thang, much older than the rest of the members of the Youth League. He was a traditional doctor and held the function of notable in charge of rites in his village, in Ben Tre province. Recruited in 1927, he had gone to Canton for training but was jailed in December during the second anti-Communist wave and spent several months in a Chinese prison. Upon his release, he returned to Cochinchina as head of the Regional Committee. Immediately, his difficult personality, his lack of education compared with the more middle-class and French-educated rank and file members, and his expensive tastes created enemies within various echelons of the Cochinchinese branch. He was feared rather than respected by his fellow adherents; some even suspected him of diverting the League's funds for his own use.

Since many new adherents were recruited locally and not sent to

South China for training, they had only a vague idea of the identity and function of the Central Committee. Not all were convinced that it should be the ultimate authority or that it knew what was actually going on within the country, and they resented having to take orders from abroad. Their distrust of the Central Committee found focus in Phat, whom they regarded as a "creature of Canton." Phat's main critic was Ton Duc Thang, who resented being passed over, especially since he had more experience in organizational work and Communist doctrine and was older as well. His resentment increased after Thiem and Phat tried to persuade him to leave his wife and children to work full-time on propaganda for the League. When he refused, the two men started to suspect him of lacking revolutionary ardor and had his movements monitored by two other League members. Feeling trapped, Thang began considering leaving the League altogether.

While Thang was still smarting over Phat's superior status, a young neophyte named Tran Thu Thuy arrived from Ben Tre for further training. In her police file picture, she looks sweet and guileless, an incongruous candidate for the role of *femme fatale*. Yet she provoked a disastrous rivalry between the two top men in the Cochinchinese branch of the Youth League. The seemingly uxorious Thang immediately fell in love with her. But it was Phat, her assigned mentor, who pressured Thu Thuy into becoming his mistress. The feminist rhetoric which had brought women into the ranks of the Youth League notwithstanding, Phat intimated that it was her duty to become his mistress, and went so far as to invoke the will of the Regional Committee. When Thu Thuy, bowing to higher authority, acquiesced, Thang's accumulated resentment boiled over. But his protests to the Regional Committee, whose members answered directly to Phat, fell on deaf ears. Still, in order not to be seen to condone Phat's immorality, the Committee assigned Thu Thuy to work with the Saigon Municipal Section, which happened to be dominated by allies of Thang. Away from the domineering Le van Phat, and perhaps goaded by Thang and Nguyen Trung Nguyet, Thu Thuy decided to lodge a formal complaint against Phat with the Municipal Section. After the Regional Committee once more declined to pursue the matter, the Municipal Section decided to adjudicate her complaint itself.

On the night of 29 November 1928, a secret meeting charged the absent Phat with committing a crime against a sister.[53] The rules were clear: the mentor must at all times treat the female neophyte like his own sister. Not only did Phat's relationship with Thu Thuy contravene party rules, but it somehow smacked of incest. A vote to execute

Phat was taken by a show of hands, and his executioners were selected at random from among those present: Tran Truong, Nguyen Trung Nguyet, Ngo Thiem, and a twenty-four-year-old tailor who was Phat's private secretary and wrote for the journal *Worker, Peasant, and Soldier*. Nguyet would procure a sleeping potion, detain Phat at home, and administer it; the men would do the rest.

In the evening of 8 December, after Nguyet had given Phat the potion, the male conspirators arrived at his house on Barbier Street. Truong slit Phat's throat with a penknife and stabbed him in the chest while the other two held him down. One of Phat's neighbors heard muffled sounds of moaning, but decided it was probably a man beating his wife: too ordinary an occurrence to worry about. And so he went back to sleep. On Thang's advice, the assassins burned their victim's face to render it unrecognizable and took away or destroyed all evidence suggesting a link with the Youth League. When the police arrived the next morning, it was confronted with the outward signs of a crime of passion: a man's body lying in a pool of blood, clad only in a pajama top. But the signs of premeditation were too obvious; within hours, the police had begun to arrest members of the Youth League, including many who had no connection whatsoever with the murder.[54] Ngo Thiem managed to go to Hong Kong to report on the affair to the Central Committee before being caught. The Central Committee agreed that Phat had deserved death and that the Regional Committee had acted reprehensibly in not curbing him, and that it should be disbanded.

At the time of the murder, the Cochinchinese branch of the Youth League counted about two hundred adherents, plus another two hundred fifty affiliates in auxiliary associations. When the affair came to trial in October 1930, sixty people were implicated in the crime, fourteen of whom, including Thu Thuy, were on the run. Nearly one-third of the membership of the Cochinchinese branch of the Youth League were thus under arrest or in flight. The disappearance of so many League members and the disorientation of the rest seriously hampered the growth of the Indochinese Communist Party in the months to come, and allowed Trotskyists returned from France to carve a niche for themselves in southern revolutionary politics.

The Demise of the Vietnamese Nationalist Party

The Barbier Street affair illustrates one possible problem arising out of confused notions of authority and fraternity and unresolved tensions over gender relations within the revolutionary movement. But real, rather than fictive, family ties, while useful for recruiting purposes, proved just as much a liability to the Vietnamese Nationalist Party as it faced colonial repression. In the end, however, the VNQDD was brought to the brink of extinction not through abuses of power, as was the southern branch of the Youth League, but because Nguyen Thai Hoc was unable to check the adventurist tendencies of some of his followers.

Although its propaganda machine was less developed and its revolutionary program less fully articulated, the organizational structure of the VNQDD closely resembled that of the Youth League. Kinship, shared regional origins, and school ties were also as much a part of the VNQDD recruitment strategy as they were for the Youth League. Like the League, the VNQDD put equal stress on national salvation and social transformation; indeed, some of its leaders gave priority to the latter over the former. Nguyen Thai Hoc, however, abhorred the idea of setting class against class, though he had only the rhetoric of Sun Yat-sen's Three People's Principles and the slogans of the French Revolution to offer as a strategy for achieving social justice. In 1928, he explored the possibility of an alliance with Nguyen An Ninh but rejected it on the ground that Ninh's ideas were too extreme.[55] That same year, before class struggle became the dominant ideology within the Youth League, leaders of the VNQDD and of the Youth League met to negotiate a merger between their two parties. The negotiations were a miserable failure. The VNQDD leaders refused to take orders from a foreign-based Central Committee. Delegates of both sides bickered over who was the more revolutionary, Nguyen Thai Hoc or Nguyen Ai Quoc.[56] After that disastrous meeting, the VNQDD and the Youth League fell into intense competition with each other for the allegiance of the same segments of the population in Tonkin.

Although it denounced class struggle, the VNQDD had an active workers' section, made up largely of employees in French stores and factories in the Hanoi area, and an equally developed women's section under the leadership of Nguyen Thai Hoc's fiancée, Nguyen thi Giang. In late 1928, a member of the workers' section named Nguyen van Vien proposed that the director of the General Office of Indochinese Manpower, Hervé Bazin, be assassinated. The Office was in charge of recruiting coolie labor, for which the overheated economy of Cochinchina had created an insatiable demand. Forty thousand coolies already worked in rubber plantations in Cochinchina, but plantation owners estimated that they would need twenty-five thousand new coolies each year for the next several years. Thirty-five thousand coolies arrived from Annam and Tonkin in 1926–1927 alone. The recruitment of coolies was characterized by corruption, misrepresentations, and coercion and had become a byword for terror in the Tonkinese countryside. Conditions in the Cochinchinese plantations were appalling.[57] A rebellion erupted in 1927 on the Phu Rieng plantation to protest the death of a coolie and general ill-treatment.[58] Its savage repression gave the Youth League its first crack at enrolling plantation workers into its ranks.

Nguyen van Vien believed that, in order to edge out the Youth League in the competition for the allegiance of workers, the VNQDD needed to prove to them that it was committed to protecting their interests. The assassination of Bazin was to furnish this proof.[59] But when he presented his scheme on behalf of the Workers' Section, Nguyen Thai Hoc refused to consider it or to take it to the rest of the membership. The Party was making headway in recruiting members in the population at large, and was particularly successful among colonial troops. Believing that the time was not yet ripe for a general insurrection, it wanted to exploit this momentum and do more recruiting. Furthermore, as Nguyen Thai Hoc argued: "If we assassinate Bazin, then the colonial authorities will repress us very severely. The majority of the leaders of our Party already figure on the Sûreté blacklist. We will all be arrested. Little profit will accrue from the assassination, but great harm will be done."[60]

This failed to convince Nguyen van Vien, who went away resolved to carry out his scheme on his own. Bazin was assassinated on 9 February 1929. Nguyen Thai Hoc's fears of reprisals were immediately realized. The Sûreté rounded up members of the VNQDD by the hundreds, extracting confessions and turning key figures in the Party into informants. In turn, the assassination squad of the VNQDD murdered informants as soon as their identity became known; but far from stopping the leaks, this allowed the Sûreté to make more arrests and to close in on Nguyen Thai Hoc and other VNQDD leaders. Nguyen van Vien's breach of discipline was not only fatal to his own party; it also loosed the colonial apparatus of repression against the Tonkinese section of the Youth League.

The campaign of repression forced members of both parties to choose between different kinds of kinship and loyalty. Among members of the Youth League arrested in the wake of Bazin's murder were

Trinh Dinh Chiem and his two sisters, Uyen and Nhu.[61] They came from the same province as Nguyen Thai Hoc and his fiancée, Nguyen thi Giang. Although relations between the Youth League and the VNQDD had become strained, the two sisters had remained friends with Giang while competing with her in recruiting women.[62] Aware of that friendship, the Sûreté extracted from them a pledge to help it capture Nguyen Thai Hoc in exchange for their brother's freedom. After being provisionally released, Nhu and Uyen contacted a cousin who belonged to the cell of Duong Hac Dinh, the head of the Tonkin Regional Committee. It is unclear whether they merely wanted advice on whether to proceed, or assistance in fulfilling their pledge. Whatever the case, Dinh convened a secret meeting of the Regional Committee in Hanoi on 28 May to discuss the deal which the sisters had struck with the Sûreté.[63] It was decided that the two sisters could not be allowed to go free, despite their relatively low ranking within the League, because they were related to too many other adherents and were therefore privy to too many of the group's secrets. Kinship, the building block of membership for the League, had become a destructive force.

According to League rules, when a guilty member was eliminated, the execution squad had to include his sponsors.[64] This grim regulation served as a screening device, and was also supposed to reinforce party loyalty over personal considerations. Ho Ngoc Lan, a shoemaker by profession and a crack marksman, was given the job of killing Nhu and Uyen, though he was engaged to Nhu. On the morning of 31 May 1929, the two sisters, unaware that their comrades had condemned them to death, took the train to Haiphong; they expected to go from there to Hong Kong, where they would fall under the protection of the Central Committee. At dusk, they went into a little lane where they were to be joined by another comrade from the Haiphong Municipal Section, and were immediately met by gunfire. Ho Ngoc Lan did not dare to contravene League orders, yet he could not bring himself to kill his fiancée, so he only shot her in the thigh. But he fired point blank at her sister Uyen, who died instantaneously. The Haiphong branch of the Youth League printed tracts to explain the killing, arguing that, in helping the Sûreté track down Nguyen Thai Hoc (whom the Youth League had declared an enemy), the sisters were guilty of aiding the French, even though they had not intended to betray their own party. The tracts bore the signature "The Assassination Squad of the Tonkin Regional Committee."[65]

Meanwhile, the continuing arrests of its members was forcing the VNQDD to jettison its insurrectionary strategy. According to this strategy, a general uprising was the last of the three stages of revolution and should be launched only if the balance of power was favorable to the insurrectionary forces, after the Party had had sufficient time to recruit adherents and mobilize popular support. But, at a plenum convened in mid-May 1929, Nguyen Thai Hoc reported somberly: "Faced with the present circumstances, our Party must lead the population in a general uprising urgently. If we leave it for later in accordance with the Party's timetable, we will certainly all be arrested and die slowly in prison. Our Party will disintegrate. This means there must be a general uprising within one year." [66]

There were calls for a less apocalyptic approach to the Party's problems; some also voiced hopes that a slow reorganization of its apparatus was possible, but Nguyen Thai Hoc's view that they were probably doomed and must go down fighting prevailed. He called on soldiers within the Party to fabricate bombs and reconnoiter for favorable sites from which to launch the uprising. The task of ensuring liaison with the colonial troops in the Yen Bay garrison in Thai Nguyen province, where the Party counted numerous adherents, was entrusted to Nguyen thi Giang, her sister, and another woman.[67] The stockpiling of weapons and bombs began, but arrests continued to deplete the ranks of the Party. In July, the authorities staged a highly publicized trial of 227 Party members who had been implicated in the murders of Bazin and of Trinh thi Uyen. In October, an explosion alerted the authorities to the fabrication of bombs in Bac Giang and further arrests were made. More bombs were discovered in different localities during the following month. The Party was falling into ever direr straits. Nguyen Thai Hoc and two other leaders of the Party barely escaped the trap which the Sûreté set for them on the advice of a traitor who had once recruited colonial troops into the VNQDD. It was soon after this nearly fatal betrayal that another meeting took place in Vong La village in Phu Tho on 26 January 1930. Nguyen Thai Hoc acknowledged to his colleagues that they were facing defeat, but said that they could not wait for the Party to be reorganized before launching a general uprising. With the recent New Year's celebrations still fresh in everyone's mind, Hoc declared:

> Life is like a game of chance; if you are dealt black cards, you stand to lose all your capital. Fortune is against us and the Party runs the

risk of dissipating all its forces. Once fear has entered the heart of people, they will lose their enthusiasm and their faith, and the revolutionary movement will become as cold as dead ashes. We will lose support, and we will be arrested sooner or later. We will die a slow and lonely death in prisons and penal camps. It is better to die now and leave behind the example of sacrifice and striving for later generations. If we do not succeed, at least we will have become men.[68]

The general uprising was fixed for the night of 9 February 1930. At Yen Bay, the insurrection proceeded as planned. An emissary was dispatched to Hoc, in Bac Ninh, to let him know that he should start an uprising there. But the emissary was arrested in Hanoi, and the Bac Ninh insurrection never materialized. In Yen Bay, the uprising was swiftly and brutally repressed. Nguyen Thai Hoc fled to Co Am village in Hai Duong. The authorities discovered his whereabouts and attacked the village on 16 February, laying waste to it and killing dozens of inhabitants. Nguyen Thai Hoc was captured five days later while trying to make his way to China.

On 17 June 1930, he and twelve other leaders of the Vietnamese Nationalist Party were brought to a scaffold at Yen Bay, where the rebellion had first started. As they faced the guillotine, several of them called out: "Long live Vietnam!"[69] With this quixotic gesture, the martyrs of Yen Bay, as they became known, joined the pantheon of heroes who had kept alive the Vietnamese sense of national identity through centuries of foreign conquest and domination, refusing to be daunted by overwhelming odds. That they had been forced against their better judgment to stage a suicidal rising and that their party was brought low by the willful lack of discipline of a self-aggrandizing individual was deemed less important than the courageous manner with which they accepted their fate.

But while the martyrs provided a link between modern anticolonialism and the resonant past, their death also brought to a close the first chapter of the Revolution. On 1 May 1930, six weeks before the leaders of the Yen Bay rising were marched to the scaffold, peasants in Nghe An had risen in protest against the insistence of the colonial state that taxes be paid on time even though the world economic crisis and natural disaster had brought starvation to the countryside. Their uprising was the first of a long series of massive demonstrations which would become the hallmark of anticolonial politics in the 1930s.[70]

In their different ways, the Vietnamese Youth League and the Vietnamese Nationalist Party had taken individualism to its limits, the Youth League by trying to channel youthful rebellion into revolutionary energy, the VNQDD by relying on personal heroism when party discipline broke down and its revolutionary strategy had to be discarded. The Vietnamese Nationalist Party never quite recovered from the failure of Yen Bay, but in mid-1930, the Vietnamese Youth League finally succeeded in transforming itself into the Indochinese Communist Party. The new party, born in the fratricidal turmoil of the previous two years, opted to shed the youthful image which the League had so assiduously cultivated when it was courting rebellious students. In its definitive statutes adopted in October 1930, the image of the party-as-family was nowhere to be found.

Even those who did not belong to an organized party no longer believed in the revolutionary potential of youth. In April 1930, the twenty-four-year-old Ta Thu Thau dismissed his former membership in the Jeune Annam party as "youthful folly."[71] Vietnamese revolutionaries now understood that revolution was not synonymous with rebellion against patriarchal authority and outmoded tradition, and that the family should not be its primary battleground or its central metaphor. The language of radicalism was giving way to the language of Marxism.

8 Communists, Trotskyists, and Progressives

> Make this the principle of your actions:
> People of the same country should love one another.
>
> Vietnamese popular saying

THE MASS POLITICS of the 1930s displaced an earlier style of public discourse which, until then, had been unabashedly elitist. This elitism reflected the Confucian-influenced notion that the primary locus and motive force of change was the individual. Even Nguyen An Ninh, the most populist of the previous decade's political figures, had no qualms about urging the creation of a new spiritual elite. Early revolutionary parties were thus an extension of the elite's self-image: the best that society could offer morally and intellectually, and its natural source of political leadership.

If the family provided the forcing ground of revolution, it did so partly because early anticolonial activists had little idea of how society operated beyond the level of the family. Their ability to analyze the workings of economic and social forces was stunted by the overwhelming fact of colonialism; they were unable or unwilling to disaggregate their own society into different components with competing claims and rights. It is possible that they shied away from acknowledging that the Vietnamese people had not presented a united front against the French, and hoped that greater unity might prevail in the fight to recapture independence: in the meantime, the less said about potential sources of divisiveness, the better.[1] Judging from their rhetoric, most revolutionaries of the early 1920s also hoped that, once the great evil of colonialism was over, the people would exercise its longed-for power to vote and create a new political system. And because such a system would be democratically run and would be untainted by colonialism, whatever conflicts arose among fellow Vietnamese would easily be solved.

Nguyen Ai Quoc himself expressed this early utopian streak when he wrote: "Revolution is the change from bad to good; it is the entirety of all acts by which an oppressed people becomes strong. The history of all societies has taught us that always through revolution has it ever been possible to improve the government, education, industry, social organization, etc. . . ."[2]

Some, however, were dissatisfied with this overly simple vision of change. Since free discussion was easier abroad than at home, it was in China and France that the most sustained attempts to arrive at a new conception of the revolutionary process were made. By the time the Youth League and the Vietnamese Nationalist Party were caught in their respective struggles for survival, Vietnamese émigrés in France and China had been exploring the implications for Vietnam of Marxist historical materialism for at least two years. They apparently were drawn to Marxism-Leninism for the same reasons as Nguyen Ai Quoc: it established a positive correlation between the struggle for national independence and the struggle to restructure society.

When organizing the Youth League, Nguyen Ai Quoc had emphasized the Leninist organizational blueprint rather than the Marxist theory of history. He resorted to the familiar metaphor of a sea voyage to explain his purpose:

> What is the first thing to be done? First of all, there must be a revolutionary party to mobilize and organize the people at home, and to link up with oppressed people and the proletarian classes abroad. Only if the party is solid can the revolution succeed, just as only when the helmsman is firmly in control can the ship sail. If we want to have a solid party, it must have an ideology as its foundation, an ideology that everyone in the party must understand and follow. A party without an ideology is like a person without intelligence, a ship without a compass.[3]

If proof was needed that a Leninist party was the best guarantee of success, there was always the example of the October Revolution, which had turned a formerly backward country on the fringes of Western civilization into what was widely imagined to be a workers' paradise. The issue was how to duplicate that success. But adherents of revolutionary parties (including the Youth League, the Phuc Viet, and the VNQDD) eventually turned their attention to the Marxist historical vision itself. Their debates show that Vietnamese revolutionaries did not accept all the premises of Marxism-Leninism unquestioningly, especially those concerning the historical role of the bourgeoisie. They were aware that the bourgeoisie of their own country was of recent origin, and that its birth was not the result of indigenous forces, but was connected with the advent of colonialism. Its revolutionary potential was highly problematic, posing a challenge to the Marxist scheme of historical progression. But the difficulties which the Youth League and the VNQDD began experiencing in 1929, the impact of the Great Depression, the reaction of the bourgeoisie to the peasant protests of 1930–1931, and above all, the continued absence of satisfactory alternative theories of history, helped push them over to the Marxist-Leninist camp.

Not every participant in the earlier anticolonial movement became a Marxist. Many exhausted their spurt of rebelliousness and returned to the bosom of their families, foreswearing politics. Others lacked the discipline required for admission into the ranks of the Indochinese Communist Party. Still others rejected the idea that for the revolution to be successful, it must follow the path of class struggle as now mandated by the Comintern. They preferred to cling to their vision of patriotic unity and of heroic individuals laying down their lives for the fatherland. They called themselves progressives, to distinguish themselves from both the Marxist revolutionaries and the neo-traditionalists who figured prominently in the imperial cabinet formed in the wake of the peasant protests of 1930–1931. But no matter what political choice each individual made, the language of revolution and counterrevolution was transformed by the injection of Marxist-Leninist terminology.

The introduction of the idiom of class-based social analysis produced a drastic intellectual reorientation which effectively ended the radical phase of the Vietnamese Revolution. This reorientation involved a rethinking of the role of the revolutionary party (and of the individual within it) and of the social processes which give rise to revolution. It substituted the masses for the individual, class for generation, society for the family, and economics for culture. Whereas radicals had believed that a unitary struggle for the liberation of the nation as a whole would serve as an operational framework for the emancipation of the individual, Marxists cast the struggle against imperialism in terms of conflicts between classes. Marxism downplayed the importance of the individual and redefined the position of the revolutionary party within society by calling attention to the role of the masses in the revolutionary process. Thus, if the 1920s were the decade of the rebellious individual, the 1930s became the decade of the proletarian masses, with class struggle replacing intergenerational conflict as the motive force of revolution.

The spread of Marxist theory among Vietnamese émigrés in France and China coincided with a shift in Comintern policy toward anticolonial movements in general and Indochina more specifically. In the early 1920s, the independent growth of Vietnamese communism had been limited by the Comintern's belief that the Vietnamese, as natives of French colonies, were not a separate national group. Furthermore, the Comintern considered the Vietnamese struggle for independence subordinate to the greater issue of the Chinese Revolution.[4] Vietnamese, therefore, were encouraged to adhere either to the French or to the Chinese Communist Party, but not to form their own. The drawbacks of such a strategy were obvious. In 1924, Nguyen Ai Quoc expressed concern over the relative lack of importance accorded to colonial questions in general, and Vietnam in particular, within the French Communist Party; in 1927–1928, the collapse of the United Front between the Chinese Communist Party and the Kuomintang had led to the arrest of key members of the Youth League who had joined the CCP. As a predominantly peasant society, Vietnam did not fit the model of a country on the threshold of a proletarian revolution. But the debacle of the United Front had eroded faith in the prior necessity of a bourgeois nationalist revolution and encouraged debate about the historical role of other social classes, including the peasantry.

There had been signs of growing Comintern interest in Vietnam even before the final unraveling of the United Front. At the plenary assembly of the Third International in Moscow in February 1927, the Javanese Communist Semaoen claimed that "the existence of a vast agricultural proletariat, the rapid development of the industrial proletariat, together with the absence of a bourgeoisie and weak contact between the French and the natives, make Indochina an easy milieu for revolutionary victory."[5] The following year, Humbert Droz, secretary for Latin American countries of the Third International, repeated this claim, but put greater emphasis on the importance of colonialism.[6] The colonial policy endorsed by the Comintern at its Sixth Congress in August 1928 put the struggle for national liberation squarely in the context of the international class struggle, thus dispensing with the idea that a bourgeois nationalist revolution was a necessary precursor to a proletarian one. Equally significant was the apparent inclusion of the peasantry in the definition of the "proletarian masses."

Like so many other concepts related to revolution, class was a recent addition to the language of Vietnamese political discourse. Phan Boi Chau had identified ten different "classes" whom he exhorted to unite together to resist French colonial rule, but he had used the term loosely to mean occupational or social groups. The translation of the term "proletariat" into Vietnamese (and Chinese) as "propertyless" (*vo san;* Ch. *wu chan*) blurred the fundamental analytic differences between the potentially revolutionary workers and the potentially counterrevolutionary peasantry of Marxist thought. Nguyen Ai Quoc himself contributed to this theoretical vagueness by regularly using the hyphenated term "worker-peasant" *(cong-nong)* in *The Road to Revolution*. As vice-president of Krestintern, he had for many years urged that more attention be given to the role of the peasantry in waging revolution at a global level.[7] His views were vindicated when, ignoring Marx's commments about "the idiocy of rural life" and the innate conservatism of peasants, the Comintern began to perceive a definite revolutionary potential in the peasantry of colonized countries.

The Transformation of the Youth League

Emigrés in China and France came at Marxism from different perspectives and with different agendas. The split between Stalin and Trotsky affected both groups, but in very dissimilar ways. Trotskyism, a major intellectual force among the expatriate community in France, hardly touched the Vietnamese living in China. This lack of interest was undoubtedly related to the desire of the China-based Central Committee of the Youth League to be admitted into the Third International. The League already had good lines of communication with Moscow through adherents enrolled in the Workers' University of the East. It had received advice, but so far had not succeeded in becoming a national branch of the Third International. It was in this context that the Youth League began to pay attention to theoretical issues it had previously ignored. Its desire to be considered ideologically correct by the Third International informed its interpretation of these issues and insulated it from "deviationist" influences.

The Youth League held a plenum in May 1929 to vote on a new organizational structure and a new program of action designed to meet Comintern requirements for recognition as a national branch.[8] When the plenum opened on 1 May in Hong Kong, it became evident that the Central Committee had not moved fast enough for some domestic adherents. In Annam and Tonkin, dissident factions had formed and were urging that the League transform itself into a proper Communist party by abandoning the concept of unitary revolution in favor of class struggle. Their representatives at the plenum suggested that the name of the organization be changed, but the Central Committee rejected their suggestion for fear of attracting further repression from the KMT. The three dissident delegates then immediately resigned from the League, declaring that they no longer wanted to obey orders from a "bourgeois group" composed of "false revolutionaries."[9] Hong Son and Le Duy Diem protested that they had worked very hard, and from the very beginning, to transform the League into a Communist party. They felt that the plenum was the wrong forum at which to propose the change, however, because too many of the delegates did not have the qualities required of Communist revolutionaries.[10]

On 9 May, the plenum approved a manifesto which was sent, adorned with a red star, a hammer, and a sickle, to the Comintern with a request for admission into the Third International. The manifesto reflected the reluctance of the delegates to the plenum to abandon the nationalist, unitary vision of revolution that had drawn them into the Youth League in favor of the idea of class struggle that now dominated Comintern policy toward colonial countries. They called on "workers, peasants, soldiers, traders, youth, and all the oppressed and exploited people of Annam to unite, to separate themselves from landowners, mandarins, and capitalists and to fight without quarter French imperialism and its running dogs."[11]

But while the plenum was in session, the three dissidents had hastened back home and begun the task of creating an Indochinese Communist Party: they wooed away adherents of the Youth League, engaged in intense (and hostile) competition for new members with the VNQDD in Tonkin, and sought to merge with the Revolutionary Party in Annam. The two dissidents from Tonkin, Ngo Gia Tu and Nguyen Tuan, first won over the Haiphong Municipal Section, then the Regional Committee, and eventually the whole Tonkin branch of the Youth League. But the emerging Indochinese Communist Party was dealt a serious setback when Nguyen Tuan was arrested in June and revealed the names of many of his colleagues to the Sûreté.[12]

Establishing the Indochinese Communist Party in Annam was more complicated. The Vietnamese Revolutionary Party had merged with another anticolonial organization, composed mainly of teachers and civil servants, and had taken yet another name, the New Vietnam Revolutionary Party (Tan Viet Cach Menh Dang). In February 1929, Dao Duy Anh had written on behalf of the New Vietnam Revolutionary Party a memorandum on the possibility of organizing a Communist party in Vietnam. He argued that there existed neither a true capitalist class nor a working class large enough to wage revolution: "Contrary to what is happening in Europe, workers are not in permanent conflict with the capitalist class; they lack 'class consciousness.'"[13] He came to the conclusion that it was premature to think of revolution and that the party he envisioned should concentrate on recruiting petty intellectuals rather than on mobilizing workers through incitement to class struggle. Nonetheless, when Tran van Cung, the dissident delegate of the Youth League, approached members of the New Vietnam Revolutionary Party with a view to forming the Indochinese Communist Party, he managed to win over quite a few of them. Negotiations were not without difficulty: Tran Mong Bach, for example, was outraged that the nineteen-year-old Cung, who had been his student and whom he had recruited into his Self-Perfection Society two years earlier, refused him the courtesy of calling him "professor."[14] Cung argued that they had achieved revolutionary equality.

Things went even less well in Cochinchina. The Regional Committee had been disbanded in the wake of the Barbier Street murder. The man who was supposed to supervise its reconstitution on behalf of the Central Committee, Pham van Dong, fell into the hands of the Sûreté when he arrived from Hong Kong after the plenum.[15] To make things worse, in August some local members of the Youth League created a rival Annamite Communist Party (An Nam Cong San Dang). But by dint of hard work, Ngo Gia Tu, who had come from Tonkin, managed to arrest the growth of this rival organization and to bring most members of the Youth League into the Indochinese Communist Party.[16] The intense competition for membership led to the absorption into the Party of a number of other anticolonial organizations, including the Nguyen An Ninh Secret Society.

A member of the Youth League had found out that Nguyen Ai Quoc was in Siam while the League was tearing itself apart and wrote to beg him to come to Hong Kong to mediate between the warring factions. But Nguyen Ai Quoc declined; his influence was not strong enough to effect a reconciliation at that point. The Indochinese Communist Party vowed to reject all compromises and would agree to fuse with the League only on the orders of the Comintern. On 4 October, its Central Committee wrote to the leadership of the League, declaring belligerently that "if Vuong [that is, Nguyen Ai Quoc] returns, we will follow the same policy toward him as we are applying to you."[17] Toward the end of the year, word came that the League's request for admission into the Third International had been rejected; so had a similar request from the Indochinese Communist Party. In both cases, confusion over the motive force of revolution had contributed to the Comintern's rejection.[18] A source close to the leadership of the Third International relayed to Hong Son its critique of the League's manifesto. According to that critique, the Party could not claim to represent all "the laboring masses" of the population and set forth different claims on behalf of each social category; this would only lead to scissions among the propertyless classes. Although it was true that "the only possible revolution was a bourgeois-democratic one, given the aspirations of the Indochinese bourgeoisie toward independence which go hand in hand with the 'struggle for land' started by the peasants, the proletariat must assume the leadership of that revolution."[19] The Third International contended that the theory of revolution in stages would only put a brake on mass action and leave the leadership of the struggle in the hands of a small number of Communist intellectuals.[20] The politics of gradual reform were repudiated in favor of accelerated proletarianization.

Only after the Third International had rejected both applications did Nguyen Ai Quoc come to Hong Kong in January 1930. With characteristic speed, he studied the situation, then convened a meeting of representatives of the warring factions. At the meeting, held on 3–7 February 1930, a new program and new statutes were elaborated. The Vietnamese Youth League was no more. In its place was the Vietnamese Communist Party, whose Central Committee was to be located in Haiphong instead of abroad. After the program and statutes of the new party were again rejected by the Comintern, another meeting was convened in October to revise both. This second meeting became known as the First Plenum of the Indochinese Communist Party. (The name, following the wishes of Comintern, reflected the inclusion of Laotians and Cambodians.)[21] Nguyen Ai Quoc was able to persuade the Eastern Bureau of the Third International to provide a monthly stipend to the Indochinese Communist Party and to get it affiliated directly with the Third International, rather than with the Singapore Federation as a branch of the Chinese Communist Party.[22]

The Rise of Trotskyism

From available documents, it would seem that those who were involved in the difficult transformation of the Youth League into the Indochinese Communist Party paid little attention to the growing rift between Stalin and Trotsky which culminated in the latter's expulsion from the Soviet Communist Party in 1928 and his banishment to Prinkipo in February of the following year. In France, however, the situation was very different. It was through the airing of differences between Stalin and Trotsky that many newly arrived Vietnamese received their first taste of Marxist ideology. And since Paris was a center of international Trotskyism, they could not but be influenced by the Trotskyist sympathies of leading intellectuals on the left.

There was nothing in France to match the organizational framework in which the metamorphosis of the Youth League into the Indochinese Communist Party took place. There was no Communist or proto-Communist organization tailored specifically to Vietnamese needs. The French Communist Party seemed to prefer "sterile agitation" among petty bourgeois elements to providing rigorous training in revolutionary work to the Vietnamese. This, at least, was the conclusion which Ta Thu Thau drew in 1930.[23]

The demise of the Intercolonial Union in 1926 had left a void which radical émigrés had difficulty filling.[24] Following a proposal which Nguyen Ai Quoc had made in 1923 but never carried out, Nguyen The Truyen brought out a Vietnamese-language newspaper, *The Soul of Vietnam (Viet Nam Hon)*, in Paris in January 1925. The journal formed the new focus of activity for Vietnamese adherents of the Intercolonial Union. Its editorial line closely followed that of *Paria*, combining articles on colonial and working-class problems, but wholly in the context of Vietnam. After it was prohibited in July 1926, it continued to appear clandestinely until September 1927 under a variety of names.[25] On 30 August 1926, the journal published an "Appeal to the League of Nations for the Right of the Annamite People to Self-Determination" in which the "total and immediate independence of the Annamite People" was advocated.[26] The group formed around the publication of *The Soul of Vietnam* organized itself into a new party called the Annamite Independence Party (AIP), which officially saw light in June 1927. Unlike the Intercolonial Union, it had no formal links with the French Communist Party.

The Annamite Independence Party was only one of many organizations in France that attracted new arrivals. The AIP and the Constitutionalists were competing for ascendancy over the students' organizations which were springing up everywhere, especially in cities such as Marseilles, Toulouse, and Lyons. The Association Mutuelle des Indochinois, originally founded by Bui Quang Chieu, had fallen into the hands of militants connected with *The Soul of Vietnam* in October 1926 and was dissolved in March 1927.[27] Leaders of the AIP at first tried to maintain good relations with the Constitutionalists. Bui Quang Chieu even published a number of articles in *The Soul of Vietnam* before the radical politics of the AIP frightened him away. Duong van Giao remained in contact with the AIP for a while longer; he even attended an organizational meeting of the AIP in early 1927 as the official representative of the Constitutionalist Party in France, though he did not sign the list of claims drafted on that occasion. The list was submitted to the first congress of the Internationalist League against Imperialism and for National Independence (better known as the Anti-Imperialist League) in Brussels in February 1927, much as the Group of Annamite Patriots had sent its claims to the Versailles Conference eight years earlier. The AIP called for the French government to return Vietnamese land to the natives. To old demands, it added calls for freedom to create trade unions and hold meetings, and advocated equal pay for equal work.[28] But when Duong van Giao, on behalf of the Constitutionalists, advocated "free Franco-Annamite cooperation," AIP delegates protested vehemently: "What the Annamite people want is not 'free Franco-indigenous cooperation' but total and immediate independence for the country . . . For this reason, the Annamites want unity that grows ever closer and therefore join the Independence Party, the party of workers, peasants, and intellectuals. Like their Chinese brothers, the Annamites turn their eyes toward the valiant proletariat of the world."[29]

In contrast to their counterparts in China, who seem to have viewed doctrinal correctness as their passport into the Third International, leftist Vietnamese in France were genuinely interested in theory for its own sake. But they encountered considerable difficulty in their attempts to study the Vietnamese situation through Marxist lenses. In matters of ideology as well as organization they were left to their own devices, because the French Communist Party made little effort either to enlist or to assist them.

Founders of the AIP were especially interested in defining the role of the bourgeoisie in the coming revolution. In Tonkin and Annam, where most of the leadership of the Indochinese Communist Party originated, the bourgeoisie was small and its economic and political power negligible.[30] Disputes over its historical role were therefore largely academic. But in Cochinchina, where many members of the AIP came from, the native bourgeoisie had acquired considerable clout both economically and politically. For them, therefore, the issue carried important strategic implications. Lenin's "Theses on the National and Colonial Question" offered contradictory clues to the potential role of the bourgeoisie. Despite the AIP founders' references to the "valiant proletariat," they had trouble figuring out the exact relationship between race and class. Should the Vietnamese revolution be a nationalist or a class-based revolution? Should an alliance be struck with the bourgeoisie? Was the bourgeoisie strong enough to lead a bourgeois democratic revolution or would it prove to be the enemy of revolution? Nguyen The Truyen argued in June 1927 that in a colonial situation such as Vietnam's, racial unity must take priority over class considerations. As he observed, "in Indochina, the highest native bourgeois is politically and socially inferior to the lowest European clerk." After all, he went on, Marxist doctrine envisaged the necessity of a national phase before the final triumph of communism. This could only mean "the impossibility of communism in the colonies in the present state of affairs."[31] Others worried that, for a bourgeois democratic revolution to become a possibility, the strength of the bourgeoisie would first have to be increased, and with it, its power to exploit the rest of its compatriots. It seemed an intolerable scenario. Stymied by their inability to resolve this theoretical conundrum, leaders of the AIP were at a loss to define the character of their organization. When the AIP made its official appearance on 13 June 1927, its political identity was so uncertain as to be defined entirely in negatives: "neither separatist, nor communist, nor even nationalist in the European sense of the word."[32] Exactly where this put AIP on the ideological spectrum was left unsaid.

This ideological confusion allowed the AIP to continue its ambiguous relations with the Constitutionalists. In late September 1927, the Constitutionalists organized a congress of Vietnamese students in Aix-en-Provence to launch a new federation of Vietnamese students. Although the agenda of the congress, launched with the support of the authorities, was ostensibly apolitical, Nguyen The Truyen and Nguyen An Ninh (who had arrived in August) intervened in debates on scholarships and educational curricula to challenge the political theses of the Constitutionalists. Under the impetus of Nguyen The Truyen and Nguyen An Ninh, the congress became the launching pad for committees of reception dominated by anti-Constitutionalist elements. These committees, designed to welcome newly arrived students from Vietnam, were crucial in drawing them into political organizations. Despite the Constitutionalist setback at the congress, Duong van Giao enjoyed a small triumph on 6 October when, to the outrage of Nguyen The Truyen and Nguyen An Ninh, he was allowed to preside over an AIP meeting.[33] But after he left for home twelve days later, the influence of the Constitutionalists in France declined rapidly.

Nguyen An Ninh and Nguyen The Truyen also returned to Vietnam in December. Nguyen An Ninh was going home to pursue his scheme to create an anticolonial movement out of the tradition of secret societies. But what prompted Nguyen The Truyen to leave France with his French wife and three children was never made clear. To those who asked, he complained that he had been used by the French Communist Party. His wife claimed that he was unhappy with its drill-sergeant mentality ("caporalisme").[34] But, as his discussion of the revolutionary role of the bourgeoisie hinted, he was also disenchanted with Marxism as an ideology. Although he was closely watched in Vietnam by the Sûreté, Truyen gave no sign of political activity. The radical phase of his career was over. This was much to the relief of his relatives, for during his militant period, he had enlisted quite a few of his cousins in the Intercolonial Union, one of whom even went to Moscow.[35]

After the departure of Nguyen The Truyen, the AIP entered a new phase. In January 1928, Ta Thu Thau, together with a group of newly arrived students, managed to revitalize it and to move it more firmly to the left. The manifesto of the new-style AIP was published on 1 April 1928 (with additions in September). To demands for immediate independence, through violent means if necessary, it added anticapitalist rhetoric. Its stated goal, after the recovery of independence and the establishment of a democratic government, was to protect "all compatriots who are oppressed by aristocrats and capitalists, and raise them to a status worthy of them in conformity with justice and humanity." The manifesto further criticized Western governments for being dominated by "rich people of little talent and small virtue." In the free Vietnam envisaged by the AIP, the parliament would include no representatives of political parties, only of trade unions.[36]

The AIP manifesto was not more specific about revolutionary strategy and theory because the AIP was still agonizing over the desirability of uniting with the bourgeoisie to achieve independence. Following a series of incidents in Cochinchina, the plight of the rural masses had begun to attract the attention of the urban elite.[37] The struggle for land had finally emerged as critical to the revolutionary process. Therefore, the potential role of the landowning bourgeoisie of Cochinchina in the process had to be clarified. On 15 October 1928 the Toulouse-based student journal *L'Avenir de l'Annam*, headed by Tran van Thach, published an article predicting that, in the event of revolution, the local bourgeoisie would betray its compatriots to protect its class interests: "The countless examples provided by liberation movements in colonial countries (China, Egypt, India) show that the upper classes tend toward collaboration with the oppressor, toward sharing with it the profits drawn from the misery, from the indescribable exploitation of the masses of colonial workers. The failure of these movements has been provoked by the treason of the national bourgeoisie, which prefers to make common cause with the colonizer than to accede to the legitimate demands of the masses."[38] The article went on to advocate a central role for the peasantry in the coming struggle: "But in order to mobilize the immense peasant masses, it is not enough to promise formal independence for the country; the struggle for independence must be linked organically to the basic needs of the people, and its most urgent need is land . . . Land to the peasants! Total independence for Annam! These are the two inseparable goals whose fulfillment alone will allow us to hope for a better future."

In November 1928, the journal further elaborated: "We want to give land to those who have been tilling it for centuries. They alone—the Annamite peasants—represent a reservoir of inexhaustible forces against imperialism . . . The only indomitable fighters are the peasant masses; without them, our efforts are doomed to failure, and the most imperious need of the masses is land. They must get it."[39]

The emerging consensus within the AIP seemed to be that whether because it was weak or because it would surely put its own interests above the good of the nation, the bourgeoisie could not be counted upon to lead the revolution. The motor force of the revolution would thus have to be the workers and the peasants. Although this conclusion brought AIP thinking close to the line adopted at the Sixth Congress of the Comintern, it did not bring the AIP any closer to the French Communist Party. Nguyen van Tao, the most prominent Vietnamese member of the FCP, played an ambiguous role in the attempt to create an Indochinese Communist Party independent of the Colonial Studies Commission.[40] Henri Lozeray, a member of the Commission, met with Vietnamese Communists on 22 April 1928, but the meeting was fruitless. There was disagreement over the possibility of a Communist revolution in the immediate future and over the desirability of winning members of the AIP over to communism. A proposal to create a Vietnamese cell within the French Communist Party was made, but nothing came of it; Vietnamese Communists continued to be scattered among various French cells.[41] The one concrete result was that Nguyen van Tao began producing a new journal, *Workers and Peasants (Cong Nong)*.

The disagreements over whether to form a separate Indochinese Communist Party foreshadowed changes in colonial policy announced at the Sixth Congress of the Comintern. As later became clear in the critique of the 1929 manifestos of the Youth League and the fledgling ICP, the Comintern rejected the possibility of an alliance with the national bourgeoisie and urged extreme caution in forging tactical alliances with non-Communist radicals. This new policy led to a considerable cooling in the relations between Communist and non-Communist émigrés. Although the AIP had no formal ties with the French Communist Party, it had, until then, maintained contacts with the latter and some AIP adherents were recruited to go to Moscow. But Ta Thu Thau, whose distrust of foreign control over the Vietnamese struggle for independence was reinforced by the new policy, refused an offer to go to Moscow.[42] This meant in practice a refusal to become a Communist and to submit himself to the discipline of the French Communist Party. Both because of Thau's refusal to go to Moscow and because of the Comintern's policy of not cooperating with non-Communist organizations, the AIP lost whatever support the French Commmunist Party had previously given it and became highly vulnerable to repression. On 16 September, the Government-General of Indochina formally requested that the metropolitan authorities dissolve the AIP. The request was granted on 21 March 1929; in the interim, the AIP functioned under the shadow of dissolution.[43] Relations between the AIP and the FCP took a turn for the worse in January 1929 after the right-wing French organization Jeunesses Patriotes staged a demonstration in front of a Parisian café frequented by Vietnamese émigrés. Several Vietnamese were arrested during the ensuing brawl. *Humanité* accused Ta Thu Thau and other members of the AIP of having stayed away from the café, knowing that their Communist compatriots were going to be attacked. In fact, however, Ta Thu Thau and his housemate Huynh van Phuong were among those arrested. The AIP responded with counteraccusations of its own in its organ, *Résurrection*.[44]

The worsening state of relations between the Communists and the AIP reflected a larger crisis within world communism. By the end of 1928, the French Commmunist Party and the Vietnamese expatriates who either belonged to it or were to some extent influenced by its doctrine were reeling from the shock of Trotsky's expulsion from the Soviet leadership. Among Trotsky's supporters, the failure of Comintern policy in China, which had culminated in the split between the KMT and the CCP, reinforced hostility toward Stalin. A group named Left Opposition (Opposition de Gauche), which was still affiliated to the mainstream French Communist Party but sympathetic to Trotsky, had already been in existence for several years. It was represented by several journals: *Contre le Courant*, edited by Maurice Paz; *La Vérité*; and *La Lutte des Classes*, edited by Alfred Rosmer and Pierre Naville. Rosmer, who had been a friend of Lenin and had once represented the French Communist Party on the Executive Committee of the Comintern, enjoyed enormous prestige; Naville was a highly respected intellectual. The stature of the French Trotskyists in the Communist world had made Paris a center of international Trotskyism. After Trotsky was banished to Prinkipo on 10 February 1929, there began a steady stream of letters and visits between Prinkipo and Paris. This traffic coincided with the move leftward of what had once been the AIP. After the AIP was disbanded by court order in March, Ta Thu Thau entered in contact with the *Contre le Courant* group of

Maurice Paz. In late 1929, he began collaborating also with *La Vérité* and *La Lutte des Classes*.[45]

Another factor in the growth of Marxism among Vietnamese émigrés in France was an increasing awareness of economic issues. Floods and typhoons laid waste large areas of Cochinchina and Tonkin in 1929 and killed hundreds of people. These natural disasters compounded shortages caused by a mediocre harvest.[46] The impact of the world economic crisis was also beginning to be felt in Vietnam as well as in France. For theoretically inclined revolutionaries such as Ta Thu Thau, this was another incentive to ponder the relationship between nation and class, and the role of the bourgeoisie in the revolution. On 8 April 1930, Ta Thu Thau and Huynh van Phuong jointly published an article in *La Vérité* in which they explored the theoretical reasons for the collusion between the bourgeoisie and the colonial regime. In the article, entitled "After Yen Bay, What to Do?," they argued that the Vietnamese bourgeoisie was fundamentally dependent on colonial capitalism, and that it was therefore bound to collude with it against fellow Vietnamese: "Born of conquest, which was a veritable economic revolution because it replaced small-scale production with capitalist production, it can only survive and expand in a regime established by conquest."[47] They condemned the bourgeoisie's double-faced strategy of making periodic appeals to national solidarity when its economic interests were at stake, and of retreating when violent revolution threatened. The article reprised themes that had already been explored by Tran van Thach in 1928. But it was also informed by an awareness of the hostility with which southern Constitutionalists and northern neo-traditionalists had greeted the Yen Bay uprising.[48] Although Ta Thu Thau remained unwilling to let non-Vietnamese dominate the direction and agenda of the Vietnamese revolution, in matters of theory he was not very far from the positions adopted by the Comintern. Ta Thu Thau and Huynh van Phuong were deported, shortly after their article appeared, for organizing a demonstration in May in front of the Elysée Palace to protest the death sentences handed out to the leaders of the Yen Bay uprising. Fifty demonstrators, including Thau and Phuong, were arrested; nineteen, all students, were subsequently deported.

Meanwhile, mass protests had erupted throughout Vietnam. Famine had already struck in the wake of the disasters of 1929 but, fearing that fund-raising campaigns and organizations would serve as fronts for anti-French activities, the authorities refused to sanction Vietnamese initiatives to collect relief for the victims. To justify their refusal, officials also denied the very existence of the famine and therefore took no measures to allay hunger.[49] The authorities thus stymied efforts by nonpolitical figures to organize relief but did not prevent, paradoxically, the recruiting activities of the revolutionaries. With the Vietnamese Nationalist Party sidelined by repression in the wake of the assassination of Bazin, the Indochinese Communist Party and the Youth League had been busy mobilizing peasants and workers. The Comintern had advised them not to wait for the Communist Party to be fully in place to begin organizing mass protests. After the fusion in February 1930 of the various groups that had issued from the League, the newly formed Communist Party threw its energies into organizing workers' and peasants' protests. Within the month, coolies went on strike again at the Michelin rubber plantation in Phu Rieng, Cochinchina. In March, workers at the textile factory in Nam Dinh in Tonkin also struck; they were followed in April by workers at the match factory and sawmill in Ben Thuy in northern Annam. As tax-paying time loomed closer, the number of workers' strikes picked up. On 1 May, the first mass protests by peasants erupted in Nghe An, followed by other demonstrations in neighboring Ha Tinh, and in scattered places in Cochinchina. Soon the hammer and sickle became familiar symbols of revolt. In Nghe An and Ha Tinh, Soviets were established in September 1930, and an attempt to do likewise was made in Cao Lanh in Cochinchina.[50]

It was when peasant demonstrations were at their peak that the successor to the AIP, a group calling itself the Organization of Vietnamese in France, wrote to Trotsky in Prinkipo.[51] The person delegated to write on its behalf was Ho Huu Tuong, who had joined the household of Ta Thu Thau and Huynh van Phuong only a week or so before the demonstration in front of the Elysée Palace. Tuong had come up from Lyons, where he had been coaching Chinese worker-students after getting an advanced degree in mathematics in Aix-en-Provence. After the demonstration, Tuong and Phan van Hum, Nguyen An Ninh's former associate, were secretly driven to Brussels by Raymond Molinier and Gérard Rosenthal, a young leftist who later became Trotsky's lawyer.[52] From Brussels, Hum and Tuong took over from Thau in writing for *La Vérité* under the joint pen name of Giai Phong ("liberation").[53] After Rosenthal ascertained that the police were not seeking to arrest or deport them, Tuong and Hum came back to Paris. It was then that he was asked to write to Trotsky. Ho Huu Tuong did not yet consider himself a Trotskyist, but he was one of a handful of radicals close to the Trotskyists who had escaped deportation.

Buoyed by the spread of mass protests at home, the Organization felt confident enough to challenge Trotsky's prediction that revolution would take place first in industrialized Europe. The letter was drafted as a resolution to the effect that "the international revolution displaces its center from Europe to Asia."[54] Ho Huu Tuong wanted to insert in the resolution the argument that this shift in center was due to the strength of the peasantry in Asia, but the Communist League, to whom the draft was submitted, excised the heretical passages dealing with this issue. When Trotsky sent back his critique of the resolution, its authors found themselves chided at length for underestimating the importance of agrarian revolution. Another exchange of correspondence took place a few months later. The two letters from Trotsky eventually formed the basis of the program of the Vietnamese Trotskyists who began to organize themselves as the Left Opposition (Ta Doi Lap) after their return from France in 1931. Thus, as a new decade began, Marxism had become entrenched in Vietnam in both its Trotskyist and Stalinist incarnations.

Neither logic nor geography alone can explain why Trotskyism appealed exclusively to natives of Cochinchina. The prominence of Paris as a center of international Trotskyism and the lack of interest on the part of the French Communist Party in recruiting and training Vietnamese émigrés both contributed to Ta Thu Thau's conversion to Trotskyism. But in another, equally important, sense so did his distinctly southern background, with its greater emphasis on individualism and its weaker communitarian ethos. The prospect of belonging to a worldwide movement which happened at the time to be paying particular attention to the problems of decolonization in agrarian societies was one of the reasons which had drawn adherents of the Vietnamese Youth League into the Indochinese Communist Party. But those who became attracted to Trotskyism were southerners like Thau. They had no prior affiliation with the Youth League and had not learned from its tumultuous history the value of Leninist organization and iron discipline. Ta Thu Thau, for one, was not inclined to submerge himself into a ready-made party. Similar reservations kept Ho Huu Tuong from joining the ICP. An attempt to persuade him to go to Moscow was made by Bui Cong Trung, a former adherent of Jeune Annam who had become a Communist.[55] Since Ho Huu Tuong had already read Marx, Trung, who had acquired the reputation of being the theoretician of the Vietnamese contingent in Moscow, emphasized the benefits of a Leninist organization. But the effect was the opposite of what he had hoped. The independent-minded Tuong was dismayed by the prospect of losing his autonomy.[56]

Trotskyism attracted men like Ta Thu Thau or Ho Huu Tuong who had traveled the road to Marxism on their own and wanted to retain their intellectual independence. Having grappled with the complexities of Marxist theory unaided made the Trotskyists formidable public speakers, but their unwillingness to accept Leninist discipline laid them open to the same weaknesses that afflicted their French counterparts. Condemned to operate on the fringes of both mainstream communism and mainstream electoral politics, the French Trotskyists had fallen prey to sectarian disputes in which personal elements were inseparable from the ideological.[57] The most brilliant among them, Naville and Rosmer, lacked the activist energy of Pierre Frank and Raymond Molinier, but were disdainful of Molinier's intellectual shortcomings. But to Ho Huu Tuong, this sectarianism appeared as a virtue. Tuong was impressed by the lack of hierarchy in the Trotskyist movement and especially by the fact that, although Molinier was in conflict with Naville and Rosmer, he was still given important jobs to do. Tuong saw Molinier's visits to Trotsky as signs of continued trust in him, though the trips to Prinkipo were the direct result of constant disputes among the three men.[58] He failed to appreciate that their intransigence made working together impossible. There was no discipline, and therefore no real party. The French Trotskyists, though intellectually attractive to young radicals such as Ho Huu Tuong, were organizationally no match for the Communists.

The archaic tendencies of Vietnamese nationalism and its deep-rooted romanticism and adulation of heroism played a role in winning sympathy for the fallen Trotsky. Ho Huu Tuong's conversion to Trotskyism was motivated in part by his inability to believe the charges which Stalin leveled against Trotsky, especially that of treason; surely, even if his policies were deemed mistaken, the patriotism of the architect of the October Revolution could not be questioned?[59] Not long after the execution in Vietnam of the leaders of the VNQDD, Tuong went for a walk in the Meudon forest outside Paris with Pierre Frank to discuss revisions of the draft resolution he had written on behalf of the Organization of Vietnamese in France. One of Frank's objections concerned the hostile and irreverent references to Stalin with which Tuong had begun the resolution: "You will admit that Stalin is successful. That must count for something," said Frank. Tuong was appalled: "In East Asia," he recalled thirty-nine years later, "success has never been reckoned a virtue."[60] He was talking about Trotsky; he could also have been talking about the recently executed VNQDD leaders. This quixotic strain vitiated the political effectiveness of the Vietnamese Trotskyists. Like their French counterparts, they suffered from a tendency to overintellectualize every detail of doctrine and an almost constitutional inability to bury personal differences for the sake of effective action.

Despite their split into Stalinist and Trotskyist camps, Vietnamese Marxists were unanimous in their agreement on the primacy of class struggle as well as in their definition of the proletariat. Both somehow sidestepped the question of a bourgeois democratic revolution. The well-publicized hostility between Trotskyists and Communists thus had more to do with assiduously cultivated differences of organizational style and strategy than fundamental disagreements over theory. Marxists had another trait in common: while looking for a framework for analyzing society and imagining the future, they had discovered a theory of history which not only validated their a priori decision to become revolutionaries but also provided them with a persuasive alternative to Social Darwinism. The previous years of searching and sacrifices had done little to advance the cause of revolution while calamities had rained on their organizations; revolutionaries understandably yearned for some clue to what the future might hold. What attracted many of them to Marxism was its promise of certain victory instead of annihilation, and national redemption instead of endless struggle for survival. Some rejected Comintern interpretations of the link between colonialism and capitalism, or questioned its willingness to leapfrog the bourgeois-democratic stage, but others chose to swallow their doubts about apparent inconsistencies in Marxist-Leninist theory because it was the only doctrine they knew that offered hope for the future. Hence their agonized and ultimately inconclusive debates over the historical role of the bourgeoisie.

From Radicals to Progressives

Debates on women were profoundly affected by the new Marxist perspective and became crucial in separating Marxists from progressives. *Youth* had tried to integrate the issue of women's emancipation with the struggle for national independence, aiming its arguments at women who had become politicized by the student strikes of 1926. The subjugation of women was explained as the result of unequal relations of power rather than lack of education, and women were portrayed as suffering from the double yoke of capitalist and feudal oppression. As they became absorbed by the concept of class struggle Marxist revolutionaries continued to lambast the family and other remnants of "feudalism," but there was a mechanical ring to their attacks. Women remained important as symbols, but they no longer represented the oppressed nation; they had become emblematic of the exploitation of the working class by the forces of colonial capitalism. Their struggle became the pursuit of economic rather than sexual equality. The issue of gender relations and the victimization of women at home was largely swept under the carpet. The Indochinese Communist Party declared in 1937: "The formation of legal and semi-legal women's associations is a necessity. But we should note that their goal is not to allow women to struggle against men as happened during the emancipation of women of 1930–1931, but to defend interests which are common to all social classes as well as the special interests of women."[61] The goal of restructuring gender relations was disparaged as an idle concern of elite women. Nguyen thi Minh Khai, the ICP's highest-ranking woman, wrote in 1938:

> Women who support the principle of female liberation think that there must be absolute equality between husbands and wives, but in order to be equal, we must not depend economically on men; everybody accepts that giving birth is the exclusive responsibility of women, but raising children is not . . . To achieve complete emancipation and equality, we must transform the current social system. I suggest to those sisters who are happy to stay in the framework of family life that not only are they allowing themselves to be imprisoned and enslaved but that they are also reducing the forces seeking to liberate the fatherland, society, and all mankind.[62]

Nguyen thi Minh Khai also found fault with the notion that, for women to achieve emancipation, all they need do was to extricate themselves from their families: "There are some impetuous sisters whose families suffocate, oppress, and torment them, and who think that emancipation means to escape from their families and flee with some vague idea of freedom. There are sisters who cannot bear the pressure of their families to marry [someone they don't like]."

But, once they had fled from the family prison, these women would have to support themselves and confront the reality of capitalist exploitation. Therefore, she argued:

> As long as society remains in the stage of capitalist oppression, exploitation and injustice, as long as contradictions between classes still exist, women will never be completely emancipated. To create a movement to promote equality between men and women, to escape from the tyranny of the family, we support that principle, but we want to advocate a higher principle, that is, we want equality among all of mankind. Therefore, in order to completely solve the question of women, we cannot stand on one side and consider only the question of inequality between men and women. On the contrary, the fundamental issue is the common dimension, the class dimension which we must solve together.

Yet inequality between men and women was exactly what preoccupied the intellectuals who became known collectively as progressives. To a certain extent, progressivism was a continuation, in attenuated form, of the radical agenda of the 1920s. It was also both a rejection of class struggle and a revolt against the brazen appropriation of tradition by the forces of repression.

Sarraut and Varenne, both new to Vietnam, had tried to present themselves as modernizers and benevolent guides leading the Vietnamese toward political maturity. The new Governor-General of Indochina, Pierre Pasquier, however, was an old Indochina hand. In 1907, just as the Reform Movement was gathering momentum, he had written a much-praised history of Vietnam, *L'Annam d'autrefois*, which combined Orientalist erudition with nostalgia for the very values and institutions which the Reformers were beginning to question. Under Pasquier's leadership, the colonial authorities made a point of appearing as stern champions of Vietnamese tradition. When peasants who had taken part in the short-lived attempt to establish a Soviet in Cao Lanh surrendered in January 1931, the Governor of Cochinchina thus called ancestral shame on their heads:

> You now see that millions of peace-loving Annamites in Cochinchina, who are hard-working and respectful of the old laws, have responded to your hypocritical invitations [to rebel] by saying that they are not your brothers and sisters, that they disapprove of your criminal actions, and that the only brothers and sisters you have are strangers who have devastated their own country and ruined every-

thing that the Annamites respect. You feel that not only have you outraged France, but that you and those who led you have offended the spirits of your ancestors in wanting to change the road they had followed, in accusing them of errors, in bringing disorder, murder, and the sad severity of repression to the country they had bequeathed to you happy and peaceful. And you know that come Lunar New Year, you will not be able to salute the tablets of your [dead] parents whose anger and contempt you have roused. And this is why, tired, disappointed, and afraid, you come today to ask that all be forgotten.[63]

Faced with colonial misappropriation of Vietnamese tradition, progressives chose to reject it rather than try to reclaim it. In the South, progressives were the conscience of the middle class that had emerged from the Franco-Annamite schools. Politically, they stood midway between the Marxists and the Constitutionalists, but their activism was mostly oratorical. Though more aware than the urban radicals of the 1920s of the plight of peasants and workers, they recoiled before mass violence and were wary of class conflict. The chief vehicle of southern progressive thought was the journal *Ladies' News*. The editorial line of *Ladies' News*, as it followed the first peasant protests, highlighted the ambiguity of the progressive political stance. On 11 April 1930, before the onset of mass protests, *Ladies' News* published an article by a Paris-based author who was clearly influenced by Marxism. The article tried to elucidate for readers of *Ladies' News* the meaning of class by summarizing the evolution of this concept since Karl Marx. It gave a history of the origins of the Russian Revolution and concluded by predicting the victory of the proletariat over the "reactionary" bourgeoisie. On 26 June, less than two months after the first protests were staged, the journal reproduced a letter from a female coolie in Tonkin in which she told of leaving home at five in the morning, to work in the Ke Bao mine for thirteen hours in appalling conditions before getting home around nine, at which point she faced additional domestic chores. She subsisted on four or five hours of sleep and twenty cents a day. She wrote: "We don't aspire to big houses and cars, usually they have been earned with the tears of the workers . . . But what kind of society do we have? Readers, please think about it." The sympathetic tone of the accompanying editor's note was typical of the journal's attitude in the early days of the protest movement: "Alas, the situation of all our working class is pitiable, but especially so is the situation of female workers. They are more exploited, and therefore more to be pitied. We are glad to print this letter in our column 'Letter to a Friend' to bring it to our readers so that they can read it and reflect on it."

But as the mass movement lost ground, demonstrators turned increasingly against other Vietnamese: mandarins, notables, landowners, or anyone suspected of collusion with the colonial regime. This development alienated certain groups and individuals who had at first expressed sympathy for the mass movement but were dismayed by the idea of setting Vietnamese against Vietnamese. As peasant violence became increasingly directed against the native middle class, the tone of *Ladies' News* changed. Before the end of the year, it was publishing gloomy reports of riots, pillages, revolts, and attempts to interfere with the right of ordinary people to go about earning their livelihood. By 1931, it was no longer talking about the "reactionary bourgeoisie" but about the "Communist menace."[64]

In 1933, *Ladies' News* fell under the control of Marxist writers: the Trotskyist Phan van Hum and the Communist Hai Trieu.[65] Though moderate in comparison with the emerging *La Lutte*, which was jointly published by southern Communists and Trotskyists, its editorial policy moved further to the left. *Ladies' News* was eventually muzzled in December 1934 under the pretext that the journal had slandered Bui Quang Chieu three years earlier when it accused him of being in the pay of the reactionary financier Homberg.[66]

But the colonial authorities were trying to hold back a veritable tide of publications that were, in varying degrees, critical of French rule. One of the Vietnamese-language newspapers that outlived the demise of *Ladies' News* by one year was *Trung Lap* (Impartial). *Trung Lap* had begun life as the Vietnamese-language edition of la Chevrotière's *Impartial*, but had been bought out by a Vietnamese publisher. After its key writers were lured away by *Ladies' News* in 1932, it acquired a new editional board that included Nguyen An Ninh and the Communist Nguyen van Tao. Even though heavily censored, the general tenor of its attacks against colonialism and capitalism was not lost on the reading public.[67] There were also single publications which were banned immediately after they appeared, but not quickly enough to prevent some copies from circulating clandestinely. And finally, there was a steady stream of pamphlets and flyers produced by different branches of the ICP which the colonial authorities were unable to stop. The political discourse in Cochinchina was thus dominated by Marxists—Trotskyists and Stalinists. Non-Marxists often defined their positions as more moderate versions of what the Marxists proposed.

The political context in which progressivism developed in the North was quite different from that in Cochinchina. The repression of the Vietnamese Nationalist Party and peasant protests had taken a heavy toll. Leaders of the VNQDD who had escaped arrest had fled to South China; there was no one to direct the activities of the remaining rank-and-file members. Though the Indochinese Communist Party was also hit hard by repression, it recovered sufficiently to resume its activities in the mid-1930s. But although the Tonkin and Annam Regional Committees were able to publish underground newsletters, their distribution was constrained by their clandestine nature. In the absence of overt challenges from the left, the main foe of northern progressivism was thus on the right. This lack of counterpoise gave it a different flavor from its southern counterpart.

The power achieved by neo-traditionalists in Tonkin and Annam in the 1930s resulted from the initial demoralized response of the mandarins to the first wave of peasant protests. Although the mandarins and village officials certainly did not support the protests (and became their targets toward the end), their assistance to the colonial authorities was either grudgingly given or ineffectual. As Grandjean, personal secretary of the Résident Supérieur of Annam, explained to Varenne, who was now Minister of Colonies:

> In truth, we have no one left on our side. The Hue Court clamors for the return of the emperor and does all it can not to be implicated in the repression. The mandarins, to whom we never gave more than an inadequate position, materially and morally, serve us only with caution, and besides, they are no longer capable of much. The bourgeoisie undoubtedly does not want Communism, but it considers that, as in China, it could be an excellent recipe for external use, even if it does not want it internally. Students are completely against us, and so is the immense and miserable population of workers and peasants. Really, we should do something else here than repress.[68]

In 1926, Varenne had welcomed the departure of potential troublemakers from Vietnam. In 1931, however, in light of the role students had played in fostering the recent wave of popular unrest, Governor-General Pasquier drew lessons about the dangers of allowing students to go abroad: "It is erroneous to believe that a precipitate rupture with their past would bring the Annamites to us more easily. Annamites uprooted from their milieu and trained in France in French ideas are, more often than not, hostile to us: we must not forget this."⁶⁹

This warning echoed the feelings of more conservative mandarins which he had noted the previous year: "Just as literati of the beginning of the century were angry at us for not bringing Western education to their country so that they had to seek it abroad, now, these same literati raise their voice to reproach us for having corrupted their children and ruined their civilization with New Learning."⁷⁰ Pasquier was actually referring to different groups of scholars. But he was concerned only with those who had always opposed educational reforms.

As a conciliatory gesture toward the mandarins, the young emperor Bao Dai was brought back from France in 1932. Bao Dai's task was self-contradictory: to appear to accede to popular demands for reform while appeasing the more conservative elements among his court. After having spent his adolescence in France, he hardly qualified as a traditional monarch. Yet the imperial cabinet which he assembled, though purportedly reformist, was largely staffed by neo-traditionalists. One of its most prominent members was Pham Quynh, who served as Minister of Education. Recent events had stifled whatever reformist impulses Pham Quynh had displayed in previous years. In the aftermath of Yen Bay, he exhorted the authorities to suppress revolutionary activities.⁷¹ After the mass movements of 1930–1931, he declared: "Since violence is not within our power, we trust that the government will know how to use it for the common good. We believe that the violence of France is always impartial and vigilant: it will strike hard and also strike in the right place."⁷² Hostility to Pham Quynh and his ideas was the driving force behind northern progressivism.⁷³ Progressives advanced many ideas for reforming society and improving the lot of the poor, but their principal concern remained the achievement of individual freedom from familial oppression. This concern found expression in literature rather than in political action and engaged them in dialogue—however acrimonious—with more conservative elements; as for Marxist revolutionaries, progressives seem to have carefully ignored them.⁷⁴

The chief vehicle of progressive thought in Tonkin was the review *Mores (Phong Hoa)*, which served as the platform of a group of authors known collectively as the Self-Reliance Literary Group (Tu Luc Van Doan). The authors in the Group were all products of the Franco-Annamite school system of Tonkin. Nhat Linh, the Group's founder, had returned to Hanoi in 1930 after being expelled from France. After trying for two years to enter the field of journalism, he succeeded in September 1932 in taking over *Mores*. The journal had originally been founded by the director of the Thang Long School where Nhat Linh taught, but its motto of reconciling the best in the cultures of East and West had not met with readers' approval.[75] When Nhat Linh and his friends took over the moribund paper, they brought its circulation from three thousand to ten thousand.[76] The staff of *Mores* included several of Nhat Linh's brothers as well as colleagues from the Thang Long School, in particular Tran Khanh Giu, who wrote under the pen name of Khai Hung. In March 1933, feeling that the effort was a success, Nhat Linh called the group which had formed around the journal the Self-Reliance Literary Group. A ten-point manifesto, drafted by Hoang Dao, a brother of Nhat Linh and the Group's chief theoretician, was published on 2 March 1933. The Group pledged, among other things, "to always be new, youthful, to love life and have the will to strive and believe in progress" (point 5). Presenting itself as a foe of neo-traditionalism and its literary organ, *Southern Wind*, the Group declared that Confucianism was no longer appropriate for the times (point 8) and advocated the rights of the individual (point 7). As Hoang Dao claimed, "the old ideals do not meet the educational standards of the young. Confucianism is teetering on the verge of collapse, ready to follow the old Confucian scholars into oblivion." Sounding like Nguyen An Ninh a decade earlier, he added: "We must find the essence of Western civilization and then create our own to respond to our needs; in order to do so, we must break the ties which bind our souls, that is, outdated customs and the submissive spirit of our people."[77]

Like the publishers of *Ladies' News*, the members of the Self-Reliance Literary Group saw themselves as patriots who repudiated class struggle. Nhat Linh, who later made the transition from literature to politics and became a leader of the Vietnamese Nationalist Party in exile in South China, perpetuated the vision of revolutionary unity without spelling out a political program or strategy. In his fictional works, making revolution seems to have been an expiatory device rather than a systematic effort to create a new order. He wrote several novels and short stories in which he described the shame and guilt of children of privilege as they became conscious of the misery of the common people and of their fathers' role in causing it. In *Two Kinds of Beauty (Hai Ve Dep)*, which was published in 1936, Nhat

Linh drew a portrait of a student newly returned from France and burning with the desire to paint. But when he went back to his mother's home in the countryside he saw the poverty in which his mother's tenants lived, and his desire to paint vanished. He realized that "all his school fees and expenses over so many years had been money extracted from these miserable peasants over there, or some other peasants in the locality where his father served as a mandarin. He saw the absurdity of looking for an elusive light playing over the roofs of their grass huts while never imagining the cold reality, the obscure lives that were led inside those hovels."

The overall impression left by the patriotic characters in the novels of Nhat Linh is that though they refused to subscribe to the neo-traditionalist policy of collaboration, their actions were not guided by some grand strategic design. Nhat Linh depicted his heroes as loners at a time when real anticolonial activists were focusing on organizing themselves and mobilizing others. Indeed, they were more like the knights-errant of old than modern revolutionaries. Whether or not this was due to literary considerations, revolutionary action was secondary to romance and to intergenerational conflicts. As a result, the writings of the Self-Reliance Literary Group figured more prominently in debates on the question of women than in revolutionary politics.

Despite their self-images as literary iconoclasts and social reformers, authors of the Self-Reliance Literary Group propounded a notion of the New Woman that was actually rather tame. By concentrating on the domestic arena as the battlefield in which the emancipation of women must be won, they unwittingly confined themselves within the perimeters set by Pham Quynh, to whom they thought themselves implacably opposed. Their fictional women were far from being helpless and were capable of earning their own living as was expected of poor and middle-class Vietnamese women. But, the focus being on their familial relationships, their economic self-reliance was downplayed; such a perspective did not turn them into independent women or lead their creators to explore marketplace relations. Women were portrayed as victims rather than free agents, a far cry from the many real women of both urban and rural backgrounds who threw themselves into politics, whether out of filial piety, patriotism, feminism, or in opposition to economic injustice.

The feminist rhetoric of the Self-Reliance Literary Group was a northern variant of the one espoused by *Ladies' News*.[78] This was particularly true after two southern feminists, Nguyen thi Kiem and Phan thi Nga, went to Hanoi in 1934 to lecture on the activities of "New Women." The previous year had seen the publication of *In Mid-Spring (Nua chung xuan)* by Khai Hung. Despite the self-proclaimed modern outlook of the Self-Reliance Literary Group, to which Khai Hung belonged, the novel also showed clear evidence of the influence of late Ch'ing fiction. It was the story of a poor country girl who married for love a man of superior background but was forced by her scheming mother-in-law to leave her husband so that he could marry a girl of his own class. The story's ending, in which the heroine and her husband agree to a platonic marriage for the sake of his unsuspecting second wife, is particularly reminiscent of the *Tale of Kieu*. The same literary influence was at work in Nhat Linh's novel *Autumnal Sun (Nang thu)*, which appeared in early 1934. The story concerned a young girl accused of being unchaste. Instead of using the occasion to explore the validity of traditional demands for female chastity, Nhat Linh resolved her problem by showing that she had been calumnied.

That Nhat Linh was deeply influenced by the more radical brand of feminism represented by Nguyen thi Kiem and Phan thi Nga is apparent in two novels which he wrote after their visit: *Loneliness (Lanh lung)* and *A Severance of Ties (Doan tuyet)*. They were serialized in *Mores* and in *Today (Ngay Nay)*, another journal of the Self-Reliance Literary Group, beginning in 1934. *Loneliness* is reminiscent of the late Ch'ing novel the *Chronicle of Tears of Bygone Days*, reworked in a more provocative register. It is the story of a young widow who falls in love with her son's tutor and decides to engage in an illicit affair with him rather than risk incurring the wrath of her late husband's family by remarrying. In one of the most controversial scenes of the novel, the two lovers hold a tryst in front of the altar to the woman's dead husband. One critic advocated that the novel be banned, and Nhat Linh was accused of condoning female promiscuity.[79] Reaction to his next novel, *A Severance of Ties*, was equally heated. In it, Nhat Linh again made use of a gallery of stock characters: the young woman of poor but scholarly background and modern ideas, the weak and doltish husband from a rich and tradition-minded family, and the domineering mother-in-law. During a fight, the wife accidentally kills her husband. Readers pointed out that the headstrong heroine would have been a trial to any husband or mother-in-law, but the author's sympathies were clearly with her. He ended the novel with a long didactic speech in which her lawyer pleaded her case by attacking the extended family system. As a literary device, the speech was clumsy and implausible, but it conveyed perfectly the philosophy of the Self-Reliance Literary Group. The critic Truong Tuu, who had advocated banning *Loneliness,* greeted the novel as "a radiant crown of flowers set on the head of individualism."[80] But another novelist, Nguyen Cong Hoan, was so incensed by the picture of family disharmony presented in *A Severance of Ties* that, in 1935, he wrote a novel called *Miss Teacher Minh (Co giao Minh)* to suggest ways in which the most hidebound conservatives could be persuaded by sweet reason to adopt more modern ways.[81]

Mores was closed down in 1936 for having shown irreverence toward the mandarinate, but the Self-Reliance Literary Group continued to dominate the literary field until the end of the 1930s with its stories of family tyranny, thwarted love, and oppressed youth. During that time, Marxist revolutionaries focused on class issues and relegated questions of gender and familial relationships to secondary importance. The trajectory followed by the debates on women and on family relationships demonstrates how an issue that had once defined radicalism had, over time, been absorbed into the cultural mainstream and largely depoliticized.

In their absorption with the exploitation of working women, Marxists underestimated the weight of domestic responsibilities working women had to shoulder and the familial oppression from which they suffered as much as their more privileged sisters. The efforts of the Indochinese Communist Party to reach out to women and recruit them into its auxiliary groups continued to be hampered by women's dual burden at home and in society. Progressive authors may have focused mainly on the concerns of middle-class women, as was suggested by their Communist critics, but their chief limitation lay in that, although they argued for the right of women to be considered as individuals, they continually situated them in a suffocating web of familial relationships as daughters, wives, and daughters-in-law. The domestic tragedies which formed the themes of their fiction arose from the fact that their female protagonists were denied the right to be individual women acting in a context larger than the family system. Their creators were not interested in what happened to them outside the home. Nguyen thi Minh Khai's well-founded critique did not find a response in the novels of the Self-Reliance Literary Group. Reading them, one often has difficulty keeping in mind that they depict a colonial society in the throes of disintegration.

Yet, for all the limitations of their approach, it is possible to argue that, by exposing the evils of the "family system" and familism, the radicals of the 1920s and the progressives of the 1930s succeeded in stripping the family of the accommodationist connotations that neoconservatives and colonial officials had foisted on it. Nhat Linh's heroes made ineffectual revolutionaries, but in trying to expiate the guilt of their fathers, they gave a new meaning to filial piety. Filial piety no longer need signify blind obedience to one's elders or the selfish pursuit of family interests; it was more reasoned and noble and could serve as the wellspring of patriotism. And the literary romanticization of revolution, however devoid of real substance, helped restore sympathy for the revolutionary enterprise among a middle class that had been shaken by the violence of the mass protests. This renewed sympathy made it possible for the rhetoric of kinship to recover its former resonance and to be put, finally, in the service of revolution.

The Revalorization of the Past

The power of this rhetoric was strikingly demonstrated soon after Nguyen Ai Quoc, who now called himself Ho Chi Minh, declared Vietnam independent on 2 September 1945.

The road to independence had been a tortuous one. After the mass protests of 1931, Nguyen Ai Quoc had been captured in Hong Kong and was rumored to have died in prison in 1932. The Comintern had even staged an elaborate funeral on his behalf for the benefit of the Sûreté, which still doubted the veracity of the rumors.[82] But he had made his escape and had somehow reemerged in Moscow in the second half of the 1930s while the ICP was struggling both to survive and to develop a strategy to deal with the mounting threat of fascism. In 1941, some leaders of the ICP learned that he had resurfaced in South China and made contacts with him there.[83] When Nguyen Ai Quoc returned to Vietnam shortly thereafter, he adopted a new alias which showed how far the man who had once been full of enthusiasm for Wilsonian self-determination had traveled on the road of Marxism. Formerly he had proclaimed himself Nguyen the Patriot; now he had become Ho Who Aspires to Enlightenment. And yet, despite his pseudonym's allusion to ideological truth, Ho's return to the helm of the Indochinese Communist Party consolidated the retreat from class warfare that had begun in his absence.

The ICP's return to a more unitary strategy had its origins in its attempts to react to the rise of fascism in Europe and the growing possibility of a Japanese invasion of Indochina. Such a strategy was made all the more necessary by the isolation of the ICP that resulted both from Stalin's policy of "socialism in one country" and from the Chinese Communist Party's struggle for survival in base areas far from the Vietnamese border. The move toward a unitary strategy was facilitated by the fact that none of the ICP leaders still at large after successive waves of arrests was identified with the ultra-proletarian line that had dominated the politics of the early 1930s.[84] The ICP convened at the end of 1939 in the aftermath of yet another wave of repression which the colonial regime had unleashed as soon as war broke out in Europe. It was at this Sixth Plenum that the policy of unitary nationalism was sketched. The slogan of national liberation which had been put in cold storage since 1930 was brought back to the fore. Instead of declaring war on the whole middle class, the Indochinese Communist Party decided to isolate the collaborators within its ranks and win over politically uncommitted patriots. To that end, class struggle was deemphasized and radical land redistribution was shelved.

After Ho Chi Minh's return in 1941, the ICP decided to create the League for the Independence of Vietnam (Viet Nam Doc Lap Dong Minh), better known as the Viet Minh. The Viet Minh was to be an ostensibly non-Communist, broad-based coalition front of all anti-colonial forces dedicated to ending both French colonial rule and the Japanese occupation of Vietnam, which had begun in September 1940. The creation of the Viet Minh could not be completed until 1943, because in the meantime, Ho was again arrested in South China. The Viet Minh also encountered competition from other anti-colonial groups. But these rivals lacked a mass following inside the country and had no strong leadership, organization, or clear strategy. The Viet Minh, by contrast, was led by seasoned activists united by the iron discipline of a Leninist party and the shared experience of fifteen years of revolutionary struggle. And, though it had abandoned class struggle, it also benefited from the existence of mass organizations of workers, soldiers, peasants, youth, and women that had been created during the ultra-proletarian phase. Thus the Viet Minh was in the best position to take advantage of the power vacuum left by the defeat of Japan before the French tried to regain control of Indochina in late 1945.

The Viet Minh took control of Hanoi on 19 August 1945. Two weeks later, on 2 September, Ho Chi Minh stood in Ba Dinh Square addressing his compatriots.[85] He began:

My dear compatriots,

"All men are created equal. They are endowed by their creator with certain inalienable rights; among these are Life, Liberty, and the Pursuit of Happiness."

These immortal words are contained in the American Declaration of Independence of 1776. More generally, they mean that every people has the right to exist, to be happy, and to be free. The Declaration of the Rights of Man and of the Citizen of the French Revolution of 1791 also states: "Men are born to be free and to have equal rights, and must always remain free and have equal rights."

Thus began the Vietnamese Declaration of Independence. Throughout his address, Ho Chi Minh chose to stress the theme of freedom rather than equality, which had come to symbolize class conflict and national disunity. But it was collective, not individual, freedom he was talking about, as his closing words made clear: "Vietnam has the right to enjoy freedom and independence, and in fact, has become a free and independent nation. The whole Vietnamese people is resolved to bring all its spirit and its power, its life, and its possessions to preserve this right to freedom and independence."

A new school year was beginning, and a few days later, Ho delivered another address, this time aimed at schoolchildren:

Previously, your fathers and older brothers, and last year still, you yourselves were forced to accept a slave's education, designed to train lackeys for the French imperialists. Today, you are luckier than your fathers and older brothers in being educated in an independent country . . . Listen to my advice, the advice of someone who always solicitously hopes that you will excel. During the coming year, be diligent in your studies, behave well, obey your teachers, and compete with your friends. After eighty years of enslavement that have weakened our country, we must now try to rebuild what our ancestors bequeathed us and catch up with other countries. In this work of reconstruction, the country pins its hopes on you, young people. Whether the Vietnamese nation can achieve glory, whether the Vietnamese people can become as glorious as the powerful countries of the five continents depends in large part on your efforts to educate yourselves.[86]

Other events which took place during that tumultuous year may stand out more sharply, but this speech represents a turning point of sorts in the political culture of the Vietnamese Revolution. Nearly twenty years had passed since the strikes of 1926. Although the intruders had not been completely driven off, it was possible to begin rebuilding the country. But there was no longer a burning need for the completely new structure that Nguyen Ai Quoc, along with others, had envisaged in the 1920s. They no longer believed that revolution entailed the "total replacement of an ancien régime by a new one." The destruction of the old order was no longer deemed crucial to the success of revolution. Marxism having vanquished the specter of national annihilation, and the taint of collaboration lifted from traditional institutions and values, Vietnamese revolutionaries could look back on their national past with renewed pride and find new uses for it, secure in the belief that History was on their side.[87] In invoking Vietnam's ancestral legacy, Ho Chi Minh demonstrated that control of national symbols and metaphors had returned to the Vietnamese. Throughout the speech, Ho referred to himself by an appellation which became familiar worldwide: Uncle Ho. In thus implying kinship and solidarity with the parents of the students he was addressing, Ho showed that it was possible once again to extol intergenerational harmony and to put the evocative language of the family at the service of the nation. With this joining of piety and patriotism, the early phase of the Vietnamese Revolution was over.

Conclusion

> And thus the entire throng of the dead themselves fashion the most beautiful creations of the living. In this manner, the present is intimately linked to the past—more than just linked: the present lives in the past.
>
> Nguyen Tinh, in *Cloche Fêlée*, 1925

THE 1920s in Vietnam are usually regarded as a period of transition from the scholarly reformism of the beginning of the century to the revolutionary mass politics of the thirties. But this description hardly does justice to the complexities of these years and to the difficulties that attended the launching of the revolution. A better way to sum up the 1920s would be to describe them as the experimental, and most individualistic, stage of the Vietnamese Revolution.

In light of the opprobrium which Marxist revolutionaries later heaped on the notion of individualism, and the revalorization of the past which began in the 1930s, one might be tempted to conclude that Vietnamese urban radicalism was, in historical terms, no more than a flash in the pan, its iconoclasm and its advocacy of individual freedom and self-realization a hiatus in an essentially nationalist and collectivist drama. But this iconoclasm was essential in getting the revolutionary process under way. Youthful alienation set in motion the great engine of revolution.

It can be argued that liberal colonial officials such as Sarraut and Varenne contributed as much as, if not more than, reactionary officials to the emergence of radicalism. Not only did their reformist rhetoric raise expectations, but their appropriation of the Vietnamese past and of the language of family attachments polluted the public discourse, thereby prompting younger Vietnamese to draw connections between Vietnamese social structures and colonial power. On the Vietnamese side, the rampant familism inherent in neo-traditionalism did more than the assimilationist policies of Bui Quang Chieu to foster the marriage of personal and political concerns that was the chief characteristic of radicalism. Another factor that contributed to the growth of radicalism was the use by French officials and native collaborators of the metaphor of the immature child to describe the Vietnamese body politic. Thus encouraged, adolescents easily fancied themselves as potential revolutionaries.

It is easy to be seduced by the self-consciously Western language of Vietnamese radicalism into overlooking the many ways in which this rhetoric resonated with traditional political culture. This is not to deny the distinctive characteristics of radicalism, which was the result of decades of change that profoundly altered the political and cultural landscape of Vietnam. The brand of Western-inspired radicalism that flourished in the 1920s is unthinkable without the growth of urban centers. In the cities and towns of colonial Vietnam there emerged a culture that became increasingly removed from the rhythms and values of agrarian society. Neo-traditionalists, who perceived the problem of cultural change mostly in terms of tradition versus modernity, realized, however vaguely, the importance of the deepening cleavage between rural and urban society. It was no coincidence that in contemporary short stories, youthful unfilial behavior and hedonism often resulted from a stay in the city. A hallmark of the new urban culture was the explosive growth of the publishing industry and in particular of journalism. The expansion was sustained by constant debates. Through this dialogue, ostensibly dominated by upholders of the status quo, the radicalist critique of colonial society took shape and spread among Vietnam's youth. The Franco-Annamite schools, whose curriculum enshrined the veneration of Western knowledge, acted as the forcing ground of radicalism. In these largely urban schools, young Vietnamese learned to disengage themselves from the peasant world and lost their attachment to the past.

Vietnamese reaction to foreign rule was remarkably uniform in its assumptions, if not in its direction. Both patriotic Reformers and accommodationists, acknowledging Western superiority, advocated the transformation of Vietnamese culture. Their belief in the transformative power of education put the chief burden of national and cultural survival, whether through accommodation or resistance, on the individual and in particular on elite youth. The differing cultural and political agendas entertained by the colonial authorities and by assimilationists, neo-traditionalists, anticolonial conservatives, and reformers contributed to educational incoherence and bred disaffection among young Vietnamese.

Yet, in their disdain for conventions, the radicals of the 1920s were unaware of the traditional character of some of their assumptions and attitudes. Among them was ingrained elitism. Urban radicals expected to be at the head of a movement of national independence of which the uneducated masses were to be the passive beneficiaries. Although their aspirations to leadership rested on grounds of moral and intellectual superiority rather than on wealth or status, they remained unexamined claims nonetheless. This gave their advocacy of equality a somewhat hollow ring. The formation of Leninist-inspired parties in the mid-1920s did not seriously challenge the radicals' basic elitism. Without being anchored in Marxist class analysis or drawing upon a true mass membership, the revolutionary vanguard was nothing more than a collection of children of privilege whose mandarin mentality had assumed a patriotic coloration and who had trouble submitting to group discipline. This kind of elitism was only laid to rest with the advent of ultra-proletarian mass politics.

The introduction of Marxist analytical categories constituted an implicit repudiation of the centrality of the individual, as both target and source of change, which had fed the earlier drive for cultural reform. The idea that class struggle rather than cultural adaptation or personal heroism was the motive force of progress meant that the reformist impulse could be directed outward, at society, the economy, or the political system, instead of inward, at culture, the family, or the self. The place of the individual in society and of his role in history was thus reconceptualized. Class provided the new context in which the individual became part of the national community, displacing the besieged family and the disintegrating village as the basic unit of social organization. Marxism's explanation of the dynamic interaction between the different classes that made up society, and of the revolutionary (or counterrevolutionary) potential of each, was in sharp contrast with earlier, static conceptions of society. It allowed revolutionaries to invest the ideals of liberty, equality, and fraternity with concrete meaning and to clarify their visions of post-revolutionary society.

Although many of the dominant figures in the mass struggles of the 1930s began their political careers as young radicals in the wake of the strikes of 1926–1927, intellectually, the link between radicalism and Marxism is fairly tenuous. Radicalism and Marxism addressed different sets of concerns which are generally subsumed under the same heading of anticolonialism. The central issue of radicalism was freedom; Marxism provided a solution to the dilemma of survival. These two issues came together at the level of the nation which was battling for both its freedom and its survival. Beyond that level, however, conceptual frameworks and analytical categories did not fully coincide. Radicalism operated at the level of the individual, Marxism at the level of the group. The radicalist critique was aimed primarily at cultural values; it conceived of society in terms of institutions such as the family. Marxism addressed problems of social justice; it spoke of economic forces and conceived of society in terms of class.

Perhaps more important than the organizational model supplied by Leninism was the answer to the long search for a new order and for historical meaning embedded in the Marxist vision. As reinterpreted by Lenin, and especially by the Sixth Congress of the Comintern, this worldview not only replaced the traditional image of an unpredictable Heaven with the notion of History, but also prophesied the triumph of colonized peoples against imperialist capitalism. The prophetic dimension of Marxist historicism thus acted as a counterbalance to the fears of national annihilation that had spurred every Vietnamese reformer and revolutionary since the notion of Heaven's Will had been superseded by the Social Darwinian theory of perpetual struggle between strong and weak nations, races, and cultures as the source of historical change and the explanation for colonial conquest. Marxist historicism also helped to counter the nihilistic fatalism of collaborators such as Hoang Cao Khai and the deficiencies of a purely voluntarist approach to anticolonialism. The Marxist theory of history did not put the whole responsibility for success or failure, for survival or extinction, on the uncertain strength of will of flawed human beings; nor did it ask them to transform themselves morally, culturally, and intellectually before they could be considered mature enough for self-rule.

The appeal of Marxism derived in no small part from its perceived parallelism with Social Darwinism. Both Marxism and Social Darwinism laid claim to scientific truth. Both combined elements of determinism and voluntarism in their theories of history. Both were based on the idea of struggle as the motive force of progress. In Marxism, the struggle was waged neither among individuals nor among nations, but among classes. More important, the Marxist theory of history promised redemption instead of endless struggle. Instead of the real possibility of extinction, Marxism offered the prospect of a workers' utopia. Marxism thus seemed to turn Social Darwinism on its head and rewrite the future: "weak and small" nations, which in the context of Social Darwinism had little hope of survival, were destined to triumph by virtue of their sheer numbers and their incorporation into the world anti-imperialist system.

Perhaps it is the power of prophecy which explains the simultaneous appeal of two belief systems as seemingly disparate as Caodaism and Marxism. Some scholars discern in this simultaneity the disaggregation of Vietnamese politics in the 1920s; others see in it signs that Vietnamese society had become open to new ideas and new experiences to a degree unmatched before or since.[1] One possible answer to this apparent conundrum is that the 1920s were above all the decade of large claims and overarching solutions: in the face of looming national annihilation, social disintegration, and overwhelming spiritual malaise, nothing less than a totally new moral, social, and political order would do. Anything else seemed timid and inadequate. The crisis of Vietnamese culture had produced a need for reassurance which Marxism and Caodaism each tried to address. The Cao Dai sect, officially created only months after the first student strikes broke out, presented itself as a totally new and universal religion. But the secret of its success lay in its capacity for revitalizing popular religion and, most of all, in its combination of millenarianism and spiritism. The Cao Dai sect reassured the faithful through the gnosticism of its millenarian rhetoric and its spirit messages; Marxism promised victory to the oppressed masses of Vietnam through its historical determinism.

Paradoxically, although its emotional appeal lay in the very immutability of the laws of historical progression, Marxism gained in relevance to the Vietnamese situation only after its central doctrine had undergone a fundamental revision which, by deemphasizing the revolutionary potential of the bourgeoisie, undercut its historicist claims. But, whether they wanted closer relations to a worldwide Communist movement based on Lenin's ideas or whether they abhorred Leninist party organization, Communists and Trotskyists embraced Marxism because its historical determinism validated their a priori decision to follow the course of revolution rather than reform. Whatever impulses led them to Marxism, they thought they had found a map of the world and an itinerary.

But the adoption of the Marxist-Leninist vision also foreclosed a whole dimension of the revolutionary discourse. By emphasizing the importance of class at the expense of the individual, Marxism-Leninism brushed aside the humanist concerns—in particular the desire for personal freedom and moral autonomy as distinct from social justice, equality, or political independence—that had brought so many young Vietnamese into revolutionary politics. Even after the wartime return to a more unitary vision of revolution, individualism retained the negative connotations it had been saddled with earlier. Some of the dominant concerns of the 1920s, including personal self-realization and the emancipation of the individual from the tyranny of the group and from ideological conformity, thus remain unaddressed. Because of the continued lack of interest in these issues, radicalism represents more than a transition from scholarly patriotism to revolutionary communism for Vietnam: it represents the unrealized ideals, the unfinished agenda of the Vietnamese Revolution.

Notes

Index

Abbreviations

AIP	Annamite Independence Party
AOM	Archives d'Outre-Mer
AP	Affaires Politiques
CCP	Chinese Communist Party
CF	*Cloche Fêlée*
EA	*Echo Annamite*
FCP	French Communist Party
ICP	Indochinese Communist Party
JAS	*Journal of Asian Studies*
KMT	Kuomintang
NB	Phan Boi Chau, *Nien bieu* (Memoirs)
NCLS	*Nghien Cuu Lich Su* (Historical Studies)
NF	Nouveau Fonds
NP	*Nam Phong* (Southern Wind)
PA	Papiers d'Agents
PNTV	*Phu Nu Tan Van* (Ladies' News)
PTI	*Petite Tribune Indigène*
SLOTFOM	Service de Liaison des Originaires des Territoires Français d'Outre-Mer
TI	*Tribune Indigène*
VNQDD	Viet Nam Quoc Dan Dang (Vietnamese Nationalist Party)

Notes

Note on Sources. In this work I make use of the unpublished memoirs of my father, Ho Huu Tuong (1910–1980). A carbon copy of these memoirs, written in French in 1969, is in my possession. I have also drawn on the written transcripts of a set of unpublished interviews with him conducted in 1966 by Walter Slote of Columbia University.

Extensive use is also made of different sets of French colonial archives. Although formerly scattered among different locations, these archives have now been brought together in a single location in Aix-en-Provence; however, they continue to be classified separately.

One set of archives consists of materials either sent to or generated by the Ministry of Colonies in Paris. These materials are referred to in the Notes as "AOM Indochine, NF–" (for Nouveau Fonds, which covers the period 1920–1954). A second set, also formerly housed at the Ministry of Colonies, is known as the SLOTFOM series. SLOTFOM is the acronym for Service de Liaison des Originaires des Territoires Français d'Outre-Mer. The Service was originally created in 1914 to address the needs of colonial troops sent to France during World War I. Most of these troops were repatriated after the war, but enough natives of French colonies remained in France to justify the continued existence of the Service. However, the Service increasingly took on intelligence-gathering functions. The SLOTFOM holdings include extremely rich data on the activities of Vietnamese expatriates in France. They also contain translations of journals and newspapers produced and circulated illegally in Vietnam in the 1920s and 1930s, some of which may no longer be extant in the original. Another important source of documentation is the Dépôt d'Archives d'Outre-Mer in Aix-en-Provence (also referred to in the Notes as "AOM Indochine"), consisting of materials formerly kept locally in Indochina and sent back to France in 1954. Among these materials are those belonging to the category F (Affaires Politiques), and most particularly the subseries 7F (Sûreté Générale). From these sources was eventually compiled the six-volume *Contribution à l'histoire des mouvements politiques de l'Indochine française* issued by the Government-General of Indochina in 1930–1933. In this study, use has been made of vol. 1, *Le "Tan Viet Cach*

Menh Dang" "Parti Révolutionnaire du Jeune Annam" (1925–1930); vol. 2, *Le "Viet Nam Quoc Dan Dang" ou "Parti National Annamite" au Tonkin (1927–1932)*; and vol. 4, *Le "Dong Duong Cong San Dang" ou "Parti Communiste Indochinois" (1925–1933).*

For further details on the French colonial archives, the reader is referred to Chantal Descours-Gatin and Hugues Villiers, *Guide de recherches sur le Vietnam: Bibliographies, archives et bibliothèques de France* (Paris: L'Harmattan, 1983).

Introduction

1. Huynh Kim Khanh compared these radicals to "prodigal sons"; *Vietnamese Communism, 1925–1945* (Ithaca: Cornell University Press, 1982), pp. 45–53. As this book will show, many of the young rebels were women, and the question of women's rights loomed large in the early phase of the Vietnamese Revolution. According to J. Dion, who wrote the introduction to the SLOTFOM archives of the French Ministry of Colonies, 607 Vietnamese students were in France as of November 1926. This contrasts sharply with the 45 applications for student visas submitted between 1 July 1923 and 31 December 1924. See AOM Indochine, 7F22: Notice d'information politique portant sur la période comprise entre le 1er juillet 1923 et le 31 décembre 1924; 2ème section: contrôle des étrangers et des immigrants. See also AOM Indochine, 7F22(4): Départs annamites, which contains a chart listing all students known to have left for France in 1926, with special comments on children of "suspects" and those known to be in correspondence with individuals mentioned in "Notes de la propagande révolutionnaire intéressant les pays d'outre-mer" of the Sûreté. The number of students who went to China, though greater, is more difficult to establish because it was easier to go undetected by the colonial authorities.
2. Nguyen Du, *The Tale of Kieu*, trans. by Huynh Sanh Thong (New Haven: Yale University Press, 1983), p. 3.
3. Letter of Tocqueville to his friend Beaumont, dated 6 December 1857, discussing the difficulties of writing *L'Ancien régime et la révolution,* quoted in André Jardin, *Alexis de Tocqueville* (Paris: Hachette, 1984), p. 486.
4. The passage of a law in 1922 which stipulated that a copy of every publication that appeared in France and its colonies be deposited at the Bibliothèque Nationale in Paris helped preserve a large number of pamphlets, monographs, and periodicals that may no longer be extant anywhere else in the world. The materials available there represent a real treasure trove for the historian of modern Vietnam.

5. Trans. by Huynh Sanh Thong, in Huynh Sanh Thong, *The Heritage of Vietnamese Poetry* (New Haven: Yale University Press, 1979), p. 207.

1. Our Fathers' House

1. My mother was six when she witnessed this scene, the teacher being her own grandfather, Dao Duy Chung.
2. A minor manifestation of this nativism was the retention of traditional hair fashion among southern men well into the middle of the twentieth century, decades after Western-style haircuts had become a sign of enlightened patriotism. See David G. Marr, *Vietnamese Anticolonialism, 1885–1925* (Berkeley: University of California Press, 1971), pp. 169–171.
3. Dao Duy Chung was known for being "loyal to Vietnam" and "upholding the old ways"; see Nguyen Lien Phong, *Dieu co ha kim thi tap* (Eulogies for the Dead, Praise for the Living) (Saigon: Dang Le Nghi, 1915). The material regarding Dao Duy Chung comes from this work as well as from family reminiscences.
4. *TI*, 14, 21 Dec. 1920.
5. Délétie, *L'Enseignement traditionel*, quoted in Gouvernement-Général de l'Indochine, Direction Générale de l'Instruction Publique, *L'Annam scolaire* (Hanoi: Imprimerie d'Extrême-Orient, 1931), p. 8.
6. For a description of the examinations of Nam Dinh of 1905, see Paul Doumer, *L'Indochine française (Souvenirs)* (Paris: Vuibert et Nouy Editeurs, 1905), pp. 134–138.
7. *Thoi Vu* (Current Affairs) 109, 1939, quoted in Phan Cu De, *Ngo Tat To, Tac Pham* (Ngo Tat To: Works), collected and edited by Phan Cu De (Hanoi: nha xuat ban Van Hoc, 1977).
8. The popular saying expressing this opinion is "nom na la cha mach que" (the demotic script is the father of argument and deviousness).
9. When modern Vietnamese rediscovered them in the 1920s, the ideas of the Ming philosopher Wang Yang-ming, credited by the Japanese for their own success in meeting the challenge of the West, appeared like newly minted truth. Dao Trinh Nhat, *Vuong Duong Minh* (Wang Yang-ming) (Saigon: Tan Viet, n.d.), preface.
10. "Nhut phu nhi su": first comes the father then comes the teacher.
11. Alexander B. Woodside, *Community and Revolution in Modern Vietnam* (Boston: Houghton Mifflin, 1976), p. 97.
12. "Tu than, te gia, tri quoc, binh thien ha"; Ch. "hsiu shen, chi chia, chih kuo, p'ing t'ien-hsia."
13. Phan Ke Binh, *Viet Nam phong tuc* (Vietnamese Customs) (Hanoi, 1941; reprinted by Song Moi, 1983), p. 134. This study originally ap-

peared as a series of articles in *Indochina Review* nos. 24–49 (1913–1914).
14. See, for example, letters addressed by students to Nguyen An Ninh and included in AOM Indochine, 7F22: Rapport annuel 1924–1926.
15. "Gai trinh khong tho hai chong; quan trung khong tho hai chua."
16. An example appears in the celebrated exchange between two brilliant scholars, the collaborationist Ton Tho Tuong and the anticolonial activist Phan van Tri: see Thai Bach, *Tho van yeu nuoc cuoi the ky muoi chin dau the ky hai muoi* (Patriotic Literature of the Late Nineteenth, Early Twentieth Centuries) (Hanoi: nha xuat ban Van Hoc, 1976); J. H. C. S. Davidson, "'Good Omens' versus 'Worth': The Poetic Dialogue between Ton Tho Tuong and Phan van Tri," in Robert Taylor and Mark Hobart, eds., *Meaning, Context, and Power in Southeast Asia* (Ithaca: Cornell University Southeast Asia Program, 1986), pp. 53–77.
17. An excellent study in English of Phan Dinh Phung appears in Marr, *Vietnamese Anticolonialism*.
18. Dao Trinh Nhat, *Phan Dinh Phung* (Saigon: Tan Viet, 1957), p. 200.
19. Dao Trinh Nhat, *Phan Dinh Phung*, pp. 84–85.
20. Marr, *Vietnamese Anticolonialism*, p. 63; Dao Trinh Nhat, *Phan Dinh Phung*, p. 86.
21. Dao Trinh Nhat, *Phan Dinh Phung*, pp. 202–206; for a slightly different translation, see Marr, *Vietnamese Anticolonialism*, pp. 66–67.
22. Phan's ancestral tombs had been desecrated several years earlier. Dao Trinh Nhat, *Phan Dinh Phung*, pp. 198, 278.
23. Dao Trinh Nhat, *Phan Dinh Phung*, p. 207.
24. Quoted in full in Chuong Thau, *Tho van yeu nuoc va cach mang dau the ky xx* (Patriotic and Revolutionary Literature of the Early Twentieth Century) (Hanoi: nha xuat ban Van Hoc, 1976), pp. 631–651; for a detailed analysis of the text, see Marr, *Vietnamese Anticolonialism*, pp. 173–175.
25. For Chinese perceptions of Social Darwinism, see Benjamin I. Schwartz, *Yen Fu: In Search of Wealth and Power* (Cambridge: Harvard University Press, 1964); James Pusey, *Charles Darwin and China* (Cambridge: Council on East Asian Studies, Harvard University, 1983).
26. Phan Boi Chau, *Viet Nam vong quoc su* (History of the Loss of Vietnam), trans. into modern Vietnamese by Nguyen Quang To (Saigon: Tao Dan, 1969). See also Phan Boi Chau, *Nien bieu* (Memoirs), trans. into modern Vietnamese by Pham Trong Diem and Ton Quang Phiet (Hanoi: nha xuat ban Van Su Dia, 1957), pp. 57–58 (the 1973 edition, annotated by Nguyen Khac Ngu and published in Saigon, omits a number of details concerning this meeting); Marr, *Vietnamese Anticolonialism*, pp. 115–116; Chuong Thau, "Anh huong cach mang Trung Quoc doi voi su bien chuyen cua tu tuong Phan Boi Chau" (The Influence of the

Chinese Revolution on the Evolution of Phan Boi Chau's Thought), *NCLS* 43 (1962), pp. 12–26, 36; and "Anh huong cua Phan Boi Chau doi voi mot so to chuc cach mang Trung Quoc" (The Influence of Phan Boi Chau on a Number of Chinese Revolutionary Organizations), *NCLS* 55 (1963), pp. 33–43, 65; *NCLS* 56 (1963), pp. 32–37.
27. Phan Boi Chau, *Viet Nam vong quoc su*, p. 71.
28. Marr, *Vietnamese Anticolonialism*, pp. 84–86.
29. Dinh Xuan Lam and Chuong Thau, "Tim hieu them ve tu tuong bao dong cua Phan Boi Chau" (To Better Understand Phan Boi Chau's Violent Ideology), *NCLS* 182 (Sept.-Oct. 1978), pp. 18–33.
30. For more on Phan Chu Trinh, see Marr, *Vietnamese Anticolonialism*. It can be argued that, since cultural change has a more profound and long-lasting impact than political change, Phan Chu Trinh's influence was more revolutionary than that of Phan Boi Chau. The point is that Phan Chu Trinh was committed to as gradual a process of cultural transformation as was necessary to avoid political violence.
31. For a sympathetic portrait of some early collaborators, see Milton Osborne, *The French Presence in Cochinchina and Cambodia: Rule and Response, 1859–1905* (Ithaca: Cornell University Press, 1969).
32. Nguyen Hien Le, *Dong Kinh Nghia Thuc* (The Tonkin Free School) (Saigon: La Boi, 1968), p. 45. For more details on the career of Nguyen van Vinh, see Pham The Ngu, *Viet Nam van hoc su gian uoc tan bien* (A New Summary History of Vietnamese Literature) (Saigon: Quoc Hoc tung thu, 1965), chap. 2. Pham Duy Ton graduated from the School of Interpreters in 1901. See Thanh Lang, *Bang luoc do van hoc Viet Nam* (A Sketch of Vietnamese Literature) (Saigon: Trinh Bay, 1967), p. 493.
33. For details of the Reform Movement in Tonkin and Annam, see Marr, *Vietnamese Anticolonialism*, and also Nguyen Hien Le, *Dong Kinh Nghia Thuc*; for a more detailed discussion of southern reformism, see Son Nam, *Thien Dia Hoi va cuoc Minh Tan* (The Heaven and Earth Society and the Reform Movement) (Saigon: Phu Sa, 1971).
34. Nguyen Hien Le, *Dong Kinh Nghia Thuc*, pp. 102–104.
35. Nguyen Hien Le, *Dong Kinh Nghia Thuc*, p. 94.
36. For more details on the events of 1908, see Marr, *Vietnamese Anticolonialism*, pp. 185–195.
37. Nguyen Hien Le, *Dong Kinh Nghia Thuc*, p. 121.
38. *NB* (1973), pp. 106–108.
39. See Hue-Tam Ho Tai, "The Politics of Compromise: The Constitutionalists and the Electoral Reforms of 1922 in French Cochinchina," *Modern Asian Studies* 18:2 (July 1984).
40. Tai, "The Politics of Compromise."
41. For a more detailed study of the League for the Restoration of Vietnam, see Marr, *Vietnamese Anticolonialism*, esp. chap. 9.

42. *NB* (1973), pp. 165–166.
43. In his memoirs, Phan Boi Chau expressed regret at these futile killings: see *NB* (1973), p. 166. One of his partisans also conceived the idea of killing Sarraut while he presided over the civil service examinations in Nam Dinh, but gave up the plan; see Hoai Thanh, *Phan Boi Chau* (Hanoi: nha xuat ban Van Hoa, 1978), pp. 81–82.
44. For an account of the riots in Cochinchina, see Hue-Tam Ho Tai, *Millenarianism and Peasant Politics in Vietnam* (Cambridge: Harvard University Press, 1983), chap. 5.
45. Nguyen Hien Le, *Dong Kinh Nghia Thuc*, p. 121.
46. Quoted by Pham The Ngu, *Viet Nam van hoc su*, p. 107.
47. Pham The Ngu, *Viet Nam van hoc su*, chap. 2.
48. The list is taken from Pham The Ngu, *Viet Nam van hoc su*, pp. 112–113.
49. Quoted in Pham The Ngu, *Viet Nam van hoc su*, p. 113.
50. Quoted in Pham The Ngu, *Viet Nam van hoc su*, p. 113.
51. Albert Sarraut, *Grandeurs et servitudes coloniales* (Paris: Editions du Sagittaire, 1931), pp. 107–108; the same language appeared in Governor-General A. Varenne's speech of 21 December 1926 to the Conseil Supérieur of Indochina.
52. On Nguyen van Vinh's cultural shift, see Pham The Ngu, *Viet Nam van hoc su*, p. 122.
53. Hanh Son, *Cu Tran Cao Van* (Tran Cao Van) (Paris: Minh Tan, 1952); see also Marr, *Vietnamese Anticolonialism*, pp. 231–234.
54. For more details, see Tai, *Millenarianism and Peasant Politics*, pp. 63–76.
55. Ferdinand Buisson, letter to the Minister of Colonies, reprinted in *Cahier de la Ligue des Droits de l'Homme* (July 1921) and excerpted in Duong van Giao, *L'Indochine pendant la guerre de 1914 à 1918* (Paris: J. Budry et Cie., 1925), pp. 326–327. At the trial, a witness said of the prison: "Ce n'était donc plus un lieu de détention, mais bien un 'crevatorium.'" Throughout the account, the French Résident of Thai Nguyen, Darles, is referred to only as D.
56. *NB* (1973), p. 62. Luong Ngoc Quyen's father had been principal of the Tonkin Free School, and both his brother and sister had taught classes there.
57. *TI*, 6 Sept. 1924, quoting from *Voix Libre*. See also AOM, SLOTFOM III-55: Affaire de Thai Nguyen: Condamnations. In *Vietnamese Anticolonialism*, p. 235n, Marr, relying on French reports cited in Trang Liet, *Cuoc doi cach mang Cuong De* (The Revolutionary Life of Prince Cuong De) (Saigon: nha in Ton That Le, 1951), lists only 163 deaths on both sides.

58. Clara Malraux, *Les Combats et les jeux* (Paris: Grasset, 1969), p. 60. For an account of the origins of the Commission of investigation, see Duong van Giao, *L'Indochine pendant la guerre*, pp. 323–324.
59. Sarraut, quoted in Francis Decaux, *Les Pouvoirs du gouvernement-général de l'Indochine* (Lille: Camille Robbe, 1919), pp. 99–100.
60. The piecemeal approach to educational policy is amply revealed in the plethora of decrees. See Indochine française, Direction Générale de l'Instruction Publique, *L'Enseignement secondaire indochinois et les humanités extrême-orientales* (Paris: Exposition coloniale internationale, 1931), pp. 6–7.
61. Decree of 26 August 1910 of Governor-General Klobukowsky, cited in *L'Enseignement secondaire*, p. 7.
62. Gail P. Kelly, *Franco-Vietnamese Schools, 1918–1938: Regional Development and Implications for National Integration* (Madison: University of Wisconsin–Madison, Southeast Asia Publications, 1982), pp. 12–13.
63. Gouvernement-Général de l'Indochine, Direction Générale de l'Instruction Publique, *L'Annam scolaire: de l'enseignement traditionel annamite à l'enseignement moderne franco-indigène* (Hanoi: Imprimerie d'Extrême-Orient, 1931), pp. 10–11.
64. Sylvain Lévi, *Indochine*, vol. 2: *Documents officiels* (Paris: Société d'éditions géographiques, maritimes et coloniales, 1931), p. 145.
65. *L'Annam scolaire*, p. 7.
66. *L'Annam scolaire*, p. 10.
67. That villagers were expected to bear all expenses connected with this school expansion program is made clear in the circular of 30 July 1919 of the Résident Supérieur of Annam quoted in *L'Annam scolaire*, p. 38. In Annam alone, 485 schools closed down in 1919–1920, according to official statistics. Ibid., p. 41.
68. These figures are included in François de Tessan, *Dans l'Asie qui s'éveille* (Paris: Renaissance du Livre, n.d.), p. 248.
69. P.L.B., "La Diffusion de l'enseignement populaire en Indochine, 1924–1925," *Revue Indochinoise* 9–10 (Sept.-Oct. 1925), p. 265, quoted in Pham Cao Duong, *Vietnamese Peasants under French Domination, 1861–1945* (Berkeley: Center for South and Southeast Asia Studies, 1985), p. 141.
70. Statistics culled from the preface of *L'Annam scolaire*.
71. Lévi, *Indochine*, vol. 2, p. 146. The population figure of 17,101,000 for 1930 appears on p. 205.
72. Pham Cao Duong, *Vietnamese Peasants*, pp. 142–143.
73. "Il n'est pas douteux que le nombre des indigènes qui savent lire le quoc ngu est très élevé relativement à l'effort scolaire qui a été réalisé en ce pays. C'est un spectacle courant de la rue ou de la route annamite que

de voir des individus déjà âgés, appartenant aux classes les plus humbles, plongés dans des lectures plus ou moins laborieuses." AOM Indochine, NF1568: Note sur l'activité des partis d'opposition antifrançaise en Indochine, 1er trimestre 1928.
74. *TI*, 27 Sept. 1924.
75. J. Buttinger, *Vietnam: A Political History* (New York: Praeger, 1968), p. 103.
76. Gail P. Kelly, *Franco-Vietnamese Schools*, pp. 12–13.
77. These were the Lycée Petrus Ky in Saigon and the Lycée du Protectorat in Hanoi. Those of Hue, Vinh (Annam), and My Tho (Cochinchina) only included the first three grades. Lévi, *Indochine*, vol. 2, p. 137.
78. See, for example, Pham Quynh's praise in *NP* 93 (Mar. 1926).
79. Lévi, *Indochine*, vol. 2, p. 140; *L'Annam scolaire*, p. 49.
80. For a translation of the text of the Indictment, see Marr, *Vietnamese Anticolonialism*, pp. 246–247.
81. Tran Dan Tien, *Nhung mau chuyen ve doi hoat dong cua Ho Chu Tich* (Anecdotes about President Ho's Career) (Hanoi: nha xuat ban Van Hoc, 1970), p. 34. The play was staged with the assistance of the left-wing Club du Faubourg.
82. *TI*, 8 Apr. 1919. The speech was originally given in 1914 at the Conseil Supérieur de l'Indochine, an advisory body to the Governor-General.
83. *TI*, 27 Apr. 1919.
84. *Projet de loi de mise en valeur des colonies françaises, presenté par M. Albert Sarraut, Ministre des Colonies* (Paris: Bibliothèque de la *Revue Indigène*, 1921), p. 26.
85. Tai, "The Politics of Compromise."
86. R. B. Smith, "Bui Quang Chieu and the Constitutionalist Party in French Cochinchina, 1917–1930," *Modern Asian Studies* (Apr. 1969).
87. Smith, "Bui Quang Chieu."
88. Sarraut, *Grandeurs et servitudes*, p. 111.
89. The text of this speech was reprinted in *TI* on 24 September 1917.
90. *Bulletin financier*, 11 Oct. 1917.
91. See Duong van Giao, *L'Indochine pendant la guerre*, pp. 145–153. Giao's dissertation seems to have been conceived as a means of furthering the political ambitions of his uncle, Bui Quang Chieu.
92. The exact figures are 43,430 soldiers and 51,000 workers; Duong van Giao, *L'Indochine pendant la guerre*, p. 38–108.
93. According to a census of 1918, of the 36,715 Vietnamese workers then in France, 25,236 were completely illiterate. AOM Indochine, NF226, quoted in J. Dion, "Introduction à SLOTFOM."
94. In a letter to the Minister of Colonies dated 23 August 1919, Pierre Pasquier, writing in his capacity as chief of staff of the Governor-General

of Indochina, suggested: "Nous devons faciliter l'obtention à ceux qui sans avoir d'obligations militaires se sont engagés pour la durée de la guerre, sont allés à feu au risque de leur vie, y ont montré de courage et même d'héroisme et ont donné ainsi des preuves certaines de leurs sentiments français." AOM Indochine, AP21, carton 279: Projet de décret modifiant la naturalisation.
95. *TI*, 8 Nov. 1917, 21 Jan. 1918, 31 Jan. 1918.
96. The electoral reforms of 1922 raised this number to 20,000; see Tai, "The Politics of Compromise."
97. Letter of Bui Quang Chieu to Ernest Outrey, Deputy for French Cochinchina, 8 November 1917, published in *TI*.
98. Interview with Bui Quang Chieu, published in *PNTV*, 20 July 1929.
99. *TI*, 26 June 1923.
100. *PNTV*, 20 June 1929.
101. Tessan, *Dans l'Asie qui s'éveille*, p. 247.
102. "L'Instruction intensive des indigènes peut-elle être nuisible à l'influence française?" *TI*, 7 Jan. 1918.
103. AOM Indochine, 7F22: Notes de Sûreté concernant la situation politique indigène au 25 mai 1923; P. Arnoux à M. Cognacq.
104. AOM Indochine, 7F22: Chef du Service de la Sûreté cochinchinoise au Gouverneur de la Cochinchine; Hérisson à M. Cognacq, 2 Apr. 1921.
105. AOM Indochine, 7F22: P. Arnoux à M. Cognacq, 25 May 1923.
106. See Chapter 4 for more details on this episode.
107. A portrait of Pham Quynh appears in Tessan, *Dans l'Asie qui s'éveille*, p. 261.
108. Pham The Ngu, *Viet Nam van hoc su*, p. 138.
109. "Rong Nam phung bac, danh do Duc tac."
110. Pham The Ngu, *Viet Nam van hoc su*, p. 129.
111. Nguyen van Trung, *Chu dich Nam Phong* (The Objectives of *Southern Wind*) (Saigon: n.p., 1972), p. 47. I am indebted to David Marr for pointing out this publication to me.
112. Bac Ha, in *Trung Lap* (Impartial) 6 (1930), quoted in Nguyen van Trung, *Chu dich Nam Phong*, p. 106. Nguyen van Trung charges that when Sarraut was Governor-General, Pham Quynh compared his rule to the Meiji Restoration; when Varenne was in power, Pham Quynh criticized Sarraut and affected more leftist ideas; when Pasquier became Governor-General, he then returned to monarchism and praised patriarchal society and the preservation of tradition.
113. *NP* 68 (Feb. 1923).
114. *NP* 106 (June 1926).
115. For a biography of Liang Shu-ming, see Guy Alitto, *The Last Confucian* (Berkeley: University of California Press, 1979); for an excellent

survey of the National Essence Movement in China, see Charlotte Furth, "Intellectual Change from the Reform Movement to the May Fourth Movement, 1895–1920," in *The Cambridge History of China*, vol. 12 (Cambridge: Cambridge University Press, 1984).

116. Tessan, *Dans l'Asie qui s'éveille*, pp. 260–261; see also Pham The Ngu, *Viet Nam van hoc su*, p. 128. Nguyen van Trung, in *Chu dich Nam Phong*, also discusses at length the involvement of Marty in both *Southern Wind* and AFIMA.
117. Quoted in Tessan, *Dans l'Asie qui s'éveille*, pp. 261–262.
118. *NP* 156 (Aug. 1930).
119. Pham The Ngu, *Viet Nam van hoc su*, p. 130.
120. The 1920s also saw the introduction of physical education in the school curriculum, though this had been advocated by the reformers of 1907.
121. *NP* 68 (Feb. 1923).
122. Kelly, *Franco-Vietnamese Schools*, p. 52. This essentially reprises McAlister's position: "The denial of the exercise of political power is the most conspicuous source of the sense of relative deprivation leading to revolution." John T. McAlister, Jr., *Vietnam: The Origins of Revolution* (New York: Knopf, 1970), p. 333.
123. AOM Indochine, 7F21(1): Service de Sûreté du Tonkin, Rapport annuel 1922–1923.
124. AOM, SLOTFOM III-44: Déclarations de Nguyen The Vinh recueillies par la Direction de la Sûreté générale indochinoise, August 1931.
125. AOM Indochine, 7F34: Agitation antifrançaise dans les pays annamites, 1905–1933. The data gathered in this file formed the basis of the six-volume work of the Gouvernement-Général de l'Indochine, Direction des Affaires Politiques et de la Sûreté Générale, *Contribution à l'histoire des mouvements politiques de l'Indochine française* (Hanoi, 1930–1933).
126. A case in point is Nguyen The Truyen, whose father continued to support him financially though Truyen's anticolonial activities—which included recruiting several of his relatives—brought much unwanted attention to his family.
127. Nguyen Khac Vien, "Marxism and Confucianism," in David G. Marr and Jayne Werner, eds., *Tradition and Revolution* (Berkeley: Indochina Research Center, 1972).
128. Nguyen Ba Hoc, "Thu tra loi ong chu but *Nam Phong*" (A Reply to the Editor of *Southern Wind*), *NP* 40 (Oct. 1920), pp. 322–324, quoted in David G. Marr, *Vietnamese Tradition on Trial* (Berkeley: University of California Press, 1981), p. 331.
129. Huynh Kim Khanh, *Vietnamese Communism, 1925–1945* (Ithaca:

2. Different Roads to Freedom

1. See in particular Georges Boudarel, "L'Extrême-gauche asiatique et le mouvement national vietnamien," in Pierre Brocheux, ed., *Histoire de l'Asie du Sud-est: révoltes, réformes, révolutions* (Lille: Presses universitaires de Lille, 1982), pp. 165–192; see also Shiraishi Masaya, "Phan Boi Chau in Japan," in Vinh Sinh, ed., *Phan Boi Chau and the Dong Du Movement* (New Haven: Council on Southeast Asian Studies, Lac Viet Series, 1988), pp. 52–100.
2. For a discussion of the controversy, see Li Yu-ning, *The Introduction of Socialism into China* (New York: Occasional Papers of the East Asian Studies Institute, Columbia University, 1971), pp. 22–24, and Martin Bernal, *Chinese Socialism to 1907* (Ithaca: Cornell University Press, 1976), pp. 134–197.
3. Luong Ngoc Quyen's younger brother, Nghi Khanh, lived for a time at the office of the *People's Journal* while learning Japanese. See *NB* (1973), p. 64.
4. *NB* (1973), pp. 101–105.
5. *NB* (1973), pp. 105–109.
6. *NB* (1973), pp. 126–127.
7. Shiraishi, "Phan Boi Chau in Japan," p. 72.
8. Arif Dirlik, "Vision and Revolution," *Modern China* 12:2 (Apr. 1986), p. 152; Shiraishi, "Phan Boi Chau in Japan," p. 73.
9. Shiraishi, "Phan Boi Chau in Japan," pp. 71–81.
10. Bernal, *Chinese Socialism,* p. 219.
11. Quoted in Bernal, *Chinese Socialism,* p. 219. See also Dirlik, "Vision and Revolution."
12. *NB* (1973), p. 148.
13. *NB* (1973), p. 149.
14. *NB* (1973), p. 155; see also David G. Marr, *Vietnamese Anticolonialism, 1885–1925* (Berkeley: University of California Press, 1971), pp. 217–218.
15. See Arif Dirlik and Edward Krebs, "Socialism and Anarchism in Early Republican China," *Modern China* 7:2 (Apr. 1981), pp. 117–151; Howard Boorman, ed., *Biographical Dictionary of Republican China,* vol. 2 (New York: Columbia University Press, 1968), pp. 413–416.
16. The scheme seems to have generated more headaches than money; see Trang Liet, *Cuoc doi cach mang Cuong De* (The Revolutionary Life of

Prince Cuong De) (Saigon: nha in Ton That Le, 1951), p. 50. Phan Boi Chau attributes the scheme to another anarchist, Teng ching-ya; see *NB* (1973), pp. 153, 164.
17. Phan Boi Chau, *Nguc trung thu* (Letter from Prison), trans. by Dao Trinh Nhat (Saigon: Tan Viet, 1950), p. 68; Boudarel, "L'Extrême-gauche asiatique," p. 171.
18. Boudarel, "L'Extrême-gauche asiatique," p. 172.
19. Archives du Ministère des Affaires Etrangères: Indochine, Rebelles annamites en Chine, vol. 2, p. 450, letter dated 27 November 1923, quoted in Boudarel, "L'Extrême-gauche asiatique," p. 172.
20. Shiraishi, "Phan Boi Chau in Japan," p. 81.
21. See his entry in Howard Boorman, *Biographical Dictionary of Republican China*, vol. 1 (New York: Columbia University Press, 1967), pp. 92–98.
22. Dirlik, "Vision and Revolution," p. 152.
23. Alexander B. Woodside, *Community and Revolution in Modern Vietnam* (Boston: Houghton Mifflin, 1976), pp. 57–58.
24. *NB* (1973), pp. 154–155.
25. Marr, *Vietnamese Anticolonialism*, pp. 218–221; Dirlik, "Vision and Revolution," p. 135.
26. See *NB* (1973), pp. 167–168, and Phan Boi Chau, *Tuong Trung Nu Vuong, Truyen Pham Hong Thai* (The Play of the Trung Queens, the Story of Pham Hong Thai) (Hanoi: nha xuat ban Van Hoc, 1967), pp. 141–144.
27. *NB* (1973), p. 155.
28. *NB* (1973), pp. 175–178.
29. Phan Ba Ngoc had been a member of the Disciplinary Department of the short-lived Constitutionalist Association. See *NB* (1973), p. 102.
30. *NB* (1973), pp. 193–196.
31. In 1923, Chang Ping-lin introduced Phan Boi Chau to Rabindranath Tagore; *NB* (1973), p. 202.
32. *NB* (1973), pp. 196–197.
33. Gouvernement-Général de l'Indochine, Direction des Affaires Politiques et de la Sûreté Générale, *Contribution à l'histoire des mouvements politiques de l'Indochine française*, 6 vols. (Hanoi, 1930–1933), vol. 1.
34. Dang Thuc Hua later went to Siam and organized the Vietnamese émigré community there. For this period of his life, see Woodside, *Community and Revolution*, pp. 238–239; Nguyen Tai, "May mau chuyen ve cu Dang Thuc Hua" (Anecdotes about Dang Thuc Hua), *NCLS* (Nov. 1965), p. 45; Hoang van Hoan, *Giot nuoc trong bien ca* (A Drop in the Ocean) (Beijing: nha xuat ban Tin Vietnam, 1986), chap. 2, esp. pp. 47–54; Boudarel, "L'Extrême-gauche asiatique," pp. 183–184.
35. *NB* (1957), p. 143. This passage does not appear in the Saigon edition

of 1973; for information about the founding of the Society of Like Hearts and for the text of its manifesto, see Trung Chinh, "Tam Tam Xa la gi?" (What Was the Society of Like Hearts?) *NCLS* 133 (July-Aug. 1970), pp. 5–9; see also Quang Hung and Quoc Anh, "Le Hong Son, nguoi chien si xuat sac thuoc the he nhung nguoi cong san dau tien of Viet-nam" (Le Hong Son, Outstanding Member of the First Generation of Vietnamese Communists), *NCLS* 184 (Jan.-Feb. 1979), pp. 11–20.
36. Trung Chinh, "Tam Tam Xa," p. 6.
37. Trung Chinh, "Tam Tam Xa," p. 5.
38. Trung Chinh, "Tam Tam Xa," p. 8.
39. *NB* (1973), p. 200.
40. *NB* (1973), p. 205.
41. *NB* (1973), p. 209.
42. Louis Roubaud, *Vietnam, la tragédie indochinoise* (Paris: Valois, 1931), pp. 50–51; see also Phan Boi Chau, *Tuong Trung Nu Vuong, Truyen Pham Hong Thai.*
43. *NB* (1973), pp. 209–210.
44. He is conventionally thought to have been born in 1890, which would have made him twenty-one at the time; but in his application for admission into the Ecole Coloniale, he gave 1892 as the year of his birth. The letter of application is reproduced in Nguyen The Anh and Vu Ngu Chieu, "Tu mong lam quan den cach mang" (From Dreams of Becoming a Mandarin to Revolution), *Duong Moi-Voie Nouvelle* 1 (1984), pp. 18–19.
45. The letter of rejection is reproduced in Nguyen The Anh and Vu Ngu Chieu, "Tu mong lam quan," p. 16.
46. AOM, SLOTFOM III-29: Note du 11 déc. 1929.
47. Another brother, a devout Catholic with French citizenship, worked as a court interpreter and was known to disapprove of anticolonial activities. See AOM, SLOTFOM III-29: Note du 11 déc. 1929.
48. AOM Indochine, AP23, carton 330(9): Condamnés politiques, Phan Chu Trinh: decree of 18 March 1911.
49. For an account of Phan Chu Trinh's life in France, see Thu Trang Cong thi Nghia, *Nhung hoat dong cua Phan Chu Trinh tai Phap, 1911–1925* (The Activities of Phan Chu Trinh in France, 1911–1925) (Paris: Dong Nam A, 1983).
50. A text of the "Revendications" appears in Daniel Hémery, "Du patriotisme au marxisme: l'immigration vietnamienne en France de 1926 à 1930," *Le Mouvement Social* 90 (Jan.-Mar. 1975), p. 48.
51. Tran Dan Tien, *Nhung mau chuyen ve doi hoat dong cua Ho Chu Tich* (Anecdotes about President Ho's Career) (Hanoi: nha xuat ban Van Hoc, 1970), pp. 31–32.

52. Tran Dan Tien, *Nhung mau chuyen,* pp. 31–32; the author suggests that Phan van Truong wrote the articles because Nguyen Ai Quoc's French was far from fluent.
53. AOM, SLOTFOM III-3: Note sur les associations d'indochinois à Paris, 14 June 1923.
54. AOM, SLOTFOM III-3. The Association Mutuelle des Indochinois en France had a membership of 150 and received subsidies amounting to 50,000 francs.
55. Letter to the Central Committee of the French Communist Party, Moscow, July 1923, from Ho Chi Minh, *Tuyen tap* (Selected Works), vol. 1: *1920–1954* (Hanoi: nha xuat ban Su That, 1980), pp. 15–19.
56. Appendix to *Le Procès de la colonisation française* (Paris: Librairie du Travail, 1925).
57. AOM Indochine, 7F19: Direction de la Sûreté du Tonkin, notes mensuelles, June-July 1927, Oct.-Dec. 1927.
58. AOM, SLOTFOM III-3: Note du 14 juin 1923, Contrôle général des indochinois en France.
59. Léon Werth, *Cochinchine* (Paris: Rieder, 1926), p. 35.
60. *CF,* 10 Dec. 1923.
61. *CF,* 26 Nov. 1925.
62. Letter to Max Nettlau, 5 March 1902, reproduced in P. A. Kropotkin, *Selected Writings on Anarchism and Revolution,* edited with an introduction by Martin Miller (Cambridge: MIT Press, 1970).
63. Woodside, *Community and Revolution,* p. 42, quoting from Lam Giang, *Giang luan ve Phan Boi Chau* (Lectures on Phan Boi Chau) (Saigon: n.p., 1959), p. 104.
64. Biographical data on Nguyen An Ninh come from a variety of sources: AOM Indochine, 7F22A: Notice d'information politique portant sur la période comprise entre le 1er juillet 1923 et 31 décembre 1924; AOM Indochine, 7F34: Gouvernement Général, Sûreté Générale, "Affaire Gilbert Chieu," Agitation antifrançaise dans les pays annamites de 1905 à 1918, tomes 1, 2; Phuong Lan, *Nha cach mang Nguyen An Ninh* (The Revolutionary Nguyen An Ninh) (Saigon: n.p., 1970).
65. Nguyen An Khuong's role in the Reform Movement is mentioned in AOM Indochine, 7F34: L'Agitation antifrançaise dans les pays annamites de 1905 à 1918, vol. 1, pp. 81–90.
66. AOM Indochine, 7F34: Agitation antifrançaise de 1905 à 1918, vol. 2, p. 52; Nguyen Hien Le, *Dong Kinh Nghia Thuc* (The Tonkin Free School) (Saigon: La Boi, 1968), pp. 128–129. Cuong De thought that this woman was a daughter of Nguyen An Khuong; Nguyen An Ninh, however, noted in his letter to the governor of Cochinchina of 2 May 1926 that he was an only son, so she can only have been his aunt.
67. *TI,* 17 Dec. 1917; of the seventeen graduates, only two were French.
68. AOM Indochine, 7F22A: Rapport annuel 1924–1926.

69. At his trial in 1926, Ninh was reminded of this scholarship and was accused of ingratitude toward the colonial regime; *Hai ngoai chau san* (Overseas Journal), 10 May 1926, in AOM Indochine, 7F22(4) rapport annuel 1924–1926.
70. *CF,* 19 May 1924.
71. AOM Indochine, 7F22A.
72. AOM Indochine, 7F22: Rapport annuel 1924–1926; Babut went back to Vietnam in 1923 and became editor-in-chief of the Hanoi-based *Argus Indochinois*.
73. Le van Thu, *Hoi kin Nguyen An Ninh* (The Nguyen An Ninh Secret Society) (Saigon: Me Linh, 1961), p. 17.
74. AOM Indochine, 7F22A.
75. *CF,* 7 Jan. 1924.
76. Bui Quang Chieu, "L'Idéal des jeunes générations," *PTI,* 20 Dec. 1919.
77. The full text of the 15 October 1923 speech appeared in *CF,* 7 Jan. 1924, and quotations from the speech in subsequent paragraphs here are all from this source.
78. The reference was to *Le Miracle français en Asie,* by Charles Régismantet, an associate of Sarraut; it was published in Paris in 1922.
79. Phan Boi Chau, *Tuong Trung Nu Vuong, Truyen Pham Hong Thai,* pp. 131–132.
80. Bergsonism, which was very popular both in the West and in China, also influenced Pham Quynh and Liang Shu-ming. See François de Tessan, *Dans l'Asie qui s'éveille* (Paris: Renaissance du Livre, n.d.), p. 261; Guy Alitto, *The Last Confucian* (Berkeley: University of California Press, 1979), pp. 96–101.
81. *CF,* 24 Dec. 1923.
82. The article also contains a peculiar interpretation of traditional polygamy as being favorable to women, while Western-style divorce is described as disadvantageous to them because it forces husbands to make public their wives' shortcomings. This can only be a reflection of Ninh's own recent experience with divorce.
83. *CF,* 10 Dec. 1923.
84. AOM, SLOTFOM III-55: Note du 18 juin 1925.
85. *CF,* 10 Dec. 1923.
86. Werth, *Cochinchine,* p. 59. Ninh probably provided the inspiration for the character of Ling in Malraux' *La Tentation de l'Occident* (The Temptation of the West), which was published in 1926, shortly after Malraux' return to France from Vietnam and well before he set foot in China. Ling's persona, with its Western erudition and its strong streak of mysticism, closely resembles that of Ninh.
87. Emma Goldman, *Living My Life,* vol. 1 (New York: Knopf, 1931), p. 194.
88. *CF,* 24 Dec. 1925.

89. Werth, *Cochinchine*, pp. 162–163.
90. Ba Nguyen An Ninh, "Hoi ky" (Memoirs), in *Con duong giai phong* (The Road to Liberation), vol. 2 (Hanoi: nha xuat ban Phu Nu, 1976), p. 151.
91. *CF*, 14 July 1924.
92. *CF*, 19 May 1924.
93. *La France en Indochine* (Paris: Debeauve, 1925); the pamphlet was serialized in *CF* later that year.
94. Ton Quang Phiet, "Du luan ve thanh nien" (Opinion on Youth), *NP* 89 (Jan. 1925).
95. *Contribution*, vol. 1, pp. 5–6.
96. *Contribution*, vol. 1, pp. 7–9.

3. Daughters of Annam

1. See, for example, Beatrice Brodsky Farnsworth, "Communist Feminism: Its Synthesis and Demise," in Carol Berkin and Clara M. Lovett, eds., *Women, War, and Revolution* (New York: Holmes & Meier, 1980); and, inter alia, Judith Stacey, *Patriarchy and Socialist Revolution in China* (Berkeley: University of California Press, 1983).
2. See, for example, David G. Marr, *Vietnamese Tradition on Trial* (Berkeley: University of California Press, 1981), chap. 1; Ngo Vinh Long and Nguyen Hoi Chan, *Vietnamese Women in Society and Revolution*, vol. 1: *The French Colonial Period* (Cambridge: Vietnam Resource Center, 1974); Mai thi Tu and Le thi Nham Tuyet, *Women in Vietnam* (Hanoi: Foreign Languages Publishing House, 1979).
3. Alexander B. Woodside, *Community and Revolution in Modern Vietnam* (Boston: Houghton Mifflin, 1976), p. 76.
4. "Tai gia tung phu, xuat gia tung phu, phu tu tung tu."
5. Tessan, however, remarked on the uniformly self-confident gait of Vietnamese women of all classes: François de Tessan, *Dans l'Asie qui s'éveille* (Paris: Renaissance du Livre, n.d.), pp. 273–276.
6. Pham Quynh, "Dia vi nguoi dan ba trong xa hoi nuoc ta" (The Position of Women in Our Society), *NP* 82 (Apr. 1924).
7. Than Trong Hue, "Con duong tien bo cua nuoc ta" (The Road to Progress of Our Country), *NP* 8 (1918), quoted in Marr, *Vietnamese Tradition on Trial*, p. 204.
8. *Gai lanh, vo hien, me tu.*
9. Huynh van Tong, *Lich su bao chi Viet Nam tu khoi thuy den nam 1930* (A History of Vietnamese Journalism from Its Origins to 1930) (Saigon: Tri Dang, 1973), pp. 100–102.
10. Nguyen Hien Le, *Dong Kinh Nghia Thuc* (The Tonkin Free School) (Saigon: La Boi, 1968), pp. 68–70.

11. See Charlotte Beahan, "Feminism and Nationalism in the Chinese Women's Press, 1902–1911," *Modern China*, 1:4 (Oct. 1975), pp. 379–416; Jacqueline Nivard, "Women and the Women's Press: The Case of the Ladies' Journal (Funu Zahi), 1915–1931," *Republican China* 10:1b (Nov. 1984), pp. 37–55; Peter Zarrow, "He Zhen and Anarcho-Feminism in China," *JAS* 47:4 (Nov. 1988), pp. 796–813.
12. Zarrow, "He Zhen," p. 796.
13. For the text of the play, see Phan Boi Chau, *Tuong Trung Nu Vuong, Truyen Pham Hong Thai* (The Play of the Trung Queens, the Story of Pham Hong Thai) (Hanoi: nha xuat ban Van Hoc, 1967); for an interpretation which puts greater emphasis on the Vietnamese context, see David G. Marr, *Vietnamese Anticolonialism, 1885–1925* (Berkeley: University of California Press, 1971), pp. 153–154.
14. Gouvernement-Général de l'Indochine, Direction Générale de l'Instruction Publique, *L'Annam scolaire: de l'enseignement traditionel annamite à l'enseignement moderne franco-indigène* (Hanoi: Imprimerie d'Extrême-Orient, 1931), pp. 109–112.
15. The numbers remained modest. In 1922–1923, when Tessan probably visited Vietnam, 226 students were enrolled in the Collège de Filles Indigènes. See Tessan, *Dans l'Asie qui s'éveille*, pp. 179–184.
16. Pham Quynh, "Su giao duc dan ba con gai" (The Education of Women and Girls), *NP* 4 (Oct. 1917).
17. Nguyen Ba Hoc, "Ban ve chu nghia tu do ket hon" (On Freedom of Marriage), *NP* 27 (Sept. 1919).
18. Pham Quynh, "Dia vi nguoi dan ba." Issues of *Southern Wind* appeared much later than their supposed date of publication; thus, the talk, given in May, was reprinted in the April issue of the journal.
19. Nguyen Don Phuc, "Guong To Nga" (The Example of the Daughters of Confucius), *NP* 55 (Jan. 1922).
20. *Southern Wind* carried numerous articles and notices supporting nursery schools. See, for example, Nguyen Don Phuc, "Van de au tri vien" (The Issue of Nursery Schools) *NP* 59 (May 1922).
21. Pham Quynh, "Su giao duc dan ba con gai."
22. Pham Quynh, "Dia vi nguoi dan ba." He had used these lines before in "Su giao duc dan ba con gai."
23. Nguyen Don Phuc, "Dan ba Dong Phuong" (Oriental Women), *NP* 101 (Dec. 1925).
24. "Con hu tai me"; see Nguyen Don Phuc, "Dan ba Dong Phuong."
25. For further details, see Pham The Ngu, *Viet Nam van hoc su gian uoc tan bien* (A New Summary History of Vietnamese Literature) (Saigon: Quoc Hoc tung thu, 1965), p. 138.
26. Pham Quynh, "Su giao duc dan ba con gai."
27. Pham Quynh, "Dia vi nguoi dan ba."

28. *NP* 56 (Feb. 1922). Nothing came of this suggestion.
29. Ngo Huy Linh, "Nam Quoc nu luu tan truyen" (A New History of Famous Women in Vietnam), *NP* 83 (May 1924).
30. Nguyen Don Phuc, "Guong To Nga."
31. Doan Ngoc Bich, "Chuyen co Phung" (The Story of Miss Phung), *NP* 65 (Nov. 1922).
32. Doan Ngoc Bich, "Ga ban cho con" (The Daughter Sold in Marriage) *NP* 67 (Jan. 1923).
33. Tran Quan Chi, "Muon chan hung phong hoa thoi phai cai cach moi duong sinh hoat cua quoc dan" (To Renovate Customs, We Must Reform All Aspects of the People's Life), *NP* 62 (Aug. 1922); "Cai hai tao hon phai kip tru" (The Scourge of Early Marriages Must Be Speedily Eradicated), *NP* 63 (Sept. 1922).
34. Perry Link, *Mandarin Ducks and Butterflies* (Berkeley: University of California Press, 1981), pp. 40–54.
35. *NP* 86 (Aug. 1924). For an extended discussion on *Tuyet Hong Le Su*, the Vietnamese version of *The Chronicle of Great Tears of Bygone Days*, see Thanh Lang, *Bang luoc do van hoc Viet Nam* (A Schema of Vietnamese Literature) (Saigon: Trinh Bay, 1967), pp. 468–478.
36. *Khai Hoa* was a daily established in 1921 by the northern industrialist Bach Thai Buoi; it ran until 1927. See Huynh van Tong, *Lich su bao chi*, p. 153.
37. An analysis of the significance of this publication is provided in Cao thi Nhu Quynh and John C. Schafer, "From Verse Narrative to Novel: The Development of Prose Fiction in Vietnam," *JAS* 47:4 (Nov. 1988), pp. 756–777.
38. *NP* 51 (Sept. 1921). For a study of late Ch'ing literary trends, see Milena Dolezelova-Velingerova, "The Origins of Modern Chinese Literature," in Merle Goldman, ed., *Modern Chinese Literature in the May Fourth Era* (Cambridge: Harvard University Press, 1974).
39. Phan Cu De, *Tieu thuyet Viet Nam hien dai* (The Contemporary Vietnamese Novel), vol. 1 (Hanoi: nha xuat ban Van Hoc, 1975), p. 21.
40. Hoang Ngoc Phach, "Van chuong voi nu gioi" (Literature and Women), *NP* 41 (Nov. 1920).
41. Quoted in Pham The Ngu, *Viet Nam van hoc su*, p. 362. Hoang Ngoc Phach was echoing Marshal Pétain's wartime motto: "famille, travail, patrie."
42. Phan Cu De, *Tieu thuyet Viet Nam hien dai*, vol. 1, p. 21.
43. For contemporary reactions, see Pham The Ngu, *Viet Nam van hoc su*, pp. 362–367; see also Phan Cu De, *Tieu thuyet Viet Nam hien dai*, vol. 1, p. 21.
44. Pham The Ngu, *Viet Nam van hoc su*, p. 366.

45. For an English translation, see Huynh Sanh Thong, trans., *The Tale of Kieu* (New Haven: Yale University Press, 1983); for a discussion of its Chinese antecedents, see Charles Benoit, "The Evolution of the Tale of Wang Cuiqiao: From Chinese Historical Event to Vietnamese Literary Masterpiece," Ph.D. dissertation, Harvard University, 1982.
46. Quoted in Pham The Ngu, *Viet Nam van hoc su,* p. 152.
47. *NP* 86 (Aug. 1924).
48. Pham The Ngu, *Viet Nam van hoc su,* p. 156.
49. *NP* 86 (Aug. 1924).
50. Huynh van Tong, *Lich su bao chi,* p. 141. On the staff were, among others, Tan Da, Dao Trinh Nhat, and Nguyen Thuong Huyen.
51. Ngo Duc Ke, "Nen quoc van" (The Foundations of National Literature), *Huu Thanh* 12 (Apr. 1924), reprinted in Chuong Thau, *Tho van yeu nuoc va cach mang dau the ky xx* (Patriotic and Revolutionary Literature of the Early Twentieth Century) (Hanoi: nha xuat ban Van Hoc, 1976), pp. 294–301.
52. Pham The Ngu, *Viet Nam van hoc su,* pp. 150–160.
53. See AOM Indochine, 7F22: Rapport annuel 1924–1926.
54. Pham Quynh, "Dia vi nguoi dan ba."

4. Scandal Sheets

1. The structure of the monopolies was largely set up by Paul Doumer, who began his tenure as Governor-General in 1897. See Virginia Thompson, *French Indochina* (New York: Macmillan, 1937), pp. 184–191.
2. See, for example, the text of a letter Sarraut wrote to the Résident Supérieur of Cambodia in 1917, reproduced in full in Nguyen Ai Quoc, *Le Procès de la colonisation française* (Paris: Librairie du Travail, 1925), p. 31. At a rally held in Montpellier on 24 October 1927, Nguyen The Truyen read aloud a circular which Sarraut, as Governor-General, had sent out to "the bureaucrats under his orders," telling them "to use their influence to promote the opening of alcohol dealerships down to the smallest villages in order to increase the revenues of the Treasury": AOM, SLOTFOM III-29, Conférence de Montpellier, 24 Oct. 1927, rapport du préfet du 25 octobre. And in 1934, Andrée Viollis reproduced the text of a recent prefectural decree ordering each taxpayer in Annam to consume seven liters of alcohol per month and stipulating that villages where consumption fell below quota were to be penalized. See Viollis, *Indochine SOS* (Paris: Gallimard, 1935), p. 29n.
3. Eugen Weber, *Peasants into Frenchmen* (Stanford: Stanford University Press, 1976).
4. Léon Werth, *Cochinchine* (Paris: Rieder, 1926), p. 59.

5. AOM Indochine, NF2640: Résident Supérieur d'Annam Pierre Pasquier reporting on the troubles of 1931.
6. *CF*, 14 May 1924, "Les Exploits du Dr. Cognacq."
7. Walter Langlois, *André Malraux: The Indochina Adventure* (New York: Praeger, 1966), p. 93.
8. *CF*, 24 Mar. 1924, "L'Affaire de Thai Nguyen à la Chambre," quoting from *L'Indépendant:* exchange between deputies Outrey and Boisneuf.
9. *PTI*, 12 Apr. 1924; Clara Malraux, *Les Combats et les jeux* (Paris: Grasset, 1969), p. 60.
10. *CF*, 19 Apr. 1926.
11. *La Lutte*, 21 Jan. and 3 June 1936. See also Walter Langlois, *André Malraux*, pp. 86–88.
12. For some examples, see Langlois, *André Malraux*, pp. 61–62.
13. *PTI*, 10 May 1924.
14. This information was divulged by the acting editor-in-chief of *Impartial*, André Peyre, during la Chevrotière's trip to Paris in 1923. After his return, la Chevrotière sacked his hapless deputy for this indiscretion. See *La Lutte*, 3 June 1936.
15. Much of this data comes from the vitriolic exchanges between la Chevrotière and the Monin-Malraux team in *Indochine*. Arnoux, the head of the Cochinchinese Sûreté, had destroyed the judicial file on la Chevrotière, but his trial had been widely reported in the press in 1917. See *Indochine*, 8, 18, 22 July 1924. In *CF*, 19 Apr. 1926, Dejean de la Batie openly referred to "le réveil des instincts mauvaix de l'ancien indicateur officieux et remunéré de la Sûreté, de l'ex-recruteur de coolies pour plantations."
16. Cognacq was accused of having destroyed the archives of the Colonial Council since 1923 and of substituting fakes: *Annam*, 24 Aug. 1926.
17. AOM Indochine, 7F22: Notice d'information politique portant sur la période comprise entre le 1er juillet 1923 et le 31 décembre 1924.
18. *EA*, 1923, quoted in François de Tessan, *Dans l'Asie qui s'éveille* (Paris: Renaissance du Livre, n.d.). The exact date of publication is not given.
19. *PTI*, 14 Feb. 1924.
20. Ho Huu Tuong, *41 nam lam bao* (41 Years of Journalism) (Saigon: Tri Dang, 1972), p. 7: "because he was councillor, my uncle was forced by the government to subscribe to *Nam Phong*."
21. Tessan, *Dans l'Asie qui s'éveille*, p. 260.
22. Pham The Ngu, *Viet Nam van hoc su gian uoc tan bien* (A New Summary History of Vietnamese Literature) (Saigon: Quoc Hoc tung thu, 1965), pp. 104–106.
23. For example, in 1933, *Trung Lap* (Impartial) was suspended for having referred to the emperor Bao Dai as "little god" *(thang troi)*; see AOM

Indochine, NF958. In 1936, *Ngo Bao* (Midday Journal) and *Phong Hoa* (Mores) were suspended between June and September for "seeking to undermine the prestige and authority of the Annamite mandarins, [who are] faithful servants of the French *oeuvre* in Tonkin." Specifically, they had satirized their mores, and in particular their "century-old practices of corruption." See Amicale des Journalistes Annamites de Cochinchine, *Le Régime de la presse en Indochine* (Saigon: n.p., 1937).
24. However, issues of newspapers that contained derogatory remarks about the Emperor or his court were banned in Tonkin and Annam even if they were allowed to circulate in Cochinchina.
25. Among them were the poet Tan Da; Ngo Tat To, who later wrote *Tents and Bamboo Beds;* Dao Trinh Nhat, author of the biography of Phan Dinh Phung; the historian Tran Huy Lieu; and Phan Khoi, the poet and essayist.
26. *CF,* 11 Nov. 1925.
27. *CF,* 17 Mar. 1924, "Sur la suppression du *Nam Ky Kinh Te Bao.*"
28. Huynh van Tong, *Lich su bao chi Viet Nam tu khoi thuy den nam 1930* (A History of Vietnamese Journalism from Its Origins to 1930) (Saigon: Tri Dang, 1973); see also C. Rageau, "Publishing in Vietnam, 1922–1945," unpublished paper, 1982. A highly personal description of the journalistic scene up to 1915 is Henri Lamagat, *Souvenirs d'un vieux journaliste indochinois* (Hanoi: Imprimerie d'Extrême-Orient, 1942).
29. In 1923, the former director of the Sûreté, Hérisson, bought *Opinion* for $60,000. *Courier Saigonnais* changed hands after 1919; bought by the Bank of Indochina, it later became the property of the Banque de Paris et des Pays-Bas. Details of ownership can be found in Virginia Thompson, *French Indochina,* pp. 310–311; see also Diep van Ky, *Le Régime de la presse en Indochine française* (Saigon: n.p., 1936); Huynh van Tong, *Lich su bao chi;* Nguyen Viet Chuoc, *Luoc su bao chi Vietnam* (A Brief History of Vietnamese Journalism) (Saigon: Nam Son, 1974).
30. Thompson, *French Indochina,* p. 311.
31. Nguyen Phan Long, *Cahier des voeux annamites* (Saigon: n.p., 1926).
32. Huynh van Tong, *Lich su bao chi,* p. 147.
33. In 1927, Devilar wrote an influential work, *Comment on perd une colonie* (Paris: Presses Modernes, 1927), in which he criticized the authorities' handling of the unrest of the previous year. He later became head of the Censorship Office.
34. AOM Indochine, 7F22(4): Rapport annuel 1924–1926.
35. Clara Malraux, *Les Combats et les jeux,* p. 36.
36. *TI,* 18 Oct. 1919, reprinting an *Impartial* article warning about the "sudden reawakening of Annamite nationalism."

37. *Impartial,* 8 May 1924, quoted in Langlois, *André Malraux,* p. 61.
38. Chavannes was the president of the Ligue pour la République; Moutet was president of the League for the Rights of Man and the Citizen, and later a member of the Popular Front cabinet of Léon Blum; see for example, Moutet's letter of 16 September 1925 to Minister of Colonies: AOM Indochine, AP23, carton 337: Régime de la presse, protestation de M. Monin.
39. *CF,* 7 Jan. 1924.
40. This biographical profile appears in AOM Indochine, 7F22(4): Rapport annuel 1924–1926.
41. In the 1930s, Dejean de la Batie moved to a more pro-colonial stance and worked for *Le Populaire,* a newspaper described by the Trotskyist paper *La Lutte* as "réactionnaire, anti-socialiste": *La Lutte,* 25 Feb. 1936.
42. *Projet de loi de mise en valeur des colonies françaises, presenté par M. Albert Sarraut, Ministre des Colonies* (Paris: Bibliothèque de la *Revue Indigène,* 1921), p. 15.
43. Clara Malraux, *Les Combats et les jeux,* p. 64.
44. Chinese from Tra Vinh were said to have provided Monin $100,000 in 1924. See AOM Indochine, 7F22: Notice d'information politique, 1923–1924.
45. *CF,* 28 Jan. 1924.
46. *PTI,* 15 Dec. 1923.
47. In 1925, Chieu opposed sending Ninh to France to lobby for reforms on those grounds; AOM Indochine, 7F22(4).
48. *CF,* 24 Dec. 1923; Monin's Chinese friends contributed to the event, but none took part in this public affair. See AOM Indochine, 7F22: Notice d'information politique, 1923–1924.
49. *CF,* 24 Mar. 1924.
50. Yet, despite the fact that the Vietnamese electorate had been enlarged to 20,000, the total of votes cast by both Vietnamese-born and French voters seldom reached 5,000. In 1913, there were 3,000 registered French voters, of whom three quarters were civil servants; see Bertrand Camilli, *La Représentation des indigènes en Indochine* (Toulouse: Thèse pour le doctorat des sciences économiques, 1914), p. 177. In the elections of 1928, 4,973 people registered to vote, and only 2,837 actually cast their vote; see AOM Indochine, 7F23: Rapport annuel 1927–1928.
51. Camilli, *La Représentation des indigènes,* pp. 116–117; see also AOM Indochine, PA28, carton 3, dossier 78: William Léonce Bazé, Rapport sur les collèges électoraux indochinois, 1937: "En Cochinchine, les Indiens sont les maîtres de l'urne électorale. L'actuel député de Cochinchine a été elu pour 4 millions de francs. Il ne connait rien des desiderata

de ses sois-disants électeurs. Il ne peut interpelller ou agir que sur les directives 'calculées' émanant d'une source viciée."
52. *CF,* 2 June 1924.
53. *EA,* 6 June 1924.
54. *CF,* 19 May 1924.
55. AOM Indochine, 7F22, 2ème section: Contrôle des étrangers et des immigrants: Notice d'information politique portant sur la période comprise entre le 1er juillet 1923 et le 31 décembre 1924.
56. J. P. Bernard, *Le Parti communiste français et la question littéraire* (Grenoble: Presses universitaires de Grenoble, 1972), p. 311, citing René Arcos, "Patrie européenne," *Europe* (15 Jan. 1923). Luc Durtain, the future author of another work set in Indochina, *Dieux blancs, hommes jaunes,* was on the administrative board of the review.
57. The offer of a job and of land is mentioned in AOM Indochine 7F22(4).
58. *CF,* 17 Mar. 1924.
59. AOM Indochine, 7F22(4).
60. Cao Chanh, *Essor Indochinois,* 7 May 1924; Cao Chanh later became an associate of Nguyen An Ninh and received financial assistance from Ninh's uncle to launch another newspaper.
61. Werth, *Cochinchine,* pp. 55, 59.
62. "Défendez vos droits," *CF,* 28 Jan. 1924.
63. A sampling of such letters can be found in AOM Indochine, 7F22(4).
64. Clara Malraux, *Les Combats et les jeux,* pp. 37–38.
65. The editorial line of *Saigon Républicain* subsequently became indistinguishable from government-subsidized papers.
66. For further details see Langlois, *André Malraux;* Clara Malraux, *Les Combats et les jeux;* and Jean Lacouture, *Malraux: une vie dans le siècle* (Paris: Seuil, 1976).
67. Clara Malraux, *Les Combats et les jeux,* p. 43. See also AOM Indochine, 7F22(4).
68. Clara Malraux, *Les Combats et les jeux,* p. 43; see also AOM Indochine, 7F22(4).
69. AOM Indochine, 7F22(4).
70. Clara Malraux, *Les Combats et les jeux,* pp. 65–67.
71. Ninh's wife, Truong thi Sau, a very resourceful woman, was able to contribute several thousand piasters to her husband's anticolonial activities. See Ba Nguyen An Ninh, "Hoi Ky" (Memoirs), in *Con duong giai phong* (The Road to Liberation), vol. 2 (Hanoi: nha xuat ban Phu Nu, 1976), p. 151. See also AOM Indochine, 7F23: 1924–1926.
72. On 15 July 1925, *Europe* published the first installment of Léon Werth's "Notes d'Indochine," in which Ninh figured prominently.
73. Although Nguyen The Truyen announced that Ninh had come to France to study communism, there is no sign that he became a Communist. See

AOM, SLOTFOM III-90: Note sur la propagande révolutionnaire intéressant les pays d'outre-mer, 30 June 1925.
74. AOM Indochine, AP23, carton 330, dossier 9: Condamnés politiques, Phan Chu Trinh.
75. Clara Malraux, *Les Combats et les jeux,* p. 175.
76. Much of this information comes from Clara Malraux's account in *Les Combats et les jeux,* p. 167. See also Langlois, *André Malraux,* pp. 95–98.
77. Labaste's term had expired in 1924, but because new elections had been postponed pending the reorganization of Indochina's Chambers of Agriculture, he was able to cling to his office. See Clara Malraux, *Les Combats et les jeux,* p. 167; see also Langlois, *André Malraux,* pp. 98–101.
78. Eventually, the Constitutionalists organized a successful boycott of French businesses, and la Chevrotière was obliged to step down. After further internal maneuvers, Bui Quang Chieu replaced him. See AOM Indochine, 7F22(4).
79. This account follows the articles that appeared in *Indochine* on the subject beginning on 11 July 1925.
80. A Vietnamese mandarin actually offered to purchase all the land so that he could give it back to the peasants working on it; he presented a certificate of solvency for one million piasters. *Indochine,* 31 July 1925, quoted in Langlois, *André Malraux,* p. 244n.
81. Clara Malraux, *Les Combats et les jeux,* p. 43.
82. AOM Indochine, NF964.
83. An excellent account of Varenne's tenure is William H. Frederick, "Alexandre Varenne and Politics in Indochina, 1925–1926," in Walter F. Vella, ed., *Aspects of Vietnamese History* (Honolulu: University of Hawaii Press, 1973), pp. 96–159.
84. *EA,* 16 Nov. 1925.
85. *EA,* 16 Nov. 1925. The statement was made in September.
86. AOM Indochine, 7F22(4).
87. Dejean de la Batie, "Pourquoi j'ai cessé ma collaboration avec *l'Annam,*" *EA,* 27 Apr. 1927.
88. Ever the romantic, Malraux described in highly dramatic tones how the type was handed to him in his preface to Viollis, *Indochine SOS.* But Clara notes in her own memoirs that he was nowhere around.
89. For a short biographical profile, see Daniel Hémery, *Révolutionnaires vietnamiens et pouvoir colonial en Indochine* (Paris: François Maspéro, 1975), p. 445. A more extended study is Phuong Lan, *Nha cach mang Ta Thu Thau 1906–1945* (The Revolutionary Ta Thu Thau, 1906–1945) (Saigon: Khai Tri, 1973).
90. AOM Indochine, 7F22. Tinh also contributed to a variety of political and religious activities.

91. André Malraux, *Antimémoires* (Paris: Gallimard, 1967), p. 433.
92. *CF*, 25 Nov. 1925.
93. Phan Boi Chau suspected his secretary, Nguyen Thuong Huyen, of having betrayed him; see *NB* (1973), p. 211. Cuong De, however, believed that the traitor was Lam Duc Thu, a member of the Like Hearts Society who was a founding member of the Vietnamese Youth League. Lam Duc Thu reportedly bragged about his part in the arrest and later fell out with an accomplice over the sharing of the reward; see Trang Liet, *Cuoc doi cach mang Cuong De* (The Revolutionary Life of Prince Cuong De) (Saigon: nha in Ton That Le, 1951), pp. 120–122. Cuong De's memoirs do not directly implicate Nguyen Ai Quoc in the kidnapping, as has been suggested by Hoang van Chi in *From Colonialism to Communism* (New York: Praeger, 1964), p. 18. Lam Duc Thu was later revealed as a French Sûreté agent. The amount of the reward is given as $100,000 by Hoang van Chi, and $150,000 by Dao Trinh Nhat in "Mot viec bi mat chua ai noi ra" (A Secret Never Before Revealed), in *Cai Tao* (Reform), Hanoi (30 Oct. 1948), quoted in J. Buttinger, *Vietnam: A Political History* (New York: Praeger, 1968), p. 159.
94. Devilar, *Comment on perd une colonie*, p. 27.
95. Clara Malraux, *Les Combats et les jeux*, p. 225.
96. *CF*, 26 Nov. 1926.
97. Letter of Nguyen An Ninh to *La Lutte* dated 17 November 1934, published on 22 November 1934.
98. Devilar, *Comment on perd une colonie*, pp. 27–28; Frederick, "Alexandre Varenne," p. 119.
99. *CF*, 28 Dec. 1925; see also Clara Malraux, *Les Combats et les jeux*, p. 226.
100. *Indochine Enchainée*, 3 Dec. 1925.
101. *CF*, 3 Dec. 1925.
102. *EA*, 30 Dec. 1925.
103. *CF*, 30 Nov. 1925.
104. AOM Indochine, 7F22: Notice d'information politique portant sur la période comprise entre le 1er juillet 1923 et le 31 décembre 1924.
105. Clara Malraux, *Les Combats et les jeux*, p. 104.
106. Relations between Monin and the Malraux must have become strained, for he did not bother to see them off. See Clara Malraux, *Les Combats et les jeux*, p. 227.
107. He died in 1928 of fever contracted while on a hunting trip in the highlands and was buried on Vietnamese soil.
108. Letter dated 2 October 1933, reproduced in Edmund Wilson, *The Shores of Light* (New York: Farrar, Strauss & Young, 1952), p. 573.
109. Clara Malraux, *Les Combats et les jeux*, p. 69.

5. Prodigal Children

1. Generational differences were revealed in the use of language. Nguyen Ai Quoc and Ho Tung Mau, both born in 1890, made notations in Chinese. Other members of the Youth League, and later of the Indochinese Communist Party, wrote in French. See Huynh Kim Khanh, *Vietnamese Communism, 1925–1945* (Ithaca: Cornell University Press, 1982), p. 115n.
2. Gouvernement-Général de l'Indochine, Direction des Affaires Politiques et de la Sûreté Générale, *Contribution à l'histoire des mouvements politiques de l'Indochine française,* 6 vols. (Hanoi, 1930–1933), vol. 1, pp. 7–9.
3. *Contribution,* vol. 1, p. 17.
4. *Contribution,* vol. 1, p. 11.
5. *Contribution,* vol. 1, pp. 6–13.
6. Hoang van Dao, *Viet Nam Quoc Dan Dang* (The Vietnamese Nationalist Party) (Saigon: n.p., 1970), p. 25.
7. AOM, SLOTFOM III-90: Note sur la propagande révolutionnaire intéressant les pays d'outre-mer, 30 Sept. 1925.
8. AOM, SLOTFOM III-48: Notes de l'agent Désiré, June 1925. Despite its moribund state, the Intercolonial Union was able to publish Nguyen Ai Quoc's *Procès de la colonisation française* and to send a steady supply of articles from *Paria, Humanité,* and other left-wing newspapers to contacts within Vietnam.
9. AOM Indochine, 7F22(4): Rapport annuel 1924–1926.
10. See, for example, the advertisements that appeared in *Cloche Fêlée* and *Echo Annamite.*
11. Phuong Lan mentions that even at the time, members of Jeune Annam entertained the possibility that Dong was an *agent provocateur;* see Phuong Lan, *Nha cach mang Nguyen An Ninh* (The Revolutionary Nguyen An Ninh) (Saigon: n.p., 1970), pp. 150–151. His rapid pardon, after he was deported to Annam, and the ambiguous references to him that appear in Sûreté reports would seem to lend credence to this suspicion; see AOM Indochine, 7F22.
12. For accounts of meetings, see *CF* and *EA,* Jan.-Mar. 1926.
13. The director had been transferred to the Collège under a cloud after provoking a strike by the staff of the school he had headed in Cambodia; he was thought to have escaped reprimand because he was the nephew of a former Governor-General. See *CF,* 2 Feb. 1926.
14. *EA,* 18 Apr. 1926.
15. It is unclear why Nguyen Phan Long waited so long to publicize their contents.
16. AOM Indochine, 7F22(4).

17. AOM Indochine, 7F22(4).
18. AOM Indochine, 7F22(4).
19. Letter to Colonna reprinted in *EA*, 3 May 1926.
20. AOM Indochine, 7F22(4).
21. The full text of the tract appears in AOM Indochine, 7F22(4); several published versions are also available. See, for example, Phuong Lan, *Nha cach mang Nguyen An Ninh*, pp. 166–168; William H. Frederick, "Alexandre Varenne and Politics in Indochina, 1925–1926," in Walter F. Vella, ed., *Aspects of Vietnamese History* (Honolulu: University of Hawaii Press, 1973), p. 136; and Thomas Ennis, *French Policy and Development in Indochina* (Chicago: University of Chicago Press, 1936), p. 184.
22. The text of the petition is included in AOM Indochine, 7F22(4).
23. This suspicion continued to follow him; in 1927, he was beaten up by Jeune Annam members. See AOM Indochine, 7F23(1): Rapport annuel 1927–1928.
24. For an analysis of the two lectures, see David G. Marr, *Vietnamese Anticolonialism, 1885–1925* (Berkeley: University of California Press, 1971), pp. 269–271.
25. *NP* 99 (October 1925). The publication date is misleading because the journal consistently appeared late. Pham Quynh had not always been an admirer of the emperor; Nguyen van Trung suggests that Pham Quynh disparaged Khai Dinh in his account of their joint travel to France. See Nguyen van Trung, *Chu dich Nam Phong* (The Objectives of *Southern Wind*) (Saigon: n.p., 1972), p. 106.
26. Sûreté reports put the size of the crowd at 8,000. See AOM Indochine, 7F22(4).
27. A far from objective account of Chieu's return comes from the pen of Trinh Hung Ngau, an adherent of Jeune Annam, in *CF*, 25 Mar. 1926.
28. The letter was reproduced in *La Lutte*, 24 Dec. 1936.
29. AOM Indochine, 7F22(4).
30. See The Nguyen, *Phan Chu Trinh* (Saigon: Tan Viet, 1949), pp. 53–78. For another description of the funeral rites, see David G. Marr, *Vietnamese Tradition on Trial* (Berkeley: University of California Press, 1981), pp. 19–23.
31. 7F22(4).
32. "Cong no chua thanh, chi chang phai. Hon co khon thieng, xin ung ho, Non song ganh vac, gai cung trai." The Nguyen, *Phan Chu Trinh*, pp. 55–56.
33. "Nhat Phan tu khu, nhat Phan hoan, ta tai to quoc. Thien co van chuong, thien co tam su, thuy vi tien sinh." The Nguyen, *Phan Chu Trinh*, p. 77.
34. *CF*, 12 Apr. 1926.

35. *EA*, 3, 9 Apr. 1926.
36. *EA*, 10 Apr. 1926.
37. AOM Indochine, 7F22(4).
38. *CF*, 12 Apr. 1926.
39. This incident, which was reported in *Echo Annamite* and *Cloche Fêlée*, is also briefly mentioned in AOM Indochine, 7F22 (4), but without details. Taboulet is not mentionned by name.
40. Camille Devilar, *Comment on perd une colonie* (Paris: Presses Modernes, 1927), pp. 33–34.
41. La Chevrotière's paper, *Impartial*, was also boycotted; its circulation plummeted from 10,000 to 3,000, leading him to get out of publishing. AOM Indochine, 7F22 (4). This suggests that readership of French-language newspapers in Cochinchina, whatever their ownership, was largely Vietnamese.
42. Ho Huu Tuong, *41 nam lam bao* (41 Years of Journalism) (Saigon: Tri Dang, 1972), pp. 8–10; also, unpublished interviews, 1966. Rotten, adulterated, or uncooked food was a constant complaint, as were clothes and shoes that fell apart after one wearing. Among those expelled: Ho Huu Tuong and Ung van Khiem, later member of the Indochinese Communist Party.
43. At the trial, Lam Hiep Chau was fined one hundred francs and sentenced to one year in prison.
44. An account of the trial appeared in the émigré paper published in South China, *Hai Ngoai Chau San*, 10 May 1926; see AOM Indochine, 7F24: Rapport annuel 1924–1926.
45. In August, Cognacq was formally accused of systematically destroying the financial records of Cochinchina since 1923 and substituting forgeries; see *Annam*, 21 Aug. 1926, and *NP* 110 (Oct. 1926), p. 429.
46. *EA*, 3 May 1926; see also letters of Nguyen An Ninh and his wife asking for a free pardon in AOM Indochine, AP14: Service de législation et d'administration, dossier 3.
47. *Annam*, 6 Jan. 1927, reprint of article from *Humanité*, 2 Dec. 1926.
48. AOM Indochine, NF2429: Affaire Colonna.
49. *EA*, 21 May 1926.
50. *EA*, 17 May 1926.
51. AOM Indochine, 7F22(5)1: Rapport annuel 1924–1926, p. 76.
52. *EA*, 5 May 1926.
53. *Annam*, 27 May 1926.
54. Pham Quynh makes frequent mentions of Chieu's efforts in this direction in *Southern Wind* beginning with the May 1926 issue. This is at variance with the histories of the Constitutionalist Party by R. B. Smith, "Bui Quang Chieu and the Constitutionalist Party in French Cochinchina, 1917–1930," *Modern Asian Studies* (Apr. 1969); and Megan

Cook, *The Constitutionalist Party in Cochinchina: The Years of Decline, 1930–1942* (Monash University Centre of Southeast Asian Studies: Monash Papers on Southeast Asia no. 6, 1977).
55. Even Sûreté informers disapproved of the selfish elitism of the Constitutionalists: "En résumé, la politique de collaboration franco-annamite prônée par ce groupement se traduit par l'entretien de bons rapports (et des avantages qui en résulteraient, naturellement) entre les représentants de tous ordres du Gouvernement français, et les membres de l'élite annamite. Quant au sort de la masse, il n'en n'est pas question." AOM Indochine, 7F22(5)1.
56. For electoral purposes, Bui Quang Chieu relied on the more extensive membership of the Société Mutuelle d'Enseignement. See AOM Indochine, 7F22(5)1.
57. *NP* 106 (July 1926).
58. *NP* 106 (June 1926), p. 545, "Le Malaise Moral."
59. *NP* 105 (May 1926), pp. 409–410.
60. *Contribution,* vol. 1, pp. 17–18.
61. "Hai cai phong trao cai cach trong the gioi doi nay, Wilson va Lénine" (Two Currents of Reform in the World Today, Wilson and Lenin), *NP* 84 (June 1924), pp. 490–497.
62. *Tribune Indochinoise,* 14 Oct. 1926.
63. *Annam,* 20 May 1926.
64. *Annam,* 25 Nov. 1926.
65. In April 1927, the Sûreté found a copy of "The ABC of Communism" and of "The Proletarian Revolution and the Renegade Kautsky" in Le The Vinh's lodgings. See AOM Indochine, 7F22(4).
66. Only sports associations were deemed to be exactly what they purported to be; see AOM Indochine, 7F1: Note sur l'activité des partis d'opposition antifrançaise en Indochine, 1er trimestre de 1928.
67. *Tribune Indochinoise,* 5 Nov. 1926. This statement, however, embroiled him in controversy with Outrey and Colonna; see *NP* 111 (Nov. 1926), pp. 528–529.
68. Ha Huy Tap used the pen name of Lam Giang.
69. *Tribune Indochinoise,* 20 Apr. 1927.
70. Strikes took place in Vinh, Qui Nhon, Thanh Hoa, Dong Hoi, and Phan Thiet. See *Annam,* 14, 21, 25 Apr. 1927, and *EA,* 15, 20, 21 Apr. 1927.
71. On 18 September 1927, 60 students went on strike at the An Nam School owned by Bui Quang Chieu. On 30 September, 80 students at Gia Long school staged a protest over uncooked food; a strike had been held there on 12 January over the same issue. After 2 students were expelled as ring-leaders, 60 of their schoolmates demanded their money back; when they did not receive satisfaction, they left school. On 12 October, 40 girls at St. Paul de Chartres stayed out, claiming that the

sisters were too strict. On 29 October, students at Taberd complained of being served uncooked rice. In December, 4 students were expelled from the Collège de Cho Quan for leading a strike; this led to a sympathy strike at the Collège Chasseloup-Laubat which ended with the expulsion of 2 of its leaders. See AOM Indochine, 7F22(5)1.
72. AOM, SLOTFOM III-2: letter from Minister of Colonies Léon Perrier to Governor-General A. Varenne, 28 Sept. 1927.
73. *EA*, 24 Apr. 1926.
74. "Autour des grèves d'écoliers—une mise au point," *EA*, 3 Aug. 1926, pp. 1–2.
75. AOM Indochine, 7F19: Direction de la Sûreté du Tonkin, notes mensuelles, June-July, Oct.-Dec. 1927.
76. *Nha Que*, 1 Jan. 1927.
77. How much the Sûreté was aware of this phenomenon is attested in the lists of departures from Vietnam included in AOM Indochine, 7F22.
78. Letter from a reader in Toulouse, *NP* 112 (Dec. 1926).
79. There was also a considerable movement of internal migration as young Vietnamese went from place to place to join clandestine organizations. Hoang van Hoan's experience is a case in point. See Hoang van Hoan, *Giot nuoc trong bien ca* (A Drop in the Ocean) (Beijing: nha xuat ban Tin Vietnam, 1986), pp. 15–27.
80. Nhat Linh, *Di Tay* (Going to France) (Saigon: Phuong Giang, 1960), pp. 20–21; see also Alexander B. Woodside, *Community and Revolution in Modern Vietnam* (Boston: Houghton Mifflin, 1976), p. 4.
81. Andrée Viollis, *Indochine SOS* (Paris: Gallimard, 1935), pp. 14–15.
82. Nhat Linh, *Di Tay*, pp. 104–105, 109–111.
83. *Tribune Indochinoise*, 23 Dec. 1927.
84. Nguyen Huu Ninh, in *L'Avenir de l'Annam*, 1 Mar. 1928.
85. Quoted in Daniel Hémery, "Du patriotisme au marxisme: l'immigration vietnamienne en France de 1926 à 1930," *Le Mouvement Social* 90 (Jan.-Mar. 1975), p. 26.
86. AOM, SLOTFOM III-2: lettre du Ministre des Colonies Léon Perrier au Gouverneur-Général A. Varenne, 30 Aug. 1927.

6. Organizing Revolution

1. A translation of this tract into French can be found in AOM, SLOTFOM V-45.
2. Nguyen Thuong Huyen, a grand-nephew of Phan Boi Chau's associate Nguyen Thuong Hien and holder of a *cu nhon* degree, worked for the Hanoi-based journal, *Friendship's Sound*.
3. One was dated 27 February and the other 1 August 1924; see Alexander

B. Woodside, *Community and Revolution in Modern Vietnam* (Boston: Houghton Mifflin, 1976), p. 166.
4. Inprecor, July 17, 1924; AOM Indochine, carton 109, dossier 1035, Aug. 31, 1924, cited in Duiker, *The Rise of Vietnamese Nationalism, 1900–1941* (Ithaca: Cornell University Press, 1976), p. 199; for the full text of his address, see Ho Chi Minh, *Tuyen Tap* (Selected Works), vol. 1: *1920–1954* (Hanoi: nha xuat ban Su That, 1980), pp. 31–47.
5. During his stay in China he mostly used the name of Li Shui (Ly Thuy), though among his compatriots he called himself Vuong Son Nhi (he used a total of more than thirty aliases during his two-year stay in China).
6. Gouvernement-Général de l'Indochine, Direction des Affaires Politiques et de la Sûreté Générale, *Contribution à l'histoire des mouvements politiques de l'Indochine française*, 6 vols. (Hanoi, 1930–1933), vol. 4, p. 15.
7. Report to the Executive Committee of the Comintern, 19 December 1924, quoted in Ban Nghien Cuu Lich Su Dang (Commission to Study the History of the Party) *Chu Tich Ho Chi Minh* (President Ho Chi Minh) (Hanoi: Su That, 1970), p. 32, and cited in Huynh Kim Khanh, *Vietnamese Communism, 1925–1945* (Ithaca: Cornell University Press, 1982), p. 66.
8. The French translation of Nguyen Ai Quoc's critique, dated 9 April 1925, can be found in AOM, SLOTFOM V-45.
9. N. M. Roy later took over the leadership of the League of Oppressed People of the East. Nguyen Ai Quoc continued to use its headquarters as a stopping point for new recruits from Vietnam. On 14 January 1926, using the alias of Wang Ta-jen, he made a speech at the Second Congress of the KMT in Canton urging the formation of a worldwide anti-imperialist movement. See King Chen, *Vietnam and China* (Princeton: Princeton University Press, 1969), p. 22.
10. They were Hong Son (aka Le van Phan), Ho Tung Mau (aka Ho Ba Cu), Lam Duc Thu (aka Nguyen Cong Vien), Nguyen Giang Khanh, Dang Xuan Hong, Truong Quoc Huy, and Le Cau (aka Tong Giao Cau). See letter to the Comintern dated 12 February 1925; Trung Chinh, "Thu tim xem chu tich Ho Chi Minh tiep thu chu nghia Lenin va truyen ba vao Viet Nam nhu the nao?" (How Did President Ho Receive Leninism and Propagate It in Vietnam?) *NCLS* 132 (May-June 1970), pp. 5–21.
11. Trung Chinh, "Tam Tam Xa la gi" (What Was the Society of Like Hearts?), *NCLS* 133 (July-Aug. 1970), p. 7.
12. "La Révolution," *Youth* 6 (26 July 1925). Nguyen Ai Quoc's statistics are incorrect. The number of Frenchmen in Indochina in 1928 was 38,236; see Sylvain Lévi, *Indochine*, vol. 2: *Documents officiels* (Paris: Société d'éditions géographiques, maritimes et coloniales, 1931), p. 205.

Of these, 8,335 were military personnel. Official statistics put the population of Vietnam at 17 million in 1925.
13. "Réponse à l'étudiante X," *Youth* 16 (18 Oct. 1925).
14. AOM Indochine, 7F2: Propagande émanant des associations antifrançaises, annexe à la note du 23 Octobre 1929.
15. One early channel was a bookshop run by Lam Duc Thu's wife. See *Contribution,* vol. 4, p. 17.
16. Nguyen Luong Bang, "Nhung lan gap Bac" (The Times I Met Him), in *Bac Ho, hoi ky* (Uncle Ho, Memoirs) (Hanoi: nha xuat ban Van Hoc, 1960), pp. 57–58.
17. Nguyen Luong Bang, "Nhung lan gap Bac," p. 61.
18. The other papers were the bi-weekly *Linh Kach Menh* (Revolutionary Soldier), which appeared between early 1927 and early 1928; *Bao Cong Nong* (Peasant-Worker Journal), which was published from December 1926 until early 1928; and *Viet Nam Tien Phong* (Vietnamese Vanguard), a monthly which appeared only four times in 1927.
19. Twenty-five issues appeared in 1925, 48 in 1926. In 1927, owing to KMT repression, the number dropped to 40. Fifty issues came out in 1928 despite turmoil and arrests. But, as a result of both internal conflict and external pressure, only 33 issues appeared in 1929, and only 8 from January to 30 May 1930, when the journal ceased to be published altogether.
20. Thep Moi, *Thoi dung Dang* (The Party-Building Phase) (Paris: Doan Ket, 1979), p. 45.
21. Le Manh Trinh, "Nhung ngay of Quang Chau va o Xiem" (Days in Canton and in Siam), in *Bac Ho, hoi ky,* pp. 93–94; see also Chen, *Vietnam and China,* pp. 21–24.
22. Chen, *Vietnam and China,* p. 24.
23. Le Manh Trinh, "Nhung ngay o Quang Chau," p. 95.
24. AOM, SLOTFOM III-44.
25. Le Manh Trinh and another trainee were sent to Siam in 1927 to organize the Vietnamese émigrés there. Le Manh Trinh, "Nhung ngay o Quang chau," p. 96.
26. The translation in the text is made from the Vietnamese; the translation directly from Lenin's original reads: "Without a revolutionary theory there can be no revolutionary movement . . . the role of the vanguard fighter can be fulfilled only by a party that is guided by the most advanced theory." V. I. Lenin, *Selected Works,* vol. 1 (London: Lawrence & Wishart, 1947), pp. 165–166.
27. *Duong kach menh,* in Ho Chi Minh, *Tuyen tap,* vol. 1, p. 249.
28. AOM Indochine, 7F2: 23 Oct. 1929, quoting from "Décisions dominantes du Ve Congrès de la IIIe Internationale, 1924."
29. Thep Moi, *Thoi dung Dang,* pp. 43–44.

30. This passage is based on AOM Indochine, 7F2: 23 Oct. 1929; see also *Contribution*, vol. 4.
31. AOM Indochine, 7F23: 1er trimestre 1928.
32. "C'est surtout le nord-Annam et plus particulièrement les provinces de Vinh et de Thanh Hoa qui semblent avoir été travaillées par la propagande conjuguée des fonctionnaires et des lettrés, dirigée par des meneurs dont l'activité occulte est devenue très prudente et difficile à suivre. La théorie de la propagande suivant les procédés de Moscou s'apprend ainsi par coeur . . . Les enfants des campagnes récitent des poésies sur la solidarité, le travail, la force du prolétariat, etc . . . . qui viennent de Canton." AOM Indochine, 7F1: Note sur l'activité des partis d'opposition antifrançaise en Indochine, 1er trimestre de 1928.
33. *Contribution*, vol. 1, pp. 7–9.
34. *Contribution*, vol. 1, p. 8.
35. *Contribution*, vol. 1, p. 15.
36. Nhuong Tong, *Nguyen Thai Hoc, 1902–1930* (Saigon: Tan Viet, 1956), p. 22.
37. See his letter to the French Chamber of Deputies written during his incarceration, reproduced in Nhuong Tong, *Nguyen Thai Hoc*, pp. 138–142.
38. Nhuong Tong, *Nguyen Thai Hoc*, p. 21.
39. Hoang van Dao, *Viet Nam Quoc Dan Dang* (The Vietnamese Nationalist Party) (Saigon: n.p., 1970), p. 38.
40. Hoang van Dao, *Viet Nam Quoc Dan Dang*, pp. 38–39.
41. The Nam Dong Publishing Society had published an admiring profile of Sun Yat-sen in 1926. See *Contribution*, vol. 2, p. 6. A translation of Rousseau's *Contrat social* appeared around the same time in a Hanoi journal, *Thuc Nghiep Dan Bao* (Journal of Practical Industry). See Nhuong Tong, *Hoa Canh Nam* (Flowers from the Southern Branch) (Barnstrup: Nguon Viet, n.d.), p. 42.
42. Dong Xuyen, "Tu Nam Dong Thu Xa den VNQDD" (From the Nam Dong Publishing House to the VNQDD), in Nhuong Tong, *Hoa Canh Nam*, pp. 106–107.
43. Nhuong Tong, *Nguyen Thai Hoc*, pp. 25–26.
44. *Youth* 57 (14 Aug. 1926).
45. Vu Tho, "Qua trinh thanh lap dang vo san o Viet Nam da duoc dien ra nhu the nao" (How Did the Process of Establishing a Proletarian Party in Vietnam Unfold?), *NCLS* 71 (Feb. 1965), p. 19.
46. *CF*, 26 Apr. 1926.
47. Nguyen An Ninh, *Hai Ba Trung* (The Trung Queens) (Saigon: nha xuat ban Bao Ton, 1928).
48. Phan van Hum, "Ngoi tu Kham Lon" (A Stay in the Central Prison), serialized in *Than Chung*, Feb. 1929.

49. Daniel Guérin, *L'Anarchisme, de la doctrine à l'action* (Paris: Gallimard, 1965), p. 16.
50. AOM Indochine, 7F1: 1er trimestre de 1928; see also AOM Indochine, 7F4: Notes périodiques, Aug.-Sept. 1930, referring to the districts of Duc Hoa, Hoc Mon, and Ba Diem as "fiefs of Nguyen An Ninh," although Ninh was then in jail.
51. For a study of the role of secret societies in Vietnamese anticolonialism, see Hue-Tam Ho Tai, *Millenarianism and Peasant Politics in Vietnam* (Cambridge: Harvard University Press, 1983).
52. Georges Coulet, *Sociétés secrètes en terre d'Annam* (Saigon: C. Ardin & Cie., 1926).
53. Ninh brought along forty students, many of whom had participated in strikes and spent time in jail as he had. See AOM, SLOTFOM III-3, 12 Oct. 1927.
54. For more details, see Tai, *Millenarianism*, chaps. 5–6.
55. AOM Indochine, 7F23: Rapport annuel 1927–1928, stating that money was raised in Gia Dinh, Hoc Mon, and Ba Diem and that Ninh possessed 600 piasters at the time of his departure; see also AOM Indochine, 7F1: 1er trimestre de 1928, and AOM Indochine, 7F2: L'Association de Nguyen An Ninh "Cao Vong Thanh Nien Dang."
56. AOM Indochine, 7F23: Rapport annuel 1927–1928: brigades mobiles.
57. AOM Indochine, 7F22: Rapport annuel 1924–1926; see also AOM Indochine, 7F22A: Notice d'information politique portant sur la période comprise entre le 1er juillet 1923 et le 31 décembre 1924, in particular "classification des lettres adressées à *Cloche Fêlée*." Hum's letter was dated 12 April 1924; Dao Duy Anh also wrote on 20 May 1924.
58. Ho Huu Tuong, *41 nam lam bao* (41 Years of Journalism) (Saigon: Tri Dang, 1972), p. 26.
59. Phuong Lan, *Nha cach mang Nguyen An Ninh* (The Revolutionary Nguyen An Ninh) (Saigon: n.p., 1970), p. 191.
60. Sûreté information gathered before Nguyen An Ninh's arrest is voluminous. See, for example, AOM Indochine, 7F24: Mar., May, June 1928.
61. *Duoc Nha Nam,* 14 May 1929.
62. *Than Chung,* 12 Apr. 1929, reprinted from *Courier Saigonnais.*
63. *Duoc Nha Nam,* 14 May 1929.
64. AOM Indochine, 7F24: Mar. 1928; AOM Indochine, 7F23(1): Rapport annuel 1927–1928.
65. AOM Indochine, 7F24: March, May 1928; see also AOM Indochine, 7F2: L'Association de Nguyen An Ninh "Cao Vong Thanh Nien Dang."
66. AOM Indochine, 7F24: Jan. 1928.
67. AOM Indochine, 7F23: Notes portant sur la période du 1er juin 1928 au 31 mai 1929: commissariat spécial de Saigon; see also *Than Chung,* 26 Apr. 1929.

68. Phan van Hum, "Ngoi tu Kham Lon."
69. Minutes of the meeting of 15 September 1928 of the Cochinchinese section of the New Vietnamese Revolutionary Party, quoted in AOM, SLOTFOM III-48, Oct. 1929; see also AOM Indochine, 7F2: L'Association de Nguyen An Ninh.
70. Hoang van Dao, *Viet Nam Quoc Dan Dang*, p. 50; see also AOM Indochine, 7F2.
71. Phan van Hum, "Ngoi tu Kham Lon."
72. Le van Thu, *Hoi kin Nguyen An Ninh* (The Nguyen An Ninh Secret Society) (Saigon: Me Linh, 1961), p. 53.

7. Freedom and Discipline

1. Nguyen Luong Bang, "Nhung lan gap Bac" (The Times I Met Him), in *Bac Ho, hoi ky* (Uncle Ho, Memoirs) (Hanoi: nha xuat ban Van Hoc, 1960), p. 60.
2. Statutes of the Youth League published in June 1929 in *Huong Dao, Ko quan chi dao kua hoi chap uy trung uong kua hoi Viet Nam Kach Menh Thanh Nien* (Guide, Directing organ of the Central Committee of the Vietnamese Revolutionary Youth League). The substitution of the letter *k* for the letter *c* in certain words is inspired by Ho Chi Minh's *Con duong kach menh*. AOM Indochine, 7F2: annexe à la note du 23 octobre 1929.
3. The most notable of her efforts was a rebuke to Hoang Ngoc Phach for lamenting the nefarious effect of romantic literature on female sensibilities. It was printed in *NP* 41 (Jan. 1921).
4. *NP* 106 (June 1926).
5. The terms of Phan Boi Chau's house arrest were extremely lenient, allowing him to receive visitors and also to make speeches.
6. See, for example, Suzette Leith, "Chinese Women in the Early Communist Movement," in Marilyn B. Young, ed., *Women in China* (Ann Arbor: University of Michigan Center for Chinese Studies, 1973), pp. 47–71.
7. Phan Boi Chau, *Nu quoc dan tu tri* (The Education of Female Citizens) (Hue: Nu Cong Hoc Hoi, 1926), pp. 16–27; see also David G. Marr, *Vietnamese Tradition on Trial* (Berkeley: University of California Press, 1981), pp. 215–216.
8. *Youth* 51 (28 June 1926).
9. *Youth* 47 (6 June 1926).
10. *Youth* 57 (14 Aug. 1926).
11. Letter from Ngoc Lan, *Youth* 81 (29 Feb. 1927).
12. *Youth* 86 (10 Apr. 1927).
13. *Youth* 87 (17 Apr. 1927).

14. *Youth* 96 (24 July 1927). See also *Youth* 100 (23 Aug. 1927).
15. *Youth* 104 (2 Oct. 1927).
16. *Youth* 113 (12 Dec. 1927).
17. AOM, SLOTFOM III-3, 12 Oct. 1927.
18. Camille Devret and Edith Pye, *Report of the I.W.L.P.F. Delegation to China*, Geneva, Women's International League for Peace and Freedom, 1928. See also AOM Indochine, 7F24: Notices mensuelles de Sûreté, Nov.-Dec. 1927.
19. *PNTV*, 20 June 1929.
20. *PNTV*, 11 July 1929.
21. AOM Indochine, 7F19: Direction de la Sûreté du Tonkin; notes mensuelles, June-Dec. 1927.
22. AOM Indochine, 7F1: 1er trimestre, 1928.
23. Her name was Mme. Nguyen Ngoc Son; see AOM Indochine, 7F19: Direction de la Sûreté—Tonkin; notices mensuelles, Apr. 1928; AOM Indochine, 7F1: 1er trimestre 1928.
24. *Youth* 106 (17 Oct. 1927).
25. *Youth* 116 (2 Jan. 1928).
26. *Youth* 126 (19 Mar. 1928).
27. *Dong Thanh* 15 (15 Nov. 1927).
28. On 1 October 1928, at the suggestion of Nguyen Ai Quoc, its name was changed to *Fraternity (Than Ai)* and its revolutionary rhetoric toned down in a move to reach a wider public among the Vietnamese exiles in Siam; see AOM, SLOTFOM V-17; AOM Indochine, 7F2: 23 Oct. 1929.
29. Bui Quang Chieu received a retainer of $800 from the financier Homberg and another retainer from the Fontaine Distillery. This led Nguyen Phan Long to distance himself from him and to renounce, at least temporarily, the "myth" of Franco-Annamite collaboration; see AOM Indochine, NF1568: Note sur l'activité des partis d'opposition antifrançaise en Indochine, 1er trimestre de 1928.
30. AOM Indochine, 7F23: Direction de la Sûreté Générale, rapport annuel 1928–1929.
31. *PNTV*, 2 May 1929.
32. Phan Khoi, "Mot la don kien cai che do gia dinh An Nam" (A Bill of Accusation against the Vietnamese Family System), *PNTV*, 17 Oct. 1929.
33. Phan Khoi, "Than oan cho Vo Hau" (In Defense of Empress Wu), *PNTV* 53 (22 May 1930) and 55 (5 June 1930).
34. *PNTV*, 9 May 1929.
35. *PNTV*, 2 Jan. 1930.
36. *PNTV*, 9 May 1929.
37. *PNTV*, 5 Sept. 1929.
38. *PNTV*, 9 May 1929; italics in the original.

39. *PNTV,* 15 Aug. 1929.
40. *Youth* 135 (21 May 1928).
41. *Youth* 137 (4 Apr. 1928).
42. *Youth* 154 (1 Oct. 1928).
43. *Youth* 149 (26 Aug. 1928).
44. Letter of 1 December 1928, *Youth* 115 (16 Dec. 1928).
45. *Youth* 166 (23 Dec. 1928).
46. The Association had branches in Nam Dinh, Bac Ninh, Thai Binh, and Bac Giang; see AOM Indochine, 7F2: Note complémentaire du 19 novembre 1929.
47. Examples include Nguyen Trung Nguyet, Nguyen thi Minh Khai, and Mai Huynh Hoa, a grand-daughter of the Widow Nguyet Anh who married Phan van Hum in 1936.
48. AOM, SLOTFOM III-129: Le Thanh Nien Cach Mang Dong Chi Hoi, rapport au sujet des mesures de répression prises contre les membres de l'Association révolutionnaire "Viet Nam Cach Mang Thanh Nien," Hue, 10 Mar. 1930.
49. *Youth* 159 (5 Nov. 1928).
50. *Youth* 166 (23 Dec. 1928).
51. *Cong Nong Binh,* 15 July 1929, AOM Indochine, 7F2, annexe à la lettre du 23 octobre 1929.
52. The material in this section is culled mainly from the voluminous information, including individual confessions, contained in AOM Indochine, 7F55: Affaire de la rue Barbier, and from the account of the trial which appeared in the official journal *Indochine* on 5 October 1930.
53. The meeting was held at the lodgings of another Kroff employee, Bui van Them, and was called by Do Dinh Tho, a staff writer for the *Morning Bell.* Ton Duc Thang did not attend, but Tran Truong and Nguyen Trung Nguyet were present, as was Ngo Thiem.
54. The first arrest was that of Nguyen Duy Trinh, a twenty-year-old from Tonkin who later became Minister of Foreign Affairs of the Democratic Republic of Vietnam.
55. Hoang van Dao suggests that Nguyen Thai Hoc objected to Ninh's Trotskyism. Hoang van Dao, *Viet Nam Quoc Dan Dang* (The Vietnamese Nationalist Party) (Saigon: n.p., 1970), p. 50. Such a label would be improbable in 1928. Louis Marty merely suggests that "Nguyen An Ninh's ideas were too far apart from those of the Tonkin Nationalists for a merger to be possible." Gouvernement-Général de l'Indochine, Direction des Affaires Politiques et de la Sûreté Générale, *Contribution à l'histoire des mouvements politiques de l'Indochine française,* 6 vols. (Hanoi, 1930–1933), vol. 2, p. 9.
56. Nhuong Tong, *Nguyen Thai Hoc, 1902–1930* (Saigon: Tan Viet, 1956), p. 42.

57. AOM Indochine, 7F1: 1er trimestre 1928, p. 46. A harrowing description of life on the plantations and of the callousness of plantation owners appears in Paul Monet, *Les Jauniers* (Paris: Gallimard, 1930).
58. For a first-hand account of the rebellion, see Tran Tu Binh, *The Red Earth,* translated by John Spragens, Jr. (Athens: Ohio University, Monographs on International Studies, Southeast Asia Series, 1985).
59. Hoang van Dao, *Viet Nam Quoc Dan Dang,* pp. 53–58.
60. Hoang van Dao, *Viet Nam Quoc Dan Dang,* p. 55.
61. In Sûreté reports, Trinh Dinh Chiem's name is erroneously given as Tran Can Chiem or Tran van Chiem. His proper name appears in Vietnamese accounts of the VNQDD. See, for example, Hoang van Dao, *Viet Nam Quoc Dan Dang,* pp. 65–68.
62. AOM Indochine, 7F2: Action auprès des femmes, 23 Oct. 1929.
63. AOM Indochine, 7F23: Rapport annuel 1928–1929. See also AOM Indochine, 7F2: Crime de la ruelle de Metz, Haiphong, 31 May 1929; AOM Indochine, 7F2: Note complémentaire, 19 Nov. 1929; AOM Indochine, 7F4: Note périodique, 1929. It is possible that, by that time, Dinh had already turned informer. See Huynh Kim Khanh, *Vietnamese Communism, 1925–1945* (Ithaca: Cornell University Press, 1982), p. 117n.
64. Statutes passed in May 1929 and published in *Huong Dao,* June 1929. AOM Indochine, 7F2: Documents de propagande émanant des associations antifrançaises, annexe à la note du 23 octobre 1929: associations antifrançaises et la propagande communiste en Indochine.
65. AOM Indochine, 7F2: 23 Oct. 1929: note complémentaire du 19 novembre 1929; AOM Indochine, 7F21: Rapport annuel de la Sûreté Générale du Tonkin, June 1928–June 1929. Hoang van Dao suggests that the decision to eliminate the two sisters came from the Haiphong Municipal Section, which had come under the control of dissidents, rather than from the Tonkin Regional Committee. See Hoang van Dao, *Viet Nam Quoc Dan Dang,* pp. 65–68.
66. Hoang van Dao, *Viet Nam Quoc Dan Dang,* pp. 89–90.
67. Hoang van Dao, *Viet Nam Quoc Dan Dang,* p. 91.
68. Hoang van Dao, *Viet Nam Quoc Dan Dang,* pp. 103–104; the phrase *Khong thanh cong thi cung thanh nhan* is usually translated "if we do not succeed then at least we will become heroes," but this wording fails to convey the sense of a rite of passage inherent in the phrase *thanh nhan.*
69. Hoang van Dao, *Viet Nam Quoc Dan Dang,* pp. 159–164.
70. For more details on this period, see Huynh Kim Khanh, *Vietnamese Communism,* chap. 3, "The Crisis of Infantile Communism."
71. "Apres Yen Bay, que faire?" *La Vérité,* April 18, 1930, quoted in Daniel

Hémery, "Ta Thu Thau: l'itinéraire politique d'un révolutionnaire vietnamien pendant les années trente," in Pierre Brocheux, ed., *Histoire de l'Asie du sud-est: révoltes, réformes, révolutions* (Lille: Presses Universitaires de Lille, 1982), p. 203.

8. Communists, Trotskyists, and Progressives

1. Bui Quang Chieu, who did acknowledge the existence of socioeconomic differences, was willing to defend and promote the rights of only a privileged few, and only within the framework of continuing colonial rule.
2. *Youth,* 28 June 1925.
3. Ho Chi Minh, *Con duong kach menh* in *Tuyen Tap* (Selected Works), vol. 1: *1920–1954* (Hanoi: nha xuat ban Su That, 1980), p. 240.
4. For illustrations of this policy, see Daniel Hémery, "Du patriotisme au marxisme: l'immigration vietnamienne en France de 1926 à 1930," *Le Mouvement Social* 90 (Jan.-Mar. 1975), pp. 19–21.
5. AOM Indochine, 7F2: Associations antifrançaises en Indochine et la propagande communiste, 23 Oct. 1929, p. 36.
6. "Les dirigeants de la IIIème Internationale estiment que pour mieux toucher la France capitaliste, c'est en Indochine qu'il faudra frapper un grand coup. A cet effet, les organisations spéciales de la 3ème Internationale ont dressé tout un plan d'activité et de propagande nationaliste pour l'Indochine. Ce plan sera pleinement réalisé en 1928 . . . La propagande devra se montrer particulièrement active dans les régiments indigènes." See AOM Indochine, 7F1: Note sur l'activité des partis d'opposition antifrançaise en Indochine, 1er trimestre de 1928.
7. Huynh Kim Khanh, *Vietnamese Communism 1925–1945* (Ithaca: Cornell University Press, 1982), p. 168.
8. Plans for the plenum had been made by Ho Tung Mau, but he was in jail at the time when the plenum convened.
9. AOM, SLOTFOM III-129: Le Thanh Nien Cach Mang Dong Chi Hoi, rapport au sujet des mesures de répression prises contre les membres de l'Association révolutionnaire "Viet Nam Cach Mang Thanh Nien," Hue, 10 Mar. 1930.
10. AOM, SLOTFOM III-129: Le Thanh Nien Cach Mang Dong Chi Hoi, letter of 25 July 1929. The Youth League had begun a successful proletarianization campaign in 1928 that had brought workers and peasants into auxiliary associations. But the membership of the Youth League was still overwhelmingly made up of members of the elite. Members of auxiliary associations did not have decision-making powers. For details, see Huynh Kim Khanh, *Vietnamese Communism,* pp. 109–112.
11. Gouvernement-Général de l'Indochine, Direction des Affaires Politiques

et de la Sûreté Générale, *Contribution à l'histoire des mouvements politiques de l'Indochine française,* 6 vols. (Hanoi, 1930–1933), vol. 4, app. 2.

12. Nguyen Tuan was assassinated in his turn on 2 February 1930; see AOM, SLOTFOM III-129: Le Thanh Nien Cach Mang Dong Chi Hoi, 1930; AOM Indochine, 7F21(7): Rapport annuel de la Sûreté Générale du Tonkin, 1929–1930. For a more detailed account of the transition from Vietnamese Youth League to Indochinese Communist Party, see Huynh Kim Khanh, *Vietnamese Communism,* chap. 2.
13. *Contribution,* vol. 1, pp. 52–53.
14. *Contribution,* vol. 2, p. 19.
15. AOM Indochine, 7F55: Affaire rue Barbier. Pham van Dong, a court mandarin's son enrolled in the Lycée Albert Sarraut, had joined the Youth League in 1927.
16. Competition generated new publications especially aimed at workers; for example, on 1 November 1929, a new journal entitled *Hammer and Scythe (Bua Liem)* and described as the "central organ of the ICP" called on workers to demand the right to form trade unions and to strike and mount demonstrations; it also listed a long set of demands ranging from increases in the minimum wage to paid maternity leaves. See AOM, SLOTFOM V-26.
17. AOM, SLOTFOM III-129: Le Thanh Nien Cach Mang Dong Chi Hoi.
18. See *Contribution,* vol. 4, annexes nos. 3 and 4, for the text of the two requests.
19. *Contribution,* vol. 4, app. 7, p. 96.
20. *Contribution,* vol. 4, app. 7, p. 97.
21. One of the sources of criticism had been the new party's name. It was therefore changed from the Vietnamese to the Indochinese Communist Party. The Party was no longer composed exclusively of Vietnamese, but included Laotians and Cambodians as well, in conformity with the Comintern definition of a national branch. For a detailed analysis of the Comintern critique of the February program, see Huynh Kim Khanh, *Vietnamese Communism,* pp. 126–129.
22. AOM Indochine, NF2639: Notice sur Nguyen Ai Quoc du 6 juin 1931.
23. Ta Thu Thau, "Après Yen Bay, que faire?" *La Vérité,* 18 April and 1 May 1930, quoted in Hémery, "Du patriotisme au marxisme," p. 44. This was not Thau's first critique. At the Second Congress of the Anti-Imperialist League in Frankfurt in July 1929, he criticized the "bureaucratic deficiencies" of the anticolonial work of the French Communist Party. See Daniel Hémery, "Ta Thu Thau: l'itinéraire politique d'un révolutionnaire vietnamien pendant les années trente," in Pierre Brocheux, ed., *Histoire de l'Asie du sud-est: réformes, révoltes, révolutions* (Lille: Presses Universitaires de Lille: 1982), p. 214.

24. The Intercolonial Union was dissolved in August 1926; see AOM, SLOTFOM III-48: Les Associations antifrançaises en Indochine et la propagande communiste, historique, 23 Dec. 1929.
25. The names included *Hon Viet Nam, Phuc Quoc, L'Ame Annamite,* and *La Nation Annamite;* see AOM, SLOTFOM V-35.
26. AOM, SLOTFOM III-3: Le Parti Annamite de l'Indépendance.
27. Hémery, "Du patriotisme au marxisme," p. 27.
28. AOM, SLOTFOM III-3: 29 June 1927, 2 Apr. 1927.
29. *Le Peuple,* 12 Feb. 1927.
30. The first Vietnamese-born industrialist in Tonkin, Bach Thai Buoi, was a supporter of the VNQDD.
31. *La Nation Annamite,* quoted in Hémery, "Du patriotisme au marxisme," p. 19.
32. AOM, SLOTFOM III-3: Le Parti Annamite de l'Indépendance.
33. AOM, SLOTFOM III-3: 12 Oct. 1927.
34. AOM Indochine, 7F1: 1er trimestre 1928.
35. AOM, SLOTFOM III-44: Déclarations de Nguyen The Vinh recueillies par la direction de la Sûreté Générale indochinoise, Aug. 1931.
36. AOM, SLOTFOM III-3: "Loi kinh cao cung dong bao cua Dang Viet Nam Doc Lap" (Declaration to the People of the Vietnamese Independence Party), 1 Apr. 1928.
37. These incidents included a highly publicized showdown in Rach Gia which led to numerous deaths in 1927, as well as an uprising in the Michelin rubber plantation that same year. On the Rach Gia conflict, see Son Nam, *Lich su khan hoang mien Nam* (A History of the Settling of the South) (Saigon, 1973; reprinted Houston: Xuan Thu, n.d.), pp. 289–296; on the Phu Rieng uprising, see Tran Tu Binh, *The Red Earth,* translated by John Spragens, Jr. (Athens: Ohio University, Monographs on International Studies, Southeast Asia Series, 1985).
38. Quoted in Hémery, "Du patriotisme au marxisme," p. 32.
39. Hémery, "Du patriotisme au marxisme," p. 33.
40. Nguyen van Tao, a former schoolmate of Ta Thu Thau, had left Vietnam in 1926; in 1928, he was a member of the Colonial Commission.
41. AOM, SLOTFOM III-44: Déclarations de Nguyen The Vinh, Aug. 1931. Vinh claimed to have defected after attending the Sixth Congress of the Comintern over differences of opinion with Lozeray and Nguyen van Tao. It should be noted that both Hémery and Khanh have doubts about the veracity of the information contained in this confession.
42. Hémery, "Ta Thu Thau," p. 211.
43. AOM, SLOTFOM V-45.
44. AOM, SLOTFOM III-23, bagarre du café Turquetti, 9 Jan. 1929.
45. AOM, SLOTFOM III-42–51: Note sur le Parti Trotskyiste Indochinois, 13 May 1933.

46. In January 1929, the harvest was reported at 2,166,838 metric tons, compared with 2,392,840 tons for the previous year. See AOM Indochine, Fo3-180: 1929.
47. Hémery, "Ta Thu Thau," p. 215.
48. Pham Quynh, for example, called on the colonial authorities to be stern in their repression. See *NP* 146 (Jan. 1930). Again, the actual date of publication was later than the printed one.
49. *PNTV,* 24 Oct. 1929.
50. For more details on this period, see Huynh Kim Khanh, *Vietnamese Communism,* chap. 3, "The Crisis of Infantile Communism."
51. Ho Huu Tuong, unpublished memoirs. See Note on Sources.
52. Ho Huu Tuong, unpublished memoirs.
53. Ho Huu Tuong's knowledge of Marxism came from reading the private collection of a French Trotskyist in Marseilles. See Ho Huu Tuong, unpublished memoirs.
54. Ho Huu Tuong's recollection of the content of the letters appears in his unpublished memoirs and in an unpublished interview of 16 July 1966; see Note on Sources.
55. Bui Cong Trung, a native of Annam, had once written articles for *Cloche Fêlée* and for the one issue of *Peasant* which Nguyen Khanh Toan had brought out.
56. Ho Huu Tuong, unpublished memoirs.
57. Isaac Deutscher, *The Prophet Outcast* (London: Oxford University Press, 1963), pp. 45–46.
58. Ho Huu Tuong, interview, 16 July 1966; Deutscher, *The Prophet Outcast,* pp. 45–46.
59. Ho Huu Tuong, unpublished memoirs.
60. Ho Huu Tuong, unpublished memoirs.
61. *Nouveaux principes d' organisation du Parti,* Bibliothèque communiste no. 13, in AOM Indochine, 7F11: Notes périodiques 1937: sommaire de la note périodique de mai 1937.
62. "The Question of Women's Emancipation," in *Dan Chung* (The People), 1938, quoted in Nguyet Tu, *Chi Minh Khai* (Sister Minh Khai) (Hanoi: nha xuat ban Phu Nu, 1980), pp. 83–85. Nguyen thi Minh Khai used the pen name Nguyen thi Kim Anh.
63. AOM, SLOTFOM III-48, no. 13: Dec. 1930–Jan. 1931, text of speech by Governor Krautheimer.
64. Huynh Kim Khanh, *Vietnamese Communism,* p. 161.
65. Hai Trieu was the son of Dam Phuong, founder of the Association for the Study of Domestic Arts.
66. Huynh van Tong, *Lich su bao chi Viet Nam tu khoi thuy den nam 1930* (A History of Vietnamese Journalism from Its Origins to 1930) (Saigon: Tri Dang, 1973), p. 176; see also David G. Marr, *Vietnamese Tra-*

dition on Trial (Berkeley: University of California Press, 1981), pp. 220–228.

67. On the severity of censorship, see Amicale des Journalistes Annamites de Cochinchine, *Le Régime de la presse en Indochine* (Saigon: n.p., 1937), p. 27: "Au moment des élections municipales de 1933, la rigueur de la censure ne tolèrait pas l'expression 'lao dong' [Labor]." The quote refers specifically to *Trung Lap*. For more on *Trung Lap,* see AOM Indochine, NF958: Revue de la presse indigène de Cochinchine, June-July, Aug.-Sept. 1932; AOM Indochine, NF2415: Revue de la presse indigène de Cochinchine, 1er & 2ème trimestres 1933.
68. AOM Indochine, PA 28-III-61, letter of 21 January 1931.
69. AOM Indochine, NF2640: Incidents du mois d'avril au 1er mai 1931: les mesures et les réformes proposées.
70. Paraphrased in Pham The Ngu, *Viet Nam van hoc su gian uoc tan bien* (A New Summary History of Vietnamese Literature) (Saigon: Quoc Hoc tung thu, 1965), p. 99.
71. *NP* 146 (Jan. 1930).
72. Pham Quynh, *Nouveaux essais franco-annamites* (Hue: Bui Huy Tin, 1937), p. 127.
73. When *Southern Wind* closed down in 1934, *Mores* "announced the news as if it were a joyous event." See Pham The Ngu, *Viet Nam van hoc su,* p. 454.
74. It need not be assumed a priori that this neglect stemmed entirely from hostility. More research needs to be done on the relationship between progressives and Marxist revolutionaries after Yen Bay.
75. Pham The Ngu, *Viet Nam van hoc su,* p. 432.
76. Pham The Ngu, *Viet Nam van hoc su,* p. 433.
77. Hoang Dao, "Muoi dieu tam niem" (Ten Points to Bear in Mind), *Mores* 87 (2 Mar. 1933).
78. *Ladies' News* had a considerable influence over northern authors; see Pham The Ngu, *Viet Nam van hoc su,* p. 454.
79. Truong Tuu: "All parents who wish to prevent their daughters from being seduced by unbridled sexuality should forbid them to read *Loneliness*"; quoted in Pham The Ngu, *Viet Nam van hoc su,* p. 455.
80. Quoted in Pham The Ngu, *Viet Nam van hoc su,* p. 454.
81. Nguyen Cong Hoan did not believe that reason alone would conquer all. In 1939, he wrote another novel, *Buoc duong cung* (Dead End), which offered a stark portrait of rural poverty and hinted at the possibility of revolt. The novel was banned by the colonial authorities.
82. Huynh Kim Khanh, *Vietnamese Communism,* p. 179n, citing Nguyen Khanh Toan, Nguyen Luong Bang, Le Manh Trinh and others, *Avec l'Oncle Ho* (Hanoi: Foreign Languages Publishing House, 1972), pp. 143–144.

83. See Vo Nguyen Giap, "Ho Chu Tich, nguoi cha cua quan doi cach mang Viet Nam" (President Ho, Father of the Vietnamese Revolutionary Army), in *Bac Ho, hoi ky* (Uncle Ho, Memoirs) (Hanoi: nha xuat ban Van Hoc, 1960), pp. 178–183.
84. Huynh Kim Khanh, *Vietnamese Communism*, p. 259.
85. For an eyewitness account of the event, see Archimedes Patti, *Why Vietnam* (Berkeley: University of California Press, 1980), pp. 248–250.
86. *Nhung loi keu goi cua Ho Chu Tich* (The Appeals of President Ho) (Hanoi: Su That, 1958), pp. 20–21.
87. Pierre Rousset, *Communisme et nationalisme vietnamiens* (Paris: Galilée, 1978), pp. 243–247. For a more extended discussion on "the uses of the past" see Marr, *Vietnamese Tradition on Trial*, chap. 6.

Conclusion

1. Huynh Kim Khanh, *Vietnamese Communism, 1925–1945* (Ithaca: Cornell University Press, 1982), p. 38; P. Brocheux, "Vietnam: le grand tournant de 1930," *Histoire* 69 (1984), pp. 105–116. Brocheux speaks of a state of generalized availability *(disponibilité)*, whereas Khanh, commenting on the nearly simultaneous rise of the Vietnamese Youth League and of the Cao Dai sect, diagnoses social breakdown.

Index

Activism, 69, 83, 157, 158, 163, 224; vs. discussion, 58, 62, 65–66, 72, 164. *See also* Anticolonialism
AFIMA. *See* Association for the Intellectual and Moral Formation of the Annamites
Agrarian Tribune (Nong Co Min Dam), 25
Aid the King Movement (Can Vuong), 16, 17, 20, 22, 23, 26
AIP. *See* Annamite Independence Party
Algeria, 40, 137
Anarchism, 57–58, 60–67, 81, 82, 125, 174; collective, 4, 57, 58, 61, 86; libertarian, 4, 57, 73, 86, 173; and revolutionaries, 173, 186–187, 188; and violence, 62, 84
Annam, 2, 6, 7, 16, 22, 82, 144, 219; anticolonialism in, 57–58, 66, 68–69, 84, 85, 90, 91, 151, 171, 172; antitax protests in, 26; bourgeoisie in, 234; communism in, 229, 233, 248; *corvée* in, 151; émigrés from, 71; intelligentsia of, 38, 146–147; journalism in, 120, 121, 142, 150, 287n24; mandarinate in, 25, 38, 39, 248, 287n23; schools in, 11, 29, 33, 34, 35, 36, 44, 50; strikes in, 160, 165, 166; women in, 94, 210; World War I protests in, 31; young revolutionaries in, 182, 186, 188, 194
Annam, 162, 164, 165
Annamite Communist Party (An Nam Cong San Dang), 230
Annamite Independence Party (AIP), 233, 234–235, 236, 237, 238, 240
Anti-Imperialist League, 6, 233, 306n23

Anticolonialism, 1, 4, 8, 31, 32, 46, 53, 58, 63, 66, 69; and culture, 22, 43, 56; and elitism, 38, 64, 71, 224; as family tradition, 55; and journalism, 84–85, 144, 146–147, 150, 182; and metaphor of family, 112–113; and monopolies, 115–116; and national liberation, 5, 195, 255, 260, 261; in 1930s, 222, 224; propaganda of, 74, 75, 299n32; suppression of, 41, 62; and women, 95, 200, 213. *See also* Expatriates, Vietnamese
Ardin, Hippolyte, 131
Argus Indochinois, 124, 154
Asian Friendship Association (Ashu Washinkai), 59
Aspirations of Youth Party (Cao Vong Thanh Nien Dang). *See* Nguyen An Ninh Secret Society
Assimilation, 43–44, 45, 48, 72, 78, 117, 258, 259; critique of, 85; and new culture, 76; total, 44, 52, 155–156
Association for the Intellectual and Moral Formation of the Annamites (Hoi Khai Tri Tien Duc; AFIMA), 50–51, 98, 100, 110, 112, 121, 199
Association for the Study of Domestic Arts (Nu Cong Hoc Hoi), 199, 200, 201, 204, 211, 303n46, 308n65
Association Mutuelle des Indochinois en France, 70, 123, 233
L'Avenir de l'Annam, 236
Avenir du Tonkin, 123

Babut, E., 76
Bakunin, M. A., 188, 189

Banque d'Indochine, 157, 159–160
Bao Dai, 37, 249, 286n23
Bao Ton publishing house, 182
Bazin, Hervé, 218, 219, 221, 240
Bergson, Henri, 79, 281n80
Bolshevism, 120, 125, 137
Book of Changes, 172, 175
Borodin, Mikhail, 67, 175
Bui Cong Trung, 241–242, 308n55
Bui Quang Chieu, 40, 42, 43–46, 70, 119, 120, 139, 193, 274n91, 290n78; as assimilationist, 43, 44, 48, 49, 51–52, 85, 258; and "bureaucratism," 76; and Constitutionalist Party, 162, 233, 294n54, 295n56; elitism of, 43–45, 124, 189, 192, 305n1; finances of, 123, 206, 302n29; *France d'Asie*, 149; and French citizenship, 42–43, 46, 138; and *Ladies' News*, 206, 247; and Nguyen An Ninh, 128, 158, 161, 288n47; opposition to equal rights for women, 203; return from France, 151, 155–156, 160, 293nn26,27; and students, 167, 295n71; transfer to Phnom Penh, 46, 132. See also *Tribune Indigène*

cach mang (changing the Mandate of Heaven), 171, 175. See also Revolution
Cahier des voeux annamites, 140–141, 151
Cahiers du Communisme, 69
Cambodia, 232, 306n21
Candelier Convention, 119–120, 122, 125, 128, 129, 134
Canton: émigrés in, 65, 66, 67, 85, 179, 216; Ho Chi Minh in, 175, 177, 202, 215; Youth League in, 182, 183
Cao Chanh, 150, 289n60
Cao Dai sect, 189–190, 192, 262, 310n1
CCP. *See* Chinese Communist Party
Chang Chi, 58, 59
Chang Ping-lin, 58, 59, 60, 61, 62, 63
Chavannes, Edouard, 125, 288n38
Ch'en Ch'i-mei, 60, 62, 63
Cheng Hsi, 208
Chevasson, Louis, 131

la Chevrotière, Henry Chavigny de, 118–119, 124, 125, 135, 160, 286nn14,15; and Bui Quang Chieu, 155, 290n78; as newspaper publisher, 123, 159, 247, 294n41
Chiang Kai-shek, 67, 205
Chin-shih huang-ti, 62
China: and anarchism, 57, 61; anticommunism in, 181, 214, 215; and France, 47; German influence in, 47; 1911 revolution in, 27, 62, 106; United Front in, 4, 181, 184, 195, 227; and Vietnam, 2, 3, 9, 13, 19, 20, 31, 57, 60–61, 147, 155, 156, 185, 214; women in, 89, 199. See also Expatriates, Vietnamese: in China
Chinese Communist Party (CCP), 65, 173, 177, 181, 214, 227, 232, 238, 255
Chinese Communist Peasants' Union, 179
Chinese Reform Movement (1898), 23
Ch'ing dynasty, 13, 60, 102, 104, 107
Chuang-tzu, 78
Citizenship, French, 42–43, 46, 125, 138
The Civilization of New Learning (Van minh tan hoc sach), 20–21, 49, 139
Class struggle, 226, 227, 229, 230, 243, 244, 260, 262; rejection of, 184, 218, 245, 246, 250, 255
Cloche Fêlée, 68, 117, 127–131, 141, 142, 151, 258, 308n55; circulation of, 127, 130, 131, 144, 178; closing of, 132, 162; compared with *Indochine*, 132–133; financing of, 127, 139; first issue of, 125–127; and Nguyen An Ninh, 72, 81, 82, 83, 91, 122, 126, 143; serialization of *Communist Manifesto* in, 160
Cochinchina, 2, 6, 7, 10, 14, 27, 28, 75, 82, 114, 144; anticolonialism in, 66, 149, 172, 173; bourgeoisie in, 40–43, 234, 236; communism in, 230, 245–246; corruption in, 115–120, 130, 134; electoral process in, 129, 288n50; émigrés from, 57, 71; floods and typhoons in, 239; Geographical Service of, 126; journalism in, 146–

Index

147, 150, 287n24, 294n41; mandarinate in, 38, 39; progressivism in, 248; Reform Movement in, 24–25; schools in, 30, 32, 33, 38; strikes in, 240; treatment of coolies in, 150; Trotskyism in, 241; women in, 90–91, 204; World War I riots in, 31. *See also* Journalism, colonial
Cochinchine Libérale, 124
Cochinchinese Colonial Council, 27, 42, 118, 120, 123, 128, 129, 134–135, 141, 153, 286n16
Cochinchinese Economic Journal (Nam Ky Kinh Te Bao), 122
Cognacq, Maurice, 75, 117–118, 125, 131, 134, 135–136, 139, 286n16, 294n45; and Bui Quang Chieu, 46, 132, 138; and *Cloche Fêlée*, 130; and Constitutionalists, 120, 128, 129; departure from Cochinchina, 161
Collège de Can Tho, 160
Collège de My Tho, 11, 33, 75
Collège de Vinh, 147, 150–151, 165, 292n13
Collège du Protectorat, 33
Colonial Exhibition (1930), 34
Colonial Studies Commission, 69, 70, 237
Colonialism, 2–7, 10, 11, 28, 30, 52, 56, 59, 77, 82, 126, 144; and capitalism, 243, 247, 261; and Constitutionalism, 143, 149, 156; and socialism, 140; view of, in France, 129, 169
Colonna (Procureur de la République), 140, 161, 163
Comintern, 4, 65, 67, 176, 179, 226, 237–238, 243, 306n21; attitude to Vietnamese revolution, 227, 239, 240; and Ho Chi Minh, 70, 174, 254; and peasantry, 228, 237; Sixth Congress of, 237, 261, 307n41; and Youth League, 181, 229, 231, 232
Communism, 1, 4, 5, 60, 140, 148, 175, 178, 179, 227, 230, 237, 242; and bourgeoisie, 234; and Confucianism, 55, 214, 224; crisis within world, 238; and feminism, 89; and Ho Chi Minh, 178, 186, 187, 194, 225; and progressivism, 247; and VNQDD,

184. *See also* Chinese Communist Party; Comintern; Indochinese Communist Party; Marxism
Communist Youth Corps (Thanh Nien Cong San Doan), 176; members of, 297n10
Con Son, 26, 68, 85, 151
Confucianism, 2, 3–4, 8, 10, 13–17, 24, 36, 37, 54, 81, 250; and commerce, 25; and communism, 55, 214, 224; in fiction, 109; and national essence, 49–50, 92; oppressiveness of, 74, 78; and self-cultivation, 78, 85–87; and women, 74, 91, 94, 101, 205, 207. *See also* Examinations, civil-service; Literati; Neo-traditionalists
Cong Luan Bao, 123
cong-nong (worker-peasant), 228
Constitutionalist Association (Cong Hien Hoi), 59
Constitutionalist Association (Paris), 149, 162
Constitutionalist Party, 41, 162
Constitutionalists, 3, 45, 58, 115, 116, 117, 126, 137–138, 139, 140, 141, 152, 294n54; and AIP, 235; as alternative to revolution, 186; boycott of, 124, 290n78; and Candelier affair, 119, 120; and collaboration, 115; and Colonial Council, 128, 129; and colonialism, 143, 149, 156; and education, 44, 101, 141, 166; elitism of, 295n55; political program of, 42; and progressives, 246; and radicals, 192; and student organizations, 233; and women, 90–91, 203, 204; and Yen Bay uprising, 239. *See also* Jeune Annam group
Continents, 130
Contre le Courant, 238
Coolies, 218–219, 240
Cooramaswamy, Ananda, 91, 127
Corsicans, in Vietnam, 117, 140
Coulet, Georges, 190; *Sociétés secrètes en terre d'Annam*, 189
Courier d'Haiphong, 123
Courier Saigonnais, 75, 170
cu nhon (Ch.: *chu jen*) degree, 12, 16, 54, 296n2

Cultural Overtures (Khai Hoa), 106, 284n36
Culture, 48, 51–52, 57–58, 74, 111, 122, 262, 271n30; call for new Vietnamese, 23, 76, 77, 162–163, 190; elite vs. popular, 49, 189–190; urban vs. rural, 259
Cuong De, Prince, 28, 64, 65, 67, 75, 291n93

Dai Phap (Great France), 56
Dam Phuong, Mme., 199, 204, 205, 211, 301n3, 308n65
Dang Thuc Hua, 63, 278n34
Dang Tu Man, 63
Dang Xuan Khu (pseud.: Truong Chinh), 179
Dao Duy Anh, 230
Dao Duy Chung, 10–11, 12, 269nn1,3
Dao thi Loan (pen name of Nguyen van Vinh), 29
Darles (Résident), 31–32, 118, 134, 272n55
Declaration of Independence, Vietnamese, 256
Dejean de la Batie, Eugène (Eugène Lien), 125–126, 132, 136, 138, 150, 152, 153, 161, 288n41; and *Annam*, 162; arrest of, 154; and *Cloche Fêlée*, 127, 130; and strikes, 158
Delong, Camille, 131
Devilar, Camille (Edouard Marquis), 123, 287n33
Devret, Camille, 203, 206
Diep van Cuong, 42
Diep van Ky, 122, 182
Dirlik, Arif, 59, 61
Doan Ngoc Bich, 102–103; "The Daughter Sold in Marriage" *(Ga ban cho con)*, 103
Dong Khanh School, 34, 96, 166, 191
Dostoevsky, Fyodor, 72; *The Brothers Karamazov*, 192
Dream of the Red Chamber, 105
Droz, Humbert, 227
Dumas, Alexandre: *La Dame aux camélias*, 105, 107
Duong Ba Trac, 26, 47
Duong Hac Dinh, 220

Duong van Giao, 149, 192, 203, 233, 235, 274n91
Duy Tan, Emperor, 26, 31

East Asia League (Toa Domeikai), 59
Eastern Travel Movement, 23, 31, 59, 75, 170
Echo Annamite, 45, 46, 120, 123, 126, 139, 141, 150, 151, 154
Ecole Coloniale, 40, 67, 279n44
Ecole Française d'Extrême-Orient, 47, 132
Education, 3, 11, 12–15, 26, 39, 256–257, 259, 273nn60,73; and *baccalauréat indochinois*, 33; degrees in, 12; expansion of, 44; in French, 30, 33, 50; introduction of physical, 276n120; pragmatic view of, 53; reform in, 29, 30–31, 32, 33–36, 37, 111, 141, 167; and revolution, 201; in Vietnamese, 29, 35, 50. *See also* Examinations, civil-service; Schools; Women: education of
Elites, 3, 11, 36, 38, 43, 63–64, 82; disdain for business, 25; duties of, 86–87; and education, 32, 98; and membership of Youth League, 305n10, 306n15; and politics, 40–41, 74, 112, 224; and reform, 39, 163; and revolution, 54, 65, 66, 84, 260; Western-educated, 40, 42, 44, 97. *See also* Confucianism
Engels, Friedrich, 188, 202
Enlightenment, European, 22, 172
Europe, 129, 289n72
Eutrope (Director of Security), 134, 135, 136
Examinations, civil-service, 11, 13, 23, 37, 269n6; abolition of, 12, 27, 33, 34, 46, 49, 55, 96; exclusion of women from, 92, 99
Expatriates, Vietnamese: in China, 9, 23, 25, 27, 60–67, 71–72, 74, 88, 147, 149, 168, 170, 173, 175, 178–179, 181, 182, 213, 225, 227, 228; in France, 24, 67–70, 71–72, 76, 133, 137, 151, 168–169, 173–174, 189, 214, 225, 227, 228, 238, 239, 248–249, 268n1; in Japan, 58–60, 61, 170

Index

Family, 89–92, 112–113, 197–198, 224, 254, 257, 258–259, 261; *che do gia dinh* (family system), 200
Feminism, 88–92, 95, 104, 251–252. *See also* Women
Ferry, Jules, 117
Fiction, 6, 101–109, 205, 208, 252; as critique of colonial society, 102, 112, 122. *See also* Literature
Filial piety, 15, 16, 47, 55, 88, 104, 251; *hieu* (Ch.: *hsiao;* piety), 15; redefinition of, 25–26, 254. *See also* Patriotism: and piety
Five Cardinal Precepts, 50
Fontaine Distillery, 116, 118, 123, 302n29
Four Classics, 50
France: anarchism in, 57, 61, 73, 76; Cartel des Gauches in, 129, 134; conquest of Vietnam, 2, 4, 10, 16, 19, 21, 52, 117; loyalty to, 80; Marxism in, 232, 233; *mission civilisatrice* of, 30, 37, 40, 72, 78, 114, 119, 138, 172; as mother country, 143; and Vietnamese imperial succession, 26, 36; Vietnamese workers in, 42, 274n93; women's suffrage in, 91. *See also* Expatriates, Vietnamese: in France; Settlers, French
Franco-Annamite schools. *See* Schools
Franco-Prussian War, 117
Frank, Pierre, 242, 243
Fraternité (Dong Bao Than Ai), 68, 69, 70
French Communist Party (FCP), 227, 233, 306n23; and AIP, 237, 238; Colonial Studies Commission of, 69, 70, 237; and Vietnamese émigrés, 54, 69, 70, 174, 232, 234, 235, 241
French Revolution, 38, 114, 172, 180, 184, 218
Friendship's Sound (Huu Thanh), 111, 285n50, 296n2
Fukuzawa, Yukichi, 22

Gandhi, 119, 172, 183, 190
Ganofsky, Edgar, 124
Gia Long, 109, 110, 295n71
Giai Phong (joint pen name of Phan van Hum and Ho Huu Tuong), 240

Gide, André, 75, 80, 169; *L'Enfant prodigue*, 80, 81
Gide, Charles, 127
Great Depression, 226, 239, 308n46
Group of Annamite Patriots, 70, 76, 233

Ha Huy Tap (pen name: Lam Giang), 147, 165, 295n68
Hai Trieu, 247, 308n65
Haiphong, 34, 71, 103, 220, 229, 231
Ham Nghi, Emperor, 16, 26
Hankow, 181, 182
Hanoi, 25, 50, 65, 67, 110–111, 138, 140, 141, 222, 250, 252; newspapers in, 38, 39, 118, 148; 1913 bombing incidents in, 28, 62, 66, 68; schools in, 24, 34, 35, 75, 84, 126, 132, 159, 167, 179, 190, 274n77; and Viet Minh, 256; women's fair in, 204. *See also* University of Hanoi
Heaven and Earth Society, 188, 189, 190, 191
Herzen, A., 188
History of Revolution, 182
"History of the War in Europe," 47
Ho Chen, 59, 95
Ho Chi Minh. *See* Nguyen Ai Quoc
Ho Dac Hien, 132, 136
Ho Huu Tuong, 240–241, 242, 243, 286n20, 294n42, 308nn53,54
Ho Ngoc Lan, 220
Ho Tung Mau, 65, 177, 179, 181 292n1, 305n8
Hoang Cao Khai, 16, 17, 18, 19, 26, 28, 261
Hoang Dao, 250
Hoang Duc Thi, 183
Hoang Ngoc Phach, 106–108; *To Tam,* 106–107, 108; "Tears from the Red District" *(Giot le hong lau),* 107
Hoang Thai Xuyen: "Twenty-Four Exemplars of Filial Piety" *(Nhi thap tu hieu),* 47
Hoang Trong Phu, 28, 51, 98, 112
Hoang van Tung, 185
Hong Kong, 182, 220, 229, 230, 231, 254
Hong Son. *See* Le Hong Son
Hsia Yu, 19

Hsu Cheng-ya: *Chronicle of Great Tears of Bygone Days (Hsueh hung lei shih)*, 104–106, 108, 252
Hu Han-min, 58, 60, 62, 66
hu nho (ossified Confucianism), 3–4, 50
Hue, 12, 34, 96, 142, 149, 200, 248; Imperial College in, 67; Public Works Bureau in, 191; School of Applied Industry in, 151
Humanité, 69, 70, 162, 214, 238
Huynh Kim Khanh, 56, 310n1
Huynh van Phuong, 238, 239, 240

Iconoclasm, 1, 55, 74, 86, 88, 114, 146
Impartial, 118, 119, 122, 123, 159, 247, 286n14, 287n36, 294n41
Imperial College, 33, 34, 67, 165
Independence, national, 5, 23, 24, 62, 64–65, 70, 86, 140, 148, 224; and AIP, 233, 236; and authoritarianism, 83; and elitism, 40, 260; and culture, 43; Ho Chi Minh on, 254, 256; preparation for, 29–30, 40, 101; and women, 244; and youth, 56, 58, 88
India, 60, 172, 178, 183, 200
Individualism, 73, 91, 102, 172–173, 196–197, 223, 253, 258, 260, 263
Indochina Normal School, 111
Indochina Review (Dong Duong Tap Chi), 28–29, 46, 47, 110, 121
Indochina Times (Dong Phap Thoi Bao), 122, 139, 157, 160, 287n25
Indochine, 127, 132–137, 138, 139, 150, 286n15
Indochine Enchaînée, 139, 141. See also *Indochine*
Indochinese Communist Party (ICP), 55, 148, 194, 226, 234, 237, 240, 292n1, 306n2; establishment of, 229, 230; and fascism, 254, 255; First Plenum of, 231–232; and Ho Chi Minh, 254–255; publications of, 247, 306n16; repression of, 248, 255; Sixth Plenum of, 255; and women revolutionaries, 244, 253; and Youth League, 214, 217, 223, 241
Indochinese Sûreté Générale, 121
Institution Taberd, 75, 158
Intercolonial Union, 69, 70, 133, 149, 176, 232, 233, 235, 307n24

International Women's League for Peace and Freedom (IWLPF), 203
Internationalism, 60–61, 83
Internationalist League against Imperialism and for National Independence. See Anti-Imperialist League
IWLPF. See International Women's League for Peace and Freedom

Jade Pear Spirit (Yu li hun), 105. See also Hsu Cheng-ya
Japan, 8, 50, 57, 200; Vietnamese in, 23, 25, 26, 27, 31, 58–60, 61
Japanese Socialist Party, 58, 59
Jaurès, Jean, 83, 133
Jeune Annam group, 144, 150, 153, 154, 155, 162, 164, 223, 242; and *agents provocateurs*, 292n11, 293n23; attacks on, 129; and Constitutionalists, 139, 140, 151–152; disintegration of, 188; and funeral of Phan Chu Trinh, 156–157; and strikes, 158, 160, 167
Jeunesses Patriotes, 238
Journalism, colonial, 120–131, 142, 143, 146, 259, 287n29. See also individual journals and newspapers

K'ang Yu-wei, 2, 20, 23
Keio University, 22
Khai Dinh, Emperor, 31, 36, 37, 51, 65, 69, 133, 154, 293n25
Khai Hung. See Tran Khanh Giu
Khanh Hoi Realty Company, 134
Kolokol, 81
Krestintern (Communist Peasant International), 70, 228
Kroff (Ba Son) Company, 215, 303n53
Kropotkin, Peter, 54, 73, 187
Kuomintang (KMT), 65, 66, 67, 124, 132, 157, 173, 185; and CCP, 181, 184, 195, 214, 227, 229, 238, 297n9, 298n19. See also China: United Front in

Labaste, Eugène, 134, 290n77
Ladies' News (Phu Nu Tan Van), 203, 206–209, 213, 246, 247, 250, 251, 309n78
Lam Duc Thu, 176, 291n93, 298n15

Index

Lam Hiep Chau, 139, 152, 154, 155, 293n23, 294n43
Land reform, 236–237, 255
Language: Chinese, 3, 22, 49–50, 292n1; French, 3, 6, 33, 50, 292n1; of revolution, 197, 223; romanization vs. characters, 3, 22, 23, 24, 29, 33, 34, 44, 47, 49, 50; Vietnamese, 3, 6, 7–8, 22, 50, 197, 269n8. *See also* Romanized script
Laos, 42, 232, 306n21
Le Duy Diem (Le Loi), 182–183, 229
Le dynasty, 109, 110
Le Fol, 16
Le Hong Phong, 179
Le Hong Son, 65, 66, 179, 180, 181, 229, 231
Le Manh Trinh, 298n25
Le Quang Liem, 153
Le Quang Trinh, 123, 125, 141
Le The Vinh, 127, 132, 152, 154, 164, 295n65
Le van Phat, 215, 216–217
League for the Independence of Vietnam (Viet Nam Doc Lap Dong Minh), 255–256
League for the Prosperity of China and Asia (Hoi Chan Hoa Hung A), 60
League for the Restoration of Vietnam (Viet Nam Quang Phuc Hoi), 27, 28, 60, 62, 63–64, 65, 66, 67, 85, 86
League for the Rights of Man, 133, 288n38
League of East Asian Lost Countries (Tung-ya Wang-kuo Tung-meng-hui), 59
League of Oppressed People of the East, 175–176, 179, 297n9
League of the Partisans of Universal Brotherhood (Dai Dong Lien Lac Cam Tinh Hoi), 61
Lenin, 70, 84, 163, 173, 238, 262, 298n26; "Theses on the National and Colonial Question," 69, 234; *What Is to Be Done*, 180
Leninism, 163–164, 185, 186, 187, 194, 195, 196, 241, 242, 255, 260, 261
Liang Ch'i-ch'ao, 2, 8, 20, 21–22, 23, 58, 59, 102, 171
Liang Shu-ming, 49, 281n80
Liao Chung-k'ai, 66
Le Libertaire, 76
Libre Cochinchine, 124
Literati: and anticolonialism, 182; attitude to student unrest, 167; Chinese, 2–3; ignorance of revolution, 171–172; Northern, 46–52; rural, 55; Vietnamese, 2–3, 13, 18, 20, 21, 23, 25, 26, 39, 67. *See also* Confucianism; Elites; Mandarins
Literature: Chinese, 74, 100, 104–105, 107; as cultural discourse, 102, 112; French, 29, 90, 100; Vietnamese, 62, 74, 90, 100, 102, 105, 109; Western, 72, 79, 82, 100, 102, 105. *See also* Fiction
Liu Shih-fu, 60, 63, 64
Liu Shih-pei, 59, 61
loan (disorder), 51, 79
Longuet, Jean, 69
Lozeray, Henri, 237, 307n41
Lung Chi-kuan, 63
luong huu (mutual friendship) association, 191
Luong Khac Ninh, 159, 160
Luong Ngoc Quyen, 31, 272n56
Luong van Can, 95
La Lutte des Classes, 238, 239, 247, 288n41
Ly Thuy (pseud.). *See* Nguyen Ai Quoc
Lycée Albert Sarraut, 33, 35, 179, 306n15
Lycée Chasseloup-Laubat, 11, 32–33, 35, 75, 76, 139, 158, 167, 168, 296n71
Lycée Dalat, 35

Mai Dang De, 157
Malraux, André, 124, 127, 131–137, 138, 139, 140, 142, 144, 286n15, 290n88; *La Condition humaine*, 136; *Les Conquérants*, 136; *La Tentation de l'Occident*, 281n86
Malraux, Clara, 127, 131, 132, 139, 144, 290n88
Mandarins, 10–11, 25, 38, 41, 46, 51, 54, 80; children of, 12, 47, 55, 96, 97; and French, 14, 15–16, 33, 34, 247, 249; and journalism, 121, 122, 132, 287n23; and peasants, 248,

Mandarins (cont.)
  290n80; servility of, 165–166, 169, 172, 197. See also Literati
Mandate of Heaven, 171, 172
mang (Ch.: *ming*; destiny), 1–2, 18–19
Marriage, 103–104, 106, 108
Marseilles Colonial Exhibition, 24, 36, 51, 69
Marty, Louis, 39, 46, 47, 51, 121, 303n55
Marx, J. A., 124
Marx, Karl, 188, 228, 242, 246
Marxism, 139, 172, 173, 209, 226, 228, 234, 235, 247–248, 257; and elites, 260; and family, 244, 253; and individualism, 258; and progressivism, 246, 249, 309n74; vs. radicalism, 1, 4, 5, 223, 260–261; and Social Darwinism, 261–262; among Vietnamese émigrés, 148, 225, 227, 232, 239, 241, 242, 243, 254, 308n53. See also Leninism
Maspéro, Georges, 45
Mau Quoc (Mother Country), 56
May Fourth Movement, 64
Mazzini, G., 23, 62
Mekong Delta, riots in, 189
Mencius, 139, 205
Merlin, Martial, 35, 50, 66, 67, 111, 129, 134, 141, 180
Michelin rubber plantation, 240, 307n37
Midday Journal (Ngo bao), 287n23
Minh Mang, Emperor, 47
Le Miracle français en Asie, 78
Molinier, Raymond, 240, 242
Monguillot, Henri, 134, 136
Monin, Paul, 124, 125, 127, 128–129, 140, 150, 153, 288nn44,48; death of, 291n107; and the Malraux, 124, 127, 131, 132, 134, 136–137, 138, 144, 286n15, 291n106
Mores (Phong Hoa), 249–250, 252, 253, 287n23, 309n73
Morning Bell (Than Chung), 182, 303n53
Moscow, 67, 70, 153, 174, 179, 181, 214, 235, 237, 241, 242, 254

Moutet, Marius, 125, 136, 288n38
My Tho, 159, 162

Nam Dinh, 179, 210, 240, 269n6, 272n43
Nam Dong Publishing Society, 148, 149, 164, 182, 183, 184, 185, 299n41
Names, Vietnamese, 7
National essence: movements, 49, 50, 276n115; *quoc tuy* (national essence), 48, 49, 92, 97
Nationalism, 83, 242, 255, 287n36. See also Independence, national
Natural Justice (Tien I), 59, 95
Naville, Pierre, 238, 242
Neo-traditionalists, 3, 50, 61, 72, 74, 76, 90, 148, 226, 249, 251; attitude to Yen Bay uprising, 239; critique of, 77, 78, 250; defense of, 92; and familism, 258; and peaceful change, 166; and rural vs. urban society, 259; and women, 97, 100, 101
Nettlau, Max, 73
New Century (Tan The Ky), 150
New Learning, 3, 28, 31, 36, 50, 92, 95, 170, 249; vs. Confucianism, 3, 24, 72. See also Reform Movement; Romanized script
New Vietnam Youth Corps (Tan Viet Thanh Nien Doan), 64
New Vietnamese Revolutionary Party (Tan Viet Cach Menh Dang), 230. See also Vietnamese Revolutionary Party
New Woman (thi tan), 97, 101, 251, 252
News from the Six Provinces (Luc Tinh Tan Van), 25, 75
News of Annam and Tonkin (Trung Bac Tan Van), 121
Nghe An, 181, 215, 222, 240
Ngo Dinh Diem, 7
Ngo Duc Ke, 111–112
Ngo Gia Tu, 229, 230
Ngo Huy Linh, 101
Ngo Tat To, 12–14; *Tents and Bamboo Beds (Leu chong)*, 12–13, 287n25
Ngo Thiem (Hue), 215, 216, 217, 303n53
Ngo Trung Tinh, 139, 290n90

Nguyen Ai Quoc (Ho Chi Minh), 4, 6, 67, 69, 70, 71, 72, 254, 279n44, 291n93, 292n1; on anarchism, 181–187; on assassination, 180; *The Bamboo Dragon* (play), 37; in China, 174, 175, 202, 215; and communism, 178, 186, 187, 194, 225; "Freedom and Laws," 186–187; and French Communist Party, 227; and language of family, 197, 200; *Le Procès de la colonisation française,* 198; pseudonyms of, 254, 297nn5,9; on reformism, 175; on revolution, 176, 180, 225; *The Road to Revolution (Con duong kach menh),* 179–180, 194, 228; in Soviet Union, 149, 174–175; survey of political movements, 186; and Vietnamese Youth League, 88, 168, 176–178, 218, 225, 231, 232; on women, 198–199, 200, 201, 212

Nguyen An Cu, 75

Nguyen An Khuong, 74–75, 76, 105, 127

Nguyen An Ninh (pen name: Nguyen Tinh), 5, 72–87, 88, 122, 125, 126–127, 128, 129–131, 139, 178, 240, 250, 258, 281n86; on action, 83; and anarchism, 73, 76, 81–82, 86, 186; arrest of, 145, 146, 153–154, 155, 160, 193; "The Aspirations of Annamite Youth" (speech), 77, 152, 191; and Bui Quang Chieu, 128, 288n47; on bureaucratism, 76–77; and communism, 289n73, 303n55; and Constitutionalists, 235; critique of Neo-traditionalists, 74, 77–78; and death of Phan Chu Trinh, 155, 157; education of, 75–76; and elitism, 74, 82, 224; European influences on, 72, 73, 76, 79, 80, 82; "The First Sound of the Bell," 81; *La France en Indochine,* 133; on liberty, 81, 82, 86, 91, 143; and nationalism, 83; on need for new culture, 76, 78–79; opposition to authoritarianism, 83, 188; "Order and Anarchy," 81–82, 281n82; in Paris, 76, 133, 141, 169; on Phan Boi Chau, 140; and populism, 190, 193, 194, 196; release of, 189; and religion, 189–190; and revolution, 84, 86, 152–153, 173; and secret societies, 235; and self-realization, 58, 72, 83, 86–87; and students, 158, 168; trial of, 160–162, 281n69; and *Trung Lap,* 247; *The Trung Queens (Hai Ba Trung),* 188, 206; and VNQDD, 218. See also *Cloche Fêlée*

Nguyen An Ninh Secret Society (Hoi Kin Nguyen An Ninh), 187–188, 191–192, 193–194, 230

Nguyen Ba Hoc, 56, 80, 96, 97, 111

Nguyen Ba Trac, 47

Nguyen Cong Hoan, 253; *Dead End (Buoc duong cung),* 309n81; *Miss Teacher Minh (Co giao Minh),* 253

Nguyen Cong Tru: "A Hero's Will," 196

Nguyen Dinh Chieu, 94, 171

Nguyen Don Phuc, 99, 101, 110, 111, 208

Nguyen Duy Trinh, 303n54

Nguyen dynasty, 13, 28

Nguyen Khac Vien, 55

Nguyen Khanh Toan, 167–168, 308n55

Nguyen Kim Dinh, 157

Nguyen Luong Bang, 177, 197

Nguyen Phan Long, 45, 120, 123, 126, 129, 132, 153, 192; and Bui Quang Chieu, 139, 302n29; and *Ladies' News,* 206; on liberation of women, 204; and Nguyen An Ninh, 77, 158, 161; and reforms, 140–141, 143, 151; *Le Roman de Mlle. Lys,* 91. See also *Echo Annamite*

Nguyen Pho, 132, 138, 150

Nguyen Phu Khai, 40, 70, 119, 123

Nguyen Tat Thanh. See Nguyen Ai Quoc

Nguyen Thai Hoc, 183, 184, 218, 219, 220, 221–222, 303n55

Nguyen The Truyen, 72, 128, 137, 234, 235, 285n2, 289n73; as elite expatriate, 54, 70–71, 149, 232, 276n126

Nguyen thi Giang, 218, 220, 221

Nguyen thi Kiem, 252

Nguyen thi Minh Khai, 244, 253, 303n47

Nguyen Thuong Hien, 60, 65, 296n2

Nguyen Thuong Huyen, 54, 60, 171–172, 173, 174, 175, 178, 285n50, 291n93, 296n2; "On Revolution" (Luan cach mang), 172, 174, 175
Nguyen Tinh. See Nguyen An Ninh
Nguyen Trai, 93
Nguyen Trung Nguyet, 88, 215, 216, 217, 303nn47,53
Nguyen Tuan, 229, 230, 306n12
Nguyen van Tao, 168, 237, 247, 307n40
Nguyen van Trung, 275n112
Nguyen van Vien, 219
Nguyen van Vinh, 29–30, 48, 51, 77, 110; and *Indochina Review,* 29, 46, 121; mysogyny of, 29; and New Learning, 24, 28, 50. See also Tonkin Free School
Nguyet Anh, 94, 303n47
Nhat Linh, 168–169, 249–251, 254; *Autumnal Sun (Nang thu),* 252; *Loneliness (Lanh lung),* 252, 253, 303n79; *A Severance of Ties (Doan tuyet),* 252–253; *Two Kinds of Beauty (Hai Ve Dep),* 250–251
Nietzsche, Friedrich, 57, 72, 73, 79, 161, 188
Nihilism, 73, 81

L'Oeuvre, 70, 126
One Heart Society (I hsin she), 64
Opposition de Gauche (Left Opposition; France), 238
Organization of Vietnamese in France, 240, 241, 242
Outrey, Ernest, 118, 119, 124, 128, 140, 163
Oxen and Buffaloes (Trau Bo), 133

Paria, 69, 76, 77, 119, 128, 154, 232
Pasquier, Pierre, 133, 245, 248–249, 274n94, 275n112; *L'Annam d'autrefois,* 245
Patriarchy, 5, 89, 195, 198, 203, 223, 275n112
Patriotism, 86, 94, 95, 145, 157, 254, 263, 269n2; and piety, 15–20, 25–26, 55, 88, 257; and women, 204, 206, 212, 251

Paz, Maurice, 238, 239
Peasant (Nha Que), 167
Peasants, 41, 42, 210, 227, 228, 236–237, 241; and intellectuals, 43, 49; vs. middle class, 247; protests of, 135, 226, 240, 248, 249
People's Journal, 58
Le Peuple, 69
Pham Duy Ton, 24, 28
Pham Hong Thai, 66, 67, 111, 136, 177, 181, 215
Pham Quynh, 30, 44, 46–49, 50, 82, 111, 120, 121, 163–165, 191, 275n112, 281n80; as defender of emperor, 154–155, 293n25; "The Education of Women and Girls," 96–97; encouragement of native fiction, 102; as Minister of Education, 249; and *Tale of Kieu,* 110–112; and tradition, 48–49, 53–57, 72, 85, 112–113, 189, 199, 275n112; and Vietnamese youth, 52–53, 78, 80, 84, 162–163, 164, 165; on women, 93, 94, 98–99, 100, 199, 207, 208, 251; and Yen Bay uprising, 308n48. See also *Southern Wind*
Pham Tuan Tai, 148
Pham van Chieu, 190, 194
Pham van Dong, 179, 230, 306n15
Pham Ba Ngoc, 63, 66, 85, 180
Pham Boi Chau, 22–23, 31, 40, 48, 51, 67, 85, 87, 146, 191, 271n30, 272n43, 296n2; and anarchism, 58–64, 65, 66, 67, 173; and anticolonialism, 38, 43, 72, 74, 86, 157, 174; arrest of, 147, 149–150, 176, 291n93, 301n5; and classes, 228; and Eastern Travel Movement, 170; *History of Pham Hong Thai,* 79; *History of the Loss of Vietnam (Viet Nam vong quoc su),* 21–22, 23; and Reform Movement, 24, 26, 27–28; and secret societies, 189; and students, 167; trial of, 140–145, 154, 156, 161; on women, 92–96, 199–200, 202, 204
Phan Chu Trinh, 6, 23–24, 26, 36, 67, 68, 69, 74, 111, 133, 145, 146, 160, 271n30; death of, 146, 147, 154–157, 158, 160, 162, 200

Phan Dinh Phung, 16–18, 19–20, 26, 38, 55, 63, 72, 287n25
Phan Khoi, 207, 287n25; "A Bill of Accusation against the Annamite Family System," 207–208
Phan thi Nga, 252
Phan van Chanh, 169
Phan van Hum, 190, 193, 240–241, 247, 303n47
Phan van Truong, 67, 68, 69, 70, 71, 139–140, 152, 158, 162, 208
Phan Xich Long, 188–189
Phnom Penh, 46, 138, 157
Phuc Viet (Vietnamese Restoration) Party, 85, 86, 142, 147, 149, 163, 164, 165; and Marxism, 148, 225; and Vietnamese Youth League, 182, 183
Populism, 186–195
Pourvourville, Albert de, 163
Progressives, 224, 226, 243–254, 309n74
Proudhon, P. J., 77
Pye, Edith, 203, 206

quan tu (Ch.: *chun tzu*; superior man), 14

Radicalism, 1–4, 67, 163, 164, 166, 243–254, 258–259, 263; causes of, 2; and cultural iconoclasm, 1, 146, 258; end of, 226; language of, 223; and Marxism, 4, 260–261; and women's emancipation, 92, 243–244. *See also* Progressives; Revolution
Radical-Socialist Party, 131
Rathenau, Walter, 82
Reform Movement, 55, 96, 154, 245, 258, 259; advocates of, 22–26; birth of, 20–22; and bourgeoisie, 39–46; and education, 32–36, 166; end of, 26–31, 139; 1904 Manifesto, 139; and Northern literati, 46–52; and romanized script, 22, 23, 24, 67; veterans of, 65, 74, 85, 127. *See also* Social Darwinism
Religion, 189–190, 262
Renovation of the People (Hsin-min ts'ung-pao), 22, 58

Restoration League, 54, 60, 61, 176
Résurrection, 238
Réunion Island, 75, 124
Réveil Saigonnais, 123
"Les Revendications du Peuple Annamite," 68–69, 151, 292n15
Revolution, 1, 4, 6, 84, 86, 87, 160, 187, 257, 276n12; agrarian, 241; beginning of, 171; bourgeois democratic, 243; *cach mang*, 171, 175; character of Vietnamese, 234; and collective action, 87, 177, 178; end of radical phase in Vietnamese, 226; vs. evolution, 175; and famine, 239–240; feminization of, 197–213; gender relations in, 218; individualistic stage of, 258; and language of family, 197–198, 224, 254, 257, 258–259; in 1920s, 224, 226, 259–260, 262, 263, 268n1; vs. reform, 24, 116, 163, 164, 175, 195, 231, 258; role of bourgeoisie in, 234, 235, 236, 237, 239, 243; in three stages, 184, 231; world, 184, 241
Revue Mondiale, 163
Rolland, Romain, 129
Romanized script, 22, 23, 24, 29, 44; and national essence, 49, 50; in schools, 33, 34, 47, 67, 110; and women, 95, 96, 100
Rosenthal, Gérard, 240
Rosmer, Alfred, 238, 242
Rousseau, Jean-Jacques, 23, 72, 205; *Contrat social*, 133, 160, 299n41

Saigon, 28, 71, 74, 140, 152, 155, 188, 189, 190, 192, 194, 203; journalism in, 38, 39, 72, 77, 94, 118, 128, 130–131, 132; port of, 46, 120, 134; schools in, 32–33, 35, 67, 75, 96, 274n77
Saigon Républicain, 131, 289n65
Sarraut, Albert, 27, 29–30, 47, 111, 117, 118, 258, 272n43; as administrator, 45, 75, 275n112; educational reforms of, 27, 32, 34, 35, 44, 96, 146; on French colonial enterprise, 37, 113, 114, 126, 142–143; and French settlers, 32, 46, 124; policies

Sarraut, Albert *(cont.)*
  of, 39, 40, 42, 63, 115–116, 138, 245, 285n2; on Vietnamese independence, 29–30, 72
Schneider, Alfred, 121
Scholar's Revolt. *See* Aid the King Movement
School for Native Young Ladies, 158–159
School of Interpreters, 24, 30, 47
Schools, 12–15, 32–36, 44, 273n67; Franco-Annamite, 11, 33–39, 44, 46, 75, 85, 92, 103, 111, 114, 129, 147, 148, 170, 179, 182, 246, 249, 259; French, 11, 15, 32–33, 36, 75, 85, 114; traditional, 32, 33, 35, 36, 37
Secret societies, 28, 31, 235, 300n51. *See also* Nguyen An Ninh Secret Society
Self-Cultivation League (Tu Than Hoi), 147–148
Self-Perfection Society, 230
Self-Reliance Literary Group (Tu Luc Van Doan), 249, 250, 251, 252, 253, 254
Self-strengthening, 21, 22, 62, 96
Semaoen, 227
Settlers, French, 31, 37, 41, 45, 46, 116, 119, 143, 161; and journalists, 39, 48, 121, 122, 124; and reform, 27, 32, 137, 163
Seven Point Indictment (That Dieu Thu), 36, 133
Shiraishi Masaya, 59, 61
Siam, 31, 60, 71, 147, 182, 205, 231, 278n34, 298n25, 302n28
Social Darwinism, 2, 3, 4, 48, 52, 61, 190, 207, 270n25; and critique of Vietnamese culture, 20–22, 29, 79, 111; and Marxists, 243, 261
Socialism, 58, 59–60, 61, 69, 140, 142; anarcho-, 60, 61, 62, 63, 173
Socialist Party, 69, 137
Société d'Enseignement Mutuel (Hoi Tri Tri), 40, 76, 77, 295n56
Société des Missions Etrangères, 123
Society for the Encouragement of Learning (Khuyen Hoc Hoi), 193
Society for the Study of Socialism, 59

Society of Like Hearts (Tam Tam Xa), 64–67, 71, 86, 175, 176, 180, 181, 279n35, 291n93
The Soul of Vietnam (Viet Nam Hon), 232–233
Southern Wind (Nam Phong), 39, 46, 47–48, 50, 52, 56, 80, 118, 121, 250; articles in, 84, 85, 163–164, 283n20, 294n54; closing of, 309n73; criticism of, 112; debates on women in, 93–94, 100, 101, 104, 199, 209; and fiction, 102, 106, 107, 110
Soviet Union, 63, 84, 89, 174, 187, 200, 225, 232, 246
Spencer, Herbert, 20
Stalin, 228, 232, 238, 241, 242, 246, 247, 255
Strikes, 53–54, 157, 159–160, 183, 196, 240, 257, 262, 295n70, 300n53; and radicalism, 1, 146, 166; and revolutionary organizations, 158, 174, 196, 257; in schools, 150–151, 159, 162–163, 165–168, 295n71; and women, 89, 159, 199, 244; workers', 240, 306n16
Suffrage, 42, 64, 119, 204
Sun Yat-sen, 58, 60, 148, 155, 156, 299n41; Three People's Principles of, 184, 187, 218
Sung Chiao-jen, 60
Sung dynasty, 13, 208
Sûreté, Cochinchinese, 45, 119, 131, 189, 190, 192, 193, 286n15; and publications, 128, 130, 136, 143–144, 162
Sûreté, French, 54, 88; and anarchism, 81; and communism, 230, 235, 254; and émigré activists, 27, 60, 68, 71, 76, 85, 182; informers of, 140, 291n93, 295n55; and revolutionary parties, 75, 198, 219, 220, 221; and suppression of *Indochine*, 138–139; and youthful activists, 168, 169, 183

Ta Doi Lap (Left Opposition; Vietnam), 241
Ta Thu Thau, 169, 223, 238–239, 240, 307n40; and AIP, 235, 237–238; criticism of French Communist Party, 232,

Index

306n23; and Trotskyism, 139, 241, 242
Taboulet, Georges, 159
Tagore, Rabindranath, 48, 72, 82, 127, 153, 190
tai (Ch.: *tsai;* talent), 1–2, 18
The Tale of Kieu (Ngyen Du), 1–2, 29, 105, 109–112, 252
T'ang dynasty, 7, 13
Tay Son dynasty, 13, 109
Teachers, 14, 35–36, 38, 54
The Tearful Story of Kim Anh (Kim Anh le su), 106
Temps d'Asie, 123
Teng Ching-ya, 60
Than Trong Hue, 51, 65, 94, 97
Thanh Thai, Emperor, 26
Thieu Bao, Princess, 98
Third International, 69, 137, 180, 227, 228, 229, 231, 232, 233–234, 305n6
Three Bonds, 15, 50
Three Submissions and Four Virtues *(tam tong tu duc),* 50, 92, 94, 99, 200
tien si (Ch.: *chin shih*) degree, 12, 16
Tocqueville, Alexis de, 5, 10
Today (Ngay Nay), 252
Tolstoy, Leo, 72, 82, 127; *Narodnaya polyana,* 188
Ton Duc Thang, 214, 215, 216, 303n53
Ton Quang Phiet, 84, 85, 86, 87, 147, 185
Tonkin, 27, 31, 44, 47, 71, 144, 219, 220, 234, 239; anticolonialism in, 58, 66, 84, 85, 90, 91, 142, 171, 172, 183; communism in, 229, 230, 248; establishment of protectorate of, 2, 7, 16, 17; intelligentsia of, 146–147; journalism in, 6, 120, 121, 122–123, 150, 287n24; mandarinate in, 25, 38, 39, 248; schools in, 11, 12, 14, 22, 24, 30, 33, 34, 35, 39, 111; strikes in, 159, 165; women in, 94, 103, 204; young revolutionaries in, 183, 186
Tonkin Free School (Dong Kinh Nghia Thuc), 22, 24, 25, 26, 28, 60, 65, 95 272n56
Tradition: colonial misappropriation of, 245, 246; vs. modernity, 46–52, 61; 275n112; and women, 212–213. *See also* Neo-traditionalists

Traditional Lady *(cuu nuong),* 97, 101
Tran Hung Dao, 205
Tran Huy Lieu, 122, 139, 157, 287n25
Tran Khanh Giu (pen name: Khai Hung), 250; *Mid-Spring (Nua chung xuan),* 252
Tran Lanh Sieu, 167
Tran Mong Bach, 147–148, 163, 230
Tran Phu, 147
Tran Quan Chi, 104
Tran Te Xuong, 8, 57
Tran thi Nhu Man, 204, 211
Tran Thu Thuy, 216, 217
Tran Truong, 215, 217, 303n53
Tran van Cung, 230
Tran van Thach, 236, 239
tri (govern; cure), 79
La Tribune Annamite, 76
Tribune Indigène, 39–40, 41, 45, 47, 48, 76, 118, 120, 123, 126; closing of, 46, 132, 162; and debates on women, 91; and mass naturalization, 43
Tribune Indochinoise, 162, 193
Trieu, Lady, 101
Trinh Dinh Chiem, 220
Trinh Hung Ngau, 139
Trinh thi Uyen, 220, 221
Trotsky, Leon, 228, 232, 238, 240, 241, 242
Trotskyism, 139, 217, 232–243, 247, 262, 288n41, 303n55; among expatriates in France, 228, 232, 238, 241, 308n53
trung (Ch.: *chung;* loyalty), 15, 17, 26, 55
Trung Lap Bao, 123, 159, 247, 286n23
Trung sisters, 90, 95, 101, 188, 205, 206
Truong Cao Dong, 149–154, 161–162, 292n11
Truong Chinh ("Long March"). *See* Dang Xuan Khu
Truong thi Sau, 84, 194, 289n71
Truong Tuu, 253, 309n79
Ts'ai Yuan-p'ei, 67
Tu Duc, Emperor, 16, 19
tu tai (Ch.: *hsiu tsai*) degree, 12

tuong cao cong kin (high walls and closed gates), 96, 106, 108
tuong te (mutual aid) associations, 191

Unison (Dong Thanh), 205–206, 302n28
University of Hanoi, 26, 33–34, 35, 75, 85, 147

Varenne, Alexandre, 137–138, 139, 140, 141, 149, 150, 151, 161, 162, 248, 275n112; and émigré students, 170; and Jeune Annam, 153; and radicalism, 164, 165, 258; and reforms, 143, 154, 163, 166, 245, 258; and Socialism, 137, 142; and strikes, 159
Vérité, 124, 125, 128, 131
La Vérité, 238, 239, 240
Vernacular script. *See* Romanized script
Versailles Conference, 68, 233
Viet Minh. *See* League for the Independence of Vietnam
Vietnamese Communist Party, 231
Vietnamese Nationalist Party (Viet Nam Quoc Dan Dang; VNQDD), 184–185, 193, 250, 307n30; demise of, 217–223, 225, 240, 248; execution of leaders of, 242, 243; and Marxism, 225, 226, 229; and women, 198, 204, 207, 209; and Youth League, 182, 185, 196
Vietnamese People's Progressive League (Viet Nam Tan Bo Dan Hoi), 163
Vietnamese Revolutionary Party (Viet Nam Cach Mang Dang), 183, 185, 193, 229, 230. *See also* Phuc Viet Party
Vietnamese Youth League, 55, 174–182, 240, 292n1, 310n1; Cochinchinese section of, 214, 215, 216, 217, 218; and elitism, 305n10, 306n15; epigones of, 182–186; and KMT, 195, 214, 227; launching of, 176, 291n93; and Marxism-Leninism, 225, 226; publications of, 177, 182, 298nn18,19; transformation of, 228–232, 237, 241; and VNQDD, 196, 218, 219, 220, 223; and women, 88, 198, 201, 203, 204, 207, 209, 211, 212, 213, 214. *See also* Indochinese Communist Party; *Youth*
Viollis, Andrée, 169, 285n2
VNQDD. *See* Vietnamese Nationalist Party
Voix Annamite, 123–124, 125
Voix Libre, 124
vong quoc (Ch.: *wang kuo*; loss of national independence), 19

Wang Ching-wei, 66
Wang Yang-ming, 269n9
Weber, Eugen: *Peasants into Frenchmen*, 117
Wen, King, 205
Werth, Léon, 72, 82–83, 117, 129, 130, 133, 289n72
Westernization, 32, 51, 56. *See also* New Learning
Whampoa Military Academy, 65, 66, 67, 179, 182
Wilson, Woodrow, 68, 163, 174, 254
Women: and anticolonialism, 89, 157, 199; biographies of famous, 101; and Confucianism, 74, 93, 94, 101, 282n5; criticism of, 29; debates on, 91–102, 112–113, 122, 199, 243, 251, 253; and destiny, 18; education of, 91, 92–103, 122, 199, 201, 206, 207, 244; elite, 98, 99, 100, 101, 106, 199, 204, 244; and Marxism, 243, 244–245; peasant, 94, 97; and polygamy, 281n82; and revolution, 198–213, 215, 218, 220, 221, 268n1, 303n47; in Soviet Union, 84, 209; and storekeeping, 25, 99, 100; and student strikes, 89, 159, 199, 244; symbolic role of, 90, 244; in United States, 209; as workers, 199, 246–247, 253. *See also* Feminism
Women's Bell (Nu Gioi Chung), 94, 207
Women's Publishing Society (Nu Luu Thu Xa), 204
Woodside, Alexander B., 61–62, 89
Worker, Peasant, and Soldier (Cong Nong Binh), 213, 217
Workers and Peasants (Cong Nong), 237
Workers' University of the East (Moscow), 6, 179, 228

World War I, 6, 30, 31–32, 42, 57, 68, 214
Worldwide League for Humanity (The Gioi Nhan Dao Hoi), 60–61
Wuchang Uprising, 66, 106

Yen Bay Uprising, 221, 222, 223, 239, 249, 309n74
Yen Fu, 20, 21, 23

Youth (Thanh Nien), 176, 177–178, 186, 200, 206, 298n19; and women revolutionaries, 201–202, 204–205, 208, 210–214, 243–244. *See also* Vietnamese Youth League
Youth Party (Thanh Nien Dang). *See* Nguyen An Ninh Secret Society
Yuan Shih-k'ai, 62, 63

Printed in Great Britain
by Amazon